Across Cultural Borders

Across Cultural Borders

Historiography in Global Perspective

Edited by
Eckhardt Fuchs
and
Benedikt Stuchtey

ROWMAN & LITTLEFIELD PUBLISHERS, INC.
Lanham • Boulder • New York • Toronto • Oxford

ROWMAN & LITTLEFIELD PUBLISHERS, INC.

Published in the United States of America
by Rowman & Littlefield Publishers, Inc.
A wholly owned subsidiary of The Rowman & Littlefield Publishing Group, Inc.
4501 Forbes Boulevard, Suite 200, Lanham, Maryland 20706
www.rowmanlittlefield.com

PO Box 317
Oxford
OX2 9RU, UK

British Library Cataloguing in Publication Information Available

Library of Congress Cataloging-in-Publication Data

Across cultural borders : historiography in global perspective / edited by
Eckhardt Fuchs and Benedikt Stuchtey.
        p.   cm.
    Includes bibliographical references and index.
    ISBN 0-7425-1767-5 (cloth : alk. paper)—
    ISBN 0-7425-1768-3 (pbk. : alk. paper)
    1. Historiography.   2. Acculturation.   3. Culture conflict.   4.
History—Philosophy.   5. Social sciences—Philosophy.   6. Historicism.
7. Eurocentrism.   I. Fuchs, Eckhardt, 1961–   II. Stuchtey, Benedikt.
    D13.A37   2002
    907'.2—dc21   2001044379

Printed in the United States of America

♾ ™ The paper used in this publication meets the minimum requirements of
American National Standard for Information Sciences—Permanence of Paper for
Printed Library Materials, ANSI/NISO Z39.48–1992.

Contents

Acknowledgments

This book is the result of a conference, titled "Science and Historical Discipline in a Transcultural Perspective, 1850–1950," held at the German Historical Institute (GHI) in Washington, D.C., in October 1997. It was sponsored by the German Historical Institutes in Washington and London and supported by the Institut für Kultur-und Universalgeschichte e.V. Leipzig. Without the interest of the directors of the two German Historical Institutes, Professors Detlef Junker and Peter Wende, respectively, the idea of this conference would not have materialized.

We also would like to acknowledge the help of Christa Brown and Bärbel Thomas of the GHI Washington in arranging the conference. Daniel S. Mattern was a careful reader and editor of the manuscript. We also appreciate Sally Robertson and Q. Edward Wang's help in translating.

We thank all twenty-two participants—representing four continents—who attended the original meeting. Although not all of the participants' work is represented in this collection, additional experts on the subject were invited to contribute. The stimulating discussions during and after the conference as well as the advice of many participants were crucial for our understanding of the issues raised at the conference. Many of the ideas are incorporated in the chapters of this book. Special thanks go to Arif Dirlik, whose advice and critical comments encouraged us to publish this collection. Lastly, we express our gratitude to Susan McEachern and Jehanne Schweitzer of Rowman & Littlefield. This volume would not have appeared without their professional and efficient work.

Introduction

Provincializing Europe

Historiography as a Transcultural Concept

Eckhardt Fuchs

Ex oriente lux, ex occidente lex.

History takes place in time and space. Anyone who writes about history must take both of these determinants into account. The selection of a specific space and a specific time prejudices the perspective of the historian as well as the result of his work. In this book, our spatial reference point is Europe, and our time frame covers the period from the 1850s to the present. Our purpose is to provide an initial stimulus for a world history of historiography since the nineteenth century by means of transcultural comparison. However, since we want this book to take a global view of historiography, we must map out the terrain with which we are concerned. This terrain is new and mostly unknown.

Our approach led us to set three particularly significant goals:

- To learn specific information about the development of the historical discipline in countries belonging to different cultures.
- To investigate intercultural relations and transfers of historical knowledge between Europe and other cultures.
- To address the question of how to overcome a Eurocentric view rooted in the belief of the universal necessity, global validity, and superiority of European ideas of norms and modernization.

1

Whereas the first two goals prompt questions with methodological consequences, especially over how to do a transcultural comparison in the field
of history of historiography, the third goal raises fundamental epistemological questions that bring us back to the issues of time and space. At
first glance the problem of defining Europe seems to be an easy one, since
it appears to be a purely geographic problem. But it becomes more complicated when one takes into account the ethnocentric perspective on
which any attempt to define Europe is based. After all, the mapping of
the world is itself a Eurocentric invention that runs counter to geographic
reality, elevating a relatively small peninsula to the status of a continent.[1]
Any terminology that selects Europe as its geographic reference point is
therefore based on assumptions that already imply value judgments (Max
Weber), regardless of whether one refers to the "rest" of the world as
"non-European," "oriental," or "non-Western." Within this conceptual
framework, Europe or the "West" becomes the hegemonic "center" from
which a Europe-centered, hierarchical world history, or world history of
historiography, is written.[2]

Thus, any attempt to escape the Eurocentric trap when using Europe
as a point of reference might be impracticable, but it seems to be useful
in differentiating heuristically between Europe as cultural construct and
as geographical entity. The term *Western* emphasizes the cultural dimension of the term *Europe*. It signifies more than the geographic landmass of
Europe since it also includes those countries that owe their cultural heritage in whole or in part to the European tradition. In addition to the European countries, we count the "neo-European" countries of Latin America
that have no significant Indian cultural element, as well as North America
and Australia as former "white settlement colonies."[3] In contrast, the use
of "Europe," "Asia," "Africa," and so forth refers to the different continents in a nonhierarchical way as solely physical entities. This avoids the
culturally predetermined contrast of Europe with non-Europe, of Orient
with Occident. It must be emphasized, however, that immense political,
cultural, and economic differences exist not only among these geographic
units but even within a single continent. Often a cultural, economic, or
political unit can be articulated only by differentiating it from the "other"
or the "Outside," and not by an inward-looking self-definition. Europe
and the other continents are each characterized as a mixture of various
cultural and historic traditions, geographic features, and values.[4] However, the geographic designation seems to be the lowest common denomi-
nator for a transcultural comparative approach, even though we are
aware of the problem that the Arab world may have more in common
with Asia than with sub-Saharan Africa.

Like the space with which we begin, the time period of this study—
from the 1850s to the present—owes its selection to a Western perspective

on the history of historiography. In the nineteenth century, historiography in Europe became professionalized and scientific in a manner that was taken as a comparative measure of international historiographic development per se. The perspective on Chinese, Indian, and Latin American historiography is constantly oriented around this European development as a reference. It is not disregard but a lack of knowledge that has compelled this reference point.[5] One objective of this book, then, shall be to discover other possible chronological and geographic arrangements by which we might understand the historiography of world historiography.

The "global" and "transcultural" perspectives that are suggested here imply an approach that takes a broader view than just a Eurocentric one, and that, therefore, does not view Europe a priori as the center and dominant force in world history and historiography.[6] Whereas *global* is used as a geographic designation, the term *transcultural* refers not only to the broad geographic approach but also to the level of *intercultural* relations. Thus, a transcultural history of historiography looks at the specific forms of thinking and writing about history in the various cultures and the relationships between them.

THE ETHNOCENTRIC PERSPECTIVE OF EUROPEAN HISTORIOGRAPHY

The development of historiography as an academic discipline in Europe is a nineteenth-century phenomenon. Embedded in the modernization of European industrial societies was a professionalization and scientification process of historical writing with its own unique forms. Historians not only began to create their own institutions but also laid down the epistemological and methodological foundations of their discipline. The scientification of history was accompanied by two important developments. First, a definitive trait of the discipline of history as compared to other sciences lies in its function in aiding national and political legitimation. Since the nineteenth century, historical scholarship has been mostly focused on national history. Despite the idea of objectivity, history has often been written for political interests. A main social purpose of historiography was to offer a scientifically authenticated and authorized historical and societal model and to create a national myth, which placed one's own nation at the center of the historical discourse. Second, the scientification process meant a geographic narrowing of its subject matter. During the Enlightenment the writing of world history was still part of the arsenal of historiography. In the seventeenth and eighteenth centuries, for example, Chinese culture was still considered exemplary.[7] However, it soon became obvious that a gulf was developing between enlightened universalism and the belief in the superiority of one's own civilization. The idea of the difference between primitive and civilized peoples, and therefore the inferiority of other cultures to Indo-European ones, has its roots in Enlightenment philosophy.[8] Johann Gottfried Herder (1744–1803) was an exception, taking the position that every culture deserved an equal place in human history. This also applies to the world historiographies of Johann Christoph Gatterer (1727–1799) and August Ludwig Schlözer (1735–1809).[9] Herder countered the historical conception of the Enlightenment, which saw the enlightened civilization of Europe and thus a progressive process of perfectibility as the ideal and the goal of other cultures, with the singularity of other peoples—that is, a cultural diversity that could not be understood with normative concepts and teleology.[10]

The universalization of European historical thought in the nineteenth century coincided with a national historiography that barely took non-European peoples into account or, with the exception of the classical civilizations, condemned them as "stagnant" or "without history." The universalist claim to represent human civilization, as contrasted with the "barbarians," found its philosophical justification in the *Philosophy of History* by Georg F. W. Hegel (1770–1831) and its historiographical foundation in *World History* by Leopold von Ranke (1795–1886).[11] Even Karl Marx, and the few supranational histories of culture and civilization produced in the nineteenth century using the ethnographic knowledge of the time, remain trapped in the Eurocentric perspective.[12] In the nineteenth century, European history was elevated to the level of a world history in which the "other" simply faded away. It was this "invention" of Europe with its unified history and culture dating back to Classical Greece that caused certain peoples and societies to be excluded from world history.[13]

This Eurocentrism was by no means a product of Europe but of a few, domineering European nations of the early modern and modern periods. The Eurocentric image of the world also was not limited to spatial classifications. As Arif Dirlik notes in chapter 10 of this book, it also encompassed such social and political dimensions as class, gender, race, ethnicity, culture, and so forth.[14] The unbreakable connection between modernity and Eurocentrism led not to a surrender of the latter but to an incorporation of the "other" into European modernity. This picture has changed little since the time of Ranke.[15]

Paradoxically, the writing of world history disappeared at a time, from the mid-nineteenth century on, when a series of analogous political, economic, and cultural crises were occurring simultaneously in nearly all regions of the world, not only influencing the development of each nation but also resulting in global consequences. These events, to name just a few, included the Taiping Rebellion (1850–1864) and civil war in China;

the Crimean War (1853–1856); the mutiny and great revolt in India (1857–1859); the U.S. Civil War (1861–1865); the reformation of Russia after 1861; the war of 1864–1870 in Paraguay; the Meiji Restoration in Japan (1868); the formation of nation-states in Italy (1861) and Germany (1871); and the reorganization and stabilization of Mexico under Díaz after 1877.[16] Notwithstanding these developments and the fact that the objective of capitalism and modernity was universal power, Eurocentrism found its initial historiographic expression in European national histories. Non-European history, therefore, became the domain of other disciplines, from folklore and ethnology to archeology and American studies. Oriental studies would soon dominate. But scholarship on the Orient in Germany, which fractured increasingly into subdisciplines according to region after the mid-nineteenth century, originated not as historical but as philological science, the primary objective of which was to decipher and compare non-European languages.[17]

The ethnocentric perspective of modern European historiography also applies to the history of historiography. In Germany, in particular, extensive research has been done during the last two decades into the history of German historical science since the eighteenth century.[18] The focus has been on the development of *historicism* (*Historismus*), under which the study of history in Germany was "scientized" over the course of the nineteenth century. For all their different interpretations, German historians of historiography have in common an approach to historicism that analyzes it from a purely German perspective while emphasizing its universality and its leading role in the institutionalization and professionalization of nineteenth-century historical science. As a component of the modernization wave, the historistic understanding of science was elevated to a guiding paradigm.

However, one can hardly speak, as has been done until very recently, of a global adoption of the "German model," that is, of a "universal triumphal procession" of historicism.[19] Its reception outside of Germany was too diverse and heterogeneous, as a number of recent bilateral comparisons have shown.[20] A look at the international Western literature shows that research outside Germany on the history of historiography continues to be written primarily from a national perspective.[21] Recent overviews describe only the European development and do not even acknowledge other cultures.[22]

HISTORIOGRAPHY AND CULTURAL IDENTITY

Part I of the book concerns the national varieties of historiography and historical thought within different cultures. A long-term perspective permits a differentiated view of processes previously interpreted as having derived largely from the German (European) model. Recent research on the historiography of China,[23] Japan,[24] India,[25] other Asian nations,[26] and Arab[27] and African[28] countries makes it clear, however, that the national history of historiography has been studied and interpreted predominantly in relation to Western concepts. In fact, the European influence was particularly great in Japan, and even greater in the colonies. Only in Latin America, as Jochen Meissner shows in chapter 1, is the situation slightly different. Despite an overwhelming European tradition, the development of Spanish American historiography was characterized by its search for intellectual independence and identity as well. The comparatively early political independence and formation of autonomous republics there, beginning at the outset of the nineteenth century, laid the foundation for an original development of historical writing. However, it remained limited largely to national and European history and its central scenery was not the academia.[29]

The chapters in Part I face the problem of how to compare the commonalties and differences of historical thinking in various cultural regions. Only a few studies have tried to develop an appropriate set of theoretical and methodical instruments.[30] Jörn Rüsen offers one such approach later in the book, in chapter 13.[31] He suggests looking for the most general, anthropologically defined, common denominators of historical consciousness as theoretical bases for the comparison. In this way he hopes to develop a theory of transcultural historical science beyond any kind of ethnocentrism by defining the various (historical) cultures as a combination of elements that are present in all cultures. His attempt to establish a general periodization of historiography is based on the process of modernity and Weber's theory of universal rationalization and disenchantment.

The case studies in Part I are Latin America, Africa, India, and Japan. These examples embody specific historic and cultural identities: Japan as a "non-Western" imperial power; India as a colonial land with an immense cultural tradition not destroyed by colonization; Latin America as a former colonial region independent since the nineteenth century; and South Africa as a colonized country whose cultural identity was neglected and suppressed by the colonial powers. Of course, such a synchronic approach could be supplemented by the inclusion of diachronic comparisons, since there existed well-developed historiographies before modern European historical science—especially in the Arab-Islamic, Chinese, Japanese, and Indian regions—that were comparable to eighteenth- and nineteenth-century developments in Europe.[32] In light of the relatively advanced state of research on European historical science in the nineteenth and twentieth centuries, we decided against such an approach, opting instead for investigating the most decisive reference points of historical consciousness, that is, for the specific concepts of history and views of history, in different cultures at the same time. This includes the specific understanding of science and the typical institutional forms in each region.

A close examination makes evident the shortcomings of an approach that seeks to interpret historic culture in other cultural regions by using a teleological, modernization-theory approach to the history of historiography proceeding from Enlightenment and historicism to modern social history, cultural history, and postmodernism. It is precisely this view of the progressive development of history, or *scientification* of history, that has led to the Eurocentric hierarchization of historiography and the elimination of other forms from the "rational discourse" of historians. Therefore, as Stefan Tanaka suggests in chapter 5, we must address the contending conceptions of native historiography instead of taking modern Western methodology as basis for our analysis.

As Benedikt Stuchtey demonstrates in chapter 2, the example of the South African *Sonderweg* illustrates how imperialism and racism neglected and oppressed the cultural identity of the indigenous people and shaped the historical consciousness of this colonized country. As his account shows, for the Boer the frontier experience has been the focus of historiography before and since the South African War (1899–1902) and also became the center of Afrikaner national identity and political ideology. The invention of the "uncivilized wild land" justified its annexation by denying the rights of African natives. However, Stuchtey investigates the complex relationship of two White colonial communities—that of the Boer and that of the British—for the hegemonic historical interpretation and, eventually, for cultural domination in South Africa. In any case, he calls for a revision of the dichotomy between British and Boer as well as Black and Boer. Whereas some elements of the Afrikaner ideology and historiography entered British thinking and originally Irish intellectuals transmitted the historiographical and political dimensions of the idea of colonial nationalism, Boer historians made use of the common European background to construct a national identity, without producing or profiting from historiographical transfer. And whereas the political rapprochement between Boers and Britons in the early twentieth century strengthened White supremacy, the integration of the Blacks into South African society was an extremely slow process.[33]

In British India, development of a Western historical consciousness was seen as a prerequisite for independence. Whereas the British, as Michael Gottlob explains in chapter 3, used historical knowledge to maintain and legitimize their power, the Indians saw historicization as an emancipatory tool for overcoming colonial rule. Herein lay the dilemma for Indian reformer historians: binding India to the universal modernization process while also questioning the (British) historicization of India and underlying premises of modern historical thinking. Expressed in a different way, Indians acknowledged and adopted historical scholarship and associated institutions that had been imported from England to India, while criticizing its Eurocentric perspective, universalist claims to power, and potential for perpetuating the power of the colonial rulers against whom indigenous traditions and Indian identity had to be protected.

In analyzing early anglophone West African historiography, Andreas Eckert, in chapter 4, shows that although African historical tradition was mainly oral, by the end of the nineteenth century the emergence of a written "amateur historiography" had begun. Its representatives, among them Carl Christian Reindorf and Samuel Johnson, can be labeled as "cultural nationalists." However, their interest in indigenous history must be understood not only as a mere rejection of an uncritical imitation of European culture, but also as the attempt to record African history and to create a model of local history in order to imagine a national community within colonial boundaries. Eckert's case-study examples demonstrate the efforts of Western-educated African intellectuals to combine projects of modernity by defending the integrity of their own indigenous culture.

As an imperial power that has never been colonized, Japan is an altogether different case compared to Latin America, Africa, and India. As Stefan Tanaka shows in chapter 5, Japan is one of those non-Western areas that integrated its history into the rational and scientific context of modernity during the Meiji period, a process that resulted in a reconceptualization of Japanese society. However, he argues that a teleological interpretation of Japanese historiography with the emphasis on methodology and the academic discipline of modern history masks the contradictions and limitations within modernity itself. In investigating the historian Yamaji Aizan, Tanaka introduces an alternative form of national history that focuses on the development of people's rights and not on the nation-state. It was the different interpretation of Japanese history, not the attempt to synchronize the history of Japan with the Western world, that differentiated academic historians from Yamaji. Yamaji, therefore, cannot be understood in terms of modernizer/traditionalist or Westernizer/native. China is another example for the nationalization of history. Historians argue whether the development of *kaozheng* research during the Qianlong and Jiaqing reigns (1736 and 1821), at a time when Chinese historiography was emancipating itself from classical Confucianism, should be interpreted as a secularization of historiography.[34] It is undisputed, however, that the turn of the twentieth century saw the beginning of a search for a new type of historiography in China no longer based on dynastic history but on national history.[35]

Comparing the different developments of historiography in various cultures, we are faced with the question of how the triad of industrialization, modernization, and the historicization process, which was decisive in the development of modern academic historiography in Europe, also is valid, albeit with a different chronology, for Africa, Asia, and Latin America.[36] This includes the problem of whether other factors such as indigenous cultural traditions, national identity, or the colonized–independence dichotomy played a more decisive role in such places. In general, in light of these essays it becomes evident that there is no simple answer to this question. It can be said, however, that historiography was initially constituted as national historiography, either in the context of formation of independent nations or in connection with a movement for independence from colonial oppression.

The chapters in Part I highlight a fundamental dilemma. On the one hand, they try to create a history of historiography from a transcultural perspective that disregards a national (European) model in favor of an approach that looks for specific processes of adoption, rejection, and mediation of historical knowledge. On the other hand, there always is "a politics of historical comparison" behind the "method of historical comparison," as Chris Lorenz has stated.[37] In any case, it becomes apparent that a transcultural comparison is not possible without reference to European historical scholarship. European concepts of history and science have conquered the world, and historians in India, China, Japan, and elsewhere—probably with the exception of sub-Saharan Africa—have adopted some of the modern institutions and epistemological standards of Europe. The spread of European cultural, political, and economic dominion around the globe led to the foundation of specific institutions of "cultural imperialism" that have influenced and shaped the historical consciousness of other cultures. It could not, however, completely control it because popular, nonacademic history written on the local level was not largely affected by the Eurocentric cultural hegemony. Moreover, the indigenous political elites often used Western institutional forms and modes of historical research to legitimate their own rule.[38]

Considering the complex phenomenon of the "Europeanization of the world," a transcultural history of historiography cannot stop with structural comparison but must be relational.[39] Therefore, the second part of the book investigates transcultural relations and inquires into the specifics of this process. It considers the transfer of ideas and institutions, mutual perceptions and apperceptions, and institutional connections between Europe and local historical knowledge in other cultures. A group of French scholars has introduced the concept of "cultural transfer" for the Franco-German relations as a social-historical approach that does not mean a transfer of "culture" but a transfer between cultures. Such an approach focuses mainly on the channels of transfers, their mediums, and the use of the transferred knowledge from one specific social and cultural system to another.[40]

ACROSS CULTURAL BORDERS

The chapters in Part II draw on the concept of "transcultural transfer." They show the ways in which historical writings both shape and are shaped in the course of cultural encounters.[41] This group of essays also addresses the question of what happens to a historical paradigm when it is introduced into another culture. This can be a direct or an indirect import.[42] An adaptation depends not only on the concrete political and cultural conditions in the importing culture but also on the status of development of the discipline in question. Interdisciplinary boundaries may determine the difference between adoption and rejection of foreign influences. In addition, certain views of science are not static, but are subject to change over time.[43] The extent and speed of the introduction of Western thought depended to a significant extent on the strength of a culture's own scientific and cultural traditions. For example, Chinese Confucianism offered heavy resistance to European scientific paradigms. History there is seen as a natural process; human history is subordinated to natural history. This is articulated in China, for example, in the dichotomy between *dao* and history (norm and fact). The different perception of time, and thus the refusal to recognize a single developmental process, hindered the kind of philosophy of history that we know from Aristotle or Hegel.[44] In China, as in India, for example, there had been no explicit philosophy of history. In principle, one may say that the import of scientific paradigms altered the indigenous tradition and generated new concepts.

However, such imports functioned only through certain channels that actively engaged in or supported the import of ideas and/or institutions.[45] It was not uncommon for the import to be a conscious process, for example, in Japan, where certain scientific concepts, technologies, and institutions were adopted from the countries in which their development was most advanced.[46] For historiography, this was to a large extent Germany. It is not surprising that Japan brought in a German historian to promote professional historical science.[47] Thus, even before the turn of the century, the Japanese Historical Association and the Office of Historiography were established as professional associations based on the European model. At the same time, this was no straightforward adoption of Western models, because those models came into contact with existing traditional concepts. This amalgamation process led to "overlapping," through which traditional ideas were elevated in a new national concept.[48]

Q. Edward Wang explains in chapter 6 that the propagation of a "new historiography" as a branch of the Chinese philosophy of history at the beginning of the twentieth century was oriented at first exclusively toward Enlightenment history and German historicism. Soon, however, this new approach attempted to combine Western historical thinking and Chinese traditions. Convinced of its universal validity, Chinese scholars who had studied abroad introduced the methodology of modern science. In historiography, this meant professionalization in the 1920s in the form of a scientific, philological source criticism, a process associated with such historians as Fu Sinian and Yao Congwu.[49] Meanwhile, the flaw in Chinese "scientific history," namely, that it neglected the function of history as the basis for Chinese nationalism in favor of methodology, led, together with the Sino-Japanese War (1937–1945), to its demise in the 1940s.

Matthias Middell describes in chapter 7 the difficulties of defining a francophone historiography, referring to the relationship between French and French-speaking African historians. It is evident that French institutions and France's system of higher education played a decisive role in the development and institutional infrastructure of francophone African historiography, a fact that shows how problematic the idea of an independent African historical writing and identity has been and how the institutional and intellectual ties between the metropolitan power and the former colonized countries have shaped the mode of historiographical production and consciousness. In this difficult process of independence from Western paradigms, francophone African historians see their multiculturalism as an advantage that might help to bridge francophone and anglophone African historiography.

A look at the scientific transfer within the Western hemisphere shows that the professionalization of U.S. history also took place via local studies in order to create a national historical consciousness. Gabriele Lingelbach makes it clear in chapter 8, however, that there was no pure export of historical science even within one "culture" but that the receiving culture altered the ideas being imported, "invented" them, or adapted them to their own traditions. This example demonstrates that there were varying concepts of historical science even within the "Western" world and shows what effects resulted when they came into contact with one another.

In chapter 9, I examine the general ideological and cultural presumptions underlying the ethos of the international republic of learning. Focussing on international congresses as institutions of academic scholarship I discuss not only the Eurocentric perspective of European historians and orientalists, but also the attempts of Pacific and Latin American scholars to establish their own international scientific structures. I show how scholars' attempts to distance themselves from European models were often defeated. Historians had to fall back on the institutional structures and the scholarly, and in some cases even their ideological, premises of the West. Congresses helped to create a specific regional scientific identity. The engagement of the United States in the establishment of an international scientific community that was not dominated by European countries led ultimately to the shift of the scientific center from Europe to the United States beginning in the 1920s.

BEYOND EUROCENTRISM

Part III addresses current problems in historiography that grow out of the global and postcolonial dimension of today's developmental processes.[50] Eurocentrism in historical science remains the main determinant of modern historiography to the present day. However, the existence of new paradoxes such as localism versus globalism, cultural homogeneity versus heterogeneity, and denationalization versus ethnocentrism, leads to new challenges for historical scholarship that are manifested primarily in a critique of universalized Eurocentrism and, therefore, the concept of Western modernity. It is no longer possible to ignore the non-Western voices who question this Eurocentrism and demand reinterpretations of history that take non-European peoples into account. Edward W. Said's book *Orientalism,* which first appeared in 1978 and subjected European orientalism to a merciless critique, doubtless prompted a significant catalyst and turning point in this regard.[51] This book has led to an intensive debate and postcolonial critique of orientalism,[52] a critique that "delegitimized and disempowered colonial knowledge at a historical time when direct political hegemony was waning, revealing societies and discourses hidden by imperial historiography and literary products."[53] In addition, it led to a blanket condemnation of Europe and indiscriminate stereotyping of the process of writing history. It is not surprising, then, that calls have been made for "de-occidentalizing" the West, whereby the "occidentalism" of Said and his supporters is seen as an epistemological category that homogenizes and dehistoricizes the West, regardless of historical variations and contexts, and conceives of the West solely in terms of colonial power and hegemony. The "occidentalization of the imperial other" in this regard produces just as vacuous and generalized a version of intellectual history as does "orientalization of the colonial other."[54]

The vehement discussion in recent years among North American and Western European historians regarding the theoretical and methodological principles of the discipline, a discussion summed up by such key-words as *linguistic turn, cultural history,* and *the end of history,* have remained rooted to this cultural region without casting so much as a glance beyond the borders of Europe. Therefore, aside from "world" his-torians and those few specialists in African and Asian history, European historians have missed a debate conducted under the heading of decolon-ialism by non-Western historians and representatives of other disciplines, the main objective of which is to deconstruct and replace the Eurocentric picture of history presented by present-day historiography.[55] For these scholars, history is not ending but only just beginning.[56] They draw on European theoretical concepts from the traditional social sciences or con-temporary postmodern philosophy.[57] The debate about so-called postco-lonialism that has been taking place since the early 1990s, particularly among non-Western intellectuals teaching at U.S. universities, reflects the search for an epistemological concept that can be used for postmodern recording and interpretation of current global political, economic, and cultural processes in the present day, that is, following decolonization.[58] Stuart Hall, for example, explains:

> It is the retrospective re-phrasing of Modernity within the framework of "globalization" in all its various ruptural forms and moments (from the Por-tuguese entry to the Indian Ocean and the conquest of the New World to the internationalization of financial markets and information flows) which is the really distinctive element in a "post-colonial" periodization. In this way, the "post-colonial" marks a critical interruption into that whole grand historio-graphical narrative, which, in liberal historiography and Weberian historical sociology, as much as in the dominant traditions of Western Marxism, gave this global dimension a subordinate presence in a story which could essen-tially be told from within its European parameters.[59]

The prefix "post" thus has both a chronological and an epistemological dimension. The critics of postcolonial discourse point to the cultural self-reflection of these intellectuals and the antifoundational basis of their cul-turalism, which excludes analysis of real global capitalism and its mecha-nisms.[60] However, the end of European colonial rule and the increasingly interwoven global networks caused Eurocentrism to be called into ques-tion from both sides.

The four chapters in Part III discuss some of the debates and current problems of a transcultural historiography. In chapter 10, Arif Dirlik criti-cizes the concept of Eurocentrism and analyzes the role of non-Western concepts in the postcolonial age from the perspective of their historio-graphical consequences, especially with regard to the universal normative necessity and practical superiority of Western ideas of modernization. Whereas the projects of postcolonialism for formulating regional identities are aimed at the local level, the global drafting of history attempts to formulate major theories on a level above cultural boundaries.

Following up the question on how world historiography generates new forms of hegemony, Maghan Keita investigates in chapter 11 the episte- mological question of why and how Africa must be included in the his- tory of mankind. After a critique of recent works on world history with regard to their treatment of Africa, Keita raises the fundamental issue of the role that history plays in the construction of knowledge and demands a rewriting of world history narratives.

Using the example of recent Chinese historical writing, Wang Hui in chapter 12 shows the shift in historical interpretation from a traditional challenge/response model to the "inner development theory" and conse- quences for defining "modernity" and "Asian" in Chinese studies. He not only introduces this new historical approach but also applies it to the real historical process. It thus becomes evident that the occurrence of "modernity" in China cannot be wholly explained by this kind of mod- ernization theory, because it does not sufficiently consider the spatial and time framework in which "modernity" occurred, namely, the rise of the nation-state, the introduction of modern knowledge, communication net- works among different world regions and their interconnectedness, and capitalist "world order." In historicizing Japanese and Chinese responses to the "world-system model," Wang raises the issues of cultural hegemony, universalism, and the construction of Asia in historiography.

Finally, in chapter 13 Jörn Rüsen discusses the problem of intercultural communication and cooperation between historians and the aforemen- tioned attempts to establish a theoretical foundation for intercultural comparison.

TRANSCULTURAL HISTORY OF HISTORIOGRAPHY

The question of whether there can be a historiography—and, thereby a history of historiography—that is based on the theoretical, methodologi- cal, and terminological concepts of the eighteenth and nineteenth centu- ries, yet not Eurocentric, is addressed collectively by the chapters in this book.[61] The practice of using European historiography as a reference point is hardly a renunciation of Eurocentrism if the questions asked by non-European historiography are European questions, and if the chrono- logical concepts are based on modern European history. The chapters make clear, however, the need to examine critically the Western scientific model, its epistemological basis, and the resulting institutional structure of scholarship. This means, first of all, giving up the idea that German historicism and the associated institutional forms for historiography have global significance per se and are *sine qua nons* for the development of academic history outside of Europe.

As Dirlik argues in his chapter, neither inclusion of the "other" in history nor rejection of Eurocentric teleology automatically means a surrender of Eurocentrism, especially if one assumes that, by virtue of the dominance of its conceptions of time and space, it has become a fundamental component of global thought and thus a deciding principle of historiography in India, the Arab world, and so forth.[62] If Eurocentrism is inextricably linked to modernity, then rejection of Eurocentrism must also entail surrendering concepts of modern provenance. Ultimately, this means giving up the concept of history as a science. Dirlik has taken this idea to its logical conclusion and found that this is no solution for the problems of contemporary historiography.

This book propounds a "softer" Eurocentrism as the basis for a world history of historiography, that is, a Eurocentrism that is conscious of its ideological, political, economic, and cultural foundations. Only with self-consciousness regarding the historicity and epistemological limits of such a view of history and the world can the historian open the door to non-European and transcultural perspectives that will allow him or her to stop seeing Europe as the center of the world. Moreover, only this kind of self-reflection will permit historians to question theoretical and methodological assumptions. If modernity is historicized and thus no longer interpreted as a universal valid project, it opens the door for competing narratives of history. This competition will lead to new conceptions of history beyond a nationally bounded historiography. In turn, structural changes within the institutions of historical production might result. Thus, instead of radically rejecting modern Eurocentric historiography, this approach should compete with a variety of other models and lead to a critique and modification of the European myth. Dipesh Chakrabarty has referred to this process as the "provincializing" of Europe.[63]

A transcultural history of historiography could be based on the concept of intercultural philosophy that historians of philosophy have been discussing for a number of years.[64] Intercultural philosophy is a philosophy without prejudice that privileges no place and no tradition and has no native language. At the same time, this *philosophia perennis* means an "emancipation of non-European thinking from its centuries-old, inaccurate images unilaterally created in Europe."[65] This also implies a methodological and epistemological modesty that favors no model or system. Applied to historical science, an approach could be referred to as a *historia perennis* if it viewed the European (occidental) historiography as one form of historical thinking among others rather than as the model of historical science having the universal claim to truth.[66] There are certainly philosophical models—for example, the Indian Jaina doctrine—both for this rejection of all absolutism and universal singularity on the part of European thinking and for a comparative approach encompassing various perspectives.[67] For example, the debates on what Shmuel N. Eisenstadt calls "the culture of the axial age" show how a transcultural comparative approach can be embraced.[68] To the extent that such a historiography critically reflects on (but not necessarily discards) the scientific and ideological corset of modernity, it will be able to free itself from Eurocentrism and become literally postmodern. Thus, it is not a matter of automatically rejecting European concepts but of rejecting their hegemonic dominance. Such an undertaking must not be content with merely showing how various cultural perspectives can be articulated and synthesized in a world history. It must also show how the necessary egalitarian communication across cultural boundaries can be achieved. The prerequisite for this achievement is knowledge and acceptance of different conceptions of history and historiography and, thereby, acknowledgment of intercultural differences without hegemonic claims.

NOTES

1. Martin Lewis and Kären E. Wigen, *The Myths of Continents: A Critique of Metageography* (Berkeley, Calif.: 1997); Winfried Schulze, "Europa in der Frühen Neuzeit—begriffsgeschichtliche Befunde," in *Europäische Geschichte als historiographisches Problem*, ed. Heinz Durchhardt and Andreas Kunz (Mainz: 1997), 35–65. For a definition of the continents in classical antiquity, and particularly in Herodotus, see Werner Gauer, "Europa und Asien: Die Entdeckung der Kontinente und die Einheit der alten Welt," *Saeculum* 46 (1995): 204–15; Ram Adhar Mall, "Mediationen zum Adjektiv 'europäisch' aus interkultureller Sicht," in *Der technologische Imparativ: Philosophische und gesellschaftliche Orte der technologischen Formation: Heinz Hülsmann zum 75. Geburtstag*, ed. Walter Blumberger et al. (Munich: 1992), 139–50; Stuart Woolf, "The Construction of a European World View in the Revolutionary–Napoleonic Years," *Past and Present* 137 (1992): 72–101.

2. Arthur P. Whitaker, *The Western Hemisphere Idea: Its Rise and Decline* (Ithaca, N.Y.: 1954). From the perspective of the history of science, see Lewis Pyenson, "The Ideology of Western Rationality: History of Science and the European Civilizing Mission," *Science and Education* 2 (1993): 329–43; Lewis Pyenson, "Prerogatives of European Intellect: Historians of Science and the Promotion of Western Civilization," *History of Science* 31 (1993): 289–315.

3. Here, we are following Jürgen Osterhammel, "Sozialgeschichte im Kulturvergleich: Zu künftigen Möglichkeiten komparativer Geschichtswissenschaft," *Geschichte und Gesellschaft* 22 (1996): 147–48.

4. On this problem, using the example of the Pacific region, see Arif Dirlik, *What Is in a Rim? Critical Perspectives on the Pacific Region Idea* (Boulder, Colo.: 1993); Arif Dirlik, "The Asia-Pacific Idea: Reality and Representation in the Inven-

tion of a Regional Structure," *Journal of World History* 3 (1992): 55–79. On the South Pacific, see Friedrich Valjavec, "Wahrnehmungen kultureller Varietät: Notizen zum Ethnonationalismus im Südpazifik," *Saeculum* 46 (1995): 60–100. On Eastern Europe, see Larry Wolff, *Inventing Eastern Europe: The Map of Civilization on the Mind of the Enlightenment* (Stanford, Calif.: 1994); Hans Lemberg, "Zur Entstehung des Osteuropabegriffs im 19. Jahrhundert: Vom 'Norden' zum 'Osten' Europas, *Jahrbücher für Geschichte Osteuropas* 33 (1985): 48–91; on northern Europe, see Sorenson Øystein and Bo Stråth, eds., *The Cultural Construction of Norden* (Oslo: 1997); on the United States, see Edmondo O'Gorman, *The Invention of America: An Inquiry into the Historical Nature of the New World and the Meaning of Its History* (Bloomington, Ind.: 1959).

5. For an Asian perspective, see Rebecca E. Karl, "Creating Asia: China in the World at the Beginning of the Twentieth Century," *American Historical Review* 103 (1998): 1096–118; Stefan Tanaka, *Japan's Orient: Rendering Pasts into History* (Berkeley, Calif.: 1993); Akira Iriye, ed., *The Chinese and the Japanese: Essays in Political and Cultural Interactions* (Princeton, N.J.: 1980).

6. On the concept of globalism, see Roland Robertson, "Mapping the Global Condition: Globalization as the Central Concept," in *Global Culture: Nationalism, Globalization and Modernity: A Theory, Culture and Society Special Issue,* ed. Mike Featherstone (London: 1994): 15–30.

7. Michael Harbsmeier, "World Histories before Domestication: Writing Universal Historie, Histories of Mankind and World Histories in 18th-Century Germany," *Culture and History* 11 (1991): 23–59; Harald Kleinschmidt, "Japan im Welt- und Geschichtsbild der Europäer: Bemerkungen zu europäischen Weltgeschichtsdarstellungen vornehmlich des 16. bis 18. Jahrhunderts," *Bochumer Jahrbuch zur Ostasienforschung* 3 (1980): 137–207; Edwin J. Van Kley, "Europe's 'Discovery' of China and the Writing of World History," *American Historical Review* 76 (1971): 358–85.

8. Martin Bernal, *Black Athena: The Afroasiatic Roots of Classical Civilization,* vol. 1: *The Fabrication of Ancient Greece, 1785–1985* (New Brunswick, N.J.: 1987). An excellent overview is available in Jürgen Osterhammel, *Die Entzauberung Asiens: Europa und die asiatischen Reiche im 18. Jahrhundert* (Munich: 1998). See also Rolando Minuti, *Oriente barbarico e storiografia settecentesca: rappresentazioni della storia dei Tartari nella cultura francese del XVIII secolo* (Venice: 1994).

9. On Johann Christoph Gatterer as a German world historian of the Enlightenment, see Horst Walter Blanke, "Von Chyträus zu Gatterer: Eine Skizze der Historik in Deutschland vom Humanismus bis zur Spätaufklärung," in *Aufklärung und Historik: Aufsätze zur Entwicklung der Geschichtswissenschaft, Kirchengeschichte und Geschichtstheorie in der deutschen Aufklärung,* ed. Horst Walter Blanke and Dirk Fleischer (Waltrop: 1991), 131ff. For general information, see Jürgen Osterhammel, "Neue Welten in der europäischen Geschichtsschreibung (ca. 1500–1800)," in *Geschichtsdiskurs,* vol. 2: *Anfänge modernen historischen Denkens,* ed. Wolfgang Küttler, Jörn Rüsen, and Ernst Schulin (Frankfurt am Main: 1994), 202–15; George S. Rousseau and Roy Porter, eds., *Exoticism in the Enlightenment* (Manchester, England: 1990); Alexander Randa, ed., *Mensch und Weltgeschichte: Zur Geschichte der Universalgeschichtsschreibung* (Salzburg: 1969).

10. Johann G. Herder, *Ideen zur Philosophie der Geschichte der Menschheit [1784–91]*, vol. 6 of *Werke in zehn Bänden*, ed. M. Bollacker (Frankfurt am Main: 1989).

11. Friedrich W. Hegel, *Vorlesungen über die Philosophie der Geschichte*, vol. 12 of *Werkausgabe* (Frankfurt am Main: 1970); Leopold v. Ranke, *Weltgeschichte*, part 9 (Leipzig: 1889). On both men, see Ernst Schulin, *Die weltgeschichtliche Erfassung des Orients bei Hegel und Ranke* (Göttingen: 1958). On the origins of the modern view of the world, see Stephen Toulmin, *Cosmopolis: The Hidden Agenda of Modernity* (Chicago: 1990).

12. On Marx see Se-Yeon Kim, *Karl Marx und die nichteuropäischen Gesellschaften: Zur Kritik der eurozentrischen Interpretation der Marxschen Auffassung über die nichteuropäischen Gesellschaften* (Frankfurt am Main: 1993). As one example for a universal historical approach in the nineteenth century, see Henry T. Buckle, *History of the Civilization in England* (London: 1857–1861). On that work, see Eckhardt Fuchs, *Henry Thomas Buckle: Geschichtsschreibung und Positivismus in England und Deutschland* (Leipzig: 1994).

13. See James M. Blaut, *The Colonizer's Model of the World: Geographical Diffusionism and Eurocentric History* (New York: 1993); Samir Amin, *Eurocentrism* (New York: 1983). For German historiography, see Andreas Pigulla, *China in der deutschen Weltgeschichtsschreibung von 18. bis zum 20. Jahrhundert* (Wiesbaden: 1996); Christoph Marx, *"Völker ohne Schrift und Geschichte": Zur historischen Erfassung des vorkolonialen Schwarzafrika in der deutschen Forschung des 19. und frühen 20. Jahrhunderts* (Stuttgart: 1988); Jürgen Osterhammel, " 'Peoples without History' in British and German Historical Thought," in *British and German Historiography: Traditions and Transfers,* ed. Benedikt Stuchtey and Peter Wende (Oxford: 2000), 265–87. The widespread history of exploration and colonization will not be addressed here.

14. See chapter 10. On the explanation of the myth of European superiority, see Blaut, *The Colonizer's Model of the World*; Andre Gunder Frank, *ReOrient: Global Economy in the Asian Age* (Berkeley, Calif.: 1998); Jack Goody, *The East in the West* (Cambridge, Mass.: 1996); Vassilis Lambropolous, *The Rise of Eurocentrism: Anatomy of Interpretation* (Princeton, N.J.: 1993).

15. This statement describes the mainstream historiography. There is no doubt that a few historians such as Karl Lamprecht, Marc Bloch, or Fernand Braudel had a global historiographical perspective. It would be a worthwhile project to investigate the global reception of the French Annales school. As a case study, see Hebe Carmen Pelosi, *Historiografia y sociedad: las fuentes de "Annales" y su reception en la historiografia argentina* (Buenos Aires: 1991).

16. On the global effects of these conflicts, see Michael Geyer and Charles Bright, "World History in a Global Age," *American Historical Review* 100 (1995): 1045ff.

17. See Thomas Philipp, "Geschichtswissenschaft und die Geschichte des Nahen Ostens," *Saeculum* 45 (1994): 166–78; Albert Hourani, *Islam in European Thought* (Cambridge, Mass.: 1991), chap. 1. In general, see Jürgen Osterhammel, "Vorbemerkung: Westliches Wissen und die Geschichte nichteuropäischer Zivilisationen," in *Geschichtsdiskurs*, vol. 4: *Krisenbewusstsein, Katastrophenerfahrungen und Innovationen 1880–1945*, ed. Wolfgang Küttler, Jörn Rüsen, and Ernst Schulin

(Frankfurt am Main: 1997), 307–13; Johann Fück, "Islam as an Historical Problem on European Historiography Since 1800," in *Historians of the Middle East*, ed. Peter M. Holt and Bernhard Lewis (Oxford: 1962); Johann Fück, *Die arabischen Studien in Europa bis in den Anfang des 20. Jahrhunderts* (Leipzig: 1955).

18. From the now immense body of literature, see Otto G. Oexle and Jörn Rüsen, eds., *Historismus in den Kulturwissenschaften: Geschichtskonzepte, historische Einschätzungen, Grundlagenprobleme* (Cologne: 1996); Gunter Scholtz, ed., *Historismus am Ende des 20. Jahrhunderts: Eine internationale Diskussion* (Berlin: 1996); Otto Gerhard Oexle, *Geschichtswissenschaft im Zeichen des Historismus: Studien zu Problemgeschichten der Moderne* (Göttingen: 1996); Frank R. Ankersmit, "Historicism: An Attempt at Synthesis," *History and Theory* 34 (1995): 143–61 (and the discussion between Ankersmit and Georg G. Iggers, same issue, 162–73); Friedrich Jaeger and Jörn Rüsen, *Geschichte des Historismus* (Munich: 1992); Annette Wittkau, *Historismus* (Göttingen: 1992). A critical overview can be found in Irmline Veit-Brause, "Eine Disziplin rekonstruiert ihre Geschichte: Geschichte der Geschichtswissenschaft in den 90er Jahren (I)," *Neue Politische Literatur* 43 (1998): 36–66.

19. See Ulrich Muhlack, *Geschichtswissenschaft im Humanismus und in der Aufklärung: Die Vorgeschichte des Historismus* (Munich: 1991), 10.

20. Peter Schöttler, "Das 'Annales-Paradigma' und die deutsche Historiographie (1929–1939): Ein deutsch-französischer Wissenschaftstranser," in *Nationale Grenzen und internationaler Austausch. Studien zum Kultur- und Wissenschaftstransfer in Europa*, ed. Lothar Jordan and Bernd Kortländer (Tübingen: 1995): 200–20; Lutz Raphael, "Historikerkontroversen im Spannungsfeld zwischen Berufshabitus, Fächerkonkurrenz und sozialen Deutungsmustern: Lamprecht-Streit und französischer Methodenstreit der Jahrhundertwende in vergleichender Perspektive," *Historische Zeitschrift* 251 (1990): 325–63; Christian Simon, *Staat und Geschichtswissenschaft in Deutschland und Frankreich 1871–1914: Situation und Werk von Geschichtsprofessoren an den Universitäten Berlin, München, Paris* (Bern: 1988); Jürgen Herbst, *The German Historical School in American Scholarship: A Study in the Transfer of Culture* (Ithaca, N.Y.: 1965); Fuchs, *Henry Thomas Buckle*; Mauna Jokipii, "Über deutsche Einflüsse auf die finnische Geschichtsschreibung am Ende des 19. Jahrhunderts," *Wissenschaftliche Beiträge der Ernst Moritz Arndt-Universität Greifswald* (1990): 73–86; M. Vakarii, "Die Tradition der finnischen Geschichtsschreibung und Karl Lamprecht," *Storia della Storiografia* 6 (1984): 33–43; Andrzej F. Grabski, "Z Zagadnien Stosunkow Polsko-Niemieckich w Zakresie Historiografii Drugiej Polowy XIX w.," *Kwartalnik Historii Nauki I Techniki* 29 (1984): 323–44; Jerzy Krasuski et al., eds., *Stosunki Polsko-Niemieckie w Historiografii*, part 2: *Studia z Dziejow Historiografi Polskiej I Niemieckie* (Poznan: 1984); D. Berindai, "L'Historiographie roumaine et la communité oecuménique des historiens jusqu'à la première guerre mondiale," in *Nachdenken über Geschichte: Beiträge aus der Ökumene der Historiker in memoriam Karl Dietrich Erdmann*, ed. Hartmut Bockmann and Kurt Jörgensen (Neumünster: 1991), 241–46; Stefan Stefanescu, "L'Historiographie Roumaine dans le contexte international de la fin de XIXe siècle et du debut du XXe," *Analele Universitatii Bucuresti: Istorie* 32 (1983): 77–90; Georg G. Iggers, "Geschichtswissenschaft und Sozialgeschichtsschreibung 1890–1914," in *Marxistische Typisierung und idealtypische Methode in der Geschichtswissenschaft*, ed. Wolfgang Küttler (Berlin:

1986), 234–44; Louise Schorn-Schütte, "Karl Lamprecht und die internationale Geschichtswissenschaft an der Jahrhundertwende," *Archiv für Kulturgeschichte* 67 (1985): 417–64; Ernst Schulin, "Geschichtswissenschaft in unserem Jahrhundert," *Historische Zeitschrift* 245 (1987): 1–30; Ernst Schulin, "German 'Geistesgeschichte,' American 'Intellectual History,' and French 'Histoire des mentalités' Since 1900: A Comparison," *History of European Ideas* 1 (1981): 195–214. See also Karl-Dietrich Erdmann, *Die Ökumene der Historiker: Geschichte der Internationalen Historikerkongresse und des Comité International des Sciences Historiques* (Göttingen: 1987)

21. Among more recent publications, see Pim den Boer, *History As a Profession: The Study of History in France (1818–1914)* (Princeton, N.J.: 1998); Ernst Breisach, *American Progressive History: An Experiment in Modernization* (Chicago: 1993); Peter Burke, *The French Historical Revolution: The Annales School, 1929–1989* (London: 1990); Christopher Parker, *The English Historical Tradition Since 1850* (Edinburgh: 1990); Peter Novick, *That Noble Dream: The "Objectivity Question" and the American Historical Profession* (Cambridge, Mass.: 1988).

22. Georg G. Iggers, *Historiography in the Twentieth Century: From Scientific Century to the Postmodern Challenge* (Hanover, N.H.: 1997); Christian Simon, *Historiographie: Eine Einführung* (Stuttgart: 1996); Guy Thuillier and Jean Tulard, *Les Ecoles Historiques* (Paris: 1990); Ernst Breisach, *Historiography: Ancient, Medieval, and Modern* (Chicago: 1983); Charles-Olivier Carbonell, *L'Historiographie* (Paris: 1981). An overview is given in Ernst Schulin, "Synthesen der Historiographiegeschichte," in *Geschichtswissenschaft vor 2000: Festschrift für Georg G. Iggers zum 65. Geburtstag,* ed. Konrad H. Jarausch, Jörn Rüsen, and Hans Schleier (Hagen: 1991), 151–63. Exceptions include Michael Bentley, ed., *Companion to Historiography* (London: 1997), and the essays in *Storia della Storiografia* 5 (1984), which resulted from a congress organized by the Commission Internationale d'Histoire de l'Historiographie in 1983 in Montpellier on the subject of "L'Historiographie dans le monde à la fin du XIXe et au début du XXe siècle." The annual German journal *Saeculum,* particularly the volumes for 1987, 1994, and 1995, should also be mentioned positively in this regard, as should the annual journal for non-European history, *Periplus.*

23. For general information, see Werner Meissner, *China zwischen nationalem "Sonderweg" und universaler Modernisierung: Zur Rezeption westlichen Denkens in China* (Munich: 1994). On historiography, see Q. Edward Wang, "Chinese Historians and the West: The Origins of Modern Chinese Historiography," Ph.D. dissertation, Syracuse University, 1992; Lionel Millard Jensen, "Manufacturing 'Confucianism': Chinese and Western Imaginings in the Making of a Tradition," Ph.D. dissertation, University of California at Berkeley, 1992; Moying Li, "Hu Shi and His Dewean Reconstruction of Chinese Historiography," Ph.D. dissertation, Boston University, 1990; George Kao, ed., *The Translation of Things Past: Chinese History and Historiography* (Hong Kong: 1982); *Extrême-Orient/Extrême-Occident, Cahiers des recherches comparatives IX: La référence à l'histoire* (Paris: 1987); Zhang Zhilian, "Aspects of Chinese Historiography at the End of the XIXth and Beginning of the XXth Century," *Storia della Storiagrafia* 5 (1984): 86–91; Lien-Sheng Yang, "Die Organisation der chinesischen offiziellen Geschichtsschreibung: Prinzipien und Methoden der der offiziellen Geschichtswerke von der T'ang- bis zur Ming-Dynastie," *Saeculum* 8 (1957): 196–209.

24. Wolfgang Schwentker, "Zwischen Weltaneignung und Selbstdeutungsz-wang: Entwicklungstendenzen der Geschichtswissenschaft in Japan 1860–1945," in Küttler, Rüsen, and Schulin, *Geschichtsdiskurs*, vol. 4, 339–54; Margaret Mehl, *History and the State in Nineteenth-Century Japan* (New York: 1998); Imai Hiroshi, "British Influence on Modern Japanese Historiography," *Saeculum* 38 (1987): 99–112; Francine Herail, "Regards sur l'historiographie de l'epoche Meji," *Storia della Storiografia* 5 (1984): 92–114; Ulrich Goch, "Die Entstehung einer modernen Geschichtswissenschaft in Japan," *Bochumer Jahrbuch zur Ostasienforschung* 1 (1978): 238–71; W. G. Beasley and E. G. Pulleyblank, eds., *Historians of China and Japan* (London: 1961).

25. Bernhard Kölver, *Ritual und historischer Raum: Zum indischen Geschichtsverständnis* (Munich: 1993); Rothermund, Dietmar, "Nationale und regionale Geschichtsschreibung in Indien," *Periplus* 3 (1993): 75–82; Ashok Aonshuman, *Nation Building in a Colonial Society: The Historiographical Responses, 1900–1930* (Patna: 1992); Pratima Asthana, *The Indian View of History* (Agra: 1992); Sugam Anand, *Modern Indian Historiography: From Pillai to Azad* (Agra: 1991); Tarasankar Banerjee, "Ramesh Chandra Majumdar: The Historian of Indian Nationalism," *Journal of Indian History* 59 (1981): 347–60; Ranajit Guha, *An Indian Historiography of India: A Nineteenth-Century Agenda and Its Implications* (Calcutta: 1981); Subodh Kumar Mukhopadhyay, *Evolution of Historiography in Modern India, 1900–1960: A Study of the Writing of Indian History by Her Own Historians* (Calcutta: 1981); Ramesh Chandra Majumdar, *Historiography in Modern India* (London: 1970).

26. Nancy K. Florida, *Writing the Past, Inscribe the Future: History As Prophecy in Colonial Java* (Durham, N.C.: 1995).

27. Ulrike Freitag, *Geschichtsschreibung in Syrien 1920–1990: Zwischen Wissenschaft und Ideologie* (Hamburg: 1991).

28. Basil Davidson, *The Search for Africa: History, Culture, Politics* (New York: 1994); D. I. Ajaegbo, "African Historiographical Traditions from the Earliest Times to the Second World War: An Analytical Study," *Transafrican Journal of History* [Kenya] 19 (1990): 139–51; E. J. Alagoa, "Towards a History of African Historiography," *Odu: A Journal of West African Studies* [Nigeria] 29 (1986): 3–16; Bogumil Jewsiewicki and David Newbury, eds., *African Historiographies: What History for Which Africa?* (Beverly Hills, Calif.: 1986); Albert Wirz, "Klio in Afrika: 'Geschichtslosigkeit' als historisches Problem," *Geschichte in Wissenschaft und Unterricht* 34 (1983): 98–108.

29. For European historians, only the history of pre-Columbian America and the era of exploration and conquest were significant. Latin America of the nineteenth and early twentieth centuries was disregarded in academic circles and was dealt with in other disciplines such as anthropology and ethnology. See Marta Canessa de Sanguinetti, "Las Historias Nacionales ante su Pasado Iberico," *Revista de Historica de America* [Mexico] 111 (1991): 99–112; Nikita H. Vallenilla, "National Identities and National Projects: Spanish American Historiography in the 19th and 20th Centuries," *Storia della Storiografia* 19 (1991): 147–56; Germán Colmenares, *Las Convenciones contra la Cultura: Ensayos sobre la Histografía Hispano Americana del Siglo XIX* (Bogotá: 1987); Bernd Mütter, "Grenzen der weltgeschichtlichen Perspektive in der deutschen Geschichtsschreibung vom Zeitalter der Auf-

klärung bis zur Epoche des Imperialismus: Das Beispiel Lateinamerika. Georg Iggers zum 65. Geburtstag," in *Geschichtsbewusstsein und Universalgeschichte: Das Zeitalter der Entdeckungen und Eroberungen in Geschichtsschreibung, Unterricht und Öffentlichkeit*, ed. Walter Fürnrohr (Frankfurt am Main: 1992), 45–72. An overview of the literature appears in Horst Pietschmann, "Lateinamerikanische Geschichte als Historische Teildisziplin," *Historische Zeitschrift* 248 (1989): 305–42.

30. See Jürgen Osterhammel, "Transkulturell vergleichende Geschichtswissenschaft," in *Geschichte im Vergleich*, ed. Heinz-Gerhard Haupt and Jürgen Kocka (Frankfurt am Main: 1996), 271–313; Sebastian Conrad, "What Time Is Japan? Problems of Comparative (Intercultural) Historiography," *History and Theory* 38 (1999): 67–83; Eckhardt Fuchs and Steffen Sammler, "Geschichtswisenschaft neben dem Historismus: Eine interdiziplinäre und internationale Perspektive," in Eckhardt Fuchs and Steffen Sammler, eds., *Geschichtswissenschaft neben dem Historismus*, special issue of *Comparativ* 5 (1995): 7–19; Ernst Schulin, "Universalgeschichtsschreibung im zwanzigsten Jahrhundert," in Ernst Schulin, *Traditionskritik und Rekonstruktionsversuch: Studien zurEntwicklung von Geschichtswissenschaft und historischem Denken* (Göttingen: 1979), 163–202. For case studies, see Sally C. Humphreys, ed., *Cultures of Scholarship* (Ann Arbor, Mich.: 1997). On the recent discussion on comparative history in Germany, see, among others, Thomas Welskopp, "Stolpersteine auf dem Königsweg: Methodenkritische Anmerkungen zum internationalen Vergleich in der Gesellschaftsgeschichte," *Archiv für Sozialgeschichte* 35 (1995): 339–67; Joachim Matthes, "The Operation Called 'Vergleichen,' " in Joachim Matthes, ed., *Zwischen den Kulturen? Die Sozialwissenschaften vor dem Problem des Kulturvergleichs* (Göttingen, 1992), 75–99.

31. See also Jörn Rüsen, "Some Theoretical Approaches to Intercultural Comparative Historiography," in *Chinese Historiography in Comparative Perspective*, ed. Axel Schneider and Susanne Weigelin-Schwiedrzik, special issue of *History and Theory* 35, no. 4 (1996): 5–22; Johan Galtung, "Structure, Culture, and Intellectual Style: An Essay Comparing Saxonic, Teutonic, Gallic, and Nipponic Approaches," *Social Science Information* 20 (1981): 817–56.

32. Heinz Bechert, *Zum Ursprung der Geschichtsschreibung im indischen Kulturbereich* (Göttingen: 1969); Franz Rosenthal, *A History of Muslim Historiography* (Leiden: 1952). On the sciences as a whole, see Toby E. Huff, *The Rise of Early Modern Science: Islam, China, and the West* (Cambridge, Mass.: 1993); George Sarton, *The History of Science and the New Humanism: With Recollections and Reflections by Robert K. Merton* (New Brunswick, N.J.: 1988), chap. 2, *East and West*; George Basalla, "The Spread of Western Science: A Three-Stage Model Describes the Introduction of Modern Science into Any Non-European Nation," *Science* 156 (May 5, 1967): 611–22. On China, see Joseph Needham, *Science and Civilization in China*, 7 vols. (Cambridge, Mass.: 1954–2000).

33. To African historical consciousness in general, the role of colonialism, and the relationship of writing and rational historiography, see Adam Jones, *Schwarze Geschichte—Weisse Historiker* (Leipzig: 1998); Adam Jones, "Kolonialherrschaft und Geschichtsbewusstsein: Zur Rekonstruktion der Vergangenheit in Schwarzafrika 1865–1965," *Historische Zeitschrift* 250 (1990): 73–92; Adam Jones, *Zur Quellenproblematik der Geschichte Westafrikas 1450–1900* (Stuttgart: 1990).

34. On this point, see Michael Quirin, "Scholarship, Value, Method, and Hermeneutics in Kaozheng: Some Reflections on Cui Shu (1740–1816) and the Confucian Classics," in Schneider and Weigelin-Schwiedrzik, *Chinese Historiography in Comparative Perspective*, 34–53.

35. Axel Schneider, "Between *Dao* and History: Two Chinese Historians in Search of a Modern Identity for China," in Schneider and Weigelin-Schwiedrzik, *Chinese Historiography in Comparative Perspective*, 57.

36. On the problem of "modernity" in the case of China, see chapter 12 in this book.

37. Chris Lorenz, "Comparative Historiography: Problems and Perspectives," *History and Theory* 38 (1999): 39.

38. For Japan, see Bernd Martin, "Deutsche Geschichtswissenschaft als Instrument nationaler Selbstfindung in Japan," in *Universalgeschichte und Nationalgeschichten*, ed. Gangolf Hübinger, Jürgen Osterhammel, and Erich Pelzer (Freiburg: 1994), 209–29.

39. Grete Klingenstein et al., eds., *Europäisierung der Erde? Studien zur Einwirkung Europas auf die aussereuropäische Welt* (Vienna: 1980).

40. Michel Espagne and Michael Werner, "Deutsch-französischer Kulturtransfer als Forschungsgegenstand: Eine Problemskizze," in *Transferts. Les relations interculturelles dans l'espace franco-allemand (XVIIIe et XIXe siècle)*, ed. Espagne and Werner (Paris, 1988), 11–34; Michel Espagne and Michael Werner, "Deutsch-französischer Kulturtransfer im 18. und 19. Jahrhundert: Zu einem neuen interdisziplinären Forschungsprogramm des C.N.R.S.," *Francia* 13 (1985): 502–10; Michel Espagne and Michael Werner, "La construction d'une référence culturelle allemande en France. Genèse et histoire," *Annales* 42 (1987): 969–92. See also Johannes Paulmann, "Internationaler Vergleich und interkultureller Transfer: Zwei Forschungsansätze zur europäischen Geschichte des 18. bis 20. Jahrhunderts," *Historische Zeitschrift* 267 (1998): 649–85. For the German–British relations, see Rudolf Muhs, Johannes Paulmann, and Willibald Steinmetz, eds., *Aneignung und Abwehr: Interkultureller Transfer zwischen Deutschland und Grossbritannien im 19. Jahrhundert* (Bodenheim: 1998).

41. Osterhammel points to four criteria on which the export of science, and thus cultural contact in general, depend: the quality of indigenous traditions, their specific condition at the time of the cultural contact, the manner of transmission and presentation of Western knowledge, and the political and cultural context. See Osterhammel, *Westliches Wissen*, 308. On important proposals for a theory of cultural relations, see Jürgen Osterhammel, "Kulturelle Grenzen in der Expansion Europas," *Saeculum* 46 (1995): 101–38. As a case study for philosophy, see Lydia Brüll, "Die traditionelle japanische Philosophie und ihre Probleme bei der Rezeption der abendländisch-westlichen," *Bochumer Jahrbuch für Ostasienforschung* 1 (1978): 318–47.

42. Nakayama refers, for example, to a case in which the Dutch version of a German anatomy textbook was introduced for use in Japanese medicine in China, Japan, and the West. See Shigeru Nakayama, *Academic and Scientific Traditions,* (Tokyo: 1984), 199.

43. For example, the term "science" in Japan had a philosophical dimension

when translated as *kyuri* during the Edo period, but as *kagaku* (specialized science) during the Meiji period, it was restricted to nonphilosophical, technical disciplines. Nakayama, *Academic and Scientific Traditions,* 208–9.

44. Hellmuth von Glasenapp, *Die Philosophie der Inder* (Stuttgart: 1974).

45. See the case study by Wolfgang Schwentker, *Max Weber in Japan: Eine Untersuchung zur Wirkungsgeschichte 1905–1995* (Tübingen: 1997).

46. Nakayama, *Academic and Scientific Traditions,* 219

47. Ludwig Riess, for example, was called to the Imperial University in Tokyo in 1887 to help establish a historical institute. Schwentker, "Zwischen Weltaneignung und Selbstdeutungszwang," 344ff.; Germany had also an enormous cultural impact on China. See Françoise Kreissler, *L'action culturelle allemande en Chine: De la fin du XIXe siècle à la Seconde Guerre mondiale* (Paris, 1989); Kuo Heng-yü and Mechthild Leutner, eds., *Deutschland und China: Beiträge des Zweiten Internationalen Symposiums zur Geschichte der deutsch-chinesischen Beziehungen Berlin 1991* (Munich, 1993).

48. On the influence of Western science in Japan, see also Erich Pauer, "Japanischer Geist—weltliche Technik: Zur Rezeption westlicher Technologie in Japan," *Saeculum* 38 (1987): 19–51, and Hiroshi, "British Influence on Modern Japanese Historiography"; on China, see David Wright, "John Fryer and the Shanghai Polytechnic: Making Space for Science in Nineteenth Century China," *British Journal for the History of Science* 29 (1996): 1–16; see his note 1 for recent literature.

49. On this topic, see also Schneider, "Between *Dao* and History," which shows the contradictory nature of different historical views.

50. For India, see Dietmar Rothermund, "Nationale und regionale Geschichtsschreibung in Indien," *Periplus* 3 (1993): 75–82; for Japan, see Carol Gluck, "The People in History: Recent Trends in Japanese Historiography," *Journal of Asian Studies* 38 (1978): 25–50; for Africa, Caroline Neale, *Writing "Independent" History: African Historiography, 1960–1980* (Westport, Conn.: 1985); for China, see Jonathan Unger, ed., *Using the Past to Serve the Present: Historiography and Politics in Contemporary China* (Armonk, N.Y.: 1993).

51. Edward W. Said, *Orientalism* (1978; reprint, New York: 1994).

52. See Jürgen Lütt, Nicole Brechmann, Catharina Hinz, and Isolde Kurz, "Die Orientalismus-Debatte im Vergleich: Verlauf, Kritik, Schwerpunkte im indischen und arabischen Kontext," in *Gesellschaften im Vergleich: Forschungen aus Sozial- und Geschichtswissenschaften,* ed. Hartmut Kaelble and Jürgen Schriewer (Frankfurt am Main: 1998), 511–67; Catherina Hinz and Isolde Kurz, "From Orientalism to Post-Orientalism? Middle Eastern and South Asian Perspectives," *Asien-Afrika-Lateinamerika* 25 (1997): 281–302. With reference to Said, see Ronald Inden, *Imagining India* (Oxford: 1990). For additional German voices in the orientalism debate, see Ulrike Freitag, "The Critique of Orientalism," in Bentley, *Companion to Historiography,* 620–38; Jürgen Osterhammel, "Edward W. Said und die 'Orientalismus'-Debatte: Ein Rückblick," *Asien-Afrika-Lateinamerika* 25 (1997): 597–607. For a review essay on imperialism, colonial rule, and culture see Benedikt Stuchtey, "New Research on the History of Imperialism," *German Historical Institute London, Bulletin* 18, no. 1 (1996): 5–20.

53. Lloyd I. Rudolph and Susanne Hoeber Rudolph, "Occidentalism and Ori-

entalism: Perspectives on Legal Pluralism," in Humphreys, *Cultures of Scholarship*, 222.

54. Rudolph and Rudolph, "Occidentalism and Orientalism," 223, 229. Among others, see also Chen Xiaomei, *Occidentalism As a Counter-Discourse in Post-Mao China* (New York: 1995); James G. Carrier, ed., *Occidentalism: Images of the West* (Oxford: 1995); Om Prakash Kejariwal, *The Asiatic Society of Bengal and the Discovery of India's Past* (Delhi: 1988); Wilhelm Halbfass, *India and Europe: An Essay in Understanding* (Albany, N.Y.: 1988). Arif Dirlik recently focused on the "complicity" of the "orientalist orientals" in creating European orientalism. Thus, instead of a one-sided ideology, orientalism becomes a "relationship" between Europeans and orientals that is subject to historical changes. See Arif Dirlik, "Chinese History and the Question of Orientalism," in Schneider and Weigelin-Schwiedrzik, *Chinese Historiography in Comparative Perspective*, 96–118.

55. Philip Pomper, Richard H. Elphick, and Richard T. Vann, eds., *World History. Ideologies, Structures, and Identities* (Oxford: 1998). Notable among the "world historians" are Immanuel Wallerstein, William H. McNeill, Bruce Mazlish, and Andre Gunder Frank. Among others, see Bruce Mazlish and Ralph Buultjens, eds., *Conceptualizing Global History* (Boulder, Colo.: 1993); the discussion in *History and Theory* 34 (1995); William H. McNeill, "History and the Scientific World View," *History and Theory* 37 (1998): 1–13. See also *World History Bulletin* and *Journal of World History*. On the twentieth-century tradition of world history, see Ernst Schulin, ed., *Universalgeschichte* (Cologne: 1974).

56. On the end of history, see Francis Fukuyama, *The End of History and the Last Man* (New York: 1992). As an example of the current historical discussion, see the historiography on American-Asian relations, including Warren I. Cohen, ed., *Pacific Passage: The Study of American–East Asian Relations on the Eve of the Twenty-First Century* (New York: 1996).

57. Thus, Chakrabarty speaks of an "inequality of ignorance." See Dipesh Chakrabarty, "Postcoloniality and the Artifice of History: Who Speaks for 'Indian' Pasts?" *Representations* 37 (1992): 2. He also addresses the paradox that non-Western thinkers use European social theories developed in ignorance of non-European cultures to analyze their society.

58. Among others, Iain Chambers and Lidia Curti, eds., *The Post-Colonial Question: Common Skies, Divided Horizons* (London: 1996); Carol A. Breckenridge and Peter Van der Veer, eds., *Orientalism and the Postcolonial Predicament: Perspectives on South Asia* (Philadelphia: 1993); Partha Chatterjee, *The Nation and Its Fragments: Colonial and Postcolonial Histories* (Princeton, N.J.: 1993); Gyan Prakash, ed., *After Colonialism: Imperial Histories and Postcolonial Displacements* (Princeton, N.J.: 1995); Gyan Prakash, "Writing Post-Orientalist Histories of the Third World: Indian Historiography Is Good to Think," in *Colonialism and Culture*, ed. Nicholas B. Dirks (Ann Arbor, Mich.: 1992); AHR Forum in *American Historical Review* 99, no. 5 (1994): 1475–545. On the controversy between postmodern postcolonial discourse and its critics, see *Social Text* 31–32 (1992); Arif Dirlik, "The Postcolonial Aura: Third World Criticism in the Age of Global Capitalism," *Critical Inquiry* 20, (1994): 328–356. For criticism of the critics from a postmodern perspective, see Stuart Hall, "When Was 'The Post-Colonial'? Thinking at the Limit," in Chambers and Curti, *The Post-Colonial Question*, 242–60.

59. Hall, "When Was 'The Post-Colonial'?" 250.

60. Dirlik, "Postcolonial Aura," 346.

61. Wang introduces a few examples on how some Asian historians refuse European concepts and terms in order to return to their "original" history. He warned, however, that such an approach can lead to another form of fundamentalism. See chapter 12.

62. Dirlik calls this the "global internalization of Eurocentrism." See chapter 10 of this volume.

63. "The idea is to write into the history of modernity the ambivalences, contradiction, the use of force, and the tragedies and the ironies that attend it" (Chakrabarty, "Postcoloniality and the Artifice of History," 20; quotation on 21). Whereas Chakrabarty assumes that this concept is impossible within the existing institutional limits, we believe that substantive and institutional change are interwoven processes that occur more or less simultaneously. See also Osterhammel, "Transkulturell vergleichende Geschichtswissenschaft." On the dichotomy of tradition and modernity, see Kai Hafez, ed., *Der Islam und der Westen: Anstiftung zum Dialog* (Frankfurt am Main: 1997).

64. Ram Adhar Mall, *Philosophie im Vergleich der Kulturen: Interkulturelle Philosophie—eine neue Orientierung* (Darmstadt: 1995); Franz M. Wimmer, *Interkulturelle Philosophie: Geschichte und Theorie* (Vienna: 1990); Herta Nagl-Docekal, ed., *Postkoloniales Philosophieren: Afrika* (Vienna: 1992); Franz M. Wimmer, ed., *Vier Fragen zur Philosophie in Afrika, Asien und Lateinamerika* (Vienna: 1988). See also Peter Brenner, "Interkulturelle Hermeneutik: Probleme einer Theorie kulturellen Fremdverstehens," in *"Interkulturelle Germanistik": Dialog der Kulturen auf Deutsch?* ed. Peter Zimmermann (Frankfurt am Main: 1989), 35–55.

65. Mall, *Philosophie im Vergleich der Kulturen,* 7. On *philosophia perennis,* see 159ff.

66. Such a *historia perennis,* nevertheless, requires certain standards that prevent historical relativism, which means a methodology that allows rational procedures to verify historical narratives.

67. This reference is found in Mall, *Philosophie im Vergleich der Kulturen,* 24.

68. Karl Jaspers, *Vom Ursprung und Ziel der Geschichte* (Munich: 1983); Shmuel N. Eisenstadt, ed., *The Origins and Diversity of Axial Civilizations* (Albany, N.Y.: 1983); and Shmuel N. Eisenstadt, ed., *Kulturen der Achsenzeit,* 2 vols. (Frankfurt am Main: 1987–1992). A critical summary is provided in Stefan Breuer, "Kulturen der Achsenzeit. Leistung und Grenzen eines geschichtsphilosophischen Konzepts," *Saeculum* 45 (1994).

Part I

HISTORIOGRAPHY AND CULTURAL IDENTITY

1

The Authenticity of a Copy

Problems of Nineteenth-Century Spanish-American Historiography

Jochen Meissner

Modern historical thought is a European phenomenon that later developed validity and became a force for change in the rest of the world.[1]

For arrogance, for pride, there is no mercy.[2]

Between 1808 and 1824 almost all the former American colonies achieved political independence against Spain. This period did not mark the beginning of historical thought and writing in and about Latin America, but it was the beginning of a profound change in the intellectual climate of this region. Independence and the evolving of new republics gave rise to great expectations about a splendid future that would leave a colonial and as well a monarchic heritage far behind. But events in the following decades, up to the end of the nineteenth century, did not live up to these hopes. Internal conflicts and political, economic, and military interventions from the outside threatened the new states. The feeling of a widening gap between Latin America on the one hand and the industrializing northern European countries and the United States on the other grew throughout the region. The distance from those societies gave them some almost utopian traits in the political imaginary of Latin American intellectuals and turned them into role models for what the Latin American nations hoped to achieve. This is true for the economic as well as the political culture and for the development of science.

Although independence signifies a break in the history of Latin America, recent scholarship places more and more emphasis on the continuities between the late colonial and the early republican period. In the pigmentocracy of these multiethnic societies the Creole element—that is, the offspring of the European immigrants—managed to hold a dominant position far beyond the end of the nineteenth century. Race remained the most important factor of social inequality. The intellectual elite was recruited almost exclusively from the male offspring of Creole families. The minds of these men were shaped and trained by educational institutions that had very similar structures, subjects, and teaching methodologies as their Spanish counterparts. European thought—known through voyages and/or studies in Europe as well as through the writings and many of the extant and newly formed personal ties—determined in many ways the intellectual horizon of the Latin American political and intellectual leaders.

But, unlike some European countries, the central scenery of nineteenth-century Spanish-American historiography was not academia. This may be one reason why a systematic study of the institutional history still has to be written.[3] Throughout the century, in most areas of the regions academic writing and teaching of history was of minor importance. Therefore the first question is what do we define as the main subject of a study of nineteenth-century Spanish-American historiography? Or, in other words, where do we encounter the published leftovers of historical reflections? What are their material forms? Four major groups of historical publications have to be taken into account:

1. Articles and letters about historical subjects in newspapers and journals. Very often, but not always, these are the published versions of conferences that had been given at learned societies, or of speeches that had commemorated a certain date or celebrated a special event. These periodicals contain as well the polemics that sometimes developed around them. Sarmiento (1811–1888), one of the towering Argentinean intellectuals of the nineteenth century, viewed the newspaper as the prime means of spreading knowledge and enlightenment throughout the country.[4]
2. Textbooks for the teaching of history at the college and university level.
3. Independently published historical studies about special subjects.
4. Books that tried to synthesize the historical knowledge in the form of dictionaries or manuals.

This means—to clarify the limits of what is said here—that the vast cosmos of mostly oral popular traditions are excluded from consideration. Because pure research about the infrastructure of publishing, printing, and book trade in the different Latin American countries is almost nonexistent, we know very little about the actual number of historical publications, circulation figures, and the social and geographical radiation of these publications. As even the literacy rates are difficult or impossible to establish, we will restrict our analysis to the statements of those who actively participated in the published discourses about history. Only one general statement can be made beyond that: History is produced for an audience that could be called a "general public" (in opposition to a more exclusively academic public). But this community consisted only of the 10 to 15 percent—to give a rough and not very well-based guess—of the total population that was able to read and belonged to the predominantly Creole upper strata. This culture was mostly based in the major cities—predominantly the capitals. In other words, although possibly affected by certain consequences of this historical discourse, the vast majority of the population was excluded from active or even passive participation in it.

The biographical and prosopographical backgrounds are far better researched. In 1978 Bradford Burns published an article based on a sample of sixty-three Latin American historians of the nineteenth century.[5] In 1984 Jack Ray Thomas presented a biographical dictionary that consists of more than two hundred bio-bibliographical sketches of people whom he referred to as the most influential Latin American historians from the colonial period to the twentieth century. In 1991 smaller samples of Brazilian and Spanish-American bio-biographical sketches were published as parts of a dictionary of great historians of the modern age.[6] A certain number of work histories (*Werkgeschichten*) of Spanish-American historiography exist as well, but they mostly try to establish the national tradition of historiographies in each country.[7] There is only one book with a broader perspective: Acevedos's *Manual de historiografía hispanoamericana contemporánea* (1992). Besides that there are of course many monographs about individual historians as well as research reports on special subjects and/or countries.[8] Although there are a few very rare exceptions, the trend of applying methods of literary criticism to the historical studies of the nineteenth century has hardly influenced the history of historiography in Spanish America so far.[9] An outstanding study of the nineteenth-century Latin American historiography—something in between a thematic approach, prosopography, work analysis, and literary criticism—was published by the Colombian scholar Germán Colmenares in 1987. I will comment on some of his arguments later. The thesis propounded by Anderson, Hobsbawm, and Ranger[10] about the invention of tradition has gained some importance in Spanish America[11] and it can be expected that more studies of this type will follow. I mostly concentrate on the cases of Mexico, Chile, and add some short comments on and examples from Argentina. The material is presented in the order of five subaspects: interests or motivations; ideological frameworks or ideas; methods; forms and styles; and functions of historical writing in Spanish America in the nineteenth century.[12] To give a more complete picture of the historical writing of this world region I thought it would be a good idea not only to formulate abstract ideas about this historical writing, but to give as many examples from the original texts as possible.

The first question is: What were the motivations, reasons, or interests of the authors who undertook historical research, wrote history, or reflected on certain historical experiences? A utopian potential in the conception of history was not absent: "History is the oracle of the gods . . . which counseled and taught people to build happier and more contented lives for themselves," wrote the Chilean historian José Victorino Lastarria (1817–1888), but obviously individual curiosity, thirst for knowledge or looking for historical answers to certain questions are only of random importance compared with the interest in teaching others certain historical facts and certain "meanings" of history. Lastarria added: "write for the people, enlighten them; combat their vices and encourage their virtues; remind them of historical facts; accustom them to worship their god and their institutions."[13] As Woll put it, the key to nineteenth-century historiography was utility.

Of course the whole group of historical textbooks are motivated by the interest to educate and to teach. But this is true for most of the historical studies as well. Lorenzo de Zavala (1788–1836) hoped that his essay about the Mexican revolution (published in 1831–1832 in Paris!) would change many of the wrong ideas Europeans had about America.[14] Lucas Alamán (1792–1853) wished that his *disertaciones* would be useful for other American nations to learn from the mistakes made in Mexico.[15] And of course the young nations should be taught about their heroic past. Sometimes the purpose that a national tradition should be founded is explicitly mentioned. José Victorino Lastarria wrote in 1842 that Chileans had "an ardent desire, very common in new nations, to earn a place alongside older civilizations and hold their head up proudly before European philosophers."[16] Another very frequently mentioned reason—especially by those who actively participated in the events they describe—was the conservation of a certain knowledge that otherwise would be lost. In many cases it is closely related to the former argument, because the facts that should be remembered were those of the foundation of the new nations. Therefore, the main reason for Carlos María Bustamante (1774–1848) to write a history of the Mexican revolution, for example, was the neglect "my compatriots show in a matter which will one day cause the greatest glory of our native country. I noticed with regret that the witnesses who survived these great events were waning very quickly and that after a few years one will only find very few, which are able to instruct us with truth."[17] And giving similar reasons Lucas Alamán wrote: "In a certain way I believed myself to be obliged . . . because of the justice I owe to posterity."[18]

Naturally there were less altruistic or patriotic reasons at hand as well. History was not mainly written by unworldly aesthetes but by military or political leaders. Fanny Calderón de la Barca, a contemporary observer of the prosaic life of the upper classes of Mexico City in the first half of the nineteenth century, commented that, if enlightened men fail in the public sphere they retire from it and dedicate themselves to write.[19] Mostly they do not write literature, but history. In Argentina Mitre (1821–1906) is an excellent example of this type of historian. He had fought in the war to expel the dictator Juan Manuel de Rosas; he had lived and worked in exile in Chile; and he had served a term as president of Argentina before he reached the age of forty-eight.[20] Reasons of state were important in these writings, but so was the justification of certain decisions and the trans-figuration of the role the authors themselves or their parties played in these events. It could cause scandals as well. The Chilean historian Ben-jamín Vicuña Mackenna (1831–1886) was fascinated by the role individu-als played in the major events of Chilean history, but his effort to report only the "pure truth" about the events of independence and its actors offended so many families whose members were mentioned in his books that he became the cause of a profound distrust of Santiago's elite against the occupation of historians in general. "Anyone," wrote a scandalized reader of one of Vicuña's books, "should be indignant at the gross insults and audacious lies that the author has used to blemish the beloved mem-ory of my father."[21]

The leading ideas that shaped the minds of those who wrote history have to be distinguished from their personal interests. Many scholars limit themselves to pointing out that most of the ideological framework that influenced the writing of history in Spanish America was imported from abroad. As a matter of fact, it is amazing to what degree this ques-tion dominates the studies of Latin American historiography. It is impor-tant to notice that this is a debate in very general terms. Very few studies have been based so far on intense research on the influence of, let's say, a Burke, a Macaulay or a Michelet. Much needs to be done in future studies on the subject.

Let me give some examples from the two most analytical studies of nineteenth-century Latin American historiography that have been pub-lished so far. The first is "The poverty of progress," first published in 1980, more an essay than a study about nineteenth-century Latin American history by E. Bradford Burns, a Californian specialist. The second is the 1987 study by the Colombian historian Germán Colmenares titled "Las convenciones contra la cultura."

Burns writes: "The Latin American historians believed Europe to be the focal point of history, regarding their own histories as extensions of European."[22] He argues that the Latin American elites showed more interest in Paris, London, or New York than in the multifaceted regional and ethnic differences in their own countries. So they alienated themselves from the Latin American realities and undertook the unsuccessful attempt to imply political and economic models in Latin America that did not really fit to their reality.

> Influenced by the political and economic ideas of the Enlightenment at the time of their political independence, the ruling elites imposed upon Latin America theories that reflected little or none of the local socioeconomic environment. . . . The elites felt they shaped their institutions in the latest European molds. They ignored the obvious fact that those models did not reflect American experience.[23]

There was an "admiration for the latest ideas, modes, values, and styles of Europe and the United States and a desire to adopt—rarely to adapt— them."[24] Progress and modernization, Burns continues, were the most sacred words in the political vocabulary and they were strongly associated with capitalism, individualizing property rights (especially over land), trying to carry through a western concept of labor, constitutional orders that copied their European and U.S.-American role models. All in all, he believes, they deepened the dependency of Latin America. He concludes: "European thought was no intellectual spring; it proved to be an ideological flood, which swept before it most American originality."[25]

Colmenares argues in a much more subtle and less polemic way. Nevertheless one can frequently find in his book sentences that aim in a similar direction as Burns: "The Spanish-American historians of the nineteenth century followed the rules which at that time dominated the European historiography."[26] A bit later he adds, "The historians of the new Spanish-American nations of the nineteenth century adopted the narrative conventions that were used to determine the historiographical profession in Europe."[27] Moreover, he states that "Latin America has maintained an obstinate monologue whose unchanging subject was the European thought."[28]

It could be asked whether similar influences cannot also be found, for example, in British, French, or German historiography, whose originality has not been questioned because they reacted to impulses from outside. Moreover, what sense does it make for a North American scholar trained in the United States and teaching history in California, or a Colombian scholar trained in France[29] who bases major parts of his analysis on concepts from Paul Ricoeur's *Temps et récits*, to criticize nineteenth-century Latin American historians for being influenced by the European historiography?[30] Finally, there is an amazing parallelism with the self-conceptions of some European historians.[31] The problem with this kind of transatlantic consensus is that it very easily can be misused "to purge" (*entsorgen*) a large amount of historical narratives, historical writings that represent a very special type of an intellectual European-Spanish-American relationship.[32]

Nevertheless, if you open only one of the historical studies that were written in the nineteenth century, it is not difficult to find much evidence that supports the mentioned judgments of Burns and Colmenares. Let me give some examples. In 1842 Simonde de Sismondi's *Recherches sur les constitutions des peuples libres* was praised in Chile with the comment: "We need not be original, we need not tire ourselves out with the study of history. . . . We may just take advantage of these proven laws of political science."[33] Lorenzo Zavala published in 1824 an *Objeto, plan y distribución del estudio de la historia* under his own name, which later proved to be an only slightly modified translation of Volney's *Leçons d'Histoire*.[34] For many decades of the nineteenth century the teaching of what was thought to have borne a classical canon of European history has been much more important to the point of even substituting the concern about American traditions during the time of the colonial empire or the rich heritage of the Indian cultures on which the colonies were founded. Criticizing the way history was taught in the institutes of higher education in Mexico in the 1840s, Gómez de la Cortina (1799–1860), an offspring of an old Creole noble family of Mexico, found the knowledge of Nahuatl, Maya, or any other Indian language obviously of no importance, but stated: "If the teacher is not able to translate correctly and immediately the historical works written in Greece, Latin, French, English and German, there is a very strong reason to suspect that he can not be a good teacher of history." He then added a list of recommended readings, mostly books that were printed in Germany in the eighteenth century used by teachers to prepare their classes.[35] Books such as Bossuet's *Discours sur l'histoire universelle* were used as textbooks in Mexican and Chilean colleges.[36] The *Discours* start literally with Adam and Eve, but the European discovery of America is not even mentioned. This was no rare exception, but the norm. In Mexico elements of regional history only very slowly entered the schoolbooks, which mostly had the form of catechisms.[37] This did not always bring an improvement though. Vázquez quotes a nice example from a schoolbook of 1882:

What happened with the Ancient México? It finished. And in its place? It was ordered to build the modern Mexico or it was conquered, and the Aztecs themselves helped to accomplish that.[38]

Chile was in a similar situation until the 1840s, when some historians started to write new textbooks and tried to reform the system of higher education. But European influence was still dominant. In 1871 the translation of the six-volume textbook of Duruy, a French politician and former secretary of Michelet, was the schoolbook used in most institutions of Chilean higher education. But additional texts by the Chilean historians Barros Arana (1830–1901) and Amunátegui (1828–1888) were used as well to teach American and Chilean history.[39]

Other European influences could be seen in the areas of methodology, forms of historical writing, and so on, that further illustrated the theses of Burns and Colmenares. But as much as their statements reveal, they belong at the same time to a historiographical tradition that covers up the other half of the story. Facing the overwhelming tradition of European historical thought the struggle for originality, intellectual independence, and the development of one or several American identities can be traced back far into the colonial period. In the eighteenth century, American writers defended their regions against the cheeks about America and its inhabitants that can be found in the works of important representatives of enlightenment such as Robertson or Adam Smith. Gómez de la Cortina, who demanded that Mexican teachers of history should know several European but no Indian languages, and further recommended the reading of an exclusive European set of historical literature, also stated:

History, that is, the science which more than any other needs comparison, the purity of the originals, the independent judgment, the certainty, the flame of criticism. . . . Here we are used, speaking generally, considering as good everything that comes from Europe. It is of giving lectures of history, immediately we leave to walk through these streets, looking in bookshop after bookshop for *any* lectures of history whatever. The important thing is that these are lectures of history, and the first we find are the best, especially if they are already translated from English or from French. . . . Nor we know which species of bird it is or who was the author, neither whether the quotations are exact, corrections of the dates etc., nothing we investigate; what is important to us is to have in our hands *any kind of lectures of history* and we believe that with them we are able to learn history and to teach it to the whole world. . . . For heaven's sake! It is time now to develop judgment, to start to correct this superficiality and thoughtlessness which makes us completely ridiculous.[40]

In Chile Lastarria and many members of the literary society demanded: "Chileans might take advantage of the discoveries of European thinkers," but "our literature must be exclusively our own, and it must be wholly national."[41]

Thus the critic of overwhelming foreign intellectual influences is in no way a new discovery of Burns and Colmenares, but rather an integral part of the ideas that shaped the Latin American historiography in the nineteenth century. And there are many counter arguments that could be mentioned:

1. Books that traveled over the Atlantic or that were translated from French, English, or German may have entirely changed their meaning when they were read in a different cultural setting.
2. The whole concept of "European thought" bears a monolithic illusion of what has to be considered a universe of very different, contradicting ideas and concepts.
3. Since its discovery America has been an important part of European thought. Reverse influences—such facts as the Chilean historian Barros Arana being a member of the Academie Francaise or the Guatemalan José Milla being a member of the Royal Spanish Academy—are much less considered.
4. Different ways of influences could be considered. There is a difference between the mere copying of a French book or, for example, studying its methodology and applying it to another historical reality. But even a mere copy could prove to have an entirely different meaning. In the above mentioned plagiarism of Volney's *Leçons d'Histoire* by Zavala, Volney's names of protagonists of the French revolution, like Robbespierre and Marat, are substituted by the names of Hidalgo and Morelos. But in many ways these leaders of the Indian rebellion in the epoch of independence are much more similar to the leaders of the farmers of the Languedoc than to the leaders of the French revolution in Paris.
5. The most interesting questions that have to be answered are, what parts of the European tradition made their way to America? Why were they influential in America? And, most important, in which way were they transformed?

Colmenares considers some of these arguments and carries them further. His study is thus an important contribution in dealing with the major problem that still lies ahead: How to construct the American context in which historiography developed in America in the nineteenth century.

Burns, on the other hand, limits the problem to a dichotomy between the "bad guys" who wrote an elitist Creole historiography and a very small number of "good guys" who were more interested in the popular culture. So the problem of men such as Alberdi (1810–1884)—who Burns considers as an example of the second type of historians, who were as well heavily influenced by European ideological currents while at the same time being members of the Creole elite—does not enter into his framework. Furthermore Burns's arguments become especially suspicious when he begins to romanticize dictators such as Francia in Paraguay or Rosas in Argentina as protagonists of the popular cultures and real expressions of the will of the people. Taking this into account, Burns himself seems to be more dependent on the nationalist ideologies of some Spanish-American countries than his corrosive attacks against them would lead one to believe.

Besides these European influences other ideological currents have to be considered—for example, Sarmiento's notion of the conflict between civilization and barbarism. This contrast can be translated to the conflict between a European shaped "progressive" urban and a more autochthonously shaped, "retarded" rural culture.[42] This idea of dichotomy was considered as the dominant trait of the American societies and the major hindrance for development and modernization. It had a strong impact far beyond the boundaries of Argentina. It is also seen in Zavala's striking contrast between his adoration for the United States on the one hand ("the political school of the United States is a perfect system; a classic work, unique: a discovery similar to the printing press, the compass and the vapor"), and his disastrous judgment about his own people ("in general, the Mexican is superficial, lazy, intolerant, extravagant and almost lavish, arrogant, aggressive, superstitious, ignorant and enemy of any effort").[43] In many aspects it shows striking similarities with twentieth-century versions of modernization theory. Frequently, it was combined with a deep disdain of Indian cultures, an obvious and mostly unbroken heritage of the Creole tradition. Sarmiento speaks about the Araucanos as "disgusting Indians." Obviously he has much more in common with the members of the concurrent Chilean nation than with those Araucanian peoples who were inhabitants of his own country, because, he adds: "we should have hung them and we would order to hang them now, if they reappeared in a war against Chile."[44]

Here we find, as my hypothesis, one of the major contradictions that help to explain much of the failure of the nation-building processes in nineteenth-century Latin America. The Creole identity exceeded the limits of the new Spanish-American states and had developed during three centuries of colonial rule. The essence of this identity was the opposition against Indian and Black culture. This "popular" culture was experienced as a danger and as a threat against European civilization, of which the Creoles felt a part. Compared with that the nation-state ideology was a conflicting model, because it required a communal spirit in each region that achieved independence from Spain: a communal spirit, which would

have negated the ethnical differences, which dominated Creole thought
for centuries. I do not know a more explicit formulation of this fundamental problem of nineteenth-century Spanish-American history as that chosen by Simón Bolívar in 1819. It perfectly describes the conflict between
competitive identities in which the Creole elites were trapped, once the
tradition of colonial rule was overcome:

> We are not Europeans, we are not Indians, but a species in between los Indig-
> enous and the Spanish People. We are Americans by birth and Europeans by
> law. We find ourselves in the conflict of questioning the claims of possession
> by the natives and keep—at the same time—our position in a country which
> saw our birth and against the opposition of the invaders; thus our case is the
> most extraordinary and complicated.[45]

Several polemics arose around the methodology that should be applied
in the study and research of history. Most nineteenth-century Spanish-
American scholars agreed that the writing of history should be based on
the intense search for documents and the critical analysis of sources. It
had already been a common practice in the colonial period. Although
other topics were chosen as well, the historical subjects that found by far
the most attention were the revolutions of the independence. Being themselves actors in the events described or personally linked to them many
of the historians had a very direct access to official documents and personal letters or diaries. In many cases the adoration of the document went
so far that the books became mere chains of quotations from the different
documents arranged into a simple chronological order. Historians such
as Lucas Alamán, who used to write in a more narrative style, very often
added transcriptions of the documents they relied on to their books.[46] Systematic editions of the documents of the independence epoch in Mexico
started in the 1870s.[47] Some scholars, such as the Argentine Vicente Fidel
López (1815–1893), chose rather to base their histories on oral tradition.[48]
Sometimes histories evolved in a process that could be called a collective
writing of history. For example, often historical writings about the independence epoch were first published in journals. The reading audience
reacted to them by writing letters that criticized the presentation of certain events or leading protagonists. The corrections and differing perspectives were later integrated in the final book edition of these writings.[49]

As the generation of the witnesses of the independence events was
waning, the search in archives became more important. Unfortunately
there is no systematic study of the development of archives and libraries.
Some were already founded during the colonial period, but we do not
know about their development in the course of the nineteenth century in
a comparative perspective looking to more than one Latin American

country. Private libraries, mostly collected by the historians themselves, seem to have provided most of the data for the historical studies throughout the first half of the nineteenth century. Mitre, for example, was determined to review all available material on a given subject and therefore his efforts to collect and look through documents were monumental. He once speculated that a projected biography of the Argentine independence hero, José de San Martín, would require the examination of 10,000 manuscripts. He expected his study to run from 1,000 to 1,200 pages in two volumes. When he finally completed the book it covered 2,000 pages in three volumes.[50]

The Chileans are considered to be pioneers in the Spanish-American historiography as well as in their efforts to build an institutional infrastructure. So Barros Arana's description of the Chilean National Library at mid-nineteenth century may give an idea of the tools that were at hand:

> In those years the Biblioteca Nacional, the only library in the nation open to the public, by its scarce source of books, by the reduced numbers of its employees (an honorary director serving without pay, one librarian, and one assistant) and by the diminution of the contribution from the State, corresponded imperfectly to the objective that had been sought in its establishment. . . . The library contained some one hundred and ten or twenty thousand volumes, was in its major part ancient, endowed with a considerable section of theological books, expositories, sermons, lives of saints, or texts of classical antiquity, gleaned in their totality from the bookshelves of the old Jesuits, in general mediocre, but among which are found some rare bibliographies, and even certain precious ones of this genre that no one knew how to appreciate. The books on history and geography of America were scarce enough; and among them were not found any books that, like the famous history of Antonio de Herrera, would not be lacking in any American library.[51]

The second half of the nineteenth century—in most Spanish-American countries even more the final decades of the century—seemed to witness the change from personally acquired documents and private libraries to public archives and libraries. As many historians were sent into exile for certain periods of time because of their political involvement, mutual influences between different national historiographical schools were frequent. This relationship was extremely strong between the Argentinean and the Chilean historians and, of course, exiled intellectuals who very often traveled to Europe. Trying to make the best of their situation, this was very often the beginning of the search in foreign libraries for documents and books that could be useful when writing the history of each of the Latin American countries. But very often the materials were in disarray and almost none of them were cataloged. Therefore, work with them was slow and nerve-wracking. The materials were so dusty and dirty that sometimes it took days or even weeks to prepare them for reading. Nevertheless, after a while visiting the Spanish archives in Madrid (Simancas) and Seville was even considered mandatory. The important Ecuadorian Federico González Suárez (1844–1917) claimed that without the consultation of the Archivo de Indias in Seville it would be "morally impossible to write the general history of America and in particularly that of each of the peoples which today are the independent republics."[52] Perhaps he exaggerated his efforts to look through and copy the documents of the Ecuadorian colonial history, because the results he relates were tragic:

> [It] cost me the almost complete loss of my teeth and molars and the considerable debilitation of my sight: I suffered headaches, twitching in the face and jaw bones and stomach ailments. The dust of the archives and the reading of documents, the traveling and the constant occupation in study, with pen in hand, destroyed my health.[53]

For other historians, such as Amunátegui, this situation seems to have made the documents only more authentic:

> It is necessary . . . to study those documents, half erased, half moldered, which give off a special smell and which leave in your hand a fine and sticky dust to understand all the frustration of a work like that.[54]

Many historians believed that the documents that were revealed in such nasty enterprises already guaranteed the authenticity of their histories, and they let these documents "speak for themselves . . . since history is the science of facts, it is more valuable to relate these facts as they occurred and leave the reader free to draw his own conclusions."[55] The reason for this attitude was not simply a naive overestimation of the document, but the simple state of research. Claude Gay (1800–1873) wrote:

> A dear friend has told me that the daily papers are criticizing my work, claiming that I have written a chronicle rather than a true history because I do not understand the philosophy of this science well enough to write a good work on the subject. Without a doubt, I enjoy these brilliant theories discovered by the modern school very much, and, I, too, would like to learn of these seductive spiritual combinations. . . . But, before this can be done, the journalists should ask themselves if the study of the bibliography of American, and, especially, Chilean historical literature is advanced enough to supply the necessary data for a work of this nature.[56]

Nevertheless, as this quote indicates, this "method" was increasingly questioned. Sarmiento commented about Gay: "In America we do not need mere collections of facts, but the philosophical explanation of causes and effects."[57] In Chile in the 1840s, in a famous debate between Andrés Bello (1781–1865) and Lastarria, and in Argentina in the 1880, in an equally known polemic between Fidel López and Mitre, these assumptions were hotly debated. These polemics have been treated extensively in the literature because they are considered to be of strong impact on the historiography throughout the century, but this influence seems to be restricted to South America.

There are many different descriptions and interpretations of these polemics, but I do not want to go too deep into detail. My thin, but short description would be: Lastarria and Fidel López could be considered as members of a younger generation that rebelled against an empiricist establishment by postulating a philosophical type of writing history. Lastarria wrote that "the truth is the vision of justice that determines life. This is the base of the new philosophy of history that we present to the New World."[58] A partidarian endorsed:

> If one does not limit himself to the memorizing of a confusing chaos of isolated facts, but, on the contrary, studies history with a philosophical method, it can be one of the most important realms of knowledge for a lawyer or public official. History, the study of mankind, gathers the collective experiences of many centuries and all of the peoples of the world, and allows one to consider all of the events which might bring happiness or disaster to a nation.[59]

This current was, however, heavily criticized for not relying satisfactorily enough on primary data. Mitre, for example, commented: "I always believed that what has been called philosophical history is only the refuge of those who do not want to understand the history, of those who want to make out of this science a set of generalities and vague and useless declarations."[60] Bello himself countered the attack: "Lastarria is not interested in the investigation of facts, but the various systems of writing history which are being disputed at this time."[61]

As a matter of fact the failure of the rebels seems to be that they did not try to reconcile their philosophical and political ambitions with the methodological and empirical objections of their adversaries. This might have allowed them to bring facts and ideology into a certain harmony. Instead they rather replaced the historical data with their ambition for progress. Thus they seem to be nearer to an enlightened type of history, or one could as well say exemplary type, than to the romantic current of European historiography that had largely inspired them in their upheaval against the authorities of the old sages. Most interpretations of these disputes agree that the empiricist position prevailed in them and that it was dominant throughout the century. More recent studies are more cautious about this assumption. They indicate that the impact of the opposing view was stronger than so far admitted. The later development can be far better understood, if one assumes that both positions formed poles between which a spectrum developed. This spectrum determined much of the historical production of the time.[62]

Another example for a special methodology can be found in Miguel Luís Amunátegui's *La dictadura de O'Higgins*. He attempted to establish that "the republic was the form of government which best corresponded to the spirit of the century, and, that every new state that appears must necessarily be republican." In order to prove his thesis, he discussed the fruitless attempts of Bernardo O'Higgins to establish a dictatorship in Chile. He concluded that "it was impossible to implant a dictatorship in any of the new nations."[63] Thus the idea was to use history to prove a certain rule of political development. Naturally this was embedded in the political controversies of the time, because there can be no doubt which was the message as Montt was a dictator of Chile at this time.

The final decades of the nineteenth century open the way to a transformation of a more problem-oriented type of historiography. In Chile Letelier (1852–1919) was an early protagonist. He differed from earlier historians, who insisted that the selection of the facts was the objective phase of historical study, and only their analysis was subject to the influence of personal or political interests. Letelier replied in 1888 that the process of fact collection could be as arbitrary as their interpretation:

> What commonly happens is that the historian finds it impossible to relate all the events; he only takes into account those which fit his own criteria and neglects to mention the others or only refers to them in an incidental manner. For example, Bossuet goes into ecstasy when discussing Martin, an obscure monk of Tours, and makes no reference to Mohammed or the influence of Córdoba and Bagdad on the intellectual developments of the Middle Ages.[64]

He tried to overcome the well-felt limits of historical writing that had been produced thus far, by writing a critical analysis of historical methodology from the time of Herodotus to the present day.[65]

Letelier did not only demand a change, but also gave examples of what a new, more scientific methodology could look like. For example, most analysts considered marriage by that time as a result of individual whim or an expression of family interests. He countered that concept by going to the *Anuario estadística de Chile* and compiled a table of the number of marriages celebrated between 1871 and 1880. He noted that many more marriages occurred during the first half of the period than the second. Letelier suggested that the economic prosperity of 1871 to 1875, followed by the economic crisis of 1876 to 1878 and the War of the Pacific (1879–

1883), may have affected the rate of marriages in Chilean society. Then he presented a law explaining that the number of marriages in a society was a function of the population size, the state of the economy, and domestic customs. He further argued that such statistical studies could be extended to an analysis of suicide and crime. Whereas he never claimed that he could predict whether a certain person would marry or commit suicide in a certain year, he asserted that if he were given certain data about a society, he would be able to predict relative rates of marriages or increases and decreases in numbers of crime.[66]

By speaking about motivations, leading ideas, and methods, much has already been said about forms and styles in which history was written. As was mentioned above the methods of literary criticism have only rarely been applied to Latin American historiography so far. Therefore most of the judgments about and classification of styles that has been done so far can be reduced to the statement that there were good and bad writers. In spite of the aforementioned literary ambitions of some historians, little attention was paid to the style of writing. As Thomas puts it:

> If there was anything approximating a consensus regarding the role of style in historiography, it was that one's work must be readable and unencumbered with grammatical problems but style must always be a secondary consideration to content. Research, analysis, and interpretation were of primary importance and must never be inhibited by literary considerations.[67]

The two prevailing types are chronicles of the independence events and biographies of the heroes of independence.

Sarmiento paraphrased an idea of Thomas Carlyle when he wrote that history was the essence of unnumbered biographies and thus he believed that the biographical form was most appropriate to bring the facts into an order that the "ordinary people" could understand. "Nobody can imagine," wrote Mitre, "all the things which can be formulated in the narrative of a human life . . . the life is a picture which can include in itself all that can be imagined; it is a universal formula which can embrace the most contradicting elements." O'Higgins, San Martin, and most extensively Simón Bolívar were considered icons, as the embodiments of the revolution, enlightenment, virtue, and of course the nations they "liberated." Benjamín Vicuña Mackenna wrote histories of O'Higgins, Carrera, and Portales, and edited a whole dictionary of the heroes of Chilean independence. The obsession with biographies was so exaggerated that the same Sarmiento who first had supported this type became unnerved about it: "The eternal praise of our historical personalities, fabulous all of them, is our disgrace and our curse."[68]

Finally, we will have a look at the social functions of historiography,

which of course influenced the individual motivations and the ideological
framework involved in writing history and is closely related to both. Nevertheless, though running the risk of repeating something that has
already been mentioned, it makes sense to have a look at them as such.
As the criticism of Burns and Colmenares revealed, Latin American historiography of the nineteenth century did not fulfill the function of organizing collective memory if this collective memory was to include the
different ethnic elements of which these societies consisted. The Indian
and the Black experience entered only slowly into the framework and did
not gain importance before the beginning of the twentieth century. Nevertheless inside of what might be called the Creole public sphere history
fulfilled several important functions. I will mention four in particular.
History:

- was an important weapon in the internal conflicts between different
  political factions;
- was a political weapon in the conflict between state and church;
- was a tool to rationalize boundary conflicts; and,
- served as an important tool in the creation of the so-called *historias
  patrias* or, in other words, in the early phases of the nation-building
  process of each republic.

It has already been mentioned that many historians were active participants in the political events they described. Of course their histories
reflect the political divisions between conservatives and liberals, but more
recent revisionist views focus more on similarities. In Mexico, for example, Bustamante, Zavala, and Mora (1794–1850) are considered as the classical representatives of the liberal current, while Lucas Alamán's writing
is reported to be of a conservative character. Especially in the Mexican
case this classification seems of limited use because it is mainly based on
the political performance of these people and not on an analysis of their
works themselves. In many respects Lucas Alamán's books are much
more innovative than those of the so-called liberals. While the so-called
liberal historians usually focus much more on the heroic deeds of individuals, Lucas Alamán seems to have a much clearer perspective on the
structural elements and social forces that influenced the history of Mexico. Furthermore Lucas Alamán is one of the rare exceptions of the first
generation of national historians who had a vivid interest in the colonial
past and refuted the general condemnation of the Spanish heritage.

  In Chile liberal historians began early to use history to endorse their
arguments against the church that was depicted as the willing partner of
Spain in the time of the Conquista and the colonial period. There was no
doubt, contended Barros Arana, that: "the Inquisition and the Catholic

religion were the causes of the literary and scientific decadence of Spain at the end of the seventeenth century . . . Spain believed that the diffusion of knowledge involved a danger to the conservation of the Catholic faith and the stability of the monarchy."[69]

Furthermore the Jesuits were described as deceptive hucksters interested only in obtaining gold and property.[70] In another book the same author added that the clerics' faith "in their own prestige was the cause of their corruption and ignorance." But these "historical" statements were deeply rooted in the political conflicts of that time. Barros Arana had been appointed rector of the National Institute in 1863 and undertook many efforts to secularize the teaching of history in the institutions of higher education—many of them Catholic. His attempt to substitute older textbooks, such as the one by Bossuet, with, for example, a translation of Duruy was met with strong Catholic opposition. When he finally had to resign from his post he blamed the Catholic Church and the clergy as most responsible and projected these experiences into his histories about the role of the church in the colonial period.

In order to answer these critiques—of which Barros Arana is by far not the only example—a new breed of historian developed: Catholic historians who tried to counter the anticlerical writing on a scientific base. Crescente Errázuriz (1839–1931) serves as an example:

> Certain historians use only those facts that add stature to the person they are discussing, and, at the same time, keep silent about any facts that can harm his image. Whoever does this lacks the prime qualities of the Catholic writer. Not being impartial and completely truthful will not aid the Church, but, on the contrary, give arms to its enemies.[71]

Another Catholic historian, José Hipólito Salas (1775–1854), presented a picture of the church operating alone during the colonial period, struggling for the "sacred rights of man" against the Spaniards. He believed that 1810 was preceded by a two-century struggle by the missionaries for the liberty of the enslaved Indians, and this triumph of social liberty was the precursor of the political liberty of 1810.

Finally, boundary disputes stimulated much of the historical research of the nineteenth century. The rule of *uti possidetis juris* dictated that the colonial limits as determined by the Spanish legislation would remain unchanged for the newly independent nations. Unfortunately as many of these regions were still unexplored or only vaguely known at the moment of independence this rule left a lot of space for interpretation. For example, the possession of Patagonia was disputed between Chile and Argentina, as well as the desert of Atacama between Bolivia, Chile, and Argentina. Miguel Luis Amunátegui was especially active in investigating the documents and searching the archives for proof of the legitimacy of the Chilean claims to these territories. His research impressed even many Argentines and it has to be assumed that it played an important role in the peaceful settlement of these disputes.[72]

The role of history in boundary conflicts closes the circle on the initial question of reasons and interests that motivated the study of history in Latin America and leads back to the importance of history in the nation-building process. Long before independence we find the beginning of a consciousness of difference to Europe. Monuments of Creole self-consciousness were written as a reaction against the negation of America in European literature as well as in the attempts of regaining control by the Bourbon state. The Jesuit Francisco Javier Clavijero (1731–1783) wrote his history of Ancient Mexico mainly in Italy after the expulsion of his religious order from New Spain. Referring to the amount of prejudice about America of which the northern European enlightened literature is so rich, he wrote in his preface that he undertook to write this history to serve his native country in the best possible way and to reestablish the gleam of truth, which had been spoiled by the incredible nonsense of modern, or European, authors.[73]

At the end of this collection of heterogeneous highlights from different authors from a variety of countries and epochs, the question remains of whether something could be described as a development or at least could help us to establish an order of time periods and phases. The problem is that the circle of interests, ideas, methodologies, forms, and functions of nineteenth-century historiography discussed here is not really closed. No attempt has yet been made to describe the development of Latin American historiography as a process with a certain internal dynamic. The given periodization follows the periodization of the political history of each country, or European periodization.[74] Brading, in his book about the colonial historiography, and Colmenares, in his book about nineteenth-century historiography, are pioneers in the attempt to construct the internal dynamic of the Spanish-American discourse about history.[75] But unfortunately neither of them has proposed an alternative periodization. Obviously, the materials have to be reviewed and reordered before this is possible. But perhaps a hint can be Colmenares's unspecified use of generation differences. Therefore, the development of such a scheme remains a task for the future.

In Spanish America the space and the tools at hand for inventions were limited. The European tradition was overwhelming. Nevertheless, the history of Spanish-American historiography also is a history of the struggle for originality, intellectual independence, and identity, in all possible ways—with, against, and without the European tradition. At a time when the European tradition is becoming conscious of its own limitations,

48 Meissner

Spanish-American historiography offers an interesting case of an European–non-European intellectual relationship from which European and Latin American historians can learn much about the possibilities of their profession in a globalizing world.

NOTES

1. Original: "Das moderne historische Denken ist ein europäischer Vorgang, der dann Gültigkeit und verändernde Kraft für die übrige Welt entwickelt hat" (foreword to Wolfgang Küttler, Jörn Rüsen, and Ernst Schulin, eds., *Geschichtsdiskurs*, vol. 2: *Anfänge modernen historischen Denkens* (Frankfurt am Main: 1994), 11.
2. Original: "Para la soberbia, para el orgullo no hay perdón." See "Las ciencias y el siglo XIX," in *El Ateneo Mexicano* (Mexico: 1844), I: 230.
3. Josefina Z. Vázquez, *Nacionalismo y educación en México*, 3d ed (Mexico City: 1979). The author focuses mainly on the educational efforts to teach history in Mexico in general. The only exception I could locate so far is Ana Guirao Massif's study about the history of the faculty of philosophy and humanities in Santiago de Chile (1957). For institutional developments in Argentina mainly in the twentieth century, see Hector J. Tanzi, *Historiografía Argentina contemporánea* (Caracas: 1976), and Michael Riekenberg, ed., *Politik und Geschichte in Argentinien und Guatemala (19./20. Jahrhundert)* (Frankfurt am Main: 1994), 179–94.
4. Many of Allen Woll's excellent studies of the Chilean historiography of the nineteenth century are based on this source. See Allen Woll, *A Functional Past: The Uses of History in Nineteenth-Century Chile* (Baton Rouge, La.: 1982). This book provided most of the examples given here for the Chilean case. All translations are by the author with the exception of the quotations taken from Woll and Thomas (see note 20).
5. E. Bradford Burns, "Ideology in Nineteenth-Century Latin American Historiography," *Hispanic American History Review* 58, no. 3 (1978): 409–31. This article is almost identical with chapter 3 in E. Bradford Burns, *The Poverty of Progress: Latin America in the Nineteenth Century*, 2d ed. (Berkeley, Calif.: 1983), 35–50.
6. See the articles by Nikita Harwich Vallenilla, Maria Nizza da Silva, Nanci Leonzo, Eduardo Pérez Ochoa, Hebe Carmen Pelosi, and Isabel de Ruschi, in Lucian Boia et al., eds., *Great Historians of the Modern Age: An International Dictionary* (Westport, Conn.: 1991), 83–94, 625–91.
7. For the Río de la Platz, see, for example, Rómulo D. Carbía, *Historia crítica de la historiografía Argentina (desde sus orígenes en el siglo XVI)* (Buenos Aires: 1940), and Alberto Pla, *Ideología y método en la historiografía Argentina* (Buenos Aires: 1972). An excellent work history on Spanish-American colonial historiography is David A. Brading, *The First America: The Spanish Monarchy, Creole Patriots, and the Liberal States, 1492–1867* (Cambridge, Mass.: 1991).
8. My own current bibliography counts already more than a thousand titles. A special interest might be the presentation of history in schools. See, for example, Vázquez, *Nacionalismo y educación*; Michael Riekenberg, ed., *Lateinamerika, Geschichtsunterricht, Geschichtslehrbücher, Geschichtsbewusstsein* (Frankfurt am Main:

1990); and Nikita Harwich Vallenilla, "La génesis de un imaginario colectivo: La enseñanza de la historia en Venezuela en el siglo XIX," *Boletín de la academia nacional de historia* 71, no. 282 (1988): 349–87.

9. See Carlos Rincón, "Historia de la historiografía y de la crítica literaria latinoamericano: Historia de la conciencia histórica," *Revista de crítica literaria latinoamericana* 11, no. 24 (1986): 7–19; and Juan Durán Luzio, "Modos de relación en historia y literatura hispanoamericana durante el siglo XIX," *Escritura* (1992): 17, 33–34, 83–100.

10. Benedict Anderson, *Imagined Communities: Reflections on the Origin and Spread of Nationalism* (London: 1983); Eric J. Hobsbawm and Terence O. Ranger, *The Invention of Tradition* (Cambridge, Mass.: 1983); and Eric J. Hobsbawm, *Nations and Nationalism Since 1780: Programme, Myth, Reality* (Cambridge, UK: 1990).

11. See, for example, Nicolas Shumway, *The Invention of Argentina* (Berkeley, Calif.: 1991), and, in some respects, Riekenberg, *Politik und Geschichte*.

12. I am choosing these aspects as a heuristic scheme to order the material. In doing so I try out the categories proposed by Jörn Rüsen's disciplinary matrix. See Jörn Rüsen, *Grundzüge einer Historik*, 3 vols. (Göttingen: 1983), 29.

13. José Victorino Lastarria as quoted and translated in Woll, *Functional Past,* 20–21.

14. Lorenzo Zavala, *Umbral de la independencia* (Mexico City: 1949), 11.

15. María E. Ota Mishima, *Lucas Alamán, tesis que para obtener el título de maestro en historia de méxico presenta* (Mexico City: 1963), 87.

16. Woll, *Functional Past*, 19–20.

17. Carlos M. Bustamante, *Cuadro histórico de la revolución mexicana,* 8 vols. (1843; reprint, Mexico City: 1985), iii.

18. Lucas Alamán, *Historia de Méjico*, 5 vols. (1849; reprint, Mexico City: 1985), 1: ii.

19. Fanny Calderón de la Barca, *Life in Mexico During a Residence of Two Years in That Country* (New York: 1966); María E. Ota Mishima, *Lucas Alamán, tesis que para obtener el título de maestro en historia de Méxicao presenta* (Mexico City: 1963), 83.

20. Jack R. Thomas, "The Role of Private Libraries and Public Archives in Nineteenth-Century Spanish-American Historiography," *Journal of Library History* 9, no. 4 (1974): 336.

21. Woll, *Functional Past*, 127, 134.

22. Burns, *Poverty of Progress*, 46.

23. Burns, *Poverty of Progress*, 8.

24. Burns, *Poverty of Progress*, 8–9. For the opposition of "adopt" and "adept" in this context, compare Woll, *Functional Past*, 175, and Arturo Ardao, "Assimilation and Transformation of Positivism in Latin America," *Journal of the History of Ideas* 24 (1963): 515–22.

25. Burns, *Poverty of Progress*, 8.

26. Germán Colmenares, *Las convenciones contra la cultura* (Bogotá: 1987), 27.

27. Colmenares, *Las convenciones*, 137.

28. Colmenares, *Las convenciones*, 13.

29. See Frank Safford, "Germán Colmenares (1938–1990)" (obituary), *Hispanic American Historical Review* 71 (1991): 865–67.

30. Compare, for example, Paul Ricoeur, *Zeitung und Erzählung*, trans. Rainer Rochlitz and Andreas Knop, 3 vols. (1988; reprint, Munich: 1991), 165–201, and the structure of chapter 2 in Colmenares, *Las convenciones*, 97–135.

31. See, for example, the first quotation above the headline on the first page. Wolfgang Küttler, Jörn Rüsen, and Ernst Schulin do not seem to be too sure about their case, because on the next page they say more cautiously that the relationship between European and extra-European historical thought has to be discussed independently in a different context. So it is clear that the authors of this statement meant it as a limitation and not as a delimiting generalization. It should assure that the mentioned book is more than anything else a meditation of the European tribe about his own scribe. So it seems obvious that they use the term "modern historical thought" to name a regional event that might—but not necessarily has to—prove to be of global importance. Nevertheless, with all its ambiguity, it is an unlimited statement as such that, as I assume and have frequently experienced, would be anticipated by many Europeans—unfortunately usually less explicit as in Küttler, Rüsen, and Schulin, *Geschichtsdiskurs*, 11–13.

32. I find it difficult to translate this German term into English. Nevertheless, it was first used in an essay by Lutz Niethammer, "Die postmoderne Herausforderung. Geschichte als Gedächtnis im Zeitalter der Wissenschaft," in Küttler, Rüsen, and Schulin, *Geschichtsdiskurs*, 31–49, about the problems of histories of historiography. I find it a most intriguing description. *Entsorgen* may have been used before, but it did not really enter the common usage before the long-term risks of atomic energy were discussed. It was used to describe the way of dealing first with atomic waste and then with waste in general. In the last decades it was used as a technical term. Politicians discussed how the atomic waste could be *entsorgt* and city councils were worried about how sewage and waste of industries and private households could be *entsorgt*. Although it has become a technical term, more than that it describes an illusion or, if you prefer this expression, a wish, a dream or a utopia. It is composed of the prefix *ent-* and contains the verb *sorgen*, which can be translated as "to care," but as well, "to worry about." Therefore, *entsorgen* describes perfectly a dream or a wish that can be fulfilled only in very rare situations. The wish is to be able to forget about a problem that has been posed by a former behavior, a problem that cannot be ignored, but may perhaps be put out of the way or, at best, be processed in a way that allows one no longer to worry about them. A problem *entsorgen* does not mean to solve the problem. It rather represents the idea of creating a situation in which we can ignore the problem. Thus, as well as it describes a wish, it describes a behavior we should not follow, if we want to deal with these problems appropriately.

33. Woll, *Functional Past*, 20.

34. Juan A. Ortega y Medina and Eugenia W. Meyer, *Plémicas y ensayos mexicanos en torno a la historia* (Mexico City: 1970), 15–74. For a critical edition, see Lorenzo Zavala, *Obras: El periodista y el traductor* (Mexico City: 1966), 35–81.

35. Letters of the Conde de la Cortina, edited in Ortega y Medina and Meyer, *Plémicas y ensayos mexicanos*, 93, 105–6.

36. Jacques-Benigne Bossuet (1627–1704), *Discours sur l'histoire universelle* (1681; reprint, Paris: 1966) appeared first in 1681 and was written for teaching purposes.

Fueter characterizes the book slightly polemically but accurately: "It is not a work of history. It is a sermon in which the ecclesiastical transformed matters of history substituted the Bible quotes"; in Eduard Fueter, *Geschichte der Neueren Historiographie*, 3d. rev. ed. (Munich: 1936), 231.

37. This process is very accurately described in Vázquez, *Nacionalismo y educación*. See also Patricia Escandón, "La historia antigua de México en los textos escolares del siglo XIX," *Secuencia* 10 (1988): 33–42.

38. Vázquez, *Nacionalismo y educación*, 77.

39. See table in Woll, *Functional Past*, 160.

40. Original emphasis. Letter of Gómez de la Cortina, printed in Ortega y Medina and Meyer, *Polémicas y ensayos mexicanos*, 93–94.

41. Woll, *Functional Past*, 20.

42. On Sarmiento, see the published collection of essays by Tulio Halperin Donghi et al., eds., *Sarmiento: Author of a Nation* (Berkeley, Calif.: 1994).

43. See Josefina Z. Vázquez, "Don Lorenzo de Zavala, político e historiador," *Anuario de historia* 1 (1962): 81–100.

44. Colmenares, *Las convenciones*, 81.

45. Jochen Meissner, *Eine Elite im Umbruch: Der Stadtrat von Mexiko zwischen kolonialer Ordnung und unabhängigen Staat* (Stuttgart: 1993), 1.

46. Alamán, *Historia de Méjico*.

47. For example, Juan Hernández y Dávalos, ed., *Colección de documentos para la historia de la guerra de independencia de México*, 6 vols. (Mexico City: 1877–1882).

48. Thomas, "Role of Private Libraries," 339.

49. Jack R. Thomas, *Biographical Dictionary of Latin American Historians and Historiography* (Westport, Conn., 1984), 35.

50. Thomas, "Role of Private Libraries," 335.

51. Thomas, "Role of Private Libraries," 28.

52. Colmenares, *Las convenciones*, 125.

53. Thomas, "Role of Private Libraries," 345.

54. Colmenares, *Las convenciones*, 124.

55. Letter of Claudio Gay, printed in Guillermo Feliú Cruz and Carlos S. Ortiz, eds., *Correspondencia de Claudio Gay* (Santiago: 1962), 76.

56. Woll, *Functional Past*, 31.

57. Woll, *Functional Past*.

58. Thomas, *Biographical Dictionary*, 42.

59. Woll, *Functional Past*, 32–33.

60. Colmenares, *Las convenciones*, 49.

61. Woll, *Functional Past*, 32–33.

62. Woll, *Functional Past*, 32–33.

63. Woll, *Functional Past*, 78.

64. Woll, *Functional Past*, 183.

65. Valentín Letelier, *La evolución de la historia*, 2 vols. (1886; reprint, Santiago: 1900).

66. Letelier, *La evolución*. See as well Woll, *Functional Past*, 184.

67. Thomas, *Biographical Dictionary*, 40.

68. Colmenares, *Las convenciones*, 137.

69. As cited in Woll, *Functional Past*, 87.

70. Woll, *Functional Past*, 87–88.

71. Woll, *Functional Past*, 90–91.

72. Woll, *Functional Past*, 109.

73. Francisco J. Clavijero, *Historia Antigua de México*, ed. and introd. Mariano Cuevas, 8th ed. (Mexico City: 1987), xxi.

74. See, for example, Vázquez, *Historia de la historiografía*, Edberto O. Acevedo, *Manual de historiografía hispanoamericana contemporánea* (Cuyo: 1992), and Carbía, *Historia crítica de la historiografía Argentina*.

75. See Brading, *The First America*, and Colmenares, *Las convenciones*.

2

In Search of Lost Identity

South Africa between Great Trek and Colonial Nationalism, 1830–1910

Benedikt Stuchtey

When he grew old, Jock of the Bushveld retired to a town settlement but he could not get used to the way of life. The famous bull terrier, hero of one of the most widely read South African novels by Percy FitzPatrick, looked back on the adventurous life he had led at the side of his White master and his Black friend. Probably more than any other figure of nineteenth-century South African literature, the three symbolize the world view of the pioneering trek: the life between fields ("veld") and mountains ("berg"), the mapmaking character, the exploration of the colonial terra incognita, the adventures in hailstorms and droughts, and exposure to the dangers of wild animals and rough nature. The protagonists reflect on "hours of almost unbearable 'trek fever,' of restless, sleepless longing for the old life, of 'homesickness' for the veld, the freedom, the roaming, the nights by the fire, and the days in the bush."[1]

Although written as a children's book, the novel clearly addresses the longing for a national identity as well as the desire of an adult metropolitan readership for romantic adventures. After its publication in 1907 it was translated from English not only into other European languages, but also into Afrikaans, Zulu, and Xhosa; truly, *Jock of the Bushveld* soon became a South African classic. This is in part because, in contrast to strongly imperialist writers such as Haggard, FitzPatrick touched on a genuine and less stereotypical South African theme that attempted to establish a compromise between British and Boer conceptions of a modern South Africa.[2] The story is easy to tell: It takes its readers to the eastern Transvaal, it takes place at a time when all travel relied on horses and teams of oxen, and it narrates the adventures that people experienced during their trek northeastward through the South African veld. The book's message is complex: the dog and his master represent the "pioneering spirit" of the frontiersman, his ethos of comradeship and missionary conduct between civilization and "wilderness," and the motif of "wanderlust" in connection with the desire to explore the unknown, mysterious land. Two other aspects of the novel also are interesting. First, the author described the landscape as unsentimentally and realistically as possible in order to disclose the peculiar attraction of a rough nature that only those who open themselves to the world of the trek understand. Second, the courageous dog's travels mirror the country's history of settlement and the division of the frontier among Boers, British, and Zulus.

In FitzPatrick's novel past and present are closely intertwined. Ideally, once the frontier movement has come to an end (symbolized by Jock and his master who remain in a town after retiring from the pioneer's life), the Boer motif par excellence for a national interpretation of history would become obsolete and make way for a reconciliation among the political powers. However, this was possible only after they had also bridged a phase of colonial nationalism. It certainly was a very long way to this concept, and it was not an easy path. It is one of the major objectives of this chapter to investigate this complex problem. In FitzPatrick's words:

> So the new life began and the old was put away. But the new life, for all its brighter and wider outlook and work of another class, for all the charm . . . was not all happy. The new life had its hours of darkness too.[3]

In this chapter, two different and yet very specific South African concepts will be discussed. To a certain extent they embody what can be subsumed under FitzPatrick's terms "old life" and "new life" respectively: the trek or the frontier, and the potentials and limits that are inherent in the concept of colonial nationalism in South Africa. Whereas the frontier motif was a peculiar nineteenth- and twentieth-century national (Boer) tradition that was hardly influenced from the outside, if at all, the idea of colonial nationalism can best be understood in the British imperial context of intellectual cross-fertilization at the turn of the century.

Two historians played an important role this context. The Afrikaner nationalist tradition of which S. J. du Toit's work is a good example had hardly any impact on English-speaking South African historians. However, George McCall Theal's "influence was enormous on generations of history students in South Africa."[4] There is no doubt that Theal was an outspoken racist who believed in superior and inferior races and thus helped, from his amateur rather than professional perspective, to formulate the peculiar South African historical patterns that included the denial of political and social equality to the Black majority. Both frontier (for du Toit) and colonial nationalism (for Theal) play a central role for the South African historiographical tradition being an example of a very slow shift from a closed intellectual border toward one that possessed the possibility for cultural transfer.[5] The role of English-speaking scholarship in forming the view of South African history outside South Africa cannot be underestimated. This is certainly also in part due to the language in which the respective historians wrote.[6]

It cannot, however, be the aim of this chapter to discuss the impact of the above mentioned aspects on present-day South African historiography. Such a discussion would need to address issues such as the contributions of amateurs to professional history, the development of oral traditions, the institutionalization of history, and the paradigm of an Africanist, Black historiography.[7] And it would also need to take account of the work of a "revisionist" school of scholars who have been working since the 1960s and have tried to bring the experience of the Black majority into the focus of research.[8] By contrast the Afrikaners' historiographical debate employed "White" methodologies and asked questions concerning race relations that entirely excluded "native" aspects or Indian and Chinese immigrants. The history of the indigenous people has remained a neglected subtheme in the historiography of South Africa until recently, but this is also the case in other colonial contexts, such as Australia and Canada. Frontier and colonial nationalism are Western intellectual problems placed in the South African context.[9] Although it would be highly problematic to use categories of historical analysis from the Western context in the African one, in particular because the frontier topos is certainly not value neutral, the South African problem is different.[10] Therefore, this chapter deals not with the Hegelian problem of "peoples without history," in terms of African versus Western culture, but with the complex relationship of two very different White colonial communities with each other.

The South African frontier and the pioneering trek ("Great Trek") were synonymous. The possession and cultivation of land was the predominant feature. The historical background of the "Voortrekkers" (frontiersmen) goes back to the early 1830s, when the settlers experienced increasingly bad conditions. Many had lost their animals and property as the result of the continuing border wars, and to make matters worse, state compensation was inefficient and slow. The new antislavery legislation, social modernization, and the Anglicization of the Cape's economy and administration caused further discontent among the Boer population.

Between 1835 and 1840 about 6,000 white settlers left the Cape, heading in the direction of the river Oranje. However, unlike the Trekboers of former times, the Voortrekkers had a clearly political objective. Their trek was an expression of resistance to the influence of the relatively liberal British imperial power, and their motivation for leaving the country was rooted in deeply conservative opinions, not seldom in racism, sometimes in a thirst for adventure, and definitely in the desire to be free from British imperial control and eventually to found an independent state for themselves. Their political worldview was anti-British; their economic aim was the acquisition of land for their animals. The British Empire could have stopped the trek only if it had controlled the whole region (as it did in Australia).[11] Because these imperial claims did not exist in South Africa, and the country was depopulated in consequence of the Zulu revolution, the Mfecane (1818–1828; the widespread destruction of organized communities resulting in migrations and the loss of political and social stability), the Boers began to fight against both British and Blacks for the establishment of their own state. This struggle became the basis of the search for, and the construction of, a national identity. Any compromise was inconceivable.[12]

As a result, the racial conflict between Boers and Blacks and the political conflict between Boers and British grew and hardened into an unbridgeable, bitter antagonism that climaxed in the South African War of 1899–1902. That the worldview expressed by the Great Trek increased the intellectual isolation of the conservative Boers has often been pointed out in British liberal historiography. But the British imperial power also helped to isolate the Boers and intensify their backwardness by preventing them from gaining any access to the sea.[13] Outer conditions and mentalities came together in the fact that the emerging Boer state was equally the result of artificial construction and political ideology. The land, being so ideologically important, came before the state, and the Trekboers settled and built their own pioneering frontiers without being controlled by any colonial power. Therefore, technically the state and the West were secondary to the settlers, who had long since distanced themselves from European culture. Settlers often lived on solitary farms.

The Voortrekker Monument near Pretoria (completed in 1949) demonstrates how the Great Trek of the 1830s was publicly commemorated until the election of the new government in 1994. This monument is one of the most important nonwritten sources for the history of the frontier. On December 16, the Boer public holiday, sunlight falls on a large stone in the center of the granite monument, highlighting the words "Ons Vir Jou,

Suid Afrika" (We are yours, South Africa). This date commemorates the terrible massacre of about 3,000 Zulus at Blood River, a military victory of the trekking Boers in 1838 that ensured their further northward movement and the foundation of the Republic of Natal.[14] The Great Trek as depicted in the frieze inside the hall and the sixty-four ox-wagons surrounding the outside wall of the monument, transmit the message of the "just domination" of the Whites over the Blacks. The making of the South African frontier greatly fostered racism and segregation.[15] Hence, Boer historiography, particularly since the Nationalists' electoral victory in 1948, has produced a mass of historical literature that "has represented the Trek as a milestone in the development of conscious Afrikaner nationalism, portraying the Voortrekkers as 'nationally aware Afrikaners' linking the Age of the Patriotten with the age of Paul Kruger."[16]

In his autobiography, Nelson Mandela recalls how in his childhood the chief of his village often gave his people political lectures. Describing the cultural clash between White and Black in his time, he tried to find the roots of "real" South African history before its official birth, which, in Boer historiography, usually dates from Jan van Riebeeck's landing on the Cape of Good Hope in 1652. But according to the chief, these roots were endangered:

> The Thembu, the Pondo, the Xhosa, and the Zulu were all children of one father, and lived as brothers. The white man shattered the *abantu*, the fellowship, of the various tribes. The white man was hungry and greedy for land, and the black man shared the land with him as they shared the air and water; land was not for man to possess. But the white man took the land as you might seize another man's horse.[17]

In contemporary South Africa the past is sometimes drawn on in order to serve reconciliation, which is certainly also the case with Mandela.[18] However, the past as written by Afrikaner historians had the primary function of legitimizing political power achieved through the policy of landownership and the movement of the frontier. And since the seventeenth-century settlers had trekked from the Cape Colony, this had been the one, if not the crucial, event in the construction of the Afrikaner past, "the central theme" of South African history.[19] Different historical forms must be distinguished: the Cape frontier, the pre-trek northern frontier, and the frontier that developed in the Transvaal as a consequence of the Great Trek.[20]

The question of the uniqueness of the frontier experience has been posed in numerous studies, and although this is not the place to recapitulate the historiography of a comparative frontier history in full, a brief comparison between the North American and the Southern African frontiers is helpful in pointing out some peculiar characteristics.[21] According to the well-known thesis of the U.S. historian Frederick Jackson Turner, westward expansion on the North American continent was one of the most significant processes in its history in forming characteristics such as individualism, the pioneering spirit, and the development of democratic institutions.[22] The validity of Turner's thesis has long been challenged, but despite its generalizations and its problematic explanatory approach, many of the questions he asked are also applicable to the South African context.

Whereas North American frontier historiography stressed the libertarian aspect of the settlement of the country and the cultivation of "wilderness," the South African frontier produced a White, Boer colony within White British colonialism. It widened the gulf between these two White communities, and between them and the Black majority of the country. For Boer frontier society, this produced a strong group consciousness.[23] This, however, sounds more clear-cut than it actually was, and it underestimates the inclusive qualities of the South African frontier. When Turner described the frontier in U.S. history he pointed to the line between "savagery" and civilization without being concerned with the possible interaction of the people on the frontier. The North American frontier was a frontier of exclusion.[24]

By contrast, in South Africa the potential of the frontier to serve as a cultural meeting point was accepted. Although the "White man's country" regarded the Blacks as "other," as enemies, it saw them as an existing factor that had to be integrated into South African life. Historians such as William M. Macmillan, especially in his most important historical work, Bantu, Boer, and Briton, have shown that the South African frontier "from the start involved inclusion as well as exclusion."[25] This is also the central thesis of Martin Legassick's Marxist approach to the frontier, which is still regarded as the most convincing attempt to relate race relations and the sociohistorical consequences of the frontier to more recent economic developments in South Africa. To this extent racial conflicts and slavery were one side of the frontier coin; the other was class problems posed by modern industrialization, for example. Thus, according to Legassick, to reduce the impact of the frontier to nineteenth-century racial segregationism without taking into account a necessary social integrationism would be a historical foreshortening. Without this social integrationism the twentieth-century labor market would not have emerged successfully for White capitalism. In consequence, Legassick differentiated among three forms of the frontier tradition: "the frontier as a place of isolation and regression, as a place of conflict over land and labour, and as a place of interaction and cooperation."[26]

As early as 1899 a history of the Great Trek was published that explained the South African nation-building process in patterns similar to those used by Turner.[27] A large number of studies written during and after this period similarly concentrated on the cultural and political implications of the frontier. They asked the same questions as Turner about the significance of the availability of land, the promotion of sectionalism, the development of laissez-faire attitudes, and the evidence of basic equality and democracy at the frontier. Naturally, these qualities were regarded as the background to the founding of the Boer republics.[28] For yet another frontier situation in British imperial history, Catherine Hall has pointed to the gender dimension: "Both overlanding and exploration were quintessentially male activities—indeed, exploration can be interpreted as the ultimate expression of frontier masculinity, the extension in the European mind of man's conquest over 'virgin' territory."[29] This is certainly also applicable to South Africa; that is, the continent was seen as female, and as a result, colonial conquest and ownership of land were regarded as male power that controlled and subdued the "wilderness."[30]

The myth of the "free land" as developed by Turner was highly problematic because life at the frontier not only encouraged Afrikaner nationalism and the growth of sectionalism but also promoted societal lawlessness and political antipathy to central state control. Old values were preserved rather than, as in the North American case, new ways of life tested, resulting in a Boer *laager* mentality that defined itself in terms of a fixed location, pride in being surrounded by an African majority and yet controlling it, and finally, the twentieth-century legacy of racial discrimination and separation.[31] Despite the existing multiracial society of Southern Africa, Afrikaner settlers invented the topos of an "uncivilised wild land" that could lawfully be taken into possession by cultivating it;[32] the rights of African natives were consequently denied, and their identity was preserved by means of constructing the other.[33]

There is hardly a South African historian of any reputation who has not devoted at least one study to the history of the settlers and the Great Trek: Gerdener, Kruger, Leipoldt, Preller, Uys, van der Walt, and many others. Floris van Jaarsveld summarized their major ideas almost forty years ago.[34] According to Richard Ford, South African historiography raised, along the lines of Turner's thesis, several major issues concerning the frontier, thereby justifying it as the most important single event in the South African past.[35] Some of these issues are:

1. The availability of "free land." The relatively easy availability of land allowed the process of expansion to be presented as a tradition, with the trek as its vehicle, as a way of life that broke away from external authorities and regarded trekking as its natural right. But in contrast to the North American frontier, expansion in South Africa was a

slow process. It had no foundation in cities and had very rudimentary communication media.

2. The function of the frontier as a safety valve that reduced violence and released social, religious, political, and other tensions. But when frontiers disappeared toward the end of the nineteenth century war became inevitable.

3. The assumption that the frontier promoted national unity must be seen as false with regard to its beginnings because the initial impact of the trek was to sectionalize and regionalize the Boer people. Laissez-faire attitudes promoted by the frontier, the freedom of the veld, the self-sufficiency of the farms, and the trekkers' antipathy to any political or economic control from outside made national unification a difficult proposition. Until the 1880s regional loyalties superseded national patriotism. The struggle against Britain as an imperial power in the later nineteenth century was instrumentalized in the creation of a nation-building image, visually symbolized in the Voortrekker Monument.

4. Trek and frontier cultivated qualities such as individualism, a readiness to work hard and accept deprivation, practicality, and inquisitiveness, which became significant elements in the Boer tradition as stressed by its historians. But (British) travelers often confirmed these historiographical accounts from their own recollections.[36] The legendary David Livingstone, for example, produced a book that became one of the nonfiction best-sellers of his time. Livingstone visited Cape Town in spring 1841, where he stayed with John Philip, superintendent of the London Missionary Society, himself a champion of the rights of the indigenous peoples and a critic of British missionary policies in South Africa. However, both saw that a major part of Afrikaner history had been a result of myth-building because frontier settlers often had slaves to do the really hard work.[37]

It is of interest in this context to note that John Philip and Donald Moodie, an ex-lieutenant in the Royal Navy, were involved in a historical debate in about 1830 that has not lost its historiographical relevance for the present.[38] The controversy was about colonial domination in the Cape, the relationship between Whites and Blacks on the eastern frontier, mainly in the seventeenth and eighteenth centuries. The series of documents that Moodie put together is *The Record, or a Series of Official Papers Relative to the Condition and Treatment of the Native Tribes of South Africa,* published in Cape Town between 1838 and 1841. Philip, for his part, was a consistent critic of British imperial policy. He documented the colonial suppression of the Khoi people and accused the European invaders of destroying an intact black civilization that had possessed high moral values and

a well-functioning political and social system.[39] Their defense of
their lives and rights led to colonial wars, and hence the picture of
the "bushmen's savagery" came into being. What emerges from
Philip's account is the message that the impact of the colonial power
on the destruction of the "native" autonomy was immense and that
the subsequent hostilities between black and white laid the groundwork for the inglorious South African tradition of conflict, a conflict
of race and class in its history.[40]

5. One of the central theses of Turner's work focused on equality and
democracy as products of the frontier. Describing the Great Trek,
Afrikaner historians worked out the same characteristics for their
entire country. Both North American and South African pioneers
had excluded the indigenous populations from this process. However, unlike the Americans, the Boers did not almost completely
exterminate the natives. As a result, the South African frontier produced a multiracial society. And while the American ethos was one
of finding new political ideals on the frontier, the Boers wanted to
preserve their old, patriarchal ones.

Turning to the modern academic discussion of the frontier tradition in
South African historiography, we can expect this to have been a well-
debated topic.[41] As early as 1930 Eric Walker published a lecture that has
been frequently quoted on this subject. He held the chair of history at the
University of Cape Town between 1911 and 1936, before he left for Cambridge. In this book and in his work on the "Great Trek," Walker's interpretation of the frontier as the touchstone of South African identity has
served as the basis for many later studies.[42] According to Walker, all South
African history before the Great Trek was a sort of preparation for it, and
"most of what has happened since has been a commentary on it."[43] And
not only Afrikaner historians such as Gustav S. Preller and C. Louis Leipoldt devoted themselves to the problem of the frontier. A substantial
English-language historiography also emerged and it asked similar questions from a different perspective.[44] Nonetheless, for obvious reasons
frontier historiography has remained the domain of Afrikaans historiography. Few scholars from other countries have developed an interest in
the subject.

The groundbreaking essay by Legassick offers a comprehensive interpretation of this phenomenon, certainly to the discomfort of many Afrikaans historians who represented the frontier as a means of identifying
positively with their country's history.[45] But according to Legassick, the
frontier was predominantly responsible for the negative legacy of South
Africa. This included the White view of non-Whites as either servants or
enemies; the color bar in all political, social, cultural, and economic sec-

tors; the opposition to urbanization and industrialization, to government and Western political structures; and a restless land hunger and waste of supposedly unlimited space.[46] Hence, the frontier was the expression of a dichotomy between two European communities on the African continent: between British southern and Boer northern South Africa; that is between liberalism, tolerance and humanitarianism, and capitalism and entrepreneurism as British values, on the one hand, and republican frontierism or Afrikaner nationalism on the other.[47] Religion, particularly Calvinism, also played a significant role in frontier ideology.[48] In churches and schools the Great Trek was taught as one of the country's great heroic epics. The British version of the civilizing mission of the Pax Britannica was thereby paralleled by the Afrikaner version that the fighting (and killing) for the frontier had been done for a good cause.

This interpretation found supporters among radical Marxist historians such as Harold Wolpe, who criticized earlier interpretations by Macmillan and his most talented student, Cornelis Willem de Kiewiet.[49] Both were highly influential in forming a liberal school of South African historiography that defended (British) missionary work against the point of view expressed in the works by G. McCall Theal, for example.[50] Whereas the English-speaking liberal school of historians in the 1930s and 1940s saw no direct connection between apartheid and the capitalist system, radical historians argued that the success of the South African industrial economy should be seen as a result of racial discrimination and social exploitation of Black labor; accordingly, race and class were closely intertwined. Liberal historiography had "argued that apartheid represented an inappropriate transposition into the twentieth century of an earlier frontier mentality characterized by prejudice and fear."[51] The radical school now put forward the thesis that segregation and racial discrimination were typical of twentieth-century South African apartheid that had benefited from the development of the modern capitalist system without resulting in a nineteenth-century frontier ideology. In essence, this was more than an intellectual debate; it possessed important political and economic implications for the present state, namely, whether one wanted to fight apartheid on solely (liberal) political terms or on (Marxist) economic ones.[52]

However, the clear-cut dichotomy between British and Boer and Black and Boer as seen by the various historians of South Africa needs revision. In his multivolume *History of South Africa,* Theal, the great amateur historian, had tried, as early as the 1890s, to show how successful plantations and settlements were as constitutive elements of the South African past.[53] But he was even more interested in the possibility of cooperation between British and Boer settlers, whether on the economic, political, religious, or social level. Although the war of 1899–1902 temporarily suppressed this option, it was not wholly destroyed. As a supporter of colonial nationalism, Theal drew attention to this idea in his historiography.[54] Therefore, and also for historiographical reasons, peace in 1902 and the subsequent negotiations for union came as the fulfillment of an outstanding goal.

As Keith Surridge has shown, the Boer War caused much dissonance among the British military and political elites.[55] One of the reasons for this was that British officers expressed sympathy for the Boer struggle insofar as they regarded the Boers as honorable soldiers and saw in their rural upbringing the ideal type of the frontiersman. British military critique of the South African War therefore was rooted to some extent in anticapitalism, antiurbanism, and even anti-Semitism traditionally associated with Afrikaans frontier mentality. This also must be set against the background of changes within British society and the decreasing political influence of the British land-owning class.

Thus, central elements of the Afrikaner nation as elaborated in its philosophy and historiography also entered British military thinking: the healthy and robust farmer and the patriotic fighter who cared for land but not business or the pleasures of the city. Winston S. Churchill expressed a great deal of sympathy for these images, and high-ranking British colonial officials saw the empire's only chance of survival in maintaining its strength with qualities such as those of the South African frontiersman.[56]

> The success of the non-urban, country-bred Afrikaners against the soldiers of the world's mightiest empire was an object lesson to Britain that the old ways were just as relevant to the present and the future as to the past—if not more so. The agencies of modernization, the cities and the economics thereof, were not capable of preserving imperial strength: they undermined it.[57]

In short, the basic conservatism if not reactionism of the Boers and their defense of class and race, both associated with the landed interest, were not linked to the frontier myth alone. And according to Legassick, a White racist ideology has been part of the cultural matrix of colonialism since its early days.[58] The common European background therefore calls for a comparison. What is important, though, is that only Afrikaner historians really made use of it in the construction of a national identity. Their case was unique in African historiography in general, with the questions of slavery, racism, and apartheid being predominant for so long. By contrast, English-speaking South Africans were much less interested in a common history as a provider of identity, probably because their position was less marked by political struggle.

Twentieth-century South African historiography, particularly its liberal wing, concentrated heavily on the two major questions of race and class, both, to a great extent, the result of the frontier.[59] A comparison between the North American and the South African experiences was therefore indispensable. Eric Walker concluded in his studies, particularly in his masterly *History of South Africa* (1928), that the South African and North American interpretations of the past share the same perspective. But whereas the former saw the frontier as the source of conflict, the latter regarded it as responsible for democracy, freedom, and wealth.

In this context the term "conflict" certainly requires clearer definition. Whereas Afrikaner historians expressed the conflict in terms of culture versus savagery, Marxist historians such as Legassick put it into class terms and spoke of a conflict over labor between Xhosa and Boer settlers. Yet the latter implied social interaction and contact between Blacks and Whites, which the segregation thesis of the frontier would not have supported. Direct opportunities for conflict lay in the possession of cattle, hunting rights, or in the control over land and water, among others. Conflict became "the essence of the relationship"[60] between Whites and Blacks; in fact, it was formative in the establishment of South African society, with its peculiar elements of slave work and frontier racism. Slave work required a close relationship between master and servant, and frontier racism was a form of violence that existed intrinsically. However, the literature repeatedly stresses that cooperation between ethnic groups was an imperative component of this society without which Voortrekkers such as Hendrik Potgieter and Louis Trichardt would not have been able to keep their team moving. This process could also be called a "strategy of attempts at mutual incorporation," in which Africans and Afrikaners alike were interested.[61] Therefore, in South Africa it was the society that formed the frontier, whereas in the United States it was the Turnerian frontier that shaped U.S. society.[62]

This idea further undermines the thesis of the frontier as a place of isolation, which explains the peculiar Afrikaner "backwardness" and exemplifies pastoralism versus industrialism. For many liberal historians, Walker among them (and also against the background of Leo Fouché's studies on the eighteenth-century trekboer), it was a short step from the socially idealized isolation of the trekboers to their ideologically justified White racism. Afrikaner historiography used the same pattern of isolationism in connection with the frontier to support social and political segregationism and for the construction of the idea of the Afrikaner "volk." J. C. Smuts based his early political ideas on this. Both historiographical strands ignored the potential risks inherent in investigating the interaction between whites and blacks. This was the task that Macmillan first took up. The classic intellectual and historiographical categories such as imperialism, colonialism, and apartheid needed to be questioned if modern approaches to the complexity of (South) African history were to be addressed.[63]

It would certainly be an oversimplification to view complex South African society merely in terms of "Bantu," "Boer," and "Briton," the components of the title of Macmillan's classic of 1963. Robert Thornton has drawn attention to a rethinking of the problematic social categorization by which the South African conflict has been reduced to the dichotomy between the colonial regime ("the Europeans") and the Black opposition ("the Africans").[64] This categorization, however, does not take into account existing tensions between the local White population that had lived in and shaped the colonies for generations, and the imperial power that merely saw the colonies from the outside. Thornton is also concerned with a second problem in the form of occidentalism, an Eastern conception of the West, deriving from the development of a politically unified South Africa that needed to distinguish itself from the other, that is, Britain. Naturally, this process is older than the Voortrekkers' movement. It probably started with the first European-derived community in South Africa, the Portuguese. The Black natives needed to distinguish between Europeans from outside who were occidentalized and local Europeans who were perceived by the Blacks in terms of White racism. In any case, according to this argument, neat bipolar models of conflict such as the frontier thesis do not respond adequately to the South African complexities. Again, there is obviously a special case that makes the South African question unique among the former colonies and the modern Commonwealth nations. In Thornton's view only Canada could possibly offer a comparison, because the South African case is characterized by its explicit internationalism. This became most obvious, of course, during the Boer War with the international participation of soldiers from Britain, the empire, and volunteers from all over Europe.

This leads directly to the issue of how South Africa needed to create a distinct identity on which was based a distinct self-conception in historiography and other cultural media:

> The region largely ceased to be a European outpost in terms of its practical identity. Instead, it acquired a local identity, even though this was not always explicit or part of the awareness of the time.[65]

In both political and cultural matters a colonial identity emerged that strongly emphasized its difference from the external imperial power. It was the expression of a colonial nationalism, carrying with it the concept that neither skin color nor religion, to name but two categories, necessarily form a homogeneous entity but that it was the geographical situation that first articulated and thus differentiated local from imperial interests.

Jock of the Bushveld with his White master and Black friend is a good example. Percy FitzPatrick's Irish background conveys a political message to the peculiar South African setting and opens up questions concerning the empire in general. In contrast to the Afrikaners' nationalism seen through the frontier model, FitzPatrick's concept is notable for its construction of a South African English identity. It is remarkable how far the Irish dimension formed the intellectuals' views of the empire and how much the demand for independence within a reformed imperial system in the late Victorian and early Edwardian era produced a colonial "sense of place" that was strongly inspired by the Irish question. It is here that intellectual transfers from center to periphery can be discerned.[66]

Clearly, the outstanding Irish transmitter of the historiographical as well as political dimensions of the idea of colonial nationalism was the historian W. E. H. Lecky. In his work he concentrated mainly on the eighteenth century, paying particular attention to the Grattan Parliament of 1782–1800.[67] This relatively independent parliament was an English concession to the Anglo–Irish Protestant Ascendancy as one of the consequences of the loss of the North American colonies. At least since William Molyneux's plea for the *Case of Ireland* (1698) in which he defended Irish parliamentary freedom and the right for more political autonomy within the imperial connection, an Irish-based argument for colonial nationalism was being developed.[68] Intellectuals such as Jonathan Swift, Edmund Burke, Henry Grattan, Henry Flood, Daniel O'Connell, and W. B. Yeats picked up the idea, and Lecky put it into the broader imperial context of the late nineteenth century. Ultimately, ran the argument, the empire would profit from the balancing of local and imperial interests as the polarity was gradually overcome. In fact, the empire could continue to exist only if local nationalism were taken into account.

As far as South Africa was concerned, this meant that the differences between the White races of Boers and Britons had to be overcome. In his essay on the South African War, Lecky wrote that inhabitants of the colonies need to be given political power and local self-government simply to reduce their dislike and distrust of the imperial government: "They rely for their security upon the largest possible extension of representation."[69] Thus, Lecky believed that the solution of the South African problem lay in the direct transfer of political power to the settlers, who should be permitted to regulate their own affairs: "If this had been accepted frankly and unreservedly, the war would never have taken place."[70] The historian's judgment was made against the background of the Irish historical experience. The British flag would remain the unifying bond for South Africa and for all other members of the imperial community, but they were expected to act for the mutual benefit of all, following the federal maxim that ultimately led to the Commonwealth. However, the envis-

aged conciliation between national home rule and British imperialism
was not without ambivalence, and this was where its weakness lay. The
attempt to combine a nonsectarian nationalism with an allegiance to both
the local and the imperial, English culture often failed and ended in frustration if not political bitterness. The Protestant Ascendancy of which
Lecky and Yeats and so many other Anglo–Irish intellectuals were members experienced this very dilemma.[71]

When Richard Jebb published his *Studies in Colonial Nationalism* in 1905,
after having traveled throughout the world, he contradicted John Robert
Seeley's famous dictum, according to which the people in the crown colonies were but 10 million Englishmen abroad. On the contrary, Jebb
demanded that the colonies be transformed into sovereign dominions
connected by an "Imperial Conference" and sharing equal rights and
duties.[72] He saw their potential for separate national careers, because they
possessed a social elite that was able to reconcile general proimperial convictions with a moderate demand for local autonomy. This white elitist
cooperation rather than confrontation not only made necessary a new
definition of South Africa (and other colonies) within the empire, but it
also secured the rule of the White settlers. The rapprochement between
Boers and Britons in the early twentieth century strengthened South African White supremacy, and also "helped to redefine South Africa's role in
the empire and, by extension, the broader relationship between Britain
and its overseas white dominions." What followed was an inclusive
White nationalism that "involved the exclusion of blacks as sovereign citizens of a new state," and to this extent it possessed an expressly *colonialist*
character.[73] Accordingly, the adherents of colonial nationalism were not
revolutionaries who wanted to leave the empire. Rather, foreseeing its
gradual decline at the beginning of the twentieth century, they tried to
influence future power relations to their benefit. Only at first glance were
their politics a contradiction. Working for colonial nationalism essentially
meant preventing a "tribal particularism," that is, that form of devolu-
tionist home-rule by which Boer society would separate itself, "slipping
back into ethnic and regional 'inwardnesses.' "[74]

Thus was the alternative to the negative effects of the frontier, taking
the moderate rather than the radical path. Yet again the South African
path was a special one, insofar as, in this critical colonial region, early
forms of decolonization were developed that did not exist anywhere else
in Africa. In this regard the South African War possessed a cumulative
effect, producing an Afrikaner "ethnic nationality" and political unity.
But after 1910 the radical nationalists, under General Hertzog, who
rejected divided loyalties as unpatriotic, put a quick end to the idea of
colonial nationalism. They formed what has aptly been termed an "anti-
imperial colonialism."[75] This also was in fact Ireland's experience when it

moved into civil war in 1916: The "center" (Ireland) where the idea was originally born and the "periphery" (South Africa) that adopted it for a short time closed their intellectual frontiers again. The failure of a moderate colonial nationalism facilitated the emergence of the apartheid regime and, since 1910, some of the characteristics that were closely associated with the mentality of the nineteenth-century frontiersmen. In 1998, F. W. de Klerk, a former South African president, published his autobiography, titled *The Last Trek*. In his book, he condemns the widespread demonization of the Afrikaner population, complains about increasing racial discrimination, and asserts that he was unaware of the human-rights violations during his presidency. The book thus tragically demonstrates how little official Afrikanerdom so far has tried to understand its own history. Jock of the Bushveld knew better.

NOTES

1. Percy FitzPatrick, *Jock of the Bushveld*, ed. Linda Rosenberg (Cape Town: 1984), 265. There are several biographies of FitzPatrick, most notably Andrew Duminy and Bill Guest, *Interfering in Politics: A Biography of Sir Percy FitzPatrick* (Johannesburg: 1987); see also Saul Dubow, "Colonial Nationalism, the Milner Kindergarten, and the Rise of 'South Africanism,' 1902–10," *History Workshop Journal* 43 (1997): especially 72ff. FitzPatrick was born of Irish Catholic parents in Cape Town and educated in England and the Cape. He moved to Transvaal in the 1890s and soon became involved in local politics and the economics of the new gold fields on the Witwatersrand during the reconstructionist era. Here he published his widely acclaimed book *The Transvaal from Within* (1899), which demonstrated his intimate knowledge both of contemporary events and of the country.

2. Compare Erhard Reckwitz, "Colonial Discourse and Early South African Literature," in *Intercultural Studies: Fictions of Empire,* ed. Vera Nünning and Ansgar Nünning (Heidelberg: 1996), 126ff.

3. FitzPatrick, *Jock of the Bushveld,* 265.

4. Still a very useful survey of South African historiography is Christopher Saunders, *The Making of the South African Past: Major Historians on Race and Class* (Cape Town: 1988), 3. According to Saunders, the amateur scholars long dominated the interpretation of South African history, while professional historiography was either resistant or very slow in taking up new ideas; du Toit's study in this respect would be *Die Geskiedenis van Ons Land in die Taal van Ons Volk* (Paarl: 1877), while Theal's first major work is *Compendium of South African History and Geography*, 3d ed. (1874; reprint, London: 1878).

5. The issue of cultural and historiographical transfers has been addressed increasingly in recent times. See the introduction in *British and German Historiography, 1750–1950: Traditions, Perceptions, and Transfers*, ed. Benedikt Stuchtey and Peter Wende (Oxford: 2000), 1–24; Piet C. Emmer and Henk L. Wesseling, eds.,

Reappraisals in Overseas History: Essays on Post-War Historiography about European Expansion (The Hague: 1979).

6. Christopher Saunders, "South African Historiography in English," in *Into the 80s: The Proceedings of the 11th Annual Conference of the Canadian Association of African Studies,* ed. Donald Ray, Peter Shinnie, and Donovan Williams (Vancouver: 1981); John Lonsdale, "From Colony to Industrial State: South African Historiography As Seen from England," *Social Dynamics* 9 (1983): 67–83.

7. Ralph A. Austen, " 'Africanist' Historiography and Its Critics: Can There Be an Autonomous African History?" in *African Historiography: Essays in Honour of Jacob Ade Ajayi,* ed. Toyin Falola (London: 1993), 203–17, especially 211; and, for a general overview, David Birmingham, "History in Africa," in *Companion to Historiography,* ed. Michael Bentley (London: 1997), 692–708, especially 701ff., and Caroline Neale, *Writing "Independent" History: African Historiography, 1960–1980* (London: 1985); Arnold Temu and Bonaventure Swai, *Historians and Africanist History: A Critique* (London: 1981).

8. In his highly stimulating study, which is central to the questions of this volume, *White Mythologies: Writing History and the West* (London: 1990), Robert Young questions the Eurocentrism of historiography and the limits of Western knowledge, but by arguing along the lines of Edward Said and Gayatri Spivak, his picture more or less neglects the African side. The relationship between colonialism and historical consciousness in the African case is elaborated by Adam Jones, "Kolonialherrschaft und Geschichtsbewußtsein: Zur Rekonstruktion der Vergangenheit in Schwarzafrika 1865–1965," *Historische Zeitschrift* 250 (1990): 73–92; Jones, *Schwarze Geschichte—Weiße Historiker: Vortrag gehalten vor der Karl Lamprecht-Gesellschaft Leipzig am 27. November 1997* (Leipzig: 1997); Christoph Marx has studied the German historiographical reception of precolonial Africa in his *"Völker ohne Schrift und Geschichte": Zur historischen Erfassung des vorkolonialen Schwarzafrika in der deutschen Forschung des 19. und 20. Jahrhunderts* (Stuttgart: 1988).

9. Christopher Saunders, *Writing History: South Africa's Urban Past and Other Essays* (Pretoria: 1992); Colin Bundy, *Re-Making the Past: New Perspectives in South African History* (Cape Town: 1986); Ken Smith, *The Changing Past: Trends in South African Historical Writing* (Johannesburg: 1988); Shula Marks, *Rewriting South African History, or the Hunt for Hintsa's Head* (London: 1996); Shula Marks, "The Historiography of South Africa: Recent Developments," in *African Historiographies,* ed. Bogumil Jewsiewicki and David Newbury (Beverly Hills, Calif.: 1986), 165–76; Shula Marks, "Towards a People's History of South Africa? Recent Developments in the Historiography of South Africa," in *People's History and Socialist Theory,* ed. Raphael Samuel (London: 1981), 297–308; Basil Alexander Le Cordeur, "The Reconstruction of South African History," *South African Historical Journal* 17 (1985): 1–10; D. Chainaiwa, "Historiographical Traditions of Southern Africa," *Journal of Southern African Affairs* 3 (1978): 175–93.

10. Compare Steven Feierman, "Africa in History: The End of Universal Narratives," in *After Colonialism: Imperial Histories and Postcolonial Displacements,* ed. Gyan Prakash (Princeton, N.J.: 1995), 40–65, especially 48ff.

11. John S. Galbraith, *Reluctant Empire: British Policy on the South African Frontier, 1834–1854* (Berkeley, Calif.: 1963).

12. Elmar Lehmann and Erhard Reckwitz, eds., *Mfecane to Boer War: Versions of South African History: Papers Presented at a Symposium at the University of Essen, 25.–27. April 1990* (Essen: 1992).

13. Jörg Fisch, *Geschichte Südafrikas* (Munich: 1991), 137.

14. Fisch, *Geschichte Südafrikas*, 134–35.

15. Consequently, "segregation" has become a key subject of research both in the field of history of historiography and in the social history of South Africa; for the most recent assessments, see William Beinart and Saul Dubow, eds., *Segregation and Apartheid in Twentieth-Century South Africa* (London: 1995); Timothy Keegan, *Colonial South Africa and the Origins of the Racial Order* (Cape Town: 1996); Paul Rich, "Race, Science, and the Legitimisation of White Supremacy in South Africa, 1902–1940," *International Journal of African Historical Studies* 23, no. 4 (1990): 665–86; Saul Dubow, *Racial Segregation and the Origins of Apartheid in South Africa, 1919–36* (London: 1989).

16. Thomas R. H. Davenport, *South Africa. A Modern History* (Toronto: 1991), 47.

17. Nelson Mandela, *Long Walk to Freedom* (London: 1994), 27.

18. Compare Sarah Nuttall, "Telling 'Free' Stories? Memory and Democracy in South African Autobiography Since 1994," in *Negotiating the Past: The Making of Memory in South Africa*, ed. Sarah Nuttall and Carli Coetzee (Cape Town: 1998), 75–88, here 76ff.; see also K. W. Smith, *A New Past for a New Present: Reflections on the Writing of South African History* (Pretoria: 1988).

19. John S. Galbraith, "The 'Turbulent Frontier' As a Factor in British Expansion," *Comparative Studies in Society and History* 2 (1959–1960): 150–68, here 163.

20. Christopher Saunders and Robin Derricourt, eds., *Beyond the Cape Frontier: Studies in the Transkei and Ciskei* (London: 1974).

21. Most illuminating is the study by Howard Lamar and Leonard Thompson, eds., *The Frontier in History: North America and Southern Africa Compared* (New Haven, Conn.: 1981).

22. Frederick Jackson Turner, "The Significance of the Frontier in American History" (1893), in Frederick Jackson Turner, *The Frontier in American History*, new ed. (Tucson, Ariz.: 1986), 1–38; compare John Mack Faragher, "The Frontier Trail: Rethinking Turner and Reimagining the American West," *American Historical Review* 98 (1993): 106–17; for a general overview, see Wilbur R. Jacobs, *On Turner's Trail: 100 Years of Writing Western History* (Lawrence, Kans.: 1994); for the British and German context, compare: Benedict Stuchtey, " 'Westward the Course of Empire Takes Its Way': Imperialism and the Frontier in British and German Historical Writing Around 1900," in Stuchtey and Wende, *British and German Historiography*, 289–334.

23. Ian Douglas MacCrone, *Race Attitudes in South Africa* (Johannesburg: 1937).

24. For a fuller theoretical discussion of the frontier problem, see the groundbreaking essays by Jürgen Osterhammel: "Kulturelle Grenzen in der Expansion Europas," *Saeculum* 46 (1995): 101–38, and "Jenseits der Orthodoxie: Imperium, Raum, Herrschaft und Kultur als Dimensionen von Imperialismustheorie," *Periplus: Jahrbuch für Außereuropäische Geschichte* 5 (1995): 119–31.

25. Quoted from Martin Legassick, "The Frontier Tradition in South African Historiography," in *Economy and Society in Pre-Industrial South Africa*, ed. Shula

Marks et al. (London: 1980): 58; William M. Macmillan, *Bantu, Boer, and Briton: The Making of the South African Native Problem* (1929; rev. ed., Oxford: 1963); compare *Africa and Empire: W. M. Macmillan, Historian and Social Critic*, ed. Hugh Macmillan and Shula Marks (Aldershot, U.K.: 1989), 11–16, 173–74.

26. Legassick, "The Frontier Tradition," 14.

27. Henry Cloete, *The History of the Great Boer Trek and the Origins of the South African Republics*, ed. W. Brodrick-Cloete (London: 1899).

28. Compare Manfred Nathan, *The Voortrekkers of South Africa: From the Earliest Times to the Foundation of the Republics* (London: 1937); George McCall Theal, *History of the Boers in South Africa: The Wanderings and Wars of the Emigrant Farmers from Their Leaving the Cape Colony to the Acknowledgement of Their Independence by Great Britain* (1887; reprint, Cape Town: 1973).

29. Catherine Hall, "Imperial Man: Edward Eyre in Australasia and the West Indies, 1833–66," in *The Expansion of England: Race, Ethnicity, and Cultural History*, ed. Bill Schwarz (London: 1996), 130–70, here 140.

30. John Maxwell Coetzee, *White Writing: On the Culture of Letters in South Africa* (Johannesburg: 1988); N. Mostert, *Frontiers: The Epic of South Africa's Creation and the Tragedy of the Xhosa People* (New York: 1992).

31. Compare Floris Albertus van Jaarsveld, *The Awakening of Afrikaner Nationalism, 1868–1881* (Cape Town: 1961).

32. Jan Hendrik Malan, *Boer en Barbaar: Of die Geskiedenis van die Voortrekkers Tussen die Jare 1835–1840: En Verder van die Kaffernasies met wie Hulle in Aauraking gekom het* (Bloemfontein: 1918); Jörg Fisch, "Der Mythos vom leeren Land in Südafrika oder Die verspätete Entdeckung der Afrikaner durch die Afrikaaner," in *Afrika: Entdeckung und Erforschung eines Kontinents*, ed. Heinz Durchardt, Jürg A. Schlumberger, and Peter Segl (Cologne: 1989), 143–64.

33. John J. Agar-Hamilton, *The Native Policy of the Voortrekkers: An Essay in the History of the Interior of South Africa, 1836–1858* (Cape Town: 1928).

34. Floris A. van Jaarsveld, *The Afrikaner's Interpretation of South African History* (Cape Town: 1964); see, for example, Gustav S. Preller, *Voortrekkermense: 'n Vijftal oorspronkelike Dokumente oor die Geskiedenis van die Voortrek, met aantekeninge en bijlae*, 6 vols. (1920; reprint, Cape Town: 1938); C. Louis Leipoldt, *Die Groot Trek* (Cape Town: 1938); for a collection of some major historical studies of the Great Trek, see *Spore van die Kakebeenwa: u' Terugblik oor die Groot Trek: Saamgestel deur Historikus* (Johannesburg: 1949).

35. The following draws on Richard B. Ford, "The Frontier in South Africa: A Comparative Study of the Turner Thesis," Ph.D. dissertation, University of Denver, 1966, 440–66.

36. Among the countless travel reports that could well serve as historiographical sources, see, for example, Alice Blanche Balfour, *Twelve Hundred Miles in a Waggon* (London: 1895); Mrs. Barkly, *Among Boers and Basutos: The Story of Our Life on the Frontier* (London: 1893); James Chapman, *Travels in the Interior of South Africa*, 2 vols. (London: 1868); John Joseph Freeman, *A Tour in South Africa* (London: 1851); Allen F. Gardner, *Narrative of a Journey to the Zulu Country in South Africa Undertaken in 1835* (London: 1836); Thomas Leask, *The Southern African Diaries, 1865–1870*, ed. J. P. R. Wallis (London: 1954); John W. D. Moodie, *Ten Years in South*

Africa: Including a Particular Description of the Wild Sports of That Country, 2 vols. (London: 1835); Edward Elers Napier, *Excursions in Southern Africa, Including a History of the Cape Colony, an Account of the Native Tribes*, 2 vols. (London: 1850); Andrew Smith, *Journal of His Expedition into the Interior of South Africa, 1834–36*, ed. W. F. Lye (Cape Town: 1975); Andrew Steedman, *Wanderings and Adventures in the Interior of South Africa*, 2 vols. (London: 1835); George Thompson, *Travels and Adventures in Southern Africa*, 2 vols. (London: 1827); Anthony Trollope, *South Africa*, 2 vols. (London: 1878).

37. John Philip, *Researches in South Africa: Illustrating the Civil, Moral, and Religious Condition of the Native Tribes*, 2 vols. (London: 1828); David Livingstone, *Missionary Travels and Researches in South Africa: Including a Sketch of Sixteen Years' Residence in the Interior of Africa* (London: 1857).

38. Robert Ross, "Donald Moodie and the Origins of South African Historiography," in Robert Ross, *Beyond the Pale: Essays on the History of Colonial South Africa* (Hanover, N.H.: 1993), 192–211, here 192.

39. For a full account, see Andrew Ross, *John Philip: Missions, Race, and Politics* (Aberdeen: 1986).

40. Deborah Posel, "Rethinking the 'Race-Class Debate' in South African Historiography," *Social Dynamics* 9 (1983): 50–66; Geoffrey Cronje, ed., *Aspekte van die Suid-Afrikaanse Historiografie* (Pretoria: 1967).

41. For some modern surveys of the subjects, see Jabulani Mzala Nxumalo, *The National Question in the Writing of South African History: A Critical Survey of Some Major Tendencies* (Milton Keynes, U.K.: 1992); H. C. G. Robbertze, *Die geskiedenis van die selfbeskikkingsgedagte by die Afrikaner* (Pretoria: 1996); Floris van Jaarsveld, *Afrikaner-geskiedskrywing: Verlede, hede en toekoms* (Pretoria: 1992).

42. Eric Walker, *The Frontier Tradition in South Africa: A Lecture Delivered . . . at Rhodes House on 5th March 1930* (Oxford: 1930); Eric Walker, *The Great Trek*, 5th ed. (London: 1965).

43. Walker, *The Great Trek*, 105.

44. Compare Sheila Patterson, *The Last Trek: A Study of the Boer People and the Afrikaner Nation* (London: 1957); Lawrence Green, *Lords of the Last Frontier: The Story of Southwest Africa and Its People of all Races* (London: 1953); Oliver Ramsford, *The Great Trek* (London: 1972); T. R. H. Davenport, *The Afrikaner Bond* (Cape Town: 1966).

45. Legassick, "The Frontier Tradition," 44–79.

46. Legassick, "The Frontier Tradition," 45–46.

47. Legassick, "The Frontier Tradition," 47.

48. J. Alton Templin, *Ideology on a Frontier: The Theological Foundation of Afrikaner Nationalism, 1652–1910* (Westport, Conn.: 1984).

49. Some of the major works by de Kiewiet are *British Colonial Policy and the South African Republics* (London: 1929); *The Imperial Factor in South Africa, a Study in Politics and Economics* (Cambridge, UK: 1937); "The Frontier and the Constitution," in *The Constitution Reconsidered*, ed. Conyers Read (New York: 1938), 329–40.

50. See Christopher Saunders, "A Liberal Descent? W. M. Macmillan, C. W. de Kiewiet, and the History of South Africa," in *Africa and Empire: W. M. Macmillan,*

Historian and Social Critic, ed. Hugh Macmillan and Shula Marks (Aldershot, U.K.: 1989), 91–102.

51. Saul Dubow, "Placing 'Race' in South African History," in *Historical Controversies and Historians*, ed. William Lamont (London: 1998), 65–79, quote on 66.

52. Dubow, "Placing 'Race,' " 67ff.

53. See Saunders, *Making of the South African Past*, 9–44; Izak Daniel Bosman, *Dr. George McCall Theal as die Geskiedskrywer van Suid Afrika* (Amsterdam: n.d.).

54. Deryck Marshall Schreuder, "The Imperial Historian As Colonial Nationalist: George McCall Theal and the Making of South African History," in *Studies in British Imperial History: Essays in Honour of A. P. Thornton*, ed. Gordon Martel (London: 1986), 95–158.

55. Keith Terrance Surridge, *Managing the South African War, 1899–1902. Politicians v. Generals* (Woodbridge, Suffolk, U.K.: 1998).

56. Compare Winston Spencer Churchill, *London to Ladysmith via Pretoria* (London: 1900).

57. Keith T. Surridge, " 'All You Soldiers Are What We Call Pro-Boer': The Military Critique of the South African War, 1899–1902," *History* 82 (1997): 582–600, quote on 599. For the intellectuals' response to the South-African War, see Benedikt Stuchtey, "The International of Critics: German and British Scholars During the South African War (1899–1902)," *South African Historical Journal* 44 (1999): 149–71.

58. Legassick, "Frontier Tradition," 48.

59. Saunders, *Making of the South African Past*, 114–15; Harrison M. Wright, *The Burden of the Present: Liberal-Radical Controversy over Southern African History* (Cape Town: 1977); Hosea Jaffe, *South African Neo-Liberal Historiography* (London: 1990).

60. Legassick, "Frontier Tradition," 63.

61. Robert Thornton, "The Colonial, the Imperial, and the Creation of the 'European' in Southern Africa," in *Occidentalism: Images of the West*, ed. James G. Carrier (Oxford: 1995), 208.

62. Legassick, "Frontier Tradition," 68.

63. Michael Cross, *Resistance, and Transformation: Education, Culture, and Reconstruction in South Africa* (Johannesburg: 1992).

64. Thornton, "The Colonial, the Imperial," 192–217.

65. Thornton, "The Colonial, the Imperial," 197.

66. Thornton gives the example of the British proconsul Sir George Grey, who, against the background of his Irish experience, supported local political autonomy in the Cape; see Thornton, "The Colonial, the Imperial," 198–99.

67. Benedikt Stuchtey, *W. E. H. Lecky (1838–1903): Historisches Denken und politisches Urteilen eines anglo-irischen Gelehrten* (Göttingen: 1997).

68. John Gerald Simms, *William Molyneux of Dublin: A Life of the Seventeenth-Century Political Writer and Scientist, 1656–1698*, ed. Patrick Kelly (Dublin: 1982), 102–19; Stuchtey, *W. E. H. Lecky*, 37–44.

69. W. E. H. Lecky, *Moral Aspects of the South African War, Women's Liberal Unionist Association* (Westminster: n.d.), 2; also published in the London *Daily News*, March 10, 1900.

70. Lecky, *Moral Aspects*, 6.

71. Stuchtey, *W. E. H. Lecky*, 217–58.

72. Richard Jebb, *The Imperial Conference: A History and Study*, 2 vols. (London: 1911); see Deryck Schreuder, "Colonial Nationalism and 'Tribal Nationalism': Making the White South African State, 1899–1910," in *The Rise of Colonial Nationalism: Australia, New Zealand, Canada and South Africa First Assert Their Nationalities, 1880–1914*, ed. John Eddy and Deryck Schreuder (Sydney: 1988), 192–226.

73. Both quotes from Dubow, "Colonial Nationalism," 55, 78.

74. Schreuder, "Colonial Nationalism," 200.

75. Christoph Marx, "Ethnische Herrschaft, Gold und der anti-imperialistische Kolonialismus Südafrikas," in *Universalgeschichte und Nationalgeschichten: Ernst Schulin zum 65.Geburtstag*, ed. Gangolf Hübinger, Jürgen Osterhammel, and Erich Pelzer (Freiburg im Breisgau: 1994), 269–89.

3

India's Connection to History

The Discipline and the Relation between Center and Periphery

Michael Gottlob

A t the beginning of the 1880s, the young Hindi poet and playwright Harishchandra of Benares (1850–1885), in his play *Bharat Durdasha*, deplored the "misery of India" under foreign rule. The domination by foreigners is here presented as a typical symptom of *kaliyuga*, the last stage in the cycle of inevitable degradation according to traditional Hindu cosmology. The same Harishchandra, however, also regretted the lack of proper historical thinking among his fellow countrymen—that there was "no moon of history" to be seen in the "pure sky of India."[1] In the last decades of the nineteenth century, when the British were at the height of their power in India and the Indians had to grasp their new status as British subjects, it became common, not only among Europeans but also among Indians themselves, to view India as changeless and non-historical.[2] For the Bengali writer Bankimchandra Chatterji (1838–1894), the Indian lack of historicity was itself one of the most important causes of foreign rule. Consequently, the creation of a Westernlike historical consciousness in India was seen as a prerequisite of autonomy.[3]

In the works of Harishchandra and Bankimchandra the encounter of the traditional Indian and modern British approach to the past becomes visible in its fundamental problematic: More than in the case of other Asiatic traditions of historical thinking and their contamination through European influence, the emergence of a local historical discipline in "unhistorical" India seems to coincide with the contamination of tradi-

75

tion. The Indian historical discipline, even in the eyes of its protagonists, was a British import. The European concept of a methodical investigation in the conditions and mechanisms of social change and its promotion through historiography was so new to the Indians that to a great extent they internalized the Western judgment on the Indian lack of history. Nevertheless, it would be wrong to assume a total affiliation of Indian historical thinking from the Western patterns and to view it as a simple relation of impact and response. As Harishchandra reveals in his complaint about the symptoms of *kaliyuga,* traditional forms of coping with contingency persisted in the interpretation of colonial rule—and the complaint about the presence of the foreigners could have even included the alienness of modern historiography itself. At the same time, recent research also shows how the process of Indian modernization during colonial rule can be traced back to precolonial, that is, indigenous reform tendencies.[4]

The attempt to understand the Indian and historical dialectic of continuity and break is rendered more complicated by the fact that historians not only asserted the modern discourse itself in the context of colonial rule, but also played a central ideological part in it. If the anthropologist Bernard S. Cohn has shown that "the colonizer's knowledge of the colonized was not and could never be neutral to the relation of dominance and subordination," this also is valid for the discipline of history.[5] Thus, as Cohn has described the complicity between anthropology and power, there was a complicity between history and colonial rule too. However, not just the colonial situation has to be taken into account but also, and in particular, the marginalizing character of the Western historical discourse itself. History was part and parcel of the colonizing enterprise—dominating it as well as being dominated by it. Comparing the Indian and British historical disciplines, one also has to be aware that in the (Western) theory of social evolution, societies and cultures are already compared.[6]

The Western historical mode was adopted by Indians and became a factor of self-improvement and anticolonial resistance. Just as the British used historical knowledge for staying in power and legitimizing it, the Indians used it as an emancipatory knowledge, serving to overcome backwardness and colonial subordination alike. Both claims, that of colonial rule and that of the emancipation from it, were proposed as attempts to connect India to history. Even self-imposed historicization, however, could become an element of colonization, oscillating between self-assertion and alienation. In the awareness of a growing one world and the important role of history in this process, this inner contradiction is at the center of the quest for a postcolonial history of India.

THE QUEST FOR HISTORICITY

Central to the discipline's claim of a scientific status in the eighteenth century was revelation of the general laws and the connectedness of universal history. Philosophically minded historians aimed at that *nexus rerum universalis* that showed the uniformity of human behavior and its interdependence throughout the world.[7] Thus, Edward Gibbon, David Hume, and others tried to reconstruct the past by its underlying laws, and they viewed the reality even of remote countries and peoples as nothing but the spatial extension of their own historical experience.[8] The discovery of distant peoples served to confirm the *nexus*, and its confirmation secured the applicability of historical knowledge. History became a mode of systematization.

It was the notion of uniformity and causal relationship of behavior and events that made knowing and mastering Indian history of interest to colonial administration.[9] However, as it soon became evident, indigenous histories of the expected kind could not be found.[10] As a consequence, the East India Company introduced specific measures to locate the required data from a variety of documents, manuscripts, inscriptions, and oral traditions. The inquiries, after the company's accession to the Diwani of Bengal, were at first mainly directed at discovering the traditional revenue system.[11] But in course of time the collections of material like that of Colin Mackenzie's Great Mysore Survey (1810–1821), which includes statistics, history, geography, and memoirs, constituted the first archives of historical research in India.[12] Moreover, the interest in Indian past and present led to the foundation of scholarly and teaching institutions such as the Asiatic Society and the Fort William College, later complemented with the Archaeological Survey and other bodies.[13]

The compilation of historical and cultural facts about India remained a constant strategy throughout the period of British colonial government. And among the historians involved in this project even the more scholarly minded left little doubt about the incorporation of their work into the structures of colonial rule and administration. The affinity to practical utility and advantage is visible even in the form of personal ambition. The inquirers of the past were mostly employees of the East India Company, the power and economic success of which determined their career and income.[14] Even James Mill (1773–1836), who never visited India, laid the groundwork for his position as examiner of correspondence in the London office of the East India Company with his *History of British India* (1817). Here, he exercised great influence over the affairs of the subcontinent.

This endeavor to know and appropriate the indigenous traditions for the sake of an efficient colonial administration became the most important interface between British and Indian approaches to the past. Local informants were involved in the inquiries, and although the British regarded them only as sources to be disposed of, this did not necessarily mean passivity. As the British adapted the knowledge to their interests as rulers, similarly the native collaborators (mostly brahmanical scholars and priests) for their part tried to bring to bear certain renderings of tradition that were conducive to their own economic and status interests. Not only economic interests and political antagonism, however, but also more fundamental cultural differences led to a reciprocal distrust that went well beyond pragmatic issues. Brahmans defended their ancient monopoly and control over collective memory and the interpretation of the past. The British for their part complained about the reluctance of the natives and suspected them of obstinacy and insincerity.[15]

However, since intercultural and innercultural reflections always tend to interfere, distrust and isolation were sometimes overcome by curiosity. It was Warren Hastings (1732–1818), the East India Company's first governor general who, following the directive to govern the country as much as possible through its own institutions and legal norms, explicitly supported the orientalist training of the British administrators.[16] And despite a general feeling of superiority and the claim to rule, the fascination for the exotic could even lead to forms of contamination. Thus William Jones (1746–1794), the major inspiration behind and organizer of orientalist research in India, saw in Indian traditions and customs signs of a great civilization and expected orientalist studies to bring about another age of renaissance both in Europe and India.[17] On the side of the Indians the traditional xenology allowed extensive assimilations of heterogenic achievements that could be taken to own advantage without altering the existing sense concepts.[18] The Hindus could even view the British as restorers of *dharma* (morals) after centuries of Muslim rule.

At the same time, in the emergent groups of the Calcutta *bhadralok* (the educated middle class) a number of people not only viewed openness to new experiences a means of taking pragmatic advantage but also assimilated British methods and concepts so much that they even risked a break with tradition. This is where the search for a new Indian self-understanding encountered the Western idea of history: To connect India to the universal process of improvement as represented by Western technological, political, and social achievements, and brought to systematic expression in the scientific concept of history, was the common aim of the various religious and social reform movements in nineteenth-century India. Among the first influential organizations attempting to set free the dynamics of social evolution was the Brahmo Samaj (Society of Brahmos), founded in Calcutta (1828) by Rammohun Roy (1772–1833), who envisioned a "reformation" of Hinduism in order to bring back to the fore its potential for rationality. Roy made the tradition systematically available in written form and through translations (both into Bengali and English), especially of the Upanishads, which had long been hidden behind the "dark curtain of the Sungscrit language."[19]

Incorporated into the new framework of interpretation, factual knowledge about the past acquired a new pragmatic meaning. Thus, social or religious reform and historical research developed in a close alliance. Leading reformers—such as Ishwar Chandra Vidyasagar (1820–1891), who followed in the steps of Roy and fought for the rights of women; Mahadev Govind Ranade (1842–1901), the Maharashtrian lawyer, economist, and leader of the Prarthana Samaj (Prayer Society); and others— conducted historical research themselves.[20] And the first prominent historians, such as Ramkrishna G. Bhandarkar (1837–1925), Romesh Chunder Dutt (1848–1909), and others, also functioned as social reformers.[21] In this combined endeavor at intellectual and social advancement Indian reality took the form of a changing entity comparable to that of the West.

In the form of an organized discipline Indian historical research was largely affiliated to British institutions. A significant example is Rajendra-lal Mitra (1824–1891), who made his career in the Asiatic Society, where he was the first Indian to conduct autonomous research and, in the end, became its secretary.[22] In the teaching of history, too, this institutional incorporation is evident. Bhandarkar taught at the Elphinstone College in Bombay, where he himself had been a student, and he acted as vice chancellor of the local university. Dutt made his career in the prestigious Indian Civil Service and, for some time, taught history at University College London. And still in the twentieth century, Jadunath Sarkar, Romesh Chandra Majumdar, and others, who wrote pioneer accounts on ancient, medieval, and modern Indian history, worked in the British-controlled education system. All of them adhered strictly to Western standards and based their judgments on the same underlying assumptions as European historians.

Notwithstanding these tendencies of approximation, the impact of the colonial situation remained dominating. For even in the case of the most benevolent British the information about the past after all established a general control over its interpretation, whereas even the most loyal Indians, while conceiving the improvement of their society, also thematized (at least implicitly) their autonomy. Again Mitra stands out as an early example: He was exposed to hostilities and suspicion on the part of British colleagues, and he personally experienced the conflict between methodical rigor and national sentiment.[23] Mitra, for the sake of improvement, advocated the priority of scientific inquiry over national sentiment:

"It is not for me to plea in favour of Indian mythology, nor am I its apologist."[24]

The priority for improvement prevailed among the British administrator historians as well as among most of the reformer historians. However, it was exactly the emerging vision of India's connection to history that gave the colonial situation a specifically historical dimension. This historical consciousness became evident with the paradigm shift in the British colonial administration during the 1830s, when Hastings's directive to acknowledge and respect indigenous traditions was replaced with a policy that aimed to systematically reshaped Indian society along liberal, progressive principles. With William Bentinck's reforms an image of India came to prevail that had been formulated earlier by Mill in his *History of British India*. The author vehemently denied the existence of a great Indian civilization celebrated so much by Jones.[25] And from the diagnosed absence of any sign of practical improvement he deduced the recommendation of radical changes in Indian society. He pleaded for a thoroughgoing education that would lead to rational thinking, directed to utility and progress. This was conceived as both obligation and legitimation of colonial rule.

The pedagogical turn is personified, above all, by Thomas Babington Macaulay (1800–1859), who stayed in India as a member of the Law Chamber from 1834 to 1838 and who, in his epochal *Minute on Education* (1835), outlined a fundamental reform of the Indian educational system. With this, history that hitherto had served as secondary information for administrative use acquired the role of a dominant ideology. If India had to be historicized, however, this could be achieved only through the mediation of the advanced historical consciousness of the West. Macaulay was convinced that "all the historical information which has been collected to form all the books written in the Sanskrit language is less valuable than what may be found in the most paltry abridgements used at preparatory schools in England."[26] What was implied in the revalorization of history was the ultimate fixation on the presupposition that India was unhistorical.[27]

In the area of research the approach also had turned from the search for historiographical texts to an awesome reconstruction of a lost past from the material remains. Since the early 1830s a general change had taken place whereby the search for evidence shifted from literary sources to coins, inscriptions, archaeological excavations, and other artifacts.[28] Under the dominance of the pedagogical program and its underlying assumption of a general Indian lack of historicity, the knowledge about India was ethnologized, naturalized, and reduced to "customs and manners." Thus, whereas the administration system was won over by the "historicists" from the "orientalists," in British research on India the decisive role shifted from history to anthropology, which presented caste and village as essential elements of an unchangeable and static India.[29]

The paradoxical consequence was that Indian reformers and historians, encouraged by orientalist research, appropriated Western techniques and patterns of interpretation and began to regard social facts as worthy of remembrance and capable of improvement, even though genuine Indian historicity was denied by the British. It was this tendency among British historians to deprive Indians of their historicity that led historically minded Indians to become skeptical of Western accounts. Doubts of this kind found first expression in the emerging vernacular prose. The vernaculars figured in the process of modernization and historicization as important idioms of mediation. Indian modernizers standing in double opposition to Hindu (or Muslim) orthodoxy and Western colonialism used the vernaculars to soften the hard contrast between Sanskrit tradition and modern science.[30] In addition to challenging the Brahmanic monopoly of tradition, they now also questioned the Western monopoly of modern knowledge regarding progress and improvement.

A mid–nineteenth-century example of a critical attitude toward British historiography was Nilmani Basak, who wrote his own history of India in Bengali. He accused British authors of textbooks, translated into the vernaculars, of bias and insufficient knowledge.[31] The British writers transmitted to the students the impression that "the religions and customs of this country were all based on falsehood and the ancient Hindus were a very stupid lot."[32] Particularly after the Mutiny of 1857, when the conflict between colonizer and colonized came to a critical point, historiography became an issue of fundamental dissent.

The most important initiator and expounder of an indigenous history was Bankimchandra, who undertook a systematic analysis of the existent history during the 1880s. He concluded in his *Bangadarsan* that "there is not a single work in English that is a true history of Bengal."[33] He also questioned the competence of Western orientalists even in principle. According to Bankimchandra, in discovering Eastern wisdom the Europeans failed to grasp the vital importance it had for the Indians themselves:

> European scholars, like Professor Max Müller, have been very eloquent on the importance of the study of the Vedas, but their point of view is exclusively the European point of view, and fails to represent the vastly superior interest Vedic studies possess of us, natives of the country.[34]

In a dispute with William Hastie, Bankimchandra accused certain Europeans of a "monstrous claim to omniscience" and stated: "No knowledge to them is true knowledge unless it has passed through the sieve of European criticism. All coin is false coin unless it bears the stamp of a Western mint." A European "will fail in arriving at a correct comprehension of Hinduism, as—I say it most emphatically—*as every other European who has made the attempt has failed.*"[35] However, even if Bankimchandra complained about the alienation between the new knowledge (*sikshita*) derived from the West and traditional Indian erudition, he himself nevertheless adhered to the modern mode of thinking and explicitly conceived India's autonomy and improvement through its connection to history. He envisioned a systematic recovery of India's agency by constituting it as a historical subject. Indians or Bengalis had to become conscious authors of their own history: "There has to be a history of Bengal . . . who is to write it? . . . Anyone, who is a Bengali, has to write it."[36]

Even the more cautious authors such as Rajanikanta Gupta and Akshaykumar Maitreya now used their newly acquired methodical skills of source critique to reject certain English interpretations, and they confronted the tendencies of devaluating all things Indian in those accounts with empirical evidence.[37] Similar forms of historical self-awareness were growing in other vernaculars as well, in Marathi, Hindi, Punjabi, Malayalam, and so forth.[38] It was during the 1880s that the first comprehensive accounts written in English also appeared, for example, R. C. Dutt's *History of Civilization in Ancient India* (1888) and R. G. Bhandarkar's *Early History of the Dekkan* (1884). These historians, even if they aimed at modernization rather than nationalization, also revealed errors in Western accounts. Dutt explicitly praised Max Müller for having made traditional wisdom available to the Indian people. On this basis, he rejected "the very common and very erroneous impression that Ancient India has no history worth studying, no connected and reliable chronicle of the past which would be interesting or instructive to the modern reader."[39]

Bhandarkar, too, criticized prejudices and monopolistic attitudes of Western researchers. For him, however, this was just another reason to adhere strictly to their method.

> [If Indians] follow their critical, comparative, and historical method . . . we may take our legitimate place among the investigators of the political, literary, and religious history of our country, and not allow the Germans, the French, and the English to monopolize the field. . . . If we shake ourselves free of such a bias, and critically and impartially examine our old records and institutions, we shall do very great service to our country; we shall be able to check the conclusions of some European scholars who are swayed by an opposite bias.[40]

According to Bhandarkar, Indian historicity was realized only through Western rationality. For scholars like him, the exemplariness and centrality of the British institutions and standards was beyond doubt. If the orthodox tradition of learning still persisted, the scientific method of the West had largely been accepted as arbiter in the appeal for truth about the past.[41] Even Bhandarkar, however, made it clear that improvement also had to be connected to Indian cultural tradition:

> It is not enough that any particular reform that may be suggested is good in itself. The question that is of vital importance is, whether it can be engrafted on the existing organism of Hindu Society, whose roots go back into prehistoric times and which contains vestiges of all that it has at any period of its life assimilated or had to struggle against.[42]

Altogether, the historical mode and the belief in a scientifically informed improvement won over the legendary tradition of the Puranas (written during the first millennium C.E.). By the end of the nineteenth century, history as a methodical endeavor was established and institutionalized in India. New periodicals began to appear all over the country, in the vernacular as well as in English.[43] Bhandarkar's extensive research activities led to the foundation of the Oriental Research Institute at Poona in 1917, which was later named after him. Rabindranath Tagore, who himself took an active interest in the new historical research institutions, spoke of a growing "hunger for history." He saw in the critical efforts a success "in breaking our mental bonds."[44] This, however, reveals a double ambivalence between change and continuity, authentic and alien agency—an ambivalence that extended on the discourse itself and made the issue of the connection to history also a question of center and periphery.

THE ASSERTION OF CENTRALITY

The use of methodically elaborated historical knowledge by Indian reformer historians corresponded largely to the role attributed to it by the British ideologists of modernization. Nevertheless, with the course of time, it became increasingly difficult to unite Indian and British aspirations with regard to India's connection to history. This is due not only to the different positions of colonizer and colonized but also to variations in the conception and use of history itself. If there has always been a tendency in historiography to marginalize the experience of "the other," in the debate over Indian historicity, this general ethnocentrism took the extreme form of a total dehistoricization. As Anwar Abdel Malek has shown, in the colonialist approach to oriental history there can be distinguished two forms of appropriation: to take history away and to deny history.[45] The denial of historicity outweighs the former in its depotentializing and subordinating effect. Whereas the British appropriation of the Indian past for purposes of administration acknowledged, at least in principle, India's autonomous agency, the construction of the "unhistorical" East presented it as something incomplete to be worked on. It made its connection to Western history appear as almost imperative and inevitable.

At the same time, the underlying assumptions of the project of Indian historicization were often expressed in essentialist terms. The experience brought to bear by Macaulay—that only Western societies had proved capable of improvement and only Western history was relevant for an improvement orientated instruction—took on the form of a discrimination of mere Indian prehistory from real history of the West. James Mill had prepared the ground for this too, by describing modern Indian history almost exclusively as the deeds of Europeans in India. Indian history, according to Mill, had to be annexed as "a portion of the British history."[46] In fact, the civilizatory approach of the utilitarians was all along close to the missionary perspective. Charles Grant, one of the early evangelicals, who like Mill blamed above all else Hinduism for the degeneration of India that had "sunk in misery by their vices," envisioned improvement rising from the conversion to Christianity.[47]

It was this tendency to append Indian history to British history that asserted itself in the new paradigm of colonial administration in the 1830s, which, inaugurating the project of historicization, at the same time replaced British adaptation to indigenous conditions with the Indian orientation along Western patterns.[48] The connection to Western history was conceived, notwithstanding the invocation of historical change, rather in political and spatial notions of the periphery's annexation to the center. It is true that Macaulay himself argued decidedly in terms of historical development. But this development was wholly centered on Great Britain, so that Indians for the sake of their historicity almost had to be anglicized.[49] Instead of expecting along with William Jones an Indian renaissance, and going even well beyond Mill's idea of rationalization, Macaulay aimed at the education of "a class of persons, Indian in blood and color, but English in taste, opinion, in morals and in intellect."[50] Siva Prasad (1823–1890) can be regarded as an example of the anglicized elite who worked to transmit the Whig idea of history to the natives. Prasad was Harishchandra's teacher and also translated English history books into Hindi. He also wrote the first history of India in Hindi, which served as a text book in the North West Provinces.[51]

Appending Indian history to British was realized in military terms with the defeat of the mutiny and in political terms in the formal incorporation of India into the British Empire. The historiographical inclusion of India (as mere prehistory or appendix) into British history, then, was only a consequence. The annexation had been preceded, however, by nothing short of an amputation of the Indian past over a long period. The historical material in the course of its utility-oriented processing had been expropriated of its original author, its subjectivity absorbed by a "new epistemic regime," which reveals from its results: "Erasing colonized histories was itself fundamental to full colonial rule."[52] On the basis of a thoroughly dehistoricized India colonialism could be presented all the more as historicization of the unhistorical. And the more the British conceived themselves as historicizers, the more the native voices were silenced, becoming "anonymous footnotes for a new kind of colonial knowledge."[53] The Indian prospect in the framework of this knowledge was the connection to a history in which colonization figured as progress.[54]

Whereas historicization became a dominant ideology, the connection to history at the same time figured more and more as a spatial concept.[55] The historicizing semantic stood in contrast to the successive vanishing of the transitional perspective giving way to the "illusion of permanence."[56] As temporal posteriorization turned into eternal subordination, historicity connotated no approximation in the relation between East and West anymore but enduring difference. The reification of the Whig idea of history went as far as basing historicity on race.[57] More than ever, the relation between center and periphery in the historical discipline corresponded to that of colonial dependence. For the British viceroy, Lord Curzon (in India from 1899 to 1905), oriental studies represented the "necessary furniture of the empire." History served only to secure the functioning of a system of rule, in which the essentially passive peoples had to be taken into tow by the active ones. The nonautonomous nations had to be subordinated to a benevolent despotism, which for the sake of a general progress had to assert itself in case of doubt even against the will of those under tutelage, doing "What's for their good, not what pleases them."[58]

The marginalization of Indian history in Western accounts made centrality a dominant issue for Indian historians, too. It was Bankimchandra who first supposed a nexus between Indian subordination and the British disregard for Indian historicity. In his critique of contemporary historiography he not only laid bare its bias but also undertook a principled reflection on the relation between historical knowledge and political power. With reference to historical writing he was assessing, Bankimchandra criticized that "there is no history of the Bengali nation in it,"[59] for it lacked the physical prowess (*bahubol*) of Bengalis, their heroism, and their force of resistance, the memory of which was of the utmost importance in constituting agency. This unmasked a strategy of depotentialization behind British accounts of the Bengali-Indian past. And it highlighted the need for an indigenous historiography: "Bengal must

have her own history. Otherwise there is no hope for Bengal."[60] Bankimchandra claimed the Indian's/Bengali's right to self-representation.[61]

Postulating a historiography centered on the self and its actual needs,
Bankimchandra adhered all the more to the Western concept of a perspec-
tivating history. However, if this was to mediate progress and self-assertion, Bankimchandra did not escape essentialism either. As it was in the
British interest to deny Indian history and thus deprive Indians of their
agency (notwithstanding the claim to historicization), so it seemed evident that true Indian history, capable of constituting Indian agency, also
had to be ethnocentric history, that is, not only written by the Indians
themselves but also related exclusively to a nation existing from time
immemorial (notwithstanding the explicit emulation of the British concept of nation). Bankimchandra's verdict about the principled cognitive
incompetence of Western Indologists, who did not grasp Indian thinking
in its vital core, corresponded to the British verdict about an essentially
unhistorical India. The quest for an India-centered history was the answer
to the experience of marginalization.

The striving for historical dynamics and the simultaneous assertion of
centrality proved to be problematical and sometimes even contradictory.
Not only that: In order to constitute agency Indian history, according to
Bankimchandra, had to be written mainly as the history of the defense
against alien invaders, thus reducing the acknowledgment of the inner
diversity of India.[62] The essentialist delimitation of Indian and Western
knowledge also was just as ahistorical as was the Western classification of
historical and unhistorical peoples. This tension between historicity and
centrality had been a basic problem of Indian historiography since the
1880s, when nationalism began to institutionalize itself on the political
level.[63] Even in the case of Harishchandra it became a tensile test when he
tried to mediate not only between *kaliyuga* and the idea of progress, but
also between *deshabhakti,* the love of country, and *rajabhakti,* the love of
government as agent of modernization.[64]

Bankimchandra and Harishchandra were at least conscious of their
borrowing from the West and reflected the dilemma of India's modernization while maintaining its identity. Others appealed in a less scrupulous manner to centrality and originality, which became guiding
principles of self-assertion. The tendencies in the Western discourse to
ethnicization, hierarchization, and even to race theory as an extreme form
of essentialism ascribing a higher degree of historicity to the Aryan peoples, further encouraged nativist speculations among Indians. Faced with
the ambiguity of modernization, some of the reformers presented India
(or Hinduism for that matter) itself as the very origin and center of civilization. This was particularly the case with the Arya Samaj (Society of
Aryans), a reform movement founded in 1875 by Swami Dayanand Saras-

wati (1824–1883), who took a critical stance on the Brahmo Samaj because of its tendencies to blind imitation of the West. In *Satyarth Prakash*, Dayanand described ancient India as the cradle of civilization where allegedly modern achievements and inventions like telegraph, fire arms, and so forth had already been known.[65] It was largely in accordance with the traditional reading of the Vedas that these included even future developments. Dayanand deduced from this a temporal priority and spiritual superiority of India or Aryavarsha (the land of Aryans) over the modern West.[66]

With the turn of the tide in the reform movements—from the fight for inner modernization against orthodoxy to self-assertion vis-à-vis the foreign ruler—interest in history increasingly was directed at centralizing modernity in Indian society. Now that historiography was used for the creation of national consciousness, politicians and ideologues, such as Bal Gangadhar Tilak (1856–1920) and Vinayak Damodar Savarkar (1883–1966), undertook their own historical research. Tilak joined in the race for the earliest possible dating of Hindu culture.[67] The earlier to which vedic culture could be dated, the more convincing the Indian claim to priority and superiority as the oldest human culture. Tilak also refused to anglicize Indian institutions, that is, to denationalize them in the name of social and political reform.[68] Savarkar, in elaborating the ideology of *hindutva*, was the first to explicitly postulate the unity of race, creed, history, and territory. He centered Indian agency by consequently selecting its constituents from the original times and places of the Hindus. According to Savarkar it was the Vedic and epic tradition that "bring us together and weld us into a race." Indian agency, in order to be homogeneous, was limited to those who regarded India as the land of their sacred texts. These reconstituted in the war of independence the original agency of the epics. Savarkar, in fact, rejected "the interested or ignorant cry that has secured the ear of the present world that the Hindus have no history." Rather, the Hindus were the only people who had preserved their history through the ages: "If the Hindus do not possess a common history, then none in the world does."[69]

Finally, even the academic discipline responded to Bankimchandra's quest for an Indian historiography of India. Stimulated by the independence movement, which gained momentum with the *swadeshi* campaign from 1905 onward, academic research too concentrated on the evidence of vigor and achievement in precolonial India. The dominant influence of nationalism resulted, sometimes in clear contrast to their self-understanding as detached researchers, in the construction of an activist image of India and the rejection of general Western assumptions that were apt to legitimate colonial rule. Radha Kumud Mookerji, who died in 1964, traced the "fundamental unity of India" to the ancient Indian empires, which in general became a favorite object of nationally minded research-ers.[70] Mookerji rejected in particular the allegation that the concepts of sovereignty and central rule had been unknown to early Indians and had been introduced to India by the Persians or the Greek.[71] The alleged absence of statehood in early Indian history or its reduction to oriental despotism also were major issues for Kashi Prasad Jayaswal (1881–1937). He criticized the Oxford historian and Indologist Vincent Smith (1848–1920), who had described Indian history as an endless decline after a golden age lasting from the third century B.C.E. to the seventh century C.E. If, according to Smith, political stability could be established and secured only from outside, Jayaswal in *Hindu Polity* reconstructed demo-cratic and republican traditions in early India and revalorized Indian kingship as constitutional monarchy.[72] Romesh Chandra Majumdar (1888–1975) discovered that India itself was the center of a colonial empire that transmitted not only civilization to others but moreover, and in clear contrast to the modern British, conceded coevalness to the colo-nized.[73]

It is evident in most of these reconstructions that Anglo-Saxon institu-tions were projected back on to early India or, at least, Indian institutions were shaped along Western patterns. In fact, it was part of the mechanism of the center's influence on the periphery that not only the Europeans imagined the history of the other in the form of contrast to their self-image, but even the others themselves tried to reconstruct their ancient institutions following European models. So, even and particularly in the openly anticolonial accounts, Indian historiography remained closely related to Western categories. The relatedness to the Western mode of thinking was not even denied by these authors. The similarity of the polit-ical contents was seen as a sign of being on par with the West. Jayaswal, therefore, could explicitly refer to the British as "the greatest constitu-tional polity of modern times," viewing the encounter as an open-ended proof of verification: "The contact is electrifying: it can either kill or reju-venate the Race."[74] The similarity, at any rate, was conceived as based in the remote past itself. This was the only way to make Indian agency credi-ble and convincing.

REHISTORICIZING PERIPHERY AND CENTER

With this claim to modern Western concepts for early India, however, not only the problem of authenticity and particularity remained unresolved, it also introduced elements of essentialism into the reconstructions of national history that narrowed the perspective of change and improve-ment. It was this emerging unhistorical historicism and ethnocentric inclusivism among nationalist politicians and historians against which Bhandarkar directed his appeal to strict adherence to the Western method and orientation toward scientific progress. In a similar attitude, M. G. Ranade asked Indian revivalists what actually they wished to revive.[75] Any so-called state of origin was itself the result of a process of development. In order to mediate modern and indigenous positions, Ranade conceived of India's development as "organic growth of society" and adopted what he called the "method of tradition."[76]

By contrast, as has been seen, even British historians made essentialist use of history. Situating the historical over the unhistorical, they were taking in the temporal notions for spatial and hierarchical concepts. Against the reduction of historicity on part of the British to ideological means for a policy of subordination, a form of anticolonial critique emerged that made the transfixed relation of historical center and static periphery flexible again. R. C. Dutt, in his *Economic History of India*, confronted colonialism with its own ideology and described it as a retarding rather than accelerating factor.[77] Dutt showed how colonial economy not only failed to bring about prosperity and progress in India but even hindered its traditional potential for development to unfold. The backwardness of India appeared as an effect of systematic deindustrialization. Dutt's arguments were backed by Dadabhai Naoroji's (1825–1917) inquiries into the "drain of wealth." Describing colonial exploitation as a form of "un-British rule in India," Naoroji linked the processes of the center and the periphery in a new way, insofar that the latter's decline hampered the progress of the center itself.[78] Dutt went beyond Naoroji and, anticipating postcolonial Third World theories, alleged that the periphery's underdevelopment was correlated directly with the development of the center. Referring to the expectations of improvement, Dutt made it clear that India's historicization was propagated by the British, who at the same time obstructed it, resulting in disconnecting India from rather than connecting it to history.

Confronting the Western ideology of historicization and progress with the actual development in India, the exponents of economic nationalism (Naoroji, Ranade, Dutt) turned the idea of progress from a legitimation of colonialism into a critique of its retarding and marginalizing effects. This reconciled the notion of historical change with the quest for autonomy and centrality. What still remains ambivalent in economic nationalism and can be interpreted sometimes as modernist and in other instances as revivalist, becomes part of a consequently modernist and progressive view in the interpretations of Western-educated intellectuals or activists inspired by Marxism and socialism.[79] Particularly in the political strategy and reasoning of Jawaharlal Nehru (1889–1964) the confidence in the historical process prevailed and outweighed the preoccupation with centrality. The leader of the independence movement, who was at the same time one of its foremost historical thinkers, trying to be aware of the world historical dimension of the Indian struggle, clearly rejected the essentialized notions of Orient and Occident. He replaced the antagonism with a historical framework of interpretation: "I do not understand the words Orient and Occident, except in the sense that Europe and America are highly industrialized and Asia is backward in this respect." Industrialization, however, was itself a product of historical development, "something new in the world's history." Those who cultivated an image of India as "religious, philosophical, speculative, metaphysical, unconcerned with this world, and lost in dreams of the beyond," Nehru suspected, had second thoughts. They hoped India would "remain plunged in thought and tangled in speculation, so that they might possess this world and the fullness thereof, unhindered by these thinkers, and take their joy of it."[80]

Nehru blamed the British (as had done Bankimchandra) for nothing short of a strategy of India's dehistoricization and criticized that "real history for them begins with the advent of the Englishman to India."[81] Going further than Bankimchandra, he also rejected their classificatory approach to Indian and Western reality. For Nehru, adopting the idea of universal progress in the very interest of Indian agency and directing the idea of history against a hierarchical world order, the connection to history was not a question of periphery and center. History was a universal phenomenon, including West and East alike and distinguishing only progressive and retarding factors in all societies. Nehru thus envisioned India's reconnection to a global historical process that it had lost at some stage of its development (lost, as he admitted, through its own guilt). He was convinced that the dominant tendencies of this process not only came in favor of Indian independence but also would lead to an active and autonomous role for India in the world as well as with regard to that nation's inner improvement.

For modernist politicians such as Nehru, who tried to bring India back to the mainstream of development, this process was not to be localized anymore—a vision that corresponds in a way to the concept of a multicentric world as propagated later by India's postindependence governments. If the Western monopolization of history implied a spatialized relation between progressive and backward, Nehru aimed at its despatialization. Premised on the ubiquity of history, Nehru tried to open a nonessentialist way of how to reappropriate history without getting annexed to alien forces and dynamics. Against the British endeavor toward annexation and against the static constructions of Indian revivalists, Nehru aimed at rehistoricizing the congealed asymmetric structure of center and periphery.

In the form of scientific reasoning about society and tradition, conceived as mobilization of agency and perspectivation of progress, history became a powerful doctrine/discourse in the liberation movement. The growing importance also is reflected by a further institutionalization of research on the national level, testified by new academic publications, such as the *Journal of Indian History*, or national institutions of historical research, for example, the Indian History Congress (1935), the Bharatiya Vidya Bhavan.[82] In academic historiography it is perhaps Jadunath Sarkar (1870–1958) who best personifies this combination of methodical research, national perspective, and progressive processualization. He expected objective research to serve social improvement and national autonomy better than political partisanship. Sarkar concluded his *Lesson of India's History* that:

> We must embrace the spirit of progress with a full and unquestioning faith, we must face the unpopularity of resisting the seductive cry for going back to the undiluted wisdom of our ancestors, we must avoid emphasizing eternally the peculiar heritage of Aryan India of the far-off past.[83]

On another occasion, Sarkar expressed his intention "to find out the true solutions of the problems of modern India and avoid pitfalls of the past."[84]

India's independence in 1947, then, should have meant both its ultimate connection to history and the emancipation from periphery to center. Modern historical thinking in postindependence India expressed its hegemony in the critical work of autonomous (old and new) research institutions, a national consciousness identifying agency with the executive power of a sovereign state, and an obligation to socioeconomic progress, as much as to the directives of the central planning commission. With this, however, the question of historicity and centrality was not altogether resolved. If political independence embodied the recovery of agency, the simultaneous partition of India for some indicated its lasting incompleteness. In the quarrel over the appropriate rendering of the freedom fight, it was maintained that the end of British rule meant only a first step on the way to realize true Hindu agency.[85]

At the same time, the dynamics of improvement and emancipation had broken up the framework of national liberation (the dichotomy of colonized and colonial ruler), bringing into play the agency of the subaltern against that of the elite. Already before the end of British rule, Marxist historians such as Rajani Palme Dutt had made it clear that colonialism was only an expression of class domination and that the process of liberation had to be continued toward universal socialist revolution.[86] For the connection to history and the unfolding of Indian dynamics one had, seen from this perspective, to overcome not only national but also social and economic marginalization. Thus, even after the formal end of colonial rule the anti-imperialist thematic was on the agenda as against the ideology of state planning development.[87] Consequent historicization, according to the group around the journal *Subaltern Studies*, necessitated a more precise (equally consequent) localization of agency.[88] Seen from a postcolonial and subaltern perspective, Indian historical dynamics as conceived by Nehru still seemed to be centered elsewhere.[89] Even if progress was not British anymore, "the universal principle and the world standards had been already set by history; there was no choice on those matters."[90] Real historicization has to go beyond centrality, but it still has to take care that agency be conceded to those deprived of it.[91]

However, in his fight for true self-rule (*swaraj*), Gandhi showed a complete absence of the desire to be connected to history, instead viewing historicization itself as a form of colonization. Gandhi rejected the concepts of development and progress. But his striving for the recovery of an authentic Indian way of life rooted in the Indian past also can be seen as an attempt to make peripheral aspects of civilization central ones (of one's own civilization as much as that of the whole world).[92] Certainly, Gandhi's alternative attitude with regard to history was almost obsolete after India gained independence. Yet today it is being recovered as a source of inspiration for a postcolonial approach to social change, one that tries to grasp the colonizing elements in the concept of history, without which the connection to history apparently was unavailable. Any attempt at global history that tries to assure itself of a comparative insight into the history of historical thinking has to become aware of the asymmetries inherent in historical conceptions of each other, coming in the way of mutual historical understanding about cultural difference.

NOTES

1. Quoted from Jürgen Lütt, *Hindu-Nationalismus in Uttar Pradesh* (Stuttgart: 1970), 80. For Harishchandra, see Vasudha Dalmia, *The Nationalization of Hindu Traditions: Bharatendu Harishchandra and Nineteenth-Century Banaras* (Delhi: 1997).

2. India had become an official part of the British Empire in 1858; Queen Victoria had assumed the title of "Kaisar-i-Hind" in 1876.

3. For Bankimchandra, see Sudipta Kaviraj, *The Unhappy Consciousness: Bankimchandra Chattopadhyay and the Formation of Nationalist Discourse in India* (Delhi: 1995).

4. For the revision of the early modern period in Indian history, see Muzaffar Alam and Sanjay Subrahmanyam, *The Mughal State, 1526–1750* (Delhi: 1997); Sanjay Subrahmanyam, "Connected Histories: Notes Towards a Reconfiguration of Early Modern Eurasia," *Modern Asian Studies* 31 (1997): 735–62.

5. Ranajit Guha, "Introduction" to Bernard S. Cohn, *An Anthropologist among the Historians and Other Essays* (Delhi: 1987), xix.

6. For the correlation between history and cultural comparison, see Friedrich H. Tenbruck, "Was war der Kulturvergleich, ehe es den Kulturvergleich gab?" in *Zwischen den Kulturen? Die Sozialwissenschaften vor dem Problem des Kulturvergleichs*, ed. Joachim Matthes (Göttingen: 1992), 13–35.

7. Johann Christoph Gatterer, "Vom historischen Plan und der darauf sich gründenden Zusammenfügung der Erzählungen," in *Allgemeine Historische Bibliothek* (Halle: 1767), 1: 15–89.

8. See the ethnographic parts of Edward Gibbon, *The Decline and Fall of the Roman Empire*, ed. J. B. Bury (London: 1896); David Hume, *The Natural History of Religion*, ed. A. Wayne Colver (Oxford: 1976).

9. "Inevitably therefore in the close encounter between Europe and Asia through colonialism, there was a search for indigenous histories which would provide an avenue to comprehending these new and different cultures" (Romila Thapar, "The Search for a Historical Tradition: Early India," in *Historical Cultures*, ed. Jörn Rüsen et al. (London: forthcoming).

10. "Real history and chronology have hitherto been desiderata in the literature of India" (Board of Control, East India Company, 1810; quoted from Nicholas B. Dirks, "Colonial Histories and Native Informants: Biography of an Archive," in *Orientalism and the Postcolonial Predicament*, ed. Carol Breckenridge and Peter van der Veer [Philadelphia: 1993], 279). For the failure, due to these expectations, to grasp the specificity of the Indian approach to the past, see Thapar, "Search for a Historical Tradition."

11. "The fiscal operations here depended for their success on an intimate knowledge of traditions, continuities and past procedures—a knowledge of history" (Ranajit Guha, *An Indian Historiography of India: A Nineteenth-Century Agenda and its Implications* [Calcutta: 1988], 4).

12. Dirks, "Colonial Histories," 285, 286. See also David Ludden, "Orientalist Empiricism: Transformations of Colonial Knowledge," in *Orientalism and the Postcolonial Predicament*, ed. Carol A. Breckenridge and Peter van der Veer (Philadelphia: 1993), 250–78.

13. For the early history of the Asiatic Society, founded by William Jones in 1784, see O. P. Kejariwal, *The Asiatic Society of Bengal and the Discovery of India's Past, 1784–1838* (Delhi: 1988). The Fort William College was established in 1800 with the purpose to train young company servants in, among other things, Indian languages. The Archaeological Survey was introduced in 1861.

14. Compare S. C. Mittal, *India Distorted: A Study of British Historians on India*, 3 vols. (New Delhi: 1995), 1:12.

15. For the antagonism and mutual suspicion, see Guha, *Indian Historiography*, 5, 7.

16. With this Hastings hoped, by the way, to "lessen the weight of the chain by which the natives are held in subjection." Quoted from Peter J. Marshall, ed., *The British Discovery of Hinduism in the Eighteenth Century* (Cambridge, UK: 1970), 189.

17. William Jones, "On the Hindus," in *The British Discovery of Hinduism in the Eighteenth Century*, 246–59. For Jones, however, the connectedness of the cultures was based on common origin rather than universal laws of human nature.

18. For the "traditional Indian xenology" and the asymmetry "in the historical

presentation of the encounter between Europe and India and their mutual approaches," see Wilhelm Halbfass, *India and Europe: An Essay in Philosophical Understanding* (Delhi: 1990), 172ff.

19. Rammohun Roy, "Abridgment of the Vedanta, The Vedanta: Introduction," in *Selected Works of Raja Rammohun Roy* (New Delhi: 1977), 261.

20. Vidyasagar was author of *Banglar Itihasa* [History of Bengal] (1848). Ranade was author of *Rise of Maratha Power*.

21. Bhandarkar was a member of the All-India Social Conference and the Prarthana Samaj. Dutt worked from 1904 onward as revenue minister of the Maharaja of Baroda, trying to put into practice his reform ideas.

22. It was as late as 1829 that the first Indians were admitted to the Asiatic Society as members.

23. For James Fergusson's polemics against Mitra, see Thomas R. Metcalf, *Ideologies of the Raj*, New Cambridge History of India, 4 parts (New Delhi: 1995), part 3, 4: 213.

24. Quoted from Sisir Kumar Mitra, "Raja Rajendralal Mitra," in *Historians and Historiography in Modern India*, ed. Siba Pada Sen (Calcutta: 1973), 13.

25. Bentinck, who was governor-general from 1828 to 1835, declared himself a follower of Mill and Bentham. Compare Eric Stokes, *The English Utilitarians and India* (Oxford: 1959), 51.

26. Quoted from David Kopf, *British Orientalism and the Bengal Renaissance: The Dynamics of Indian Modernization, 1773–1835* (Berkeley, Calif.: 1969), 249–50. In another frequently quoted remark, Macaulay compared the worth of the entire Sanskrit literature with that of a single shelf of European literature.

27. In fact, the absence of historiographical text material in India for a long time to come was explained like this: "Early India wrote no history because it never made any" (A. A. MacDonell, *A History of Sanskrit Literature* [London: 1900], 11).

28. Compare Kejariwal, *Asiatic Society*, 164.

29. Compare Cohn, *Anthropologist*, 158.

30. For the multilingualism in colonial India, see Halbfass, *India and Europe*, 203, passim.

31. It was mainly the Christian missionaries who availed themselves of the vernaculars. See, for example, J. C. Marshman, *Bharatvarsher Itihas* (Outline of the History of India), 2 vols. (1831).

32. Nilmani Basak, *Bharatvarsher Itihas* (History of India), 3 vols. (1857–1858); quoted from Guha, *Indian Historiography*, 40–41.

33. Bankimchandra Chatterji, "Bangalar itihas sambandhe kayekti katha" (A few words about the history of Bengal), in *Bankim Rachanavali*, ed. Jogesh Chandra Bagal, 2 vols. (Calcutta: 1965), 2:337; quoted from Guha, *Indian Historiography*, 56.

34. Chatterji, "Bangalar itihas sambandhe kayekti katha," quoted from Guha, *Indian Historiography*, 56.

35. *Bankim Rachanavali* (English works), ed. Jogesh Chandra Bagal (Calcutta: 1969), 150, 210, 205; quoted from Partha Chatterjee, *Nationalist Thought and the Colonial World—A Derivative Discourse?* (London: 1986), 60–61.

36. Chatterji, "Bangalar itihas sambandhe kayekti katha," quoted from Guha, *Indian Historiography*, 57.

37. Rajanikanta Gupta, *Sipahi Juddher Itihas* (History of the Sepoy's War) (1880); Akshaykumar Maitreya, *Sirajuddowla* (1898).

38. See the respective contributions in Cyril Henry Philips, ed., *Historians of India, Pakistan and Ceylon* (London: 1961); Tarasankar Banerjee, ed., *Historiography in Modern Indian Languages, 1800–1947* (Calcutta: 1987); K. N. Panikkar, "In Defence of 'Old' History," *Economic Political Weekly*, October 1, 1994, 2595–97.

39. Romesh Chunder Dutt, *History of Civilization in Ancient India* (London: 1888), quoted from the fourth edition under the title *Early Hindu Civilization B.C.200 to320* (Calcutta: 1963), 2.

40. Ramkrishna G. Bhandarkar, "The Critical, Comparative, and Historical Method of Inquiry, As Applied to Sanskrit Scholarship and Philology and Indian Archeology," in *Collected Works of Sir R. G. Bhandarkar*, ed. Narayana Bapuji Utgikar and Vasudev Gopal Paranjpe, 4 vols. (Poona: 1927), 1: 392.

41. See Ramkrishna G. Bhandarkar, "Presidential Address at the Opening Session of the First Oriental Conference of India, Held at Poona on the 5th of November 1919," in *Collected Works*, 1:316–31.

42. Bhandarkar, *Collected Works*, 1:478.

43. See, for example, *Bengal Past and Present* (Calcutta: 1907ff.); *Journal of the Bihar and Orissa Research Society* (Patna: 1915ff.).

44. Quoted from Guha, *Indian Historiography*, 53. Tagore welcomed the publication of the new Bengali periodical *Aitihasik Chitra* (Images of History) (1899ff.), viewing it as "a crusade to free Indian history" and "to rescue our history from the hands of the foreigners" (quoted from A. R. Mallick, "Modern Historical Writing in Bengali," in *Historians of India, Pakistan and Ceylon*, ed. Cyril Henry Philips (London: 1961), 450.

45. Anwar Abdel Malek, "Orientalism in Crisis," *Diogenes* 44 (winter 1963): 107–8; quoted from Dirks, "Colonial Histories," 279.

46. Quoted from Guha, *Indian Historiography*, 50.

47. Charles Grant, *Observations on the State of Society Among the Asiatic Subjects of Great Britain, Particularly with Respect to Morals, and the Means of Improving it* (1792); quoted from Cohn, *Anthropologist*, 143–44.

48. For the change from Hastings's orientalist to Bentinck's westernizing or anglicizing policy, see David Kopf, *British Orientalism and the Bengal Renaissance: The Dynamics of Indian Modernization 1773–1835* (Berkeley, Calif.: 1969).

49. For the coincidence of national history and the process of civilization, see Jürgen Osterhammel, "Nation und Zivilisation in der britischen Geschichtsschreibung von Hume bis Macaulay," *Historische Zeitschrift* 254 (1992): 313–14.

50. Quoted from Benedict Anderson, *Imagined Communities: Reflections on the Origin and Spread of Nationalism*, 2d ed. (London: 1991), 91.

51. *Itihasa Timirnasak* (History as Destroyer of Darkness) (1864). An English translation titled *History of Hindustan* appeared in 1873. For Siva Prasad, see Lütt, *Hindu-Nationalismus*, 65–98.

52. See Dirks's examinations of "competing histories, and historicities, before colonized histories were snared and silenced" in "Colonial Histories," 280.

53. Dirks, "Colonial Histories," 280, 308.

54. Guha describes how the discovery of the sea route to India was presented to

Indian students as a triumph of European history. Compare *Indian Historiography*, 20–21.

55. Anthropology also "sanctioned an ideological process by which relations between the West and its other, between anthropology and its object, were conceived not only as difference, but as distance in Space *and* Time" (Johannes Fabian, *Time and the Other. How Anthropology Makes Its Object* [New York: 1983], 147).

56. See Francis G. Hutchins, *The Illusion of Permanence: British Imperialism in India* (Princeton, N.J.: 1967).

57. For the impact of the Aryan race theory on Indian studies, see Joan Leopold, "British Applications of the Aryan Theory of Race to India, 1850–1870," *English Historical Review* 89 (1974): 578–603; Metcalf, *Ideologies of the Raj*, 81–88, passim.

58. See T. G. P. Spear, "British Historical Writing in the Era of the Nationalist Movements," in *Historians of India, Pakistan and Ceylon*, ed. Cyril Henry Philips (London: 1961), 409.

59. Quoted from Guha, *Indian Historiography*, 56, 59.

60. "Bangalar itihas sambandhe kayekti katha" (A few words about the history of Bengal); quoted from Guha, *Indian Historiography*, 1.

61. Compare Guha, *Indian Historiography*, 57.

62. For the debate over the correlation between the striving for historicity and the emergence of communalist conflicts in India, see Michael Gottlob, "Communalism, Nationalism, Secularism: Historical Thinking in India before the Problem of Cultural Diversity," in Rüsen, *Historical Cultures*.

63. In 1885 the Indian National Congress (INC) was founded.

64. Compare Lütt, *Hindu-Nationalismus*, 78–84.

65. Dayanand Saraswati, *Satyarth Prakash* (Light of Truth) (Allahabad: 1884). The Arya Samaj has produced a school of historians writing in Hindi such as Ramadeva (*Vedic India*, 1911) and Raghuvir Sharan Dubli (*The True History of India*, 1913). Compare H. L. Singh, "Modern Historical Writing in Hindi," in Philips, ed., *Historians of India*, 463, 466.

66. This could even result in the notion of a colonizing mission on the part of India. Swami Vivekananda, disciple of the Hindu saint Ramakrishna and founder of the Ramakrishna-Mission, another important reform movement, on the one hand propagated modernization on Western lines and criticized the Arya Samajist's isolationism. On the other hand he too rejected the imitating approach of the Brahmo Samaj and called instead for a conquest of the world by Indian spirituality. For Vivekananda too, all cultural diversity and future development were included in Indian tradition.

67. Thus, the emergence of the Vedas was dated back to 4,000 B.C.E. Compare B. G. Tilak, *Orion* (Bombay: 1893); *The Arctic Home of the Vedas* (Bombay: 1903).

68. Compare V. P. Varma, *Modern Indian Political Thought*, 5th ed. (Agra: 1974), 195.

69. Vinayak Damodar Savarkar, *Hindutva: Who Is a Hindu?* 6th ed. (Delhi: 1989), 94–95.

70. Mookerji taught history at the Bengal National College and in the Universities of Mysore and Lucknow. In *The Fundamental Unity of India* (London: 1914) he probed also into geography as a factor of history.

71. Mookerji, *Fundamental Unity*, 70.

72. Kashi Prasad Jayaswal, *Hindu Polity: A Constitutional History of India in Hindu Times* (Patna: 1936).

73. Romesh Chandra Majumdar, *Ancient Indian Colonies in the Far East* (Lahore: 1927).

74. Jayaswal, *Hindu Polity*, 367.

75. Mahadev Govind Ranade, "Social Conference Address" (1897); quoted from *Sources of Indian Tradition*, ed. William Theodore de Bary and Steven Hay, 2d ed., 2 vols. (New Delhi: 1991), 2: 105.

76. Mahadev Govind Ranade, *The Miscellaneous Writings*, ed. by Ramabai Ranade (Bombay: 1915), 158.

77. Romesh Chunder Dutt, *Economic History of India*, 2 vols. (London: 1901–1903).

78. Dadabhai Naoroji, *Poverty and Un-British Rule in India* (London: 1901). Naoroji's critique of "Un-British Rule in India" may be read as an ironic reminder of Macaulay's program of anglicization.

79. For the Marxist interpretation of Indian history, see M. N. Roy, *India in Transition* (Geneva: 1922).

80. Jawaharlal Nehru, *The Discovery of India* (New Delhi: 1989), 151–52.

81. Nehru, *Discovery*, 28.

82. The *Journal of Indian History* began publication in 1921 in Allahabad; it is now published in Trivandrum.

83. Jadunath Sarkar, *India Through the Ages* (1928), 85.

84. Jadunath Sarkar, *Fall of the Mughal Empire*, 4 vols. (1932; reprint, New Delhi: 1988), 1: xv.

85. For Indian historiography after Partition, see Gyanendra Pandey, "Partition and the Politics of History," in *The Nation, the State: Indian Identity*, ed. Madhusree Dutta et al. (Calcutta: 1996), 1–26.

86. Rajani Palme Dutt, *India Today* (Calcutta: 1989).

87. See Bipan Chandra, "Presidential Address [Colonialism and Modernization]," *Proceedings of the 32d Session of the Indian History Congress*, vol. 2 (Jabalpur: 1970), 20. The quest for centrality is also taken up through the demand of a non-Eurocentric Marxism. See Ashok Rudra, *Non-Eurocentric Marxism and Indian Society* (Calcutta: 1988).

88. For the subaltern perspective of history, see Ranajit Guha, "On Some Aspects of the Historiography of Colonial India," *Subaltern Studies* 1 (1982): 1–8.

89. "World History resides *Elsewhere*" and India looks for the "place within that universal scheme of things" (Chatterjee, *Nationalist Thought*, 161–62). However, it found a certain consideration in the socialist pattern and nonalignment of politics.

90. Chatterjee, *Nationalist Thought*, 159.

91. For the concept of "passive revolution" as "the *general* form of the transition from colonial to postcolonial national states in the 20th century," see Chatterjee, *Nationalist Thought*, 50–52.

92. See Ashis Nandy, "Final Encounter: The Politics of the Assassination of Gandhi," in Ashis Nandy, *At the Edge of Psychology: Essays in Politics and Culture* (Delhi: 1990), 72.

4

🌺

Historiography on a "Continent without History"

Anglophone West Africa, 1880s–1940s

Andreas Eckert

THE CONTEXT: "NOTHING
EVER HAPPENED THERE"

A small elite of Western-educated journalists, lawyers, medical doctors, and teachers had a formative influence on most national movements in the African colonies after World War II. Consequently, the political profile of these movements was largely characterized by the visions of this elite, whose members espoused European ideas of progress and development. One important project of this elite was the creation of "another" Africa using science and technology. Oriented toward Western concepts of democracy, political organization, national self-determination, and economic growth, they set as their goals the ending of colonial rule and the creation of nation-states. Aside from the dominant criticism of colonial politics, the political program of the nationalist elites fell back on the heritage of African culture. Partly as a reaction to the European denial that there was any African history worth knowing, the westernized elite developed a high esteem of African culture and history. In the view of the nationalist elite, the positive and usable elements of this culture and history were necessary foundations for the new African nations.[1] What was the starting position to write a "truly African history" at the end of the colonial period?

In Africa, history became an academic discipline only after World War II.[2] However, the recording of African history is as old as the reading of history itself. Neither classical European nor medieval Islamic historians were uninterested in tropical Africa, but their horizons were limited by the extent of the contacts that were made with it, whether across the Sahara to Ethiopia or the Bilad al-Sudan, or down the Red Sea and Indian Ocean coasts to the limits of monsoon navigation.[3] During the nineteenth century, however, the (contemporary) history of Africa—and the history of the non-European world in general—disappeared from the general historiography. World history dealt from this time on until the 1920s and 1930s with the history of Europe.[4]

Hegel provides a good and often quoted example for the patterns of thought that gained ground during this period. One important element was the idea of a unilinear evolutionism: Only a gradually advancing world history could exist, culminating in bourgeois society, whereas the history of non-European societies was reduced to prehistory.[5] As Hegel wrote in *The Philosophy of History* (posthumously published in 1837): "The peculiarity of the African character [is its lack of] . . . the principle which naturally accompanies all our ideas—the category of Universality." Hegel then goes on to discuss other assumed lacks:

> [Africa] is no historical part of the World, it has no movement or development to exhibit. . . . What we properly understand by Africa, is the Unhistorical, Underdeveloped Spirit, still involved in the conditions of mere nature, and which has to be presented here as the threshold of the World's History.[6]

Western pseudoscientific theories of race in the nineteenth century assigned positions, on a scale of ability, to physical differences; the most obvious physical difference was skin color, so "scientists" automatically put Africans at the bottom of the scale, because they seemed to be the most different from the scientists themselves.[7] They went on to claim that African history had no importance or value because Africans could not have produced a true civilization and any trait worthy of admiration must have been borrowed from their neighbors. Africans thus were made objects of history, never its subjects, because they were held to be capable of absorbing foreign influences without contributing anything to the world at large. Pseudoscientific racism virtually disappeared from respectable scientific circles after 1945, but its heritage lived on. Its insidious survival was based on the fact that conclusions relying on racist evidence could live on after the supporting evidence has died. The proposition that Africa has no significant history because Africans are racially inferior became untenable, but intellectuals in the West still vaguely remembered that Africa has no history, even though they may have forgotten why.[8]

The established history during the colonial period tended to emphasize European activities and leave out the African factor. At its worst, it showed Africans as barbarians whose will and judgment were weak or ill-directed. Therefore, it implied, superior beings from elsewhere came in and did what the Africans could not do for themselves.[9] Even at its best, colonial history allowed Africans only secondary roles on the historical stage.[10] Africa, it was generally believed, had languished in a state of nature from the Stone Age to the present time. It had a past, but never any kind of history, and it was therefore a suitable field for nobody but the anthropologist.

Anthropology was in fact the European discipline that dealt most seriously with Africa during the colonial period. But the dominant, functionalist-oriented British social anthropology created a static, antihistorical picture of African societies by assuming that the nature of every "traditional" society could be discovered by taking present, observed data and subtracting everything that seemed to be an external influence. The result was what they called the "anthropological present." The effort to abstract this present from the real present again furthered the assumption that change in Africa must come from an outside influence because it made African societies appear changeless until the Europeans arrived. Moreover, by their insistence on prolonged and careful field investigation through participant observation, anthropologists tended to seek out simple societies and isolated cultures. This very selectivity distorted Western knowledge of African culture by leaving great gaps in the accounts of large and complex societies, thus adding to the myth of a primitive Africa.[11]

African historical tradition has been mainly oral, which in the view of European historians was not acceptable.[12] In parts of West Africa there was a long tradition of historical record-keeping in the form of *griots*, professional and casted praise singers and storytellers. However, Africa also has a written historiographical tradition. The academic historiography in sub-Saharan African does not predate the 1950s, but it was preceded by historical accounts written by local amateur historians that stretched back well into the nineteenth century. The academic historians of the post-World War II period owe a great deal to these nonprofessional predecessors: Much of the "oral tradition" used by academic historians is in fact gleaned from the writings of these amateurs.

One factor in the emergence of a written "amateur historiography" was that the growth of European interest in Africa gave Africans themselves a wider range of literatures in which to express their concern for their history. This especially was the case in West Africa. The breadth and depth of native contact with Christian missionaries seems to have been an important factor here. The authors of history books or pamphlets here could be labeled "cultural nationalists."[13] Early historical writing has often been seen as either emergent anticolonial nationalism or as acceptance of the colonizers' vision of the African past. However, motives far more complex than cultural assertion alone shaped early African historical writing after the late nineteenth century. Although rejecting uncritical and unqualified imitation of European culture, the cultural nationalists did not substitute it for an unqualified or uncritical defense of local African culture. Thus their interest in the study of indigenous cultures and history should be understood not simply as a project of discovery but also as a project of creation, of constructing a model of local history that would function in the legitimation of their modernizing aspirations.

This chapter attempts to analyze this early African historiography by using the example of two classics of this genre written by Africans who were active in the religion of the incoming culture and took their names from it: Carl Christian Reindorf's *A History of the Gold Coast and Asante* (1895) and Samuel Johnson's *History of the Yorubas* (completed in 1897, although not published until 1921).[14] The main emphasis here is on examining how their works were shaped by diverse interests and influences within the constraints of the colonial situation. Understanding the patterns of change during this period can only better illuminate historiographical patterns since then.

REINDORF AND EARLY
GOLD COAST HISTORIOGRAPHY

In a wide-open situation on the Ghanaian coast in the last decades of the nineteenth century some Africans had begun to compile a general history, albeit from different viewpoints. Up to this point there had been a history carried orally within specific groups, states, and local families, but no public discourse about the past in a Western sense.[15] The years from circa 1880 to the end of World War I can be described as the first or formative phase in the local African production of literary versions of the history of what became the British Gold Coast in 1901 and the independent state of Ghana in 1957.[16] The authors wrote in local African (mainly Akuapem-Twi and sometimes Fante-Twi) and European languages, but most accords were written in English. Gold Coast history was a collaborative effort involving researchers, bibliophiles, family archivists, and benevolent patrons. It was and remains remarkable in the sense that so few wrote so much in a relatively short period of time, in circumstances that were not wholly favorable to the process of researching, writing, and publishing Gold Coast history. As part-time historians, often with limited resources and without immediate access to modern archives, libraries, and publication outlets, the "amateur historians" nevertheless managed to publish an extensive corpus of history.[17] A distinction must be made between north-central Islamic versions of the Gold Coast Ghanaian past,[18] written in Arabic or Hausa by Muslim teachers (usually described as scholars) in the commercial towns of north-central Ghana,[19] and the already mentioned southern coastal or Christian versions, written by teachers, preachers, journalists, and lawyers (never described as scholars). The latter histories were published in the commercial towns on the southern Gold Coast, principally Cape Coast, Accra, and Akropong, and later in Britain, Germany, and Switzerland.

This chapter is more concerned with the second, Christian/southern-coastal branch of historiographical production. Unlike their Muslim counterparts to the north, these men were not seen as scholars and only rarely were described as members of an intelligentsia or intellectual community. Today they tend to be regarded as more or less skillful amateurs and their writings are seen as more or less valuable primary sources for the use of modern professional historians.[20]

Early Gold Coast historiography cannot be regarded in essentialist ways, neither as a nationalist response, designed to challenge the legality of British rule and to counter the racist "book history" of the imperialists, nor as an elitist response, calculated to secure the interests of the local African bourgeoisie within the new colonial state. The idea of homogenous, undifferentiated nationalism and elitism is not necessarily an effective analytical aid to furthering understanding of this historiography. Raymond Jenkins has meticulously worked out the different and often overlapping categories into which these historians could be placed.[21]

1. Those who undertook basic research. These men collected oral traditions and folklore, compiled biographies, and endeavored to procure and peruse standard texts or "ancient authorities." Their work was written up and filed as mission reports, included in their own collections of papers, or occasionally published, often anonymously, in local newspapers and periodicals.

2. A small number who published their research in books, booklets, newspapers, and journals, both within the Gold Coast colony and elsewhere. They often incorporated in their publications the allied research undertaken by their colleagues.

3. Writers who could be labeled as "general practitioners" or "essayists." They relied mainly on recently published secondary material. These were often journalist-historians who tended to use newspa-

pers and journals, foreign and local, both as sources of information
and ideas as well as vehicles for their work.
4. Those who provided information and inspiration, together with the
   resources and press outlets for local historians, whether specialists
   or general practitioners.

The majority of Gold Coast historians suffered under limited and limiting
publishing opportunities. Only very few, such as James Africanus Horton,
seem to have had the private resources and metropolitan publishing contacts to match the books produced by British authors. Most Gold Coast
authors, however, relied on newspapers as their outlets or on groups in
Europe with commercial and humanitarian interests in West Africa.[22]

As Jenkins has shown in formidable detail, the early experiences of and
early training in formal, European-derived historical studies differed
sharply among the first generations of amateur historians.[23] Reindorf and
other students of the Basel Mission all had been taught and had themselves taught history. As a result of its intimate link with language study,
which was accorded primacy by the mission, history had achieved a prestigious status as a compulsory subject and as a discipline in which written
and oral traditions were regarded as appropriate sources for reconstructing the past. Uniformity was the essence of their experience of history in
terms of content, interpretation, and medium of instruction. They had
been taught, or had taught, world or general history in local languages,
from prescribed textbooks produced by mission personnel. Moreover,
school-taught history was not an end in itself. It was a point of departure
for further (postgraduate) research, including the collection of oral traditions, and formed the foundation on which future Gold Coast African
nations would be built.

It is evident that all initiatives in the study and teaching of history,
whether Euro-African or European, were contained or sustained within
the centralized and hierarchical structure of the mission's educational
system. By 1880 European missionaries dominated the publication of history. However, Gold Coast Euro-Africans with an anglophone educational background had hardly been taught any history at all. Only those
who had been educated in Britain or Sierra Leone had probably received
some instruction in history. Before 1880 those Euro-Africans in the anglophone sphere of interest who had attempted to research, write on, or
teach English, European or Gold-Coast history, or aspects of local African
cultures, including language, had done so despite rather than because of
official British colonial or Wesleyan policy and patronage.

The history of the development of early Gold Coast historiography is
intimately connected to the history of the small, cosmopolitan Euro-African communities that had emerged to form an internally diverse and dif-

ferentiated society in the southern Gold Coast in and after the middle decades of the nineteenth century. In early colonial Accra, for example, a significant minority of the town's population, including many Western-educated individuals, were of mixed European and African ancestry, identifying themselves as being part of the wider Ga community but at the same time retaining a distinct identity as so-called mulattos.[24] The role and identity of Euro-Africans is central to a whole range of issues in Gold Coast historiography: the changing mercantile economy, the relationship between indigenous polities and British imperial power, the spread of Christianity, and the emergence of elite culture and notions of modernity. Whereas some treatments have emphasized sociocultural affiliations stretching to Europe and to the anglophone Creole communities from Freetown to Fernando Póo, others have stressed the importance of local African affiliations.[25]

In his pioneering work on the antecedents of Gold Coast nationalism, David Kimble characterized nineteenth-century mulattos "as Africans rather than Europeans, since they generally thought of themselves as such."[26] There is some evidence of the relative strength of the ties between the emerging literate elites on the Gold Coast and the indigenous communities from which they emerged. In his reexamination of the intellectual milieus of late nineteenth- and early twentieth-century urban elites, Jenkins also concludes that Euro-African communities are best characterized as a "prominent but integrated feature of the local African sociocultural landscape, rather than a distinctive 'ethno-cultural constellation.' "[27]

Reindorf, too, belonged to the Euro-African community of Western-educated individuals and was a clergyman of the Basel Mission.[28] He began his research into the history of the Gold Coast and the Asante in the early 1860s. His decision to collect and record oral histories appears to have been stimulated by the death of his grandmother in 1860 and by the Basel Mission, which in 1864, under the direction of Johann Gottlieb Christaller, entered an important phase in its study of the languages, traditions, and folklore of the Gold Coast societies.[29] Some thirty years later, in 1895, Reindorf's *History of the Gold Coast and Asante Based on Traditions and Historical Facts Comprising a Period of More Than Three Centuries from about 1500 to 1860* was published in Basel. The manuscript was finished in 1889. Having taken more than twenty years to prepare, the manuscript seems to have been printed at the author's expense, apparently because he was unable to secure direct involvement by the Basel Mission or an English publisher.

At first only a few Gold Coast Africans were aware of this book, and although it eventually achieved a wide distribution within what is now southern Ghana, it was only in the form of a "heavily revised, truncated and distorted second edition of 1951–66, which is now far better known than the original."[30] The 1966 edition published in Ghana especially met the increasing demands from a new generation of historians for a "new look" at the history of Ghana and the part played in it by Africans.[31] Already during the interwar years the book seems to have played a significant role in court cases.[32] Outside Ghana, Reindorf's impact both on the public and on subsequent historical work remained small, whereas his British contemporary, A. B. Ellis, for example, published seven very successful books on the Gold Coast.[33] Some have extolled Reindorf as a pioneer of "modern" African thought or historiography but more on account of his part-African descent than of familiarity with what he wrote.[34]

In his book, Reindorf strove to provide both a sourcebook for future historians and a guide to the past, useful for identifying appropriate development strategies.[35] These two aims contradicted each other to some extent. The more he sought to measure progress and provide a unified narrative, the further he distanced himself from the traditions he collected. His modernizing spirit thus created a number of conceptual problems for him as a writer and thinker.[36] On the one hand, he was very proud of his African background and culture, which he constantly praised; on the other, he saw many signs of what he called "retrogression" among his compatriots and propounded radical change. According to Reindorf, the main purpose of history is to measure progress and assess what has been achieved, after which a society can better tackle the future. Here we have a notion of history as a teleological process culminating in the establishment of a modern nation-state. A typical modernizer, Reindorf denied the past, and the normative power it possesses in more traditional cultures, and relegated it to the status of a mere prelude to the future. This approach does not preclude admiration for heroic deeds on the part of ancestors. In *History*, as in European history books written during the same period, great men make history.

Reindorf's *History* does not fit easily into any category. In his attempt to combine different sources, Reindorf anticipated the approach that was to dominate African historiography—at least in declarations of intent—from the 1960s onward. He relied mainly on a wealth of oral material but frequently tried to supplement it with material drawn from other sources. It is, however, difficult to evaluate Reindorf's historical reconstruction because of the virtual absence of source references and the predominance of oral material. What is striking is the richness of the ethnographic material scattered through the narrative, not yet fully recognized perhaps because it is presented not as conventional ethnography but as history.[37] Reindorf tells us a great deal about aspects such as body language, court procedure and concepts of adultery, symbolic means of communication, and military organization.

Reindorf's friend and patron Christaller, who had become acquainted with *History* through the press, wrote in his prefatory remark:

> It is the first comprehensive history of an important part of Africa written by a native and from the viewpoint of a native. . . . Here we have a history written by a native who has a warm heart for his country and people, and is at home in their language and way of thinking, whereby he could attain a truer aspect of facts than a European who has to gather his information by interpreters.[38]

Christaller's assumption that there was such a thing as "the standpoint of a native" surely is problematic, but it leads to another central aspect of Reindorf's work: *History* mirrors the new role that history had to play under colonial rule. Twaddle has argued with reference to Uganda that history became "a continuation of war by other means."[39] It became of vital concern to secure a "favorable relationship" not just with the colonial power but with the colonial state—in this case, the Gold Coast colony.[40] Reindorf was directly involved in the colony's political life, and the information he recorded reflected the desire and ability of certain local rulers to influence what became, in southeastern Ghana, the authoritative historical view. What Reindorf was doing was imagining a national community within the colonial boundaries, with himself firmly rooted in its midst.[41] He also was trying to show his educated compatriots, most of whom also were of African-European descent, that they, too, were part of this nation-in-waiting. He even assigned them a vanguard role in the development of the country, calling on them to "diffuse their better qualifications, their Christian and moral qualifications, into the rest." Only then would a change for the better be achieved.

SAMUEL JOHNSON AND YORUBA HISTORIOGRAPHY

Samuel Johnson's *The History of Yoruba from the Earliest Times to the Beginning of the British Protectorate*, completed in 1897 and published in 1921 in London, ranks high among the classics in African historiography.[42] It is quite rightly celebrated as a major work in Nigerian cultural and nationalist literature.[43] Johnson (1846–1901) worked as a schoolmaster and catechist in Ibadan, then acted as an intermediary and peace negotiator on behalf of the British in the Kiriji War between Ibadan and the Ekitiparapo. The last fifteen years of his life he spent as a missionary of the Church Missionary Society in Oyo.[44] It is extremely important to consider Johnson's Christian background when explaining his historiographical enterprise. According to John Peel, the purpose of Johnson's *History* was "an attempt to discern the purposes of God operating through the turbulent history of his times and his people, and (as a corollary) to give a secure place to Christianity in that history."[45]

Although his book occupies a rather outstanding position within the canon of early African historiography, Johnson's case provides a good example of the efforts of African intellectuals of late nineteenth-century West Africa who sought to combine projects of modernization with a defense of the integrity of the indigenous cultures. On the one hand, Johnson was a staunch supporter of mission policies and British colonial expansion as a means to civilize Yoruba society. On the other, his intention was to educate his fellow countrymen on the history of their own country. Johnson was one of the most prominent men in a group of Western-educated "historians" who emerged in the second half of the nineteenth century among the Yoruba in southwestern Nigeria. This group of amateur historians translated oral traditions and orally transmitted stories into written histories, thus creating a new form of Yoruba history.[46] This development can be understood only against the backdrop of major political, social, and economic changes in Yorubaland during the nineteenth century, which culminated in the establishment of British colonial rule.[47]

After the 1850s a tradition of history writing in English and Yoruba developed, mainly in Lagos and Abeokuta.[48] The authors were either European missionaries or Western-educated Yoruba, mostly with missionary backgrounds. The motivation to write these usually short histories, more often in pamphlet than in book format, was part of the general movement of cultural nationalism that took root among the Western-educated Yorubas between the 1880s and the early twentieth century. From the 1840s onward these individuals developed an interest in their cultural and historical background, especially after 1880, when they were increasingly barred from higher functions in the mission and the colonial government, due to the development of racialist attitudes and the formation of a more formal colonial system. This put the Western-educated Yoruba in a position of relative deprivation. In order to better their positions independent of the colonial structure, they were forced to search for alternative modes of development.

These alternatives were found in a cultural identity based on Yoruba culture, the formation of African churches, cooperation with local political elites, and eventually the formation of a nationalist movement. The prolific output of local histories and chronicles of Yoruba history during the same period should be seen in this light.[49] With it these Yoruba historians founded a school of Yoruba history that was to influence not only the attitudes of the British government toward the Yoruba hinterland, but also many of the actions of indigenous Yoruba in their dealings with the British far into the twentieth century. Moreover, by recording on paper what before had been a wholly oral affair, the Yoruba historians provided a new and unprecedented outlook on the history of the region. Because it was printed, in the eyes of the British it was much more valuable than any oral tradition. In the British system of indirect rule it was essential for the colonial authorities to know the workings of traditional society and the base on which it rested. Thus the importance of the availability of a range of historical treaties cannot be overestimated.

The opinion that the use of written material as evidence was decisive in matters of government was then quickly adopted by the rulers of Yorubaland. There are numerous examples of books that were specially written to persuade the British that the standpoint of certain interest groups was correct.[50] To what extent did this historiography contribute to the "invention of the Yoruba?"[51] In this respect, Peel has pointed out that:

> It was the body of work produced by the Christian Yoruba intelligentsia—the creation of an orthography and a literary language, the translation of the Scriptures, local and ethnic histories large and small, written in English and Yoruba, studies of the Yoruba traditional religion variously interpretative, polemical or historical—through which the Yoruba have come to know themselves precisely as such. . . . That we study a people called "the Yoruba" at all is due largely to them.[52]

Not surprisingly, the precise views held by the early Yoruba historians differed according to their relative position in Yoruba society and their level of erudition. Their works vary greatly in styles of writing, from travelogues in the tradition of early nineteenth-century travelers to history as part of a philological exercise, to history as a political instrument. The Church Missionary Society played a crucial role in publishing these works.[53] In the 1920s the emphasis shifted toward ethnographical and anthropological studies as tools of colonial administration. However, local historians in southern Nigeria continued to produce local histories, especially in those areas that did not possess a published local history of their own, because they feared a loss of authority within the framework of the colony without having a written history.[54] Only in the 1950s did the first academically trained Nigerian historians start work at the University of Ibadan. The so-called Ibadan School of History sprung from this group and became perhaps the most remarkable branch of African history on the continent. Their historiographical affinities lay within the liberal, empiricist, and archive-oriented English tradition that emphasized description over analysis in the study of history. Most historical attention was devoted to "trade and politics."[55] In recent years there was a new wave of local histories written by nonacademics.[56]

With *History*, Johnson had produced a unique historical work in more than one sense: It was the first comprehensive written history of the Yoruba people. Incorporating topics such as the development of language and grammar, religion, mythology, and government, ethnographic material, and descriptive, chronological history from the beginning of time to his own day, Johnson created an opus magnum. However, as Robin Law has pointed out in detail, Johnson's *History* is a somewhat complicated work to characterize because it makes use of rather different sorts of sources for different periods of Yoruba history.[57] Johnson relied on his own observations and experiences, on the testimony of eyewitnesses and participants (he was able to record numerous personal recollections, even if some of these were secondhand rather than strictly eyewitness accounts), on the "bards" or "national historians" of the Oyo court, and on written documents and newspapers. Curiously, Johnson seems to have made virtually no use of the numerous published accounts of European visitors to the Yoruba country from the 1820s onward.

The history of the book's publication also was complex.[58] The manuscript was completed in 1897 but then was lost. Johnson died in 1901, leaving his brother Obadiah to reconstitute the work from Samuel's notes and drafts, a task that Obadiah apparently completed in 1916. The extent to which Obadiah rewrote his brother's text remains unclear; in any case, certain parts of *History* as published refer to events after Samuel's death in 1901.

Clearly, Johnson's principal aim was "that the history of our fatherland might not be lost in oblivion, especially as our old sires are fast dying out." He continues:

> Educated natives of Yoruba are well acquainted with the history of England and with that of Rome and Greece, but of the history of their own country they know nothing whatever! This reproach it is one of the author's objects to remove.[59]

Johnson here avows a classic cultural nationalist motivation, involving both "the recording and preservation of a heritage of oral history presumed to be in danger of being lost and the overcoming of the alienation of Western-educated Yoruba from their own culture and history."[60]

But which "fatherland" is meant? This was an especially problematic question with regard to the Yoruba, who had not represented any sort of political unit in the precolonial period. Johnson conceptualized the Yoruba as defined by common descent. This, of course, was neither his invention nor that of any other contemporary nationalist intellectual. It can be suggested that the assumed identity of culture, language, and common descent probably owed more to contemporary European anthropological (and nationalist political) thought than to indigenous Yoruba conceptions. Although Johnson sought to assert a distinctively African rather than European cultural identity, the concepts of race and nationality through which he sought to do so were themselves of European derivation.

Although Johnson claimed to have written the history of all Yoruba, he offered for the most part the history of a particular (albeit the largest) subgroup of the Yoruba, the Oyo. Ironically, despite his avowed aim of fostering a sense of Yoruba national identity, Johnson's work had the effect of exacerbating rather than assuaging internal Yoruba divisions. Another instructive aspect of his *History* is that, like many other cultural nationalists, Johnson interpreted Yoruba traditional religion as being essentially monotheistic rather than truly polytheistic. For cultural nationalists like Johnson, who wished to remain Christian, this perspective evidently had the dual advantage of making Yoruba religion appear more respectable and Christianity less alien. Johnson even suggested a historical connection between Yoruba and Christian religions. The implication, evidently, is that Christianity was not alien to the Yoruba and that their conversion to it would in effect represent the restoration of a purer form of their existing (or at least their original) religion; conversion to Christianity therefore would not compromise the integrity of the national culture.

Moreover, Johnson was not just concerned with local sources and conditions. He was also reacting to European images of West Africa and the Yoruba, setting out his opinions on contemporary issues for a European audience interested in African and Yoruba affairs.[61] Johnson rejected some European images. For instance, according to him, Yoruba warfare is a noble pursuit, not a childish game. He further adopted and manipulated other ideas available to him from the discourses on Africa. Thus, pawnship became an institution suited to African development, and the Yoruba national character epitomized Victorian virtues. His overall historical framework asserted degeneration from Christian roots and inherent progressive potential, thus incorporating two models logically opposed in European thought. Johnson was reacting to European images of Africa "largely created in Europe to suit European needs," constructed more on the basis of European notions than from African data.[62] When Johnson reacted to these inventions by helping found and define the Christian Yoruba cultural nationalist tradition, he was reinventing his past with material partly provided by European inventions in response to these selfsame inventions.

CONCLUSION

Early West African historiography as represented by Reindorf and Johnson is rooted in a complex tradition of critical dialog with European ideas.

The spread of literacy, the influence of Christian missions, and especially the creation of a Pax Britannica directly affected the role that history had to play. Written history (though mainly based on oral traditions) became "a continuation of war by other means,"[63] and it became a vital concern to secure a favorable position within the colonial state. What is striking in both cases are ideas of historical recursion, whereby hopes of future progress are formulated in terms of recovery of a lost past. Another important aspect is that both authors made efforts to reinvent the past with material partly provided by European inventions. Their struggle to define their world within this strange matrix at least partly explains their apparent eclecticism.

NOTES

1. See, for example, Ali A. Mazrui and Michael Tidy, *Nationalism and New States in Africa* (Nairobi: 1984); Philip S. Zachernuk, *Colonial Subjects. An African Intelligentsia and Atlantic Ideas* (Charlottesville, Va.: 2000).

2. The emergence of African history as a field of academic study has been the subject of countless articles and books. See, for example, Bogumil Jewsiewicki and David Newbury, eds., *African Historiographies: What History for Which Africa?* (Beverly Hills, Calif.: 1986); Toyin Falola, ed., *African Historiography: Essays in Honour of Jacob Ade Ajayi* (Burnt Mills, U.K.: 1993); Simon McGrath et al., eds., *Rethinking African History* (Edinburgh: 1997); Andreas Eckert, "Historiker, 'Nation-Building' und die Rehabilitierung der afrikanischen Vergangenheit: Aspekte der Geschichtsschreibung in Afrika nach 1945," in *Geschichtsdiskurs*, vol. 5: *Globale Konflikte, Erinnerungsarbeit und Neuorientierungen seit 1945,* ed. Wolfgang Küttler et al. (Frankfurt am Main: 1999), 162–87. Joseph C. Miller, "History and Africa/Africa and History," *American Historical Review* 104 (1999): 1–32. Two of the pioneers of academic African history have published their autobiographies: Jan Vansina, *Living with Africa* (Madison, Wis.: 1994), and Roland Oliver, *In the Realms of Gold: Pioneering in African History* (Madison, Wis.: 1997).

3. See John D. Fage, "The Prehistory of African History," *Paideuma* 19–20 (1973–1974): 146–47; John D. Fage, "The Development of African Historiography," in *General History of Africa*, vol. 1: *Methodology and African Prehistory*, ed. Joseph Ki-Zerbo (London: 1981), 25. See also Heinz Duchardt et al., eds., *Afrika: Entdeckung und Erforschung eines Kontinents* (Cologne: 1989); Michael Herkenhoff, *Der dunkle Kontinent: Das Afrikabild im Mittelalter bis zum 12. Jahrhundert* (Pfaffenweiler: 1990).

4. See Jürgen Osterhammel, "Neue Welten in der europäischen Geschichtsschreibung (ca. 1500–1800)," in *Geschichtsdiskurs*, vol. 2: *Anfänge des modernen historischen Denkens,* Wolfgang Küttler et al. (Frankfurt am Main: 1994), 202.

5. See Albert Wirz, "Klio in Afrika. 'Geschichtslosigkeit' als historisches Problem," *Geschichte in Wissenschaft und Unterricht* 34 (1983): 101.

6. G. W. F. Hegel, *The Philosophy of History*, trans. J. Sibree (reprint; New York: 1956), 93, 99.

7. See generally Robert Miles, *Racism* (London: 1989).

8. See Philip D. Curtin, "Recent Trends in African History and Their Contribution to History in General," in *General History of Africa*, 1: 57.

9. The most infamous approach in this respect was the "Hamitic Hypothesis." It included a variety of historical models that begin African history in foreign lands rather than in Africa itself. For the most part, these beginnings were in the biblical and classical history of Egypt and Western Asia. The internal links were often used to argue explicitly that Africans—deemed black and inferior—owed whatever progress and improvement they had known to foreign "Hamites" rather than indigenous forces. For an example of this literature, see C. G. Seligman, *Races in Africa* (London: 1930). A good introduction is provided by Edith R. Sanders, "The Hamitic Hypothesis: Its Origin and Function in Time Perspective," *Journal of African History* 10 (1969): 521–32. The debate of Nigerian historians about the Hamitic Hypothesis is analyzed by Philip S. Zachernuk, "Of Origins and Colonial Order: Southern Nigerian Historians and the 'Hamitic Hypothesis,' c. 1870–1970," *Journal of African History* 35 (1994): 427–55.

10. See John D. Fage, "Continuity and Change in the Writing of West African History," *African Affairs* 70 (1971): 236–51; Andrew D. Roberts, "The Earlier Historiography of Colonial Africa," *History in Africa* 5 (1978): 153–67.

11. The history of (social) anthropology has been dealt with in numerous recent publications. See, among many others, Sally Falk Moore, *Anthropology and Africa: Changing Perspectives on a Changing Scene* (Charlottesville, Va.: 1994); George W. Stocking, *"After Tylor": British Social Anthropology, 1888–1951* (London: 1996); Jack Goody, *The Expansive Moment: The Rise of Social Anthropology in Britain and Africa, 1918–1970* (Cambridge, Mass.: 1996); Henrika Kuklick, *The Savage Within: The Social History of British Anthropology, 1885–1945* (Cambridge, Mass.: 1991); Adam Kuper, *Anthropology and Anthropologists. The Modern British School*, 3rd ed. (London: 1996).

12. In fact, we know very little about the historical conceptions of precolonial African societies. For some exceptions, see Robin Law, "History and Legitimacy: Aspects of the Use of the Past in Pre-Colonial Dahomey," *History in Africa* 15 (1988): 431–56; Thomas C. McCaskie, "Komfo Anokye of Asante: Meaning, History and Philosophy in an African Society," *Journal of African History* 27 (1986): 315–39; Thomas C. McCaskie, *State and Society in Pre-Colonial Asante* (Cambridge, Mass.: 1995), chap. 4; Donald Wright, "Koli Tengala in Sonko Traditions of Origin: An Example of Change in Mandinka Oral Traditions," *History in Africa* 5 (1978): 257–71.

13. The term "cultural nationalism" in this context presents some difficulty, since it was not a contemporary usage, though terms such as "patriotism" and "nationality" were used in the late nineteenth century with a cultural rather than a political reference. The term "cultural nationalism" was apparently first used of early West African intellectual thought by James Coleman, *Nigeria: Background to Nationalism* (Berkeley, Calif.: 1958).

14. A number of other important "schools" of early African (local) historiogra-

phy has to be omitted here. On Uganda, see, for example, Michael Twaddle, "On Ganda Historiography," *History in Africa* 1 (1974): 85–100; John A. Rowe, "Myth, Memoir, and Moral Admonition: Luganda Historical Writing, 1893–1969," *Uganda Journal* 33 (1969): 17–40; John A. Rowe, " 'Progress and a Sense of Identity': African Historiography in East Africa," *Kenya Historical Review* 5 (1977): 23–34. For other examples, see Jean Boulègue, "A la naissance de l'histoire écrite sénégalaise: Yoro Dyao et ses modèles (deuxième moitié du XIXème siècle, début du XXème siècle)," *History in Africa* 15 (1988): 395–405; Jeffrey Peires, "The Lovedale Press: Literature for the Bantu Revisited," *History in Africa* 6 (1979): 155–75. For an excellent general analysis of the change of conceptions of history in Africa during colonial rule, see Adam Jones, "Kolonialherrschaft und Geschichtsbewußtsein: Zur Rekonstruktion der Vergangenheit in Schwarzafrika 1865–1965," *Historische Zeitschrift* 250 (1990): 73–92.

15. Paul Jenkins, "Introduction," in *The Recovery of the West African Past: African Pastors and African History in the Nineteenth Century: C. C. Reindorf & Samuel Johnson*, ed. Paul Jenkins (Basel: 1998), 14.

16. The definitive account of Gold Coast historiography is Raymond G. Jenkins, "Gold Coast Historians and Their Pursuit of the Gold Coast Pasts, 1882–1917: An Investigation into Responses to British, Cultural Imperialism by Intellectuals of the Christianised, Commercial Communities of the Townships of the Southern Gold Coast, During the Years of British Imperial Conquest and Early Occupation, 1874–1919," 2 vols., Ph.D. dissertation, University of Birmingham, 1985. See also his "Intellectuals, Publication Outlets, and 'Past-Relationships'—Some Observations on the Emergence of Early Gold Coast–Ghanaian Historiography in the Cape Coast, Accra and Akropong 'Triangle': c. 1880–1917," in *Self-Assertion and Brokerage: Early Cultural Nationalism in West Africa*, ed. Paulo Fernando de Moraes Farias and Karin Barber (Birmingham: 1990), 68–77. His chapter on Reindorf from his dissertation is reprinted in P. Jenkins, *Recovery*, 163–96. The following sketch of early Gold Coast historiography relies heavily on R. Jenkins's work.

17. See R. Jenkins, "Gold Coast Historians," 1: 4.

18. See R. Jenkins, "Intellectuals," 68.

19. See, for example, Ivor Wilks, Nehemiah Levtzion, and Bruce Haight, *Chronicles from Gonja: A Tradition of West African Muslim Historiography* (Cambridge, Mass.: 1986).

20. See R. Jenkins, "Gold Coast Historians," 1: 21.

21. See R. Jenkins, "Gold Coast Historians," 205–7.

22. See R. Jenkins, "Gold Coast Historians," 192. On Horton see Christopher Fyfe, *Africanus Horton 1835–1883. West African Scientist and Patriot* (New York: 1972).

23. See R. Jenkins, "Gold Coast Historians," 1: 72–155.

24. See John Parker, "*Mankraloi*, Mechants, and Mulattos—Carl Reindorf and the Politics of 'Race' in Early Colonial Accra," in P. Jenkins, *Recovery*, 32. More generally, see John Parker, *Making the Town. Ga State and Society in Early Colonial Ghana* (Oxford: 2000).

25. For an overview of the literature and discussion of the term "Euro-African," see R. Jenkins, "Gold Coast Historians," 43–90; see also Parker, "*Mankraloi*, Merchants, and Mulattos," 32.

26. David Kimble, *A Political History of Ghana: The Rise of Gold Coast Nationalism, 1850–1928* (Oxford: 1963), 65.

27. R. Jenkins, "Gold Coast Historians," 1: 52.

28. A bibliographical outline can be found in R. Jenkins, "Gold Coast Historians," 2: 541–43, appendix A. Some information on Reindorf as a young catechist and missionary are provided by Peter Haenger, *Sklaverei und Sklavenemanzipation an der Goldküste* (Basel: 1997), 121–31.

29. Hans W. Debrunner, *A History of Christianity in Ghana* (Accra: 1967), 144; Raymond Jenkins, "Impeachable Source? On the Use of the Second Edition of Reindorf's *History* As a Primary Source for the Study of Ghanaian History, Part 1," *History in Africa* 4 (1977): 123.

30. Adam Jones, "Reindorf the Historian," in Paul Jenkins, *Recovery*, 115. Raymond Jenkins, "Impeachable Source I and II" (part 2 was published in *History in Africa* 5 [1978]: 81–99) provides an assessment of the nature and extent of the revisions made in the second edition.

31. See, for example, Adu A. Boahen, "A New Look at the History of Ghana," *African Affairs* 65 (1966): 212–22.

32. R. Jenkins, "Impeachable Source I," 141.

33. See Raymond Jenkins, "Confrontations with A. B. Ellis, a Participant in the Scramble for Gold Coast Africana, 1874–1894," *Paideuma* 33 (1987): 313–35.

34. Jones, "Reindorf the Historian," 115. See Robert W. July, *The Origins of Modern African Thought: Its Development in West Africa During the Nineteenth and Twentieth Centuries* (London: 1968), who praised Reindorf to be "a self-conscious, purposeful historian who wrote to fill an informational gap, whose techniques were based on a thoughtful analysis of the task before him and the tools at hand. Reindorf has a surprisingly modern and prophetic view of national history" (256). See also July, "West African Historians of the Nineteenth Century," *Tarikh* 2 (1968): 19–21.

35. The following paragraphs are based on Jones, "Reindorf the Historian," and R. Jenkins, "Gold Coast Historians," 1: 294–358.

36. For the following aspect, see Albert Wirz, "Bridging the Gulf between Centuries, Continents and Professions—An Encounter with C. C. Reindorf's *History*," in P. Jenkins, *Recovery*, 161–62.

37. See Adam Jones, "Zwei indigene Ethnographen der Goldküste im 19. Jahrhundert," in *Afrikaner schreiben zurück: Texte und Bilder afrikanischer Ethnographen,* ed. Heike Behrend and Thomas Geider (Cologne: 1998), 27–40.

38. J. G. Christaller, "Prefatory Remarks," x–xi, quoted by Jones, "Reindorf the Historian," 127.

39. Twaddle, "On Ganda Historiography," 86.

40. Jones, "Reindorf the Historian," 128. See on this aspect John D. Y. Peel, "Making History: The Past in the Ijesha Present," *Man* n.s. 19 (1984): 111–32.

41. See Wirz, "Bridging the Gulf," 157.

42. Two collective volumes provide an excellent tool to Johnson's work and to Yoruba historiography in general. See Toyin Falola, ed., *Yoruba Historiography* (Madison, Wis.: 1991); Toyin Falola, ed., *Pioneer, Patriot, and Patriarch: Samuel Johnson and the Yoruba People* (Madison, Wis.: 1993). On Johnson, see especially Michel

R. Doortmont, "Recapturing the Past. Samuel Johnson and the Construction of Yoruba History," Ph.D. dissertation, University of Rotterdam, 1994.

43. Jacob F. Ade Ajayi, "Samuel Johnson: Historian of the Yoruba," *Nigeria Magazine* 81 (1964): 141–46.

44. See the biographical sketch by Michel Doortmont, "Samuel Johnson (1846–1901): Missionary, Diplomat, and Historian," in *Yoruba Historiography*, ed. Toyin Falola (Madison, Wis.: 1991), 167–82.

45. John D. Y. Peel, "Two Pastors and Their Histories: Samuel Johnson and C. C. Reindorf," in P. Jenkins, *Recovery*, 81.

46. It should be made clear that before the nineteenth century, political, cultural and economic circumstances were such that it is hard to speak of "the Yoruba," though there were of course common traits in myths of origin, religion and other cultural aspects. Yoruba culture was, however, not homogenous. Only during the nineteenth century we face the "invention" of the Yoruba as a cultural group with a uniform language, and an ethnic identity that did not exist before this period. For this process, see John D. Y. Peel, "The Cultural Work of Yoruba ethnogenesis" in *History and Ethnicity*, ed. Elisabeth Tonkin et al. (London: 1989), 198–215, reprinted in Falola, *Pioneer, Patriot and Patriarch*, 65–75. Throughout this article I refer to the latter version. For the role of historians in this process, see below.

47. For different dimensions of this transformation, see, for example, Jean Herskovits Kopytoff, *A Preface to Modern Nigeria: The 'Sierra Leonians' in Yoruba, 1830–1890* (Madison, Wis.: 1965); Anthony G. Hopkins, "Innovation in a Colonial Context: African Origins in the Nigerian Cocoa Farming Industry, 1880–1920," in *The Imperial Impact. Studies in the Economic History of Africa and India*, ed. Clive Dewey and Anthony G. Hopkins (London: 1978), 83–96; Robin Law, *The Oyo Empire, c. 1600–c.1836: A West African Imperialism in the Era of the Atlantic Slave Trade* (Oxford: 1977); Kristin Mann, *Marrying Well. Marriage, Status and Social Change among the Educated Elite in Colonial Lagos* (Cambridge, Mass.: 1985); John D. Y. Peel, *Ijeshas and Nigerians: The Incorporation of a Yoruba Kingdom, 1890s–1970s* (Cambridge, Mass.: 1983); Robert S. Smith, *Kingdoms of the Yoruba*, 3rd ed. (London: 1988).

48. For the following paragraph I rely on Doortmont, "Recapturing the Past," 3–4, 15–16.

49. Many examples of this are provided by Robin Law, "Early Yoruba Historiography," *History in Africa* 3 (1976): 69–89, reprinted in Falola, *Pioneer, Patriot, and Patriarch*, 9–25. For other authors not mentioned by Law, see Toyin Falola, "Kemi Morgan and the Second Reconstruction of Ibadan History," *History in Africa* 18 (1991), 93–112; Toyin Falola, "The Minor Works of T. O. Avoseh," *History in Africa* 19 (1992): 237–62; H. O. Danmole and Toyin Falola, "The Documentation of Ilorin by Samuel Ojo Bada," *History in Africa* 20 (1993), 1–13; Toyin Falola and Michel Doortmont, "Iwe Itan Oyo: A Traditional Yoruba History and Its Author," *Journal of African History* 30 (1989): 301–29; John D. Y. Peel, "Kings, Titles, and Quarter: A Conjectural History of Ilesha, I: The Traditions Revisited," *History in Africa* 6 (1979): 110–53. See also Toyin Falola, *Yoruba Gurus. Indigenious Production of Knowledge in Africa* (Trenton, N.J.: 1999).

50. See, for example, P. A. Afolabi, ed., *In Truth and Justice: A Handbook of the Oyo Progressive Union* (Lagos: 1938). This book was especially written to convince the British administration of the standpoint of the Oyo Progressive Union in the 1930s administrative reforms. See Doortmont, "Recapturing the Past," 15. Robin Law argued that both oral and written historiography in the precolonial period were invented within contemporary constraints. See his "The Heritage of Oduduwa: traditional history and political propaganda among the Yoruba," *Journal of African History* 14 (1973): 207–22.

51. See Michel Doortmont, "The Invention of the Yorubas: Regional and Pan-African Nationalism Versus Ethnic Provincialism," in *Self-Assertion and Brokerage: Early Cultural Nationalism in West Africa*, ed. Paulo Fernando de Moraes Farias and Karin Barber (Birmingham: 1990), 101–8; Doortmont, "Recapturing the Past," 59–63; Peel, "Cultural Work;" Robin Law, "Local Amateur Scholarship in the Construction of Yoruba Ethnicity, 1880–1914," in *Ethnicity in Africa. Roots, Meanings, and Implications*, ed. Louise de la Gorgendière et al. (Edinburgh: 1996), 55–90.

52. Peel, "Cultural Work," 65.

53. For details, see Doortmont, "Recapturing the Past," 38–54.

54. See Stefan Eisenhofer, "Jacob Egharevba und die Rekonstruktion der Geschichte des Königtums von Benin (Nigeria)," *Paideuma* 42 (1996): 151–68; Stefan Eisenhofer, "Lokalhistoriographien in Südnigeria und die Schriften Jacob Egharevbas über die Geschichte des Reiches Benin (Nigeria)," in *Afrikaner schreiben zurück: Texte und Bilder afrikanischer Ethnographen*, ed. Heike Behrend and Thomas Geider (Cologne: 1998), 105–28; Stefan Eisenhofer, "The Origins of the Benin Kingship in the Works of Jacob Eghareuba," *History in Africa* 22 (1995): 141–63.

55. See Lidwien Kapteijns, *African Historiography Written by Africans, 1955–1973: The Nigerian Case* (Leiden: 1977); Paul Lovejoy, "The Ibadan School of History and Its Critics," in *African Historiography: Essays in Honour of Jacob Ade Ajayi*, ed. Toyin Falola (Burnt Mills, U.K.: 1993), 195–202; Wolfgang Kaese, *Akademische Geschichtsschreibung in Nigeria. Historiographische Entwicklung und politisch-soziale Hintergründe, ca. 1955–ca. 1995* (Hamburg: 2000).

56. See Axel Harneit-Sievers, "Igbo Community Histories: Locality and History in South Eastern Nigeria," *Working Papers on African Societies* 24 (1997).

57. See Robin Law, "How Truly Traditional Is Our Traditional History? The Case of Samuel Johnson and Recording of Yoruba Oral Tradition," *History in Africa* 11 (1984): 195–211, reprinted in Falola, *Pioneer, Patriot and Patriarch*, 47–63. I am quoting from the latter version. See also Robin Law, "How Many Times Can History Repeat Itself? Some Problems in the Traditional History of Oyo," *International Journal of African Historical Studies* 15 (1985): 33–51.

58. Law, "How Truly Traditional," 47.

59. Johnson, *History*, vii.

60. Robin Law, "Constructing 'A Real National History': A Comparison of Edward Blyden and Samuel Johnson," in *Self-Assertion and Brokerage: Early Cultural Nationalism in West Africa*, ed. Paulo Fernando de Moraes Farias and Karin Barber (Birmingham: 1990), 89. The following paragraphs rely on this article as well as on Doortmont, "Recapturing the Past," 77–117.

61. For this paragraph, see Philip S. Zachernuk, "Johnson and the Victorian Image of the Yoruba," in Falola, *Pioneer, Patriot and Patriarch*, 33–46.

62. See Philip D. Curtin, *The Image of Africa* (Madison, Wis.: 1964), 480. On this aspect, see also Valentin Mudimbe, *The Invention of Africa. Gnosis, Philosophy, and the Order of Knowledge* (London: 1988).

63. Twaddle, "On Ganda Historiography," 86.

5

Alternative National Histories in Japan

Yamaji Aizan and Academic Historiography

Stefan Tanaka

In a recent book on the emergence of the modern historical discipline in Japan, Margaret Mehl concludes that the historians at the Historiographical Institute, in contrast to German historians at comparable periods, "did not become interpreters of the nation; their lives and works did not help shape the Japanese empire."[1] Mehl is writing about the historians most responsible for the institutionalization of a professional modern history of Japan. They had positions at Tokyo Imperial University, the most prestigious university; served as founders, directors, and researchers at the Historiographical Institute, the premier repository of historical documents; were purveyors of the empirical methodologies that dominate twentieth-century historiography; and are considered the experts of a national history. But if they were not the principal interpreters, we must ask about the relation between history, nation, state, and belief.

As in Mehl's book, standard accounts of the rise of a modern discipline in late-nineteenth-century Japan focus on intellectuals who drew upon Western ideas. Early enlightenment writers such as Fukuzawa Yukichi and Taguchi Ukichi focused on Guizot and Henry Thomas Buckle, while empirical historians at the public universities were influenced by their colleague or teacher Ludwig Riess (Riess taught at the Tokyo Imperial University from 1887 to 1902), a distant student of Leopold von Ranke.[2] This narrative is characterized within a teleology of westernization, a rising rationalism and objectivity against more conservative elements that seek to maintain (often implying irrationality) the myths of an anachronistic past, an interesting concept for historians.

The historiography on the transformation of Japan's historical practices, then and now, has used empirical methodology as the basic criteria for judging historical writing. It is generally seen as rational, thus some interpretations have recognized a similarity in the rational and critical methods of the textual criticism (*kōshō*) of Confucian learning and the empiricism of historians such as Kume Kunitake (1839–1931) and Shigeno Yasutsugu (1827–1910).[3] And it is generally connected with westernization, especially the contrast between those with more global perspective (some universalism, like *bunmeishi* [enlightenment history]) and a conservative/nationalistic reaction. But in all cases, standard historiography emphasizes this transformation from indigenous to Western forms of history.

Transformation is usually described in some language of incompleteness, misunderstanding (of the modern), or failure. When historians have tried to extract themselves from this framework, they have tended to emphasize the presence of modern or modernlike forms prior to contact with the West. The problems of transformation, then, are located within the non-Western places, especially the conservatives who seemingly resist the adaptation of modern history, not the process itself. There are two groups who are placed in opposition to these academic historians: the conservative (*kokugaku* [nativism]) historians, who seek to maintain aspects of the histories that had guided elite societies and were quite critical of the new historical research that challenged what had been accepted as canonical texts, and the populist (*minyusha*) historians. Iwai Tadakuma's evaluation of the latter is rather familiar: "The strength of their history (*shiron*) was in their sharp contemporary criticism, but there was no careful academic methodology."[4]

A principal problem with this emphasis on methodology is the masking of contradictions within modernity itself; for history in particular, it is in the use of the particular and ideational to describe universalistic and mechanical processes as if they speak for the human. This approach fails to adequately address the contending conceptions and positions of historical understanding, instead lapsing into some variation of a debate between objectivity/truth/rationalism/Occident versus subjectivity/relativism/emotion/Orient. For example, Iwai argues that the *minyusha* historians, because of inadequate empirical methods, failed to develop a critical perspective toward the imperial household and the emperor system that organized imperial Japan. But this interpretation masks the limitations and narrow mindedness of empirical methodologies as the basis of history, and of modernity more broadly. Whereas populist historians are criticized for not being empirical enough, as Mehl's description suggests, academic historians failed from too much empiricism. Peter Duus's now quite familiar statement describes this succinctly:

> These academic historians were as much in revolt against the praise-and-blame approach of traditional historiography as men like Fukuzawa and Taguchi, but they fought not by seeking out general laws of civilization, but by careful verification of historical facts. . . . They devoted themselves to gathering facts, compiling chronologies, and subjecting classic works of historiography (such as Rai Sanyô's *Nihon gaishi*) to rigorous textual criticism. They were capable, critical, and dedicated scholars, but basically uninspiring, without an axe to grind or the passion of political commitment.[5]

To create some gap between my object of study—the discipline of modern history in Japan—and the teleology through which a study of a particular pivotal moment (especially in the modern era) becomes an explanation that secures our own uncertainties, I will focus on Yamaji Aizan (1864–1917), a powerful critic of the emerging discipline of history. Yamaji, who is included among the populist historians, wrote prolifically on historical figures, on history, and about history. Yet he received no formal academic training and principally wrote for newspapers and weekly magazines, such as *Kokumin no tomo*, *Dokuritsu hyôron*, *Shinano mainichi shinbun*, and *Kokumin zasshi*, where he gained his reputation as an independent historian and a trenchant critic of the orthodox historiography. This is the obverse of the critique based on methodology. As a popular historian or historicist Yamaji is located into an ambiguous category that allows us to marginalize what does not fit our normal historical categories and narratives: he was a Christian, proponent of economic development, nationalist, imperialist, and critic of government and of the history that scholar/bureaucrats developed. In other words, he was neither (or both) modernizer nor traditionalist, westernizer nor native, universalist nor nationalist, and so forth.

Through Yamaji it becomes possible to call attention to a particular moment in which history becomes separated from the people it purportedly represents. To write "becomes separated" suggests prior integration that did not exist. But this is where we need caution in discussing the nation and nation-state. In late-nineteenth-century Japan (and I believe throughout the world), at the same time that history was being reformulated as the story of the nation (that is, the people), objectivist methodologies that presumed mechanistic and universalistic processes described through the nation-state were central to the separation of history from those same people. For example, in a remarkably direct (by today's standards) criticism of the nascent academic history, Yamaji wrote in 1897: "Two thousand five hundred years of Japanese history is a record of hell in which the sacrifice of people's (*jinmin*) lives and blood for the government should make one shudder."[6] The history he is criticizing is the one the state and its representatives (including academic historians) were promoting as objective history in the 1890s. But while recent historians tend to describe the academic historians as unfortunates who gradually were overwhelmed by the ideology of the nation-state, Yamaji sees them as missionaries of that ideology. In particular he singles out the "ignorant historians, superstitious teachers, and stupid men like Shinagawa Yajirō."

Shinagawa was a functionary of the new government, a conservative politician from Choshu, a domain from which many leaders of the new government originated. Yamaji was reacting to Shinagawa's statement that Japan's *kokutai* (national essence) is in its monarchical system of government, what today we call the emperor system, in which sovereignty is held by the emperor and administered through his ministers. More broadly, he was critical of the *hanbatsu*, the oligarchs who were tightening their reigns over the government, despite the implementation of the Meiji Constitution in 1890. Such statements that located the emperor as the sovereign of the new government (he promulgated the Meiji Constitution in 1889 and issued in 1890 the important Imperial Rescript on Education) were rather common, though not necessarily widely accepted, in the 1890s. But in response, Yamaji queries:

> If we rephrase his words, [Shinagawa] has to be saying that Japanese people were nothing in Japanese history. Does this place it outside us, oppress us, endanger our existence, and then give us no rights to rise and resist? How can human beings endure this? The government coerces us, inflicts harm upon us, and exploits our children (*shitei*). Outside of completely prostrating to it, can one not do something? How could this be a truth (*dōri*) that human instinct allows?[7]

The most obvious point in Yamaji's attack is the relation between this historical narrative and political oppression. In the 1890s a common element in public discussion was the utility of certain pasts to the new government. As Mehl points out, from the 1869 rescript that begins, "Historiography is a forever immortal state ritual and a wonderful act of our ancestors," the government and various officials sought to determine the contents of that wonderful act as a part of its power and authority.[8]

Yamaji's writings throughout the 1890s and 1900s are peppered with criticism of academic historians, especially those at the Imperial University. In contrast to recent interpretations, Yamaji depicted the academic historians, whom Duus generously describes as uninspiring and without political commitment, as agents of the new government. In a 1911 essay,

"The Four Pillars of Imperial Japan," Yamaji writes that the government has initiated many "interesting" things, among which is the collection of data connected to the restoration.[9] He did not condemn this activity, only the historical framework in which it is used. He continues that the interpretation that the restoration brought about, by the men of Satsuma and Choshu (*hanbatsu*), is "self-flattery," like a cat chasing its tail. He contends instead that the restoration was a result of the nation (*kokumin*) that created a climate of change; then the samurai of these domains seized upon the opportunity and succeeded in overthrowing the bakufu. He writes:

> We appeal for an attitude that believes that the country's prosperity is based in the full vitality of the nation (*kokumin*) and is instead established prior to the government and encourages the government; therefore in no way should it give in to the government.[10]

A NATION OF THATCHED-HUT COMMONERS

Yamaji shares an important point with the academic and enlightenment historians. Each was trying to synchronize a history of Japan with the modern/Western world. That, of course, is difficult at best, because of the multiple forms of history in Europe at that time. The different interpretations of the Japanese historians, in part, reflect these differences. Yamaji recognized the necessity and difficulty of understanding and adapting a world historical framework. He writes, "As one member of the world, Japanese must know Japan's position in the world."[11] He is resigned to the inevitability of the historical models provided by Western historians. Thus, throughout his writing one finds a cautious embrace (despite a rhetoric critical of excessive Europeanization) of Western historical ideas. It is rooted in the idea of progress, the constant change and improvement of society. Like the academic historians he criticized, he does not question the idea of Japan—the place of the nation is naturalized as a unitary space. In his division of history into three general categories—West, Orient, and Japan—he accepted the geocultural units of Western discourse. This division is also the same as the organization of the history department at Tokyo Imperial University, the home of the academic historians he so vehemently criticized.

A principal difference in his writings is the relocation of the subject of history from the state to the nation (*kokumin*), the "thatched-hut commoners." By differentiating the nation from the nation-state, he raises an important issue of late-nineteenth-century history, the locus of the subject of the new history. Even though he accepted the new conditions of modern societies that necessitates the formulation of the nation as a fundamental part of the nation-state, his criticism of Shinagawa suggests that he did not accept the efforts of elites to maintain possession of history, thereby maintaining their power and position over the newly important nationals. His narrative is centered on the struggle for and development of people's rights, that is, on the hopes and will of humans rather than on political institutions or material goods.

In 1897 Yamaji outlined his historical narrative in an essay, "Evidence of the Development of Human Rights in Japanese History." The most important difference is the rise of rights as the subject of development, rather than some rationality or material improvement. Clearly, his horizon of expectation is in the greater freedom of individuals as a nation. Yamaji's historical narrative describes a long-term struggle to expand the rights and power of people within the archipelago. This historical narrative follows the chronology of the academic historians, which begins with the mythical emperor Jimmu, but because he historicizes moments when power and culture merge, he shifts the importance and value of these moments to emphasize nascent struggles among the people for their rights. This struggle is contrasted, not to some primitive form from which institutions emerged and improved, but to an elite that has tried to maintain institutions that oppress the masses.

Yamaji begins with the myriad clans of ancient Japan, their oppression of people, and the unification of Japan by the first emperor, Jimmu (now known to be a mythical figure), which he sees as fulfilling the needs of the oppressed masses for protection from the aristocracy. This is the first moment of the development of rights, where an enlightened ruler unifies the land and rules benevolently. In this admittedly very limited freedom that gives rise to what he calls theocracy (*shintō seiji*),[12] Yamaji shifted the subject from timeless institutions—the emperor and ideology toward the emperor—to the deeds and the needs of the masses. For Yamaji, the hallmarks of this theocratic period were the personification of the nation in the emperor, and the emergence of loyalism and patriotism because of the emperor's support of the rights of the people. Yamaji's chronology is familiar; the difference is his attempt to restore some human agency. He argues that the ideas of filiation and loyalty are ideals that emerged in support of people's rights, but bureaucrats later used these ideals to enforce obedience by turning them into timeless qualities of all Japanese. This institutionalization occurred from the seventh century as Buddhism separated society into good and vulgar, and the Fujiwara strengthened the idea of ministerial responsibility. In other words, the Nara (710–794) and Heian (794–1185) periods were a step backward, a stain on that history.

The rise of manors during the Kamakura period (1185–1333) was a second manifestation of this slow development of rights. In this case, he saw the fragmentation of power from the aristocracy in Kyoto to the warriors and lords of the manors as well as the reliance of the Hojo (the family that dominated the shogunate during this period) on regional landholders as a nascent republican government in Japan. He recognized the limitations of this development. Power was now dispersed to approximately forty-eight major landholders. But this time, efforts to limit this movement came from the imperial household itself; the Kemmu Restoration (1333–1336) marks the attempt of the retired emperor Go-Daigo to reestablish a monarchic administration. According to Yamaji, Go-Daigo's attempted restoration of imperial power was not in the interest of the nation, and his failure is evidence that "the people (*jinmin*) of Japan could protect these rights by themselves."[13]

The significance of Yamaji's narrative becomes more apparent when placed within the context of the developing academic history. The Meiji government selected the imperial governments of the Nara period and the Kemmu Restoration as key historical symbols to assert its legitimacy to power. The idea of the new government as a restoration (the Meiji Restoration, 1868) was intended to refer back to a period of imperial rule, the Nara and Heian periods. The new government chose the name Dajōkan for the new governmental administration, a direct reference to the Grand Council of State, the bureaucracy that administered in the name of the emperor during the Nara period. The Kemmu Restoration was the last major effort to wrest power from the manors and samurai and return administration to imperial hands. Even though Go-Daigo failed, Meiji accomplished those long dormant ambitions and the many stories of fourteenth-century loyalty and bravery became tools to connect subjects to the imperium.

Yamaji's project to center the nation (that is the people) in history brings out a central problematic of modern historiography, the removal of key ideas from time as a way—consciously or unconsciously—of authenticating one's own narrative. Concepts and ideas that are believed to be natural are virtually eliminated from debate. Yamaji's history attempts to recover two historical ideas that have usually been rendered as natural or ahistorical in modern histories: the idea of rights and, in Japan, the idea of the emperor. Rather than using rights as given, as in "natural rights," he recognized its historical nature, and that rights have been slow in developing in the course of human history. The institution of the emperor also gains some history. The idea of Japan having a long history that goes back to the founding emperors is a common iteration of pre-World War II Japan as well as today. Even though he accepts Jimmu, the originative beginning of Japan, his historicization of the emperor separates that institution from the state and ethics. Instead, he emphasizes the historical moments when the imperial institution was an important force in the development of rights and points out when emperors behaved ineptly or badly, which was not infrequent. In both instances, he does not denigrate these ideas; in fact, he values them. But he recognized that in the removal of these ideas from time, that is history, their meanings become circumscribed by an ethical system that are often in contradiction.

The next major era for Yamaji is what he sees as the revolutionary fifteenth century. The Onin Wars (1467–1477) set off the further devolution of power to approximately 5,000 to 6,000 small lords. He even attempted to resurrect the pirates who plied the Inland Sea and settled on the southeastern coast of China. He wrote:

> When we consider the human condition when various forces below struggled to maintain their own life and asserted their own existence, and the central government lost its power, even those like the pirates were part of this condition. And when seen as part of the progress of history they are not pirates but people who produced a magnificent state (*tangen na kokka*).[14]

Even though Yamaji described this is an important movement in the development of rights, he did not romanticize this period, which most historians describe as chaotic or an inverted world (*gekokujō*) where the tail wags the dog (literally, the bottom overcomes the top). Instead, he recognized that these petty lords ruled the people on their lands ruthlessly treating them as property, which he compared to the Russian serfs. Nevertheless, the devolution of power to the myriad lords is another step toward greater rights.

The Tokugawa period ushered in a development of a different kind of freedom, that of the body and material desire. According to Yamaji, in the Tokugawa period for the first time the people were removed from the oppression of the lord, could choose their occupation freely, and could live where they wished. This did not lead to political rights; instead, he concluded: "for the first time the people gained a bodily freedom."[15] He pointed to the Genroku period (1688–1704) as further evidence of the weakening of the lords (now approximately 270) and a benevolent policy toward urbanites. He tied this latter policy to the migration of samurai to the cities and castle-towns where they became the consumers that propelled the economic transformation in which "gold is the lineage of merchants." This was, in Yamaji's mind, the beginning of capitalism, the shift of the basis of power and prestige from land to money. He emphasized: "From this time the possessors of gold became aware that they themselves held the greatest key that controlled their affairs."[16] In short, where official historians have seen strength, Yamaji found oppression, while in moments of decline and chaos, he saw a rise of people's desires and efforts to take charge of their own lives.

Unfortunately, Yamaji never completed a general history of Japan. But his writings on history include numerous essays that argue for and against different tools—concepts and data—that promote particular types of histories. First, Yamaji's history alters the normal understanding of modern historiography that divides a traditional and modern punctuated by the Meiji Restoration and the introduction of "modern" historical methods from the West. An essential element of modern historiography is the separation of the present from a completed, that is dead, past. Michel de Certeau writes:

> Historical discourse makes a *social identity* explicit, not so much in the way it is "given" or held as stable, as in the ways it is *differentiated* from a former period or another society. It presupposes the rupture that changes a tradition into a past object.[17]

Yamaji's narrative and criticism of academic history is a contestation over the social identity made possible in these historical discourses. But it is a difference that has often been blurred by our acceptance of the same premises and temporal categories that he was contesting. First there is an important commonality that lends to this obfuscation. By lining up the multiple pasts into a developmental narrative of Japan, Yamaji, too, naturalizes the place of Japan. His, too, is a historical discourse that makes the identity of the nation explicit and is maintained through differentiation; he was a strong advocate of a unified nation and avid supporter of Japanese imperialism. The transformation of outsiders and the foreign into those of another nation-state facilitated and was facilitated by the domestication of the alterity of pasts into the nation. Modern linear narratives transform the strange and unknown into one's own past or dismiss such phenomena as superstition or deviant forms. Here, Yamaji was attempting to alter the subject, but without moving out of a principal problematic of the modern nation-state—that is the need for change (progress) and the demand for stability and continuity provided by the idea of nation. But importantly, in his history the nation is differentiated from the state, not subsumed into it. Change then is not in the transformation of the political system and its institutions that guide the nation. Instead, it is the increasing ability of the people to protect and govern themselves.

This newfound importance of pasts brings up an important difference between Yamaji and the professional historians; it is in the separation of history from the people. Yamaji critiques empirical history as dead history. Yamaji was not sanguine about the enlightenment premise of a clear break between past and present.[18] He writes:

> Truly good history cannot be written by people who are secluded only in their world of written material. If one only reads books and does not interact

with actual society (*seken*), then that person's history is dead history (*shinda rekishi*).[19]

His criticism of dead history is recognition that the rhetoric that distinguishes pasts forms a social identity that masks a continuity of power. This is part of the problem of modernity, the necessity of differentiating from the past as a way to give oneself an identity within the framework of modernity. Here, dead takes on several meanings. On the one hand, the present enjoys an identity as modern, because of its distinction from a premodern; in the case of Japan, it becomes the now past period prior to the Meiji. (This stability is always uncertain in non-Western places because of the presence of the West as modern and the non-West as past.) On the other hand, it signifies separation from the human. He criticizes those specialists who knew European historical methods but did not have an understanding of the human spirit (*jinshin*) of Japan. For example, he argued that Mikami Sanji's history of the Tokugawa period "does not engage the world and is no more than a trivial study made public." Chronological accounts, he complained, are the "unremarkable" results of experts who contribute to the alienation of Japanese from the world.[20] At another point he calls chronology "miscellany (*zuihitsu*)." One is reminded here of de Certeau's warning that "Chronology becomes the alibi of time."[21]

Here, Yamaji pointed out that the distinction between an anachronistic historiography of the Tokugawa period (and earlier) from modern methodologies masks a similarity in the uses of narratives of a particular past to maintain, and even to establish, power. Whereas standard historiography sees the development of a neutral, more modern and scientific practice, Yamaji saw a close tie to political power. He writes:

> Today, history is under pressure to completely reconstruct itself, it is in the changing times to reconstruct a true history that eliminates dry and meaningless records, it is blood, it is flesh, and it is interesting. But in this reconstruction, when one only changes the form without changing the materials, as when one replaces a Japanese-style house with a Western building, we see only a slight change.[22]

This returns us to the evaluation of populist historians by Iwai and others. Their focus on methodology obscured the separation of the nation-state from the nation, which bore potential for a history more focused on the people of the nation, rather than on the institutions of the state. Importantly, such ideas that seek to elevate the people and reduce the power of the emperor were rather common during this period. For example, Minobe Tatsukichi, professor of law at Tokyo Imperial University, argued that the emperor was one—albeit the most important—of many organs of the state. Yoshino Sakuzo, political scientist at that university, struggled over the historical relation among the individual, society, and the emperor.[23]

In 1894 Yamaji directly addressed the issue of methodology. His essay is part of a heated debate that took place during the last two decades of the Meiji period (1868–1912). Canonical texts, such as the sections in the age of the gods and the *Taiheiki* became the objects of greatest controversy on the utility of history. Shigeno and Kume, the two most influential members of the Historiographical Institute and the first professors of Japanese history at Tokyo Imperial University, began to question the veracity of passages in the *Kojiki* and *Nihon shoki* as well as the heroic deeds of figures described in tales such as the *Taiheiki*. Beginning in the mid-1880s Shigeno published essays on the fiction of Kojima Takanori and the inaccuracy of events attributed to Kusunoki Masashige, both described in the *Taikeiki*. He became known as Professor Obliterator (*massatsu hakase*) for these essays. Kume went further by questioning any utility of the *Taiheiki*, until then the accepted account of the events surrounding the Kemmu Restoration. Kume became infamous for his 1892 essay "Kamiyo wa shinsai no kozoku nari," in which he pointed out that the section on the age of the gods, in the earliest extant chronicles, the *Kojiki* and the *Nihon shoki*, is made up from legends created by the early clans.

Today, few would question the conclusions of Kume and Shigeno. Yet Kume was forced to resign after public criticism of his essay, and historians have generally seen the Kume incident as early moments of the ascendancy of the ideology of the state over historical reason. In 1910 Kita Sadakichi revised an elementary school history textbook, *Jinjō shōgaku Nihon rekishi,* in which he reiterated the existence of two imperial courts— the Northern and Southern—that resulted from the Kemmu Restoration. Though long accepted and empirically verifiable, the presence of two courts raises questions about the sacredness of the imperial institution and the notion of an unbroken imperial line of rule since Jimmu, the mythical founding emperor. The controversy subsided after the Meiji emperor declared the southern line the official line (even though he is descendent of the northern line), the offending part was deleted, and Kita was suspended for two years. Both incidents are cited as key moments in the rise of national ideology at the expense of an objective, rational history.[24] Including Yamaji in this controversy alters such prevailing interpretations that separate history from the state. Yamaji argued that there are two general historical methods that do not have precise boundaries for the former is a part of the latter: 1) minor positivism—the determination of historical fact; and 2) higher-level positivism—the inquiry into the customs and feelings of the people. In other words, for Yamaji, time is not a suitable evaluative category; as a mode of differentiation it changes a "tradition into a past object."

In his mind, then, minor positivism, that history that ascertains the validity of singular things or events, has two problems. First, by treating themes and events as past objects, they become fixed, shorn of the mutability and contexts of which they had been an integral part. Second, describing important political landmarks stops short of achieving the purpose of history—an understanding of the major social transformations and everyday life of the nation. He suggested that such a history that focuses on such monuments emphasizes political, economic, and philosophical/ideological growth, a narrative of elite rule or in his words, the 2,500 years of "hell," that has oppressed people and limited their rights (*jinsei*). In the historiography of Japan, the word for this early form of minor positivism is *kōshō*, translated either as textual criticism or positivism, the former being the critical studies of primarily Confucian scholars during the Tokugawa period, and the latter the empirical methods learned from Ranke via Riess. Yamaji did not denigrate the latter; facts, he believed, are important, but only as a part of the historical enterprise. He pointed out that:

> Of course uncovering old documents and even investigating facts (*jijutsu*) is good, but the purpose of history is not just the investigation of facts. The work of the historian is also to observe general affairs like how this nation (*kokumin*) grows and how it develops.[25]

By questioning the connotation of the past as anachronistic, Yamaji denied that earlier histories should be completely swept away just because they are old and opened the possibility for different kinds of evaluative categories. This is evident in his grouping of historians. He included among those who practice minor positivism those with who have enjoyed the patronage of some elite or bureaucratic power. He mentions Shigeno, Kawada Takeshi, Oka Rokumon (1833–1914), Gamo Keitei (1833–1901), Fujino Tetsu, and Konakamura Kiyonori as some of the most erudite whose history is either connected to the Historiographical Institute or continues the Tokugawa tradition of textual criticism. In a separate essay he calls the careful parsing of sentences of this exegetical style meaningless.[26]

The combination of Shigeno and Konakamura indicates Yamaji's anti-establishment historiography. Though both were professors at the Imperial University, they are oppositional figures in the standard historiography: Shigeno the empirical historian, and Konakamura the conservative who was tearing away at a pure scientific history.[27] From Yamaji's perspective, the issue was not over a mythical versus objective or an applied versus a pure history; it was over who would determine the historical content of the nation-state. These scholars were working for the state and vying to impose their version of the past as the history of the nation-state.

As in his historical narrative, Yamaji does not dismiss the work of those he criticizes; he shares points with both, but only to assert his own position. Even though he does not like empirical histories, Yamaji shared Kume's skepticism and used Kume's ideas when appropriate to his own narrative. For example, he built upon Kume's notion of fiction to create his narrative of this originating moment of the Japanese nation. Yamaji writes, "It is clear in texts like the *Kojiki* and the *Manyōshu* that in the beginning, Japan's *kokutai* was part of one clan leader's government and changed to a theocracy."[28] Here, Yamaji is agreeing that there was history prior to that recorded in the *Kojiki* and the *Nihon shoki*: in his narrative outlined above, he found a past of clan conflict and the historical moment in which Jimmu unified the clans, removing Jimmu from his mythical and quasi-religious status. Yamaji's account was potentially quite critical to the new government, for it shifts the source of nation from the emperor to the people. But unlike Kume's criticism, he built upon the existing narrative, never questioning Jimmu's symbolic value as the originating moment, while historicizing it. Kume, however, was in a highly public position and questioned texts in which many still wanted to believe.

Yamaji's similarity to Konakamura is evident in his defense of the *Taiheiki* as well as other historical tales that had been the canonical texts for knowing the events surrounding the Kemmu Restoration. In the extension of history to the human sciences, and his plea that history not separate past from present, Yamaji sought to formulate a history that is more mutable and not possessed by any particular segment of society, in particular the political elite. To establish this mutability, or to prevent its takeover by the state, Yamaji proposed expansion of the realm of historical evidence, and an eye for an interesting narrative style. He argued poetry, novels, travelogues, war tales, sutras, and anthologies also contain valuable historical information. He did not accept these at face value. He writes, "the *Taiheiki* is not proper history (*seishi*), but the author probably represents popular sympathy for the southern court and at the very least represents a segment of social feelings (*kanjō*)."[29] By extending the range of evidence, he sought not the antithesis of a positivistic history, but recognition of the human in history. But perhaps this act is threatening, for to accept a reality in "fiction" questions the claim to the real made by empirical historians. The incorporation of texts that we still categorize as literature, while not facts as a record of events, does serve as evidence of conditions of life of earlier people (here the nation), their emotions, and social interaction. Yamaji does not dispute the relegation of what had been considered history to the realm of literature, but he was not accepting the distinction between truth (fact) and fiction (story). Instead, his incorporation of literature to understand those undercurrents, the thoughts and feelings of people, proposes a different "reality"; it was not one dictated by elites on what the nation-state should be, but what the nation, as a collective of myriad experiences, has been and still is.

It is easy here to conclude that Yamaji is a conservative and that this is an antimodern or romantic stance. Certainly he criticized the westernization and mechanization of society in Japan. He emphasized that "a materialist civilization produces materialist people."[30] He also called those who accepted this positivistic claim that the *Taiheiki* is worthless as a historical document are akin to an obese man who does not understand reason because he is locked up in a tower.[31] But Yamaji was concerned about this problem, for it was a site of the separation of history from people. He writes that the old adage that one grows wise with time is based on experience and that the passage of time gives rise to real (*kakujitsu*) experience. Theory on the other hand is not dependent (*ataranai*) on time. In other words, academic history that is based on the ideal of objectivity is using abstract criterion that is separate from the nation. In his characteristic style of citing examples from everyday life, he writes:

> Captains cannot expound on the tides of Mexico, but they can understand winds and read the clouds; farmers do not know Linnaeus, but they do know the quality of soil and character of water. With their unlearned knowledge, they are probably laughing at the folly of scholars.[32]

And if there is any doubt of the importance of inherited knowledge, he writes, "theory raises doubt and experience makes people believe."[33]

It is this transformation of tradition into a past object, "in academic history that Yamaji found most troubling. He asserts in numerous places that the past is not separate from the present, that history is not talk about the past. It is talk about the living present. It is visiting the past to know the new."[34] This brings out Yamaji's higher positivism: the purpose of history is to inquire into the everyday life of people and the customs and human feeling. In his mind, life and feelings are in the realm of history, but it is an expanded history that encompasses society. He argued that this history is a science, but his understanding of science is not the same as those academic historians. He emphasized, "history is science. However, it is also religion. It is that which teaches the secrets connected to both heaven's will (*tenmei*) and human affairs."[35] He argued that in order for historians to develop an understanding of the shortcomings of empirical history they must have a concern for human beings: the human condition, how people work, why they act, how they are seduced, and why they are troubled. This he believed must be trained. (What historian does not believe him/herself to be concerned with the human being?)

In his 1892 essay, *Literature and History*, he drew from Hegel's invocation of the Idea to claim that politics, economics, literature, religion, and so on are all part of that society and that any narrative of that period should reflect this breadth because they are all connected to that Idea. He likened academic historians' focus on politics to a ship on the ocean during a thunderstorm. All one sees is the violent surface, not the calmer undercurrents. In society, wars, revolutions, riots, and struggles are the surface, while people's sensibilities (*jinshin*) exist underneath.[36] He writes that "the purpose of history is not just an inquiry into facts (*jijitsu*). It is also the task of the historian to observe overall things, such as how the people (*kokumin*) have grown and how they have developed."[37] His ideal was to find a history that touches those underlying sensibilities.

> *However, the historian is not a fatalist.* The laws of human affairs, like a chain, connects the before and after through the inevitable law, and so-called freedom of will is not something metaphysical as if saying it does not exist historically. *We already believe the hero, the force of the individual, and the birth of mysterious.* But how does freedom of will operate within the fixed law that permeates human affairs? At what point do both the great law of the world and the small will of the world harmonize? This is the secret. It is the hidden principle. It exists behind the so-called veil of advocates (*ronsha*) of the inexplicable.[38]

Yamaji's higher positivism was a history that encompassed all of society, but because of the dominance of empirical methods, he pushed for histories that elevate the everyday lives of commoners, the nation. Having eschewed chronology and finding incidents too specific, he argues that topics and syntheses are closer to that higher positivism. His preferred historians quite consciously, he argues, keep the part in relation to the whole. He writes:

> When one tries to clarify influential conditions where all historical things face these central issues, that research inevitably encompasses all of Japanese history. In this way, we call the convergence of a focus on one problem with all of the historical (*subete no shijitsu*) an organic research method.[39]

As examples of this kind of history, he cites Yokoi Tokifuyu's histories of Japanese industry and of the development of cities and towns; Ariga Nagao on the history (*enkaku*) of the political system; and Konakamura Kiyonori on the Japanese legal system.

STORYTELLING

Yamaji's higher positivism was meant to address another tendency of empirical histories—to write in a boring style. Because of the importance Yamaji gave to history, he argues that above all it is important to produce history that moves the reader. If it doesn't, books won't be read. Indeed, in his essay, "Contemporary Japanese History and Historians" Yamaji modified his earlier distinction between a minor and major positivism and contrasted minor positivism (*kōshō*) with pleasurable (*kōkan*) history. He cited a long tradition of writing for the enjoyment as well as edification of the reader in Japan as well as Europe. From the West he mentions Gibbons and Macaulay, and in Japan he mentions Oka, Gamo, Shimada Saburō (1852–1923), Fukuchi Genichirō, Tokutomi Sohō, and Takekoshi Yosaburō. (As the presence of Oka and Gamo in both categories indicates, Yamaji did not see these as pure types.) He then warns, "If there are few things to read [that move the reader] and few books that can create feeling (*kanka*), and if one cannot affect the human spirit (*jinshin*), history too will probably lose its connection to actual society."[40] If Mehl is correct, this fear has come true, but because of the success of empirical history, not its failure.

For Yamaji, then, storytelling is an important historical genre that can both convey information and entertain. As with Walter Benjamin in his "The Storyteller," Yamaji finds in storytelling the connection between experience and inherited and learned knowledge. And like Benjamin, Yamaji decries the decline of experience in modern society. For Yamaji, storytelling combines the utility of the past without separating the past from the present. It is that mutable discourse that generates belief, and in his case, belief in the nation. Benjamin writes, "The storyteller takes what he tells from experience—his own or that reported by others. And he in turn makes it the experience of those who are listening to his tale."[41]

Yamaji's preferred genre for his own stories was biography. Interestingly, he argued that using heroes was perhaps the best way to achieve an interesting history that is not dead. He argued that one of the ways to interest readers is to write about the past in a way that readers can imagine that they are a part of it. He wrote many biographies of major figures in Japanese history, for example Tokugawa Ieyasu, Ashikaga Takauji, Ogyū Sorai, Arai Hakuseki, Katō Kiyomasa, Minamoto Yoritomo, Katsu Kaishū, Sakuma Shōzan, Saigō Takamori, and so on. Most are military leaders. Here, he saw heroes as models: "it is without doubt that the positive model of a hero gives rise to other heros."[42] He used an analogy with biology: Just as living things beget similar things, a materialist civilization produces materialist people and heroes produce herolike people. The aspect that he was trying to keep in the present was the idea of ancestors and ethics of loyalty and patriotism.

These figures obviously come dangerously close to the history that he was writing against, those great men who make up the historical backdrop to the emperor-centered state. But if we connect these heroes to his historical narrative, most are exemplars in the development of rights throughout Japanese history. Yamaji recognized the small number of individuals actually involved in this development. His was a narrative that emphasized a struggle against entrenched power. Moreover, he characterized heroes as indicators (he used the analogy of a weathervane) of social change rather than as creators of change. Most of his heroes were important as representatives of a national (not state) achievement, not because of the person himself (his heroes are all male). Leaders, he writes, become great because they seize the moment of transformation. For example, he characterized the Meiji Restoration as the culmination of a national movement rather than a restoration of the emperor by a small band of samurai. He also wrote that while Ito Hirobumi deserves credit for establishing the constitution, he cautioned that without some fundamental understanding of constitutional government by the populous, the constitution would be worthless. His optimism that he was fostering a sense of nation rather than falling into the nation-state is evident in the following statement from 1900:

> Along with my older peers . . . the focus of my work, by believing in people is turning the biographies of heroes into human history. And then, by believing that philosophy it is in writing biographies of heroes in the East and West. My hope is that in depicting heroes who shed tears and blood it will revive our minds from the waste pile and teach the present. Those who besiege me as the enemy scorn my plan. However, whether one should be thankful or not, my endeavors are certainly not empty. The concept of hero worship is suddenly percolating among the hearts of the nation (*kokumin*). The biographical holdings of collectors grow like a grove of bamboo shoots in spring. The study and research of people is becoming a popular trend.[13]

There was a popular increase in historical interest at the turn of the century. But we must wonder whether Yamaji's optimism was warranted, for perhaps the rise in historical interest he saw was framed not in his development of the nation, but in the rise of the nation-state. Even though Yamaji was rather well known, his critique against academic history did not alter or weaken the state's possession of history. Had he succeeded in resituating the subject, his alternative history would have led to a rather different understanding and practice of how we interact with the past. But despite a quite different horizon than that of the academic historians, he used the same symbols. Indeed, many of the figures he singled out for biographies were also singled out as representatives of the nation-state. In the school textbooks, historical icons such as Tokugawa Ieyasu became exemplars of the rise of Japan and the growing power of the state, and in literature and ethics classes, figures in the *Taiheiki* were used to emphasize loyalty and filiation toward the emperor as inherent Japanese characteristics. In short, the same figures to which Yamaji turned to historicize history have been used by the government to elide the relation among power, national ideology, and history.

In short, Yamaji identified several sites where history, in the name of the people of Japan, reinforced their continued submission to the state (and where historiography today still perpetuates some of those instruments of power). But his shift of subject is rather subtle and certainly abstract. His narrative of the development of rights in Japan is certainly as plausible as the progress of the nation-state. But his turn to icons and stories as symbols of the development of those rights paralleled the narrative he criticized, and in the end served to reinforce the state history rather than his narrative that criticized the state. Ultimately, even though the academic historians wrote a history that few people read, they did establish the relation of the past to the nation-state's liberal-capitalist horizon of expectations that was replicated in all the schools and set the parameters for debate. The question that still remains is to what extent is it possible to write a history that allows space for experience within a modern nation-state.

NOTES

1. Margaret Mehl, *History and the State in Nineteenth-Century Japan* (New York: 1998), 159.

2. Most recent studies rely on the considerable work of Okubo Toshiaki. See for example, Mehl, *History and the State*; John S. Brownlee, *Japanese Historians and the National Myths, 1600–1945* (Vancouver: 1997); Jirō Numata, "Shigeno Yasutsugu and the Modern Tokyo Tradition," in *Historians of China and Japan*, ed. W. G. Beasley and E. G. Pulleyblank (London: 1961), 264–87 ; Peter Duus, "Whig History, Japanese Style: The Min'yusha Historians and the Meiji Restoration," *Journal of Asian Studies* 33 (1974): 419–20; Carol Gluck, "The People in History: Recent Trends in Japanese Historiography," *Journal of Asian Studies* 38 (1978): 25–50; Leonard Blusse, "Japanese Historiography and European Sources," in *Reappraisals in Overseas History*, ed. P. C. Emmer and H. L. Wesseling (Leiden: 1979), 193–221.

3. See, for example, Brownlee, *Japanese Historians and the National Myths*.

4. Iwai Tadakuma, "Nihon kindai shigaku no keisei," in *Iwanami koza nihon rekishi* (bekkan 22) (Tokyo: 1963), 81.

5. Duus, "Whig History, Japanese Style," 415–36.

6. Yamaji Aizan, "Nihon no rekishi ni okeru jinken hattatsu no konseki,"

Kokumin no tomo (January 9, 16, 23, 1897), in Yamaji Aizan, *Meiji bunka zenshū*, vol. 35 (Tokyo: 1965), 314.

7. Yamaji, "Nihon no rekishi," 315.

8. Mehl, *History and the State in Nineteenth Century Japan*, 1.

9. "Nihon teikoku no yonhonchū," *Kokumin zasshi* 2/6 (June 1911) in *Yamaji Aizan shū*, ed. Oka Toshirō, vol. 2 (Tokyo: 1985), 406–7.

10. "Nihon teikoku no yonhonchū," 404.

11. Yamaji Aizan, "Nihon gendaishi no shigaku oyobi shika" *Taiyo* (9–1909), in Yamaji, *Meiji bunka zenshū*, 402.

12. He wrote theocracy in a Japanese syllabary next to *shintō seiji.*

13. Yamaji, "Nihon no rekishi," 318.

14. Yamaji, "Nihon no rekishi," 322.

15. Yamaji, "Nihon no rekishi," 321.

16. Yamaji, "Nihon no rekishi," 323.

17. Michel de Certeau, *The Writing of History* (New York: 1988), 45.

18. This separation is succinctly described in Immanuel Kant's elegant essay, "What Is Enlightenment?'" He writes that "enlightenment is mankind's exit from its self-incurred immaturity." See James Schmidt, ed., *What Is Enlightenment: Eighteenth-Century Answers and Twentieth-Century Questions* (Berkeley, Calif.: 1996), 58–64.

19. Yamaji Aizan, "Rekishi no hanashi," *Kokumin shimbun* (April 29, 1894), in MBz35 Yamaji, *Meiji bunka zenshū*, 264.

20. Yamaji, "Nihon gendaishi no shigaku," 404, 402. Mikami was one of the first students of the new history department. Although Riess, Shigeno, and Kume were the principal professors, Mikami gives more credit to Konakamura and Naitō Chissō for his historical training. He joined the faculty at the Imperial University in 1892 and between 1899 and 1919 he served as director of the Historiographical Institute. Yamaji recognized Mikami as an authority on Tokugawa history, but it is this tendency toward fragmentation (or more positively, specialization) that he is criticizing.

21. Michel de Certeau, "History: Ethics, Science, and Fiction," in *Social Science As Moral Inquiry*, ed. Norma Haan, Robert N. Bellah, Paul Rabinow, and William M. Sullivan (New York: 1983), 145.

22. Yamaji, "Bungaku to rekishi" (first presented August 27, 1892), in *Yamaji Aizan shū*, 438.

23. See Frank O Miller, *Minobe Tatsukichi* (Berkeley, Calif.: 1965), and Tetsuo Najita, "Some Reflections on Idealism in the Political Thought of Yoshino Sakuzo," in *Japan in Crisis*, ed. Bernard Silberman and H. D. Harootunian (Princeton, N.J.: 1974), 29–66.

24. For an account of the Kume incident, see Mehl, *History and the State*, 126–33, and Brownlee, *Japanese Historians and the National Myths*, 92–106. For a description of the 1911 textbook controversy surrounding Kita, see Mehl, *History and the State*, 140–47, and Brownlee, *Japanese Historians and the National Myths*, 118–30.

25. Yamaji, "Rekishi no hanashi," 264.

26. Yamaji, "Bungaku to rekishi," 438.

27. Konakamura did not lead the public criticism against Kume and Shigeno. Instead, other supporters of *kokugaku*, of which he was influential, led the charge.

28. Yamaji, "Nihon no rekishi," 315.

29. Yamaji, "Bungaku to rekishi," 438.

30. Yamaji Aizan, "Eiyūron," *Jogaku Zasshi* 1 (1891), in Yamaji, *Meiji bunka zen-shū*, 248.

31. Yamaji is referring to Shigeno. Yamaji, "Bungaku to rekishi," 438.

32. Yamaji Aizan, "Keiken," *Kokumin shimbun*, November 12, 1893, in Yamaji, *Meiji bunka zenshū*, 260.

33. Yamaji, "Keiken," 259

34. Yamaji, "Rekishi no hanashi," 264.

35. Yamaji Aizan, "Shigakuron: inaka yori shufu e," *Kokumin shinbun*, July 12, 1900, in Yamaji, *Meiji bunka zenshū*, 325.

36. Yamaji, "Bungaku to rekishi," 437.

37. Yamaji, "Rekishi no hanashi," 264.

38. Yamaji, "Shigakuron," 325 (emphasis in original).

39. Yamaji, "Nihon gendaishi no shigaku," 404.

40. Yamaji, "Nihon gendaishi no shigaku," 399.

41. Walter Benjamin, *Illuminations*, ed. Hannah Arendt, trans. Harry Zohn (New York: 1968), 87.

42. Yamaji, "Eiyūron," 249.

43. Quoted in Obi Toshito, "Kaisetsu: Yamaji Aizan ni tsuite," in Yamaji Aizan, *Shironshū* (Tokyo: 1958), 469.

Part II

ACROSS CULTURAL BORDERS

6

German Historicism and Scientific History in China, 1900–1940

Q. Edward Wang

Ancient Chinese civilization is noted for many scientific inventions. Yet "science," or *kexue*, is a translated neologism not known by most Chinese until the late nineteenth century.[1] After the term entered the Chinese vocabulary, however, it evoked a "science fever," or "worship," that has dominated the lives of the Chinese educated youth and intelligentsia for more than a century.[2] Many scholars have noticed that the yearning for "Mr. Science" in the May Fourth Movement of 1919, which marked the beginning of the rising tide of "science fever" in twentieth-century China, has never waned. For example, Li Zehou, a PRC scholar, and Vera Schwarcz, an American historian, have both noticed the recurrence of the May Fourth ideals in contemporary China.[3]

The fact that Chinese intellectuals have been so intrigued by "the study of science," as the term *kexue* connotes, is related to China's relations with the West. China's military defeats by Western powers in the late nineteenth century taught the Chinese that in order for their country to fend off the Western intrusion, they must update their knowledge of science and technology. Learning science therefore was a political choice for Chinese students. They hoped that by arming themselves with modern scientific knowledge, they could reinvigorate Chinese civilization. Moreover, studying science served a moral purpose, as noticed by some scholars.[4] It was hoped, by its advocates, to provide a new standpoint for the collapsing Chinese moral system in the face of Western cultural challenge. For

Chinese intellectuals, their purpose of scientific learning was not simply for obtaining a new knowledge. Rather, scientific education had a profound social meaning, hence the term "scientism," which referred to both a research method as well as a sociopolitical attitude. The sociology of science determined, to a great extent, how science was perceived and practiced in China.[5]

WHAT IS "SCIENTIFIC HISTORY"?

The pursuit of scientific history reflects the general trend of scientific learning in China. Writing "scientific history" constituted the main content of the so-called new history (*xin shixue*) beginning in the early twentieth century, which, to some extent, marked a break from the age-old tradition of historiography in China. Xu Guansan, a modern historian who has done a comprehensive survey of the writing of "new history," states that since Liang Qichao (1873–1929) first introduced the concept of "scientific history" to China, "the main trend in the development of new history has always been scientization."[6] What prompted Liang Qichao to take an interest in scientific history was his nationalist concern for China's shattering status in the modern world. In the beginning of his *New Historiography* (*Xin shixue*), published in 1902, Liang proclaims that historical study ought to serve the nationalist cause, or the project of nation-building. He noticed that "the rise of nationalism in Europe and the growth of modern European countries are owing in part to the study of history," and asked, rather acutely, why historical studies in China failed to play the same role.[7]

To Liang, the problem is the way in which Chinese historians wrote history in the past. He believes that without a *shixue geming* (historiographical revolution), China will not be able to respond to all the challenges associated with the appearance of Western powers in Asia. Nationalist sentiment, therefore, not only accounts for why Chinese historians were interested in making changes in historiography; it also determines what type of "scientific history" they were looking for.

In the Western historiographical tradition, the writing of scientific history that occurred in the eighteenth and nineteenth centuries involved efforts, on the one hand, to search for lawful interpretations of historical development; and on the other, an Enlightenment project aimed to emulate the work of scientists by exercising reason to discover laws in human society as that in nature, and to deliver accurate, factual accounts of historical evolution through critical methods and from an objective perspective. The latter was conventionally associated with the German tradition of historicism, exemplified by the work of Leopold von Ranke (1795–

1886).[8] The attempt at a general interpretation of world history, or "Enlightenment historiography," has produced many influential works in the West that were authored by important modern thinkers such as Comte, Hegel, Marx, and Toynbee. German historicism, or "Rankean historiography," has also exerted a great influence in the academic community. Its emphasis on faithfully describing the past based on source criticism, or *Quellenkritik*, has become a quintessential feature of modern Western historiography, despite skepticism about Rankean historians' claim on objectivity.[9]

To be sure, it is a bit arbitrary here to draw a line between Enlightenment and historicist/Rankean historiography. Developed around the same time, they had juxtaposed one another in many aspects. Both, for example, regarded history as a meaningful process. In fact, some have argued that German historicism extended the influence of the Enlightenment in central Europe.[10] But insofar as Enlightenment historiography is concerned, there were indeed different manifestations. As French Enlightenment historians advocated the idea of progress and identified the driving forces, for example, class struggle, in history, German historicists such as Ranke stressed the importance of describing historical reality to present the particulars in the past and the methodological difference between the studies of *Geisteswissenschaft* and *Naturwissenschaft*. In contrast to the confidence shown by the philosophes in historical interpretation, German historicists posited that one could understand (*verstehen*) history only through experience.[11] Ranke, for example, believed that the best way to study history was to present the past as it really was, lest the historian missed the presence of God, or divine will, in the human world.[12] This focus on historical reconstruction led to the work of source collection and criticism, representing a "paradigm" in modern historiography.[13]

When Liang Qichao published his *New Historiography* in 1902, he noticed the stark difference between the ways in which Chinese and Western historians wrote history. Referring to Chinese historiography as "old history" (*jiushi*), he though it necessary for Chinese historians to experiment with the writing of new history. According to him, the new history should serve three purposes, or give three kinds of "descriptions" (*xushu*):

1. describing the evolution in both natural and human history;
2. describing phenomena in human evolution, or presenting the idea of progress in history; and
3. describing the common laws and principles in this progressive human history.

Liang's interest in searching for lawful generalizations in human history suggests that he followed the Enlightenment line of thinking as well as ideas of Darwinism and positivism. According to him, human history demonstrates a linear progress, comparable to that in nature. The duty of a "real historian" (zhen shijia) is to display this progress and find its laws.[14]

While defining the "new history" clearly along the lines of the Enlightenment form of scientific history, Liang has not used the term "science." In fact, he seems oblivious of the difference in nomenclature, that is, "study" (xue) versus "scientific study" (kexue), as in Chinese.[15] Liang's oblivion suggests that by his time, although science as a form of new learning had entered Chinese schools, its methodological and epistemological implication was not yet fully understood. Liang shared the positivist belief that like scientists, historians should describe evolution in human history. But he failed to explain how the "new" scientific historian could discover and describe laws in history as do scientists in nature, namely the epistemological questions that concerned German historicists Wilhelm Dilthey and Heinrich Rickert. At the time when Liang wrote his New Historiography, his primary concern was to remind his compatriots about China's weaknesses in comparison with Western powers. To this end, the positivist belief served the purpose; it offered descriptions of a hierarchically structured process of historical development, in which countries in the world were ranked according to their statuses in social progress. China's backward position, given its military weakness, in such a scheme became a starting point for Liang and others to address the nationalist need for restoring their country's wealth and power (fuqiang).[16]

If nationalism was an impetus for Liang to call for a new history, or "Enlightenment historiography," it disappointed him later on. There are apparent reasons. First, if evolution, or the idea of progress, is indeed the common law in human history, could this law be applied to the course of Chinese history in the past few thousand years? Liang is not so optimistic, considering his iconoclastic criticism of the Chinese cultural tradition. Second, a linear progress of human history is premised on the notion of a unitary time, against which all histories in the world move in the same direction.[17] This linear view of history allows Liang to remind his compatriots about China's weak and backward position in comparison with the West; however, it dose not point to a bright future for Chinese civilization. How could there be a future if China's past history never displayed a progressive pattern? Thus "Enlightenment historiography" has a paradoxical effect on Liang's campaign of a new history. This paradox also troubled Marxist historians in their attempt at a "scientific interpretation" of China's past.[18]

In 1922, when Liang Qichao got another chance to study history, he published his Methods for the Study of Chinese History (Zhongguo lishi yanji-

ufa, hereafter *Methods*). In this book, we find that he modified his original belief in scientific history. First, the term "evolution" (*jinhua*), which was placed at the center of the new history, disappeared in his discussion of the meaning of history. Instead, Liang wrote that historical writing merely describes "various forms of human activity" (*huodong zhi tixiang*). Obviously, Liang did not think that these activities form a process of evolution any more. Rather, they are merely "continuous activities" (*gengxu huodong*). Second, since there is no evolution, there is no need for the historian to discover "common laws and principles" in history. What the historian needs to do is simply summarize the achievement of the activities and establish causal relations among them (it is noticeable that Liang later abandoned the attempt to find causal relations). Third, as Liang made these changes, he also assigned a new task to the historian. He wanted the historian to make history a useful mirror for the present so that the modern people can reflect their conducts.[19] Liang's use of this history-mirror analogy, an age-old notion about the role of history in China, suggests that once he had forsaken his belief in evolutionism, he moved closer to his own cultural roots.

Indeed, when Liang wrote *Methods*, he was prepared to embark on the project of reconciling Western and Chinese historiographical traditions. This reconciliation constituted a new attempt at scientific history, in which the focus became source criticism, as was in Rankean historiography, rather than lawful generalizations. The title of *Methods* shows Liang's new interest: It was written about historical methodology and discusses the methods for studying Chinese history. In his discussion, Liang compared Chinese and Western traditions in source criticism, hence presenting an equivalence between the two traditions. According to Liang, Chinese historians in the past acquired ample experience in source collection, collation, and correction; their skills and methods, therefore, are comparable to those of their Western counterparts.

SOURCE CRITICISM—BRIDGING
EAST AND WEST

Liang's attempt to redefine scientific history and compare Chinese and Western culture was concomitant with the main trend of historical study in China. During the 1920s, when he published his *Methods*, Chinese historians, especially those working in an academic setting, more or less accepted the notion that science was a methodology, or a method of scientific research (*kexue yanjiu de fangfa*), which had a universal application. This notion was particularly favored by a group of students who had returned from the West, among them Hu Shi (1891–1962), a doctoral student from Columbia University. At Columbia during 1915 and 1917, Hu worked with John Dewey and completed a thesis on the logic method in ancient Chinese philosophy. After his return to China, he became a chief spokesman of Western science. Hu preached Deweyan pragmatism and translated it into "experimentalism" (*shiyan zhuyi*). He believed that Deweyan doctrines embodied the essence of scientific method that requires "a boldness in setting up hypotheses and a minuteness in seeking evidence" (*dadan de jiashe, xiaoxin de qiuzheng*).[20]

Hu's advocacy of Western science suited the need of professionalization of history in China at the time. After the abolition of the civil service examination system (1905) and the founding of modern type universities, such as National Peking University,[21] staffed by many returned students from Japan and the West, historical study underwent a quick transformation. The establishment of the history department at Peking University (1918) indicates that history gradually gained its autonomous status and severed its traditional tie with the study of the classics. In 1920, three years after Hu Shi returned to China, the department produced its first graduates.[22] About the same time, professional associations and scholarly journals also appeared in major cities. During the 1920s, therefore, historical study in China was on its way to becoming a modern profession.[23]

Hu's appropriation of modern science in American pragmatism played a crucial role in making history a disciplinary study as well as a scholarly pursuit in China. Hu understood scientific method from a positivist perspective; after some culpable reduction, he equated scientific method with the effort to search for useful facts. In doing so, he made a claim on its universal applicability. This ecumenism of science seems to have worked in this time (judging by Hu's tremendous influence in shaping modern Chinese historiography); it appealed to the Chinese academics who were eager to reform and rejuvenate Chinese culture with the help of modern science. By considering scientific method simply a technique in collecting evidence, Hu compared the method with the rich Chinese experience in textual and historical criticism, exemplified most distinctly by Qing "evidential" (*kaozheng*) scholarship, and thus offered a cross-cultural perspective on scientific history.[24]

By attesting to the universal value of scientific method, Hu Shi applied it to reexamine the Chinese literary tradition. He believed that scientific methods were "the instruments by means of which and in the light of which much of the lost treasures of Chinese philosophy can be recovered."[25] To recover Chinese "treasures," one must assure the validity of ancient texts, because through them great ideas were conveyed. To implement his belief, Hu taught students the importance of source criticism in his course on ancient Chinese philosophy. He also initiated a collective research project, known as "constructing the national past and recreating civilization" (*zhengli guogu, zaizao wenming*), through which he helped launch a movement that came to be called National Studies. At its core, the movement aimed to apply source criticism to all extant texts for verifying their authenticity, authorship, and accuracy. They applied techniques that had been used by their ancestors. What differentiates their work in the 1920s and their ancestors' work, say, that of Qing "evidential" scholars in the eighteenth century, is that Hu and his followers pursued source criticism in the name of science. Thus, science was accepted in China not because it embodied the characteristic of modern Western culture. Rather, it was accepted because it helped the Chinese to reclaim the validity of their own culture.

This sinicization of scientific method served well with the growth of Chinese historical profession. By placing source criticism at the center, Hu Shi and his comrades worked out an equivalence between Chinese and Western culture and standardized the techniques of historical study with a concentration. "The development and standardization of technique," as Peter Novick points out in his study of the U.S. historical profession, "was, of course, the whole point of professional training."[26] The emphasis on source criticism helped modern Chinese historians to set up the standard of the historical profession, as it had done earlier to the historical professions in theUnited States and Germany. More importantly, as stated above, it enabled them to revive the Chinese tradition in textual criticism. It is not coincidental that by the 1920s, while Ranke's name was not well known to the Chinese his ideas of history became well integrated with the Chinese practice of scientific history.

SCIENTIFIC HISTORY IN PRACTICE

During the first half of the twentieth century, when scientific history was in vogue, most historians' career achievements in China were measured by their success in source criticism. In fact, history seems to be a "standard" profession to many May Fourth "teachers" and "students." In addition to Hu Shi, He Bingsong (1890–1946) and Chen Hengzhe (1890–1976) were also well-known historians. Among the "students," Gu Jiegang (1893–1980), Fu Sinian (1896–1951), Yao Congwu (1894–1970), and Luo Jialun (1897–1969) were the most famous. If nationalist impulses accounted for their choice in studying history—inspired by Liang Qichao, they considered history an important means in nation-building—their training and interest in source collection and criticism characterized their major contribution to the study of Chinese history.[27]

Indeed, during the 1920s and the 1930s, the work of Chinese historians was centered around applying source criticism to examine the Chinese cultural tradition. A famous example, well known to most China scholars, is the "Discussion of Ancient History" (*gushi bian*), which was precipitated by Hu Shi's correspondence with his student Gu Jiegang. Inspired by Hu's exemplary research on the works of ancient Chinese philosophers, Gu used critical method to examine the authenticity of ancient texts in order to distinguish legend from history, fiction from facts, and reconstruct the history of China's high antiquity. To this end, he conducted scrupulous research to examine the Chinese literary tradition, in which he detected many forgeries, most of which were related to the history of ancient China. Gu hence declared that not only was the longevity of Chinese history doubtful, but that there also was a continual practice among Chinese literati in embellishing, interpolating, and even forging and falsifying texts. His finding outraged many of his peers and caused a great controversy in the intellectual community. Yet whether or not one agreed with Gu, one had first to adopt his method. Techniques in source criticism therefore became a necessary preparation for anyone who aspired to enter the history profession.[28]

This source-oriented scientific history received strong support from two German-educated historians: Fu Sinian and Yao Congwu. They both spent several years in Germany and were exposed to the German historical tradition. After they returned to China, they became main exponents of German historicism in China, helping to reconstruct Chinese history on a scientific ground. They campaigned for expanding the source material for historical study and emphasized the importance of source criticism with the method of philology.

Fu Sinian, who was Gu Jiegang's classmate and Hu Shi's student at Peking University, returned to China in 1927 after a seven-year sojourn in Europe. Although it is unclear whether Fu indeed received a solid training in Rankean historiography while in Germany—he pursued a rather broad interest in education, psychology, geology, archaeology, philology, and history—he became an outspoken advocate of the alliance between history and philology in China. Fu's interest in science emanated from his friendship with Hu Shi at Peking University; under Hu's encouragement, he and his collegemates, such as Luo Jialun and Gu Jiegang, edited the campus journal *New Tide* (*Xinchao*). While a literature student, Fu contributed many essays to the journal, introducing Western scientific theories into China. After graduation, he continued his interest in learning about science, which he regarded as "real learning" (*zhen xuewen*). Upon receiving a scholarship, Fu went to Britain to study psychology at the University of London in 1920.[29] However, three years later he decided to transfer to the University of Berlin, ending his degree program in Britain.

It is unknown why Fu Sinian forsook his original goal to obtain a degree in science. But judging by what he did after arriving in Germany, it appears that he made that decision partially because he became attracted to the German tradition of historicism, which helped him to rediscover the value of the humanities and place them on a scientific basis. To his delight, Fu found that the study of the humanities, in which he received good training from his family and early schooling, could also become scientific, as shown in the works of German scholars, and the process of achieving the scientization was simply to employ the philological method of source criticism. At the University of Berlin, while continuing his study of science, he took courses in philology and tried to learn some foreign languages. His combined interest in both science and the humanities did not help him to excel in his courses.[30] In fact, during his stay in Berlin, Fu was not always a full-time, matriculated student. He would rather take courses randomly to satisfy his own interest and/or curiosity. His main goal, it seems to me, is not to receive a degree, but to obtain some scientific training necessary for the project of reviving Chinese cultural tradition.

It is from his German stay, therefore, that Fu Sinian arrived at a new understanding of science; it was not limited to the study of natural sciences. Inspired by German historians, he established the Institute of History and Philology (*Lishi yuyan yanjiusuo*), first at Sun Yat-sen University in Guangzhou (1927) and later at Beijing, joining the newly founded Academia Sinica (1928). Among his friends, Fu was well known for his slogan that "no historical sources, no history" and his admiration for Rankean historiography. Despite some obvious discrepancies between his and Ranke's ideas of history, Fu appropriated two important ideas from Rankean historiography that were considered by most Western historians as the most important contributions to modern historical discipline: one was his emphasis on using primary/archival sources in writing history, and the other the application of critical/philological methods to examining historical sources.

Indeed, Fu's idea of establishing the Institute of History and Philology reminds us of the legacy of Rankean historiography. For example, in his "Congratulatory Remarks" to the *Historische Zeitschrift*, a journal edited by Ranke's disciples, Ranke called for establishing a research organization on a national level and publishing a scholarly journal.[31] In founding the institute, we see that Fu tried the same. Besides establishing the institute, he and his colleagues also published a journal, titled *Bulletin of the Institute of History and Philology, Academia Sinica*. The journal remains today a prestigious professional publication for original research in Taiwan.[32] In one of his prefaces to a source collection project, the *Ming Qing shiliao* (Ming and Qing archives)—a small replica of Georg Waitz's (Ranke's favorite student) *Monumenta Germaniae Historica*—Fu confessed that it was Ranke and Theodor Mommsen who inspired him to catalog and publish archives.[33]

But Fu Sinian's interest in natural sciences also left some marks in his pursuit of scientific history. While in Europe, he was exposed and receptive to the influence of positivism through the writings of Ernst Mach (1838–1916) and Karl Pearson (1857–1936). From the positivist perspective, Fu analogized history to natural sciences and emphasized their methodological compatibility. His understanding of scientific history, therefore, is a complex mixture. On the one hand, following the tradition of Rankean historiography, Fu stressed the importance of source criticism and advocated the alliance between history and philology. On the other hand, he urged his fellow historians to go beyond written sources and to broaden the scope of historical sources in order to place history on a par with natural sciences. His colleagues at the institute recalled that although Fu took charge of the publication of archival sources of the Ming and Qing Dynasties, he showed more interest in archaeological discoveries.[34] His proposal for founding the institute included plans to seek out sources in new areas for the study of history. In that proposal, he emphatically declared that "we are not book readers. We go all the way to Heaven above and Yellow Spring below, using our hands and feet, to look for things."[35]

The organization of the Institute of History and Philology reflected Fu's mixed ideas of scientific history. The institute was made up of three programs—history, philology, and archaeology—and each possessed an equal importance. For Fu Sinian, the basis of scientific research was experimentation, regardless of disciplinary difference. To that end, he equipped, for example, the philology program with a modern phonetic laboratory, whose advanced equipment, incidentally, left a strong impression on the Swedish sinologist and linguist Bernhard Karlgren in his visit. In Fu's mind, therefore, modern philological study was essentially different from that of ancient times when scholars basically conducted their research on examining texts. By doing laboratory work, he hoped that his colleagues in the institute would surpass the achievement of Qing evidential scholars in textual criticism and solve the problems that had puzzled their predecessors, such as the prominent Qing philologist Qian Daxin (1728–1804).[36]

Fu pursued the same goal in studying history. Amid the controversy regarding the history of ancient China in the early 1930s, Fu organized an archaeological team at the institute and sent it to the Henan Province to conduct excavations in the area of Anyang, a capital of the Shang Dynasty (1600–1027 B.C.E.). He believed that the real answer to the question of whether the Shang Dynasty was a Stone-Age culture, posited by Gu Jiegang and Hu Shi, or a highly civilized culture as revered by most people in traditional China, lay in the material remains in the site. Although the focus of the project was initially placed on finding more inscribed oracle bones, which turned out to be a disappointment because not many were found, it led to important discoveries of other things, including pottery, stone, shells, and soil, all of which were valuable for historians to understand the cultural level of Shang civilization. By unearthing and presenting these remains, the institute obtained ample and reliable information about China's high antiquity.

Paul Pelliot, the famous French sinologist who had helped discover the oracle bones in the Shang remains in the early twentieth century, enthusiastically praised the accomplishment as "the most spectacular discovery made in the field of Asiatic Studies in recent years."[37] In his report, Li Ji (1896–1979), the archaeologist who was in charge of the project, states that the investigation proved not only that the inscribed oracle bones were authentic Shang remains, but also that Shang society was not a Stone-Age culture, but was much more sophisticated and well developed than previously thought.[38]

Fu's enthusiasm for historical sources had finally paid off. By presenting the archaeological evidence, he and his colleagues re-created the history of Chinese antiquity on a scientific basis and refuted Gu Jiegang's skepticism. In the face of the "hard" evidence, Hu Shi changed his position and endorsed Fu's work.[39] Nevertheless, though Fu Sinian arrived at a different conclusion from Gu Jiegang in regard to ancient Chinese history, he did not undermine Gu's emphasis on source criticism. Rather, he helped strengthen such emphasis by broadening the use of sources for historians.[40] Fu's success, therefore, reflected the influence of Rankean historiography in modern China.

Compared to his famous friend Fu Sinian, Yao Congwu remained a college professor throughout his career. But this "pure" scholar—as one of his friends called him on his death—was an authority on German historiography in China. Yao spent eleven years in Germany, from 1923 to 1934, an impressive record unrivaled by most of his friends at the time.[41] During that period, Yao studied with two historians at the University of Berlin: Otto Franke (1863–1946) and Erich Haenisch (1880–1966).[42] Although sinologists by training, these two Germans passed on to Yao influences of Rankean historiography. For example, Yao was impressed by Franke's knowledge of Chinese history and his training in Rankean historiography. In one of his articles introducing his mentor's career, Yao particularly pointed out:

> Because Franke was a student of Johann Droysen, he could grasp the historical method of the Prussian school. He knew the importance of comparing

what appeared in the Chinese Standard Histories with contemporary sources.[43]

He insisted that Franke's treatment of sources was superior to that of other Western sinologists because Franke had received a rigorous training from Droysen in Rankean historiography.

Erich Haenisch was an authority on Mongolian history in Germany. With him, Yao studied the Mongolian empire in both Asian and Europe and the Mongolian language. In Germany, Yao translated Haenisch's introduction to Mongolian history into Chinese and published it in China. To investigate the impact of the Mongol conquest on Europe, he also made trips to Hungary, Austria, and Czechoslovakia, to search for traces of Mongols there.[44] In 1934, Haenisch and Yao worked hand in hand in annotating two source books of Mongolian history that became a foundation for a complete translation later in the twentieth century.[45] Again, it appears that working on source materials was the focus of Yao's education with Haenisch. An article written by Yao in German during this period, "Ein Kurzer Beitrag zur Qullenkritik der Kin-und Yuan-Dynastie," suggests that he was interested in applying German historical method—source criticism—to the study of Chinese history.

Yao maintained this interest after returning to China. At Peking and Taiwan universities, where he was appointed as a history professor, he taught two courses: one about China's relations with its northern neighbors, be they Manchus, Mongols, and Turks; the other on historical methodology, based on his understanding of the German historiographical experience. For his colleagues and students, Yao was without doubt an authoritative figure on German historiography; after his return to China, he taught the historical methods course (*lishi fangfalun*) for forty years. Through his teaching, most history students, regardless of their future interests, gained some knowledge about German historiography and major historical figures in Germany. Du Weiyun, Yao's student at Taiwan University, recalled that in teaching the methodology course, Yao usually spent more than half the time introducing the works of German historians, ranging from Ranke to Ernst Bernheim. Yao often become excited when he mentioned Ranke's name in discussing German historiography; his voice became louder and his face shined. Out of his admiration, Yao deemed the publication of Ranke's *Geschichte der Romanischen und Germanischen Volker, von 1498 bis 1535* in 1824 a breakthrough in modern historiography, because in its epilogue Ranke used critical method to judge the works of Renaissance historians and pointed to the new direction of modern historiography. In addition, Yao translated some chapters of Bernheim's book for use as class-handouts.[46]

Like his friend Fu Sinian, Yao regarded philology-assisted source criticism as basis for modern historical research. In his opinion, while philological study also existed in China, the extent to which philological method was widely used to criticize and interpret historical sources represented a Western tradition. Using the German word "hermeneutik" (hermeneutics), Yao explains the evolution of the "philologisch-kritischen Methode" (method of philological criticism). He writes that hermeneutic study emerged from the biblical study of early modern Europe, which constituted the foundation of modern philological criticism. Drawing on Bernheim's work, Yao categorizes three types of sources: literary, antiquities, and legendary. The historian should apply different methods to treating these sources. In working with literary sources, for example, historians ought to be armed with philological method, while with antiquities, they should learn chronology, paleography, and sphragistics.[47]

In introducing the German method in historiography, Yao nevertheless was not just a translator. Rather, he incorporated well-known Chinese phrases and proverbs to emphasize the importance of collecting and examining source materials. Indeed, many of his students might have forgotten the German terms Yao used in class, but they well remember the Chinese phrases. Yao's two favorite ones: "To learn how to swim, one must jump into the water" and "To look at flowers on a horseback is not as good as get off the horse and pick up flowers." Both of them stress the need to seek and scrutinize historical sources with a hands-on approach.[48] In both China and Taiwan, Yao's appreciation and appropriation of German historiography influenced students of history for a few generations.

THE END OF SCIENTIFIC HISTORY?

While an achievement in professional historiography and a boon to the nationalist cause (many Chinese were delighted to see that their civilization once again displayed its enviable longevity), this scientific history was short-lived, ending quite abruptly at the mid-1940s. China in the 1930s witnessed a serious national crisis, caused by Japan's escalated military invasion, first in Manchuria and later extending to the whole country. Under this tumultuous circumstance, few historians could retain the integrity of their research. University faculty and students, as well as the research staff in the Academia Sinica, had to retreat from northern and central China to the south and/or southwest, often at the expense of many losses. Moreover, regarding the Japanese invasion as a grave endangerment to Chinese civilization, many chose to come out from their research ivory tower and take political actions; among them were China's most devoted professional historians mentioned above.

Hu Shi and his protégé, Fu Sinian, for example, were quite typical in regard to the change of attitude of Chinese intellectuals during the 1930s. In the 1920s when they were preoccupied by the work in promoting scientific history, they had avowed to concentrate their energy on scholarly research and not to participate in political activities. But in 1931, in the face of the Japanese military invasion, they and others published the journal *Duli pinglun* (Independent Critique), aimed to offer historical wisdom for the government in drawing up war-time policy toward Japan. In explaining why they edited the journal, Hu Shi wrote:

> Fire is already burning and national disaster has befallen everybody. . . . *Independent Critique* is a single thing that my friends and I thought we could do for this country under such a situation.[49]

Although their editorship of the journal deviated from their original intention to commit themselves fully to scholarship, they still pursued an independent voice in politics, as the title suggests. Many of the essays published in the journal showed concern for China's political future and defense policy, which were at times different from the position of the government.[50] However, they were unable to hold on to this "independence" for long. One after another, many contributors of the journal were lured to the government, offering their direct service. Their departure, coinciding with the escalation of the Japanese invasion in China's coastline, forced the journal to cease publication. In 1941, after the Pearl Harbor, Hu Shi himself accepted the position as China's ambassador to the United States. Fu Sinian, likewise, was involved in the work of political consultation for the government while complaining about his inability to devote his time for serious research.[51]

In addition to the external challenge resulting from the Sino-Japanese military confrontation, there was internal challenge to the exercise of the scientific history of Rankean historiography in China. The war not only made it almost impossible for scholars to do original research, but it also caused scientific research on source criticism to lose its original appeal to the people. If the early success of scientific history was drawn on both the achievement of Qing evidential scholarship and Rankean historiography, neither of them encouraged active sociopolitical participation of intellectuals needed at the time. Qing evidential scholarship, to some extent, was amounted to a passive resistance of the Han Chinese intellectuals to the Manchu rule; for those who were concerned about the cultural crisis resulting from the downfall of the Ming Dynasty (168–1644), it offered an alternative that allowed them to continue their interest in the Confucian tradition rather than collaborating with the Manchu ruler. Likewise, Rankean historiography represented a conservative political trend, rebutting the high revolutionary tide in mid–nineteenth-century Europe. By exalting the role of the state in the rise of modern nations, it helped confirm the establishment of political and social institutions in nineteenth-century Europe.[52] Qing evidential scholarship and Rankean historiography are important intellectual heritages in the study of history. They offer useful perspectives on affirming the past and interpreting tradition, but little help in guiding actions.

This said, I do not want to imply, as claimed by most Rankean historians, that source criticism is value-free. It is certainly not, as shown in the historiographical practices in both China and the West. What I argue here is that although the Chinese exercise of scientific history—focusing on source criticism—reflected a nationalist sentiment, which allowed them to pursue a dialogue between China and the West, tradition and modernity, the urgent need of national salvation in World War II made this dialogue difficult to continue, if not totally impossible. Chinese intellectuals realized that to conduct such a dialogue meant making compromises and negotiating between two very different cultures. As shown above, in order to make scientific history work in China, participating historians appropriated elements from both Chinese and Western cultures. In fact, their choice of Rankean historiography over Enlightenment historiography was both the work and outcome of such appropriations. Historians made appropriations according to the circumstances. When the circumstances change, they would have to make adjustment.

As professional historians succumbed their scientific history to Chinese nationalism, Marxist historians began to come to the center of the stage. Despite the ideological divergence, Marxists continued the pursuit of scientific history in modern China, albeit in a different direction. To a great extent, their work falls in the category of the "Enlightenment historiography," which Liang Qichao had first introduced to the Chinese in his *New History*. Aiming to situate Chinese history in the Marxian framework of social development, the Marxists appropriated history to espouse their ideological agenda. While their dogmatic approach contains obvious fallacies, especially in the use and interpretation of sources, their historiography seemed to have better served the need of Chinese nationalism, which constituted a driving force for the Communist victory in 1949.[53]

In conclusion, I would like to recapitulate the importance of the Chinese scientific historiography from the 1900s to the 1930s. First, though their cause was interrupted by war and revolution, Chinese professional historians' experiment with scientific history helped set up the academic criteria in the discipline of history. In fact, it was largely due to their work that history in China was developed into a profession. Second, despite its traditional inheritance, this scientific phase of Chinese historiography signaled the rise of modern historical consciousness, characterized by the historians' skepticism toward tradition and their attempt at reconstructing the past. Third, their endeavor to bridge Chinese culture and Western science and tradition and modernity has proven to be a lasting intellectual legacy for modern-day Chinese. Their practice of scientific history has shown us the underlying dynamics in cultural configuration that are not only recurrent and important in today's China, but also pertinent to the study of cross-cultural communication worldwide.

NOTES

1. Joseph Needham's multivolume *Science and Civilization in China*, 7 vols. (Cambridge, Mass.: 1954–2000) has detailed the scientific achievement in Chinese civilization. *Kexue* in traditional Chinese means to study for the civil service examination, here "ke" means "status" and "xue" refers to "study." When Western science entered China, Chinese scholars such as Liang Qichao first translated it into *gezhi,* which connotes its meaning of doing research. See Federico Masini, *The Formation of Modern Chinese Lexicon and Its Evolution toward a National Language: The Period from 1840 to 1898* (Berkeley, Calif.: 1993), 186. Using the term *kexue* is due to the Japanese influence. For a recent study on the Chinese acceptance of foreign terms and its cultural impact, see Lydia Liu, *Translingual Practice: Literature, National Culture, and Translated Modernity—China, 1900–1937* (Stanford, Calif.: 1995).

2. For a history of how the Chinese accepted and worshiped science, see Danny Kwok, *Scientism in Chinese Thought, 1900–1950* (New Haven, Conn.: 1965). Yet Kwok's book is not complete, for "science" entered China before the time period of his coverage. Charlotte Furth also discusses how the modern Chinese viewed "science" in her biographical study of *Ting Wen-chiang: Science and China's New Culture* (Cambridge, Mass.: 1979), 8–15.

3. Li Zehou, *Zhongguo xiandai sixiangshi lun* (On Contemporary Chinese Intellectual History) (Beijing: 1985) and Vera Schwarcz, *The Chinese Enlightenment: Intellectuals and the Legacy of the May Fourth Movement of 1919* (Berkeley, Calif.: 1986).

4. Yan Bofei, for example, points out that the introduction of modern science into early twentieth-century China helped the Chinese to reestablish their moral system, which was on the verge of collapse after the country's shattering military defeats in the mid-nineteenth century. "Lun wusi shiqi zhongguo zhishi fenzi dui fexue de lijie" (On the Understanding of "Science" by Chinese Intellectuals in the May Fourth Period), *Wusi: duoyuan de fansi* (May Fourth: A Variety of Reflections) (Hong Kong: 1989), 198–214.

5. H. Lyman Miller's book *Science and Dissent in Post-Mao China: The Politics of Knowledge* (Seattle, Wash.: 1995) describes how science was used by both the government and political dissidents for political purposes. Although the author focuses on contemporary China, his book is useful for the discussion here. In his well-documented study, Peter Buck also describes how the Chinese accepted science as a result of "cultural collapse" and how they would like to use the methods of science to transform Chinese culture. Peter Buck, *American Science and Modern*

China, 1876–1936 (Cambridge, Mass.: 1980), 171–208. For the Chinese admiration of science in the May Fourth/New Culture Movement of 1915–1930, see Chow Tse-tsung's *The May Fourth Movement* (Stanford, Calif.: 1960) and the previously mentioned Kwok's and Schwarcz's works.

6. *Xin shixue jiushi nian* (New History in the Last Ninety Years) (Hong Kong: 1986), I: xi.

7. *Xin shixue* (New History), *Liang Qichao shixue lunzhu sanzhong* (Liang Qichao's Three Historical Works) (Hong Kong: 1980), 3. There have been quite a few English monographs on Liang Qichao; see Joseph R. Levenson, *Liang Ch'i-ch'ao and the Mind of Modern China* (Cambridge, Mass.: 1959); Hao Chang, *Liang Ch'i-ch'ao and Intellectual Transition in China, 1890–1907* (Cambridge, Mass.: 1971); and Philip C. Huang, *Liang Ch'i-ch'ao and Modern Chinese Liberalism* (Seattle, Wash.: 1972).

8. According to Leonard Krieger, the term "scientific history" means two things: critical methods and the search for a lawful generalization. "European History in America," in *History: The Development of Historical Studies in the US*, ed. John Higham et al. (Englewood Cliffs, N.J.: 1968), 255–67.

9. These two types of "scientific history" serve only as working concepts in this paper. There are, of course, intrinsic correlations between them. What I would like to emphasize here is that while Rankean historiography had its ideological agenda, as Georg Iggers and many others have noticed, it attempted to distinguish history from philosophy by emphasizing source criticism and the delivery of historical details. See Georg Iggers, *The German Conception of History: The National Tradition of Historical Thought from Herder to the Present* (Middletown, Conn.: 1983) and Ranke's own works in *The Theory and Practice of History: Leopold von Ranke*, ed. Georg Iggers and Konrad von Moltke (Indianapolis: 1973). Some German historians have argued that Rankean historiography represented an exemplary practice of German historicism, which made a significant contribution to the growth of history as a modern profession in the nineteenth century; for example, Friedrich Jaeger and Jörn Rüsen's *Geschichte des Historismus* (Munich: 1992).

10. See Peter Reill, *The German Enlightenment and the Rise of Historicism* (Berkeley, Calif.: 1975), and his article "Aufklärung und Historismus: Bruch oder Kontinuität?" in *Historismus in den Kulturwissenschaften*, ed. Otto Gerhard Oexle and Jörn Rüsen (Vienna: 1996), 45–68.

11. Compare Charles Bambach, *Heidegger, Dilthey, and the Crisis of Historicism* (Ithaca, N.Y.: 1995), and Jaeger and Rüsen, *Geschichte des Historismus.*

12. For Ranke's ideas of history, see Iggers and von Moltke, *The Theory and Practice of History.*

13. See Iggers, *The German Conception of History*, and George Iggers, "The Crisis of the Rankean Paradigm in the Nineteenth Century," *Syracuse Scholar*, 9:1 (1988): 43–50.

14. *Xin shixue*, chap. 2, "shixue zhi jieshuo" (Definitions of History), *Liang Qichao shixue lunzhu sanzhong*, 10–15.

15. Liang in the book uses *kexue* to refer to the study of nature, but not history and social sciences. Even for the former, Liang's use of *kexue* is far from consistent.

He sometime uses the term *tianran kexue* (natural sciences) but other time he uses *tianran jie zhi xue* (the study of the natural world) instead.

16. *Xin shixue,* 3.

17. Xiaobing Tang, in his book, *Global Space and the Nationalist Discourse of Modernity: The Historical Thinking of Liang Qichao* (Stanford, Calif.: 1996), has observed the effect of this unitary time on Liang Qichao's historical thinking. Prasenjit Duara's *Rescuing History from the Nation: Questioning Narratives of Modern China* (Chicago: 1995) also discusses its impact on Enlightenment historiography from a comparative perspective.

18. For Chinese Marxist historiography, see Arif Dirlik, *Revolution and History: The Origins of Marxist Historiography in China, 1919–1937* (Berkeley, Calif.: 1978); *History in Communist China,* ed. Albert Feuerwerker (Cambridge, Mass.: 1968); Dorothea Martin, *The Making of a Sino-Marxist World View: Perceptions and Interpretations of World History in the PRC* (Armonk, N.Y.: 1989); and *Using the Past to Serve the Present: Historiography and Politics in Contemporary China,* ed. Jonathan Unger (Armonk, N.Y.: 1993). This issue is also discussed in Chinese Marxist historiography in Q. Edward Wang, "Interpreting the Chinese Revolution: Chinese and American Scholarship on Chinese Peasant Rebellions," *Asian Thought and Society,* 20:60 (September–December 1995): 221–40.

19. *Zhongguo lishi yanjiufa,* chap. 1, "shi zhi yiyi jiqi fanwei" (The Meaning and Scope of History), *Liang Qichao shixue lunzhu sanzhong,* 45–47.

20. Hu Shi's own words read: "In its essence, [scientific method] consists of a boldness in suggesting hypotheses coupled with a solicitous regard for control and verification. . . . This laboratory technique of thinking deserves the name of Creative Intelligence because it is truly creative in the exercise of imagination and ingenuity in seeking evidence, and devising experiment, and in the satisfactory results that flow from the successful fruition of thinking." *Living Philosophies: A Series of Intimate Credos* (New York: 1931), 255.

21. Peking University, or Jingshi daxuetang, was founded in the wake of China's defeat in the Boxer Rebellion in 1898, when the reigning Qing Dynasty decided to make some adjustment to the new world that was forced on it. Its name was changed to Peking University in 1912 after the founding of the People's Republic of China. This change indicates the change of the nature of higher learning in the country.

22. Peking University had a history department prior to 1913, but it was discontinued afterward. When Cai Yuanpei became the chancellor in 1917, he began to admit students majoring in history. A year later the history department, with fifty-nine students, was formally established. In 1920 the department produced thirty-six graduates. See Niu Dayong, "Beijing Daxue shixuexi yange jilue" (A Brief History of the History Department in Peking University), *Beida shixue* (Beida Journal of History), 1 (June 1993): 257–58, and *Guoli Beijing Daxue jinian kan* (Commemorative Volume for the National Peking University), 3 (Taipei: 1971), 47. I am indebted to Diana Chen Lin for the above information.

23. One such journal was titled *Shidi xuebao* (Journal of Historical and Geographical Society), first published in 1921. That the journal was edited by members of the "Historical and Geographical Society" (shidi xuehui) also suggests

that academic historians had been organized into professional associations. A more detailed study of this society and the journal is found in Peng Minghui, *Lishi dilixue yu xiandai zhongguo shixue* (Historical Geography and Modern Chinese Historiography) (Taipei: 1995), 61–138.

24. Many Chinese scholars have pointed out that Hu understood scientific method against his background knowledge of textual criticism. In other words, Hu filtered Western scientific method with his Chinese "screen." See Yü Ying-shih, *Zhingguo jindai sixiangshi shang de Hu Shi* (Hu Shi in Modern Chinese Intellectual History) (Taipei: 1984), 84; Lu Yaodong, *Qiezuo shenzhou xiushouren* (A Bystander to My Motherland) (Taipei: 1989), 180–81.

25. See Hu's introduction to his dissertation, *Development of Logical Method in Ancient China* (New York: Paragon Book Reprint Corp., 1963), 9.

26. *That Noble Dream: The "Objectivity Question" and the American Historical Profession* (New York: 1988), 52.

27. For the careers of these historians, see Q. Edward Wang, *Inventing China Through History: The May Fourth Approach to Historiography* (Albany, N.Y.: 2001).

28. Source criticism was not only the method in the historians' research, but was also the center of their teaching. Gu Jiegang's lecture notes on ancient Chinese history, for example, are basically his studies of history texts. See Gu Jiegang, *Zhongguo shanggu shi yanjiu jiangyi* (Lecture Notes on the Study of Ancient Chinese History) (Beijing: 1988). Another historian, Chen Yinke (1890–1969), received his fame in the historians' circle for his philological comparison of various texts, probably indebted to his sinological training in the West.

29. On January 8, 1920, Fu wrote to Hu Shi from Britain and said he was happy to be able to study science in the West. He also regretted that he had not done so earlier when he was in China. See *Hu Shi laiwang shuxin xuan* (Selected Correspondences of Hu Shi) (Beijing: 1983), I: 103–8.

30. Wang Fansen, who wrote a dissertation on Fu Sinian, has looked up Fu's library, preserved at the Academia Sinica in Taiwan, and found that Fu did not purchase Ranke's books until 1941. Axel Schneider, a German scholar, also told me that when Fu studied in Germany, he failed a couple of courses in philology and Sanskrit. Fu's many friends also testified that Fu pursued a broad interest in his European sojourn and seemed not to have a focus in his study. See Wang Fansen, "Fu Ssu-nien (Sinian): An Intellectual Biography," Ph.D. dissertation, Princeton University, 1993. Schneider's study of Fu Sinian is partially written into his article, "Between Dao and History: Two Chinese Historians in Search of a Modern Identity for China," *History and Theory*, 35:4 (1996): 34–53.

31. See Theodore H. von Lane, *Leopold Ranke: The Formative Years* (Princeton, N.J.: 1950), 28–35.

32. The journal's Chinese title is *Zhongyang yanjiuyuan lishi yuyan yanjiusuo jikan*; it is published quarterly by the institute. Interestingly, the motive of Ranke's disciples, who formed the "Prussian School" in German historiography, for publishing the *Historische Zeitschrift* is to make history useful for contemporary politics, as indicated in Heinrich von Sybel's "Forward." But Fu Sinian does not seek such a pragmatic goal. Instead, he calls for historians to hold a detached position when conducting research. In this regard, Fu is closer to Ranke's image as per-

ceived by most historians in the nineteenth century as an "objective" historian. On Ranke's influence in Euro-American historiography, see Georg Iggers, "The Image of Ranke in American and German Historical Thought," *History and Theory*, 2 (1962): 17–40.

33. "Ming Qing Shiliao fakan liyan" (Preface to Ming Qing archives), *Fu Sinian quanji* (The Complete Works of Fu Sinian) (Taipei: 1980), IV: 357–59.

34. Fu Sinian compares Qing evidential work with scientific method, but he has also noticed their differences and insists that one must use both, meaning to combine written and material sources in historical study. *Fu Sinian quanji*, IV: 408, 414.

35. *Fu Sinian quanji*. Fu's remark here was coined in G. M. Trevelian's phrase: "Collect the facts of the French Revolution! You must go down to Hell and up to Heaven to fetch them." *Clio A Muse* (London: 1913), quoted in Xu Guansan, *Xin shixue jiushinian*, I: 221, footnote 47.

36. *Fu Sinian quanji*, 1307.

37. "The Royal Tombs of An-yang," in *Independence, Convergence, and Borrowing in Institutions, Thought, and Art*, Harvard Tercentenary Conference of Arts and Sciences, Cambridge, Mass., 1936 (New York: 1964), 272.

38. Li Ji, *Anyang: A Chronicle of the Discovery, Excavation, and Reconstruction of the Ancient Capital of the Shang Dynasty* (Seattle, Wash.: 1977). Also Fu Sinian, "Bensuo fajue anyang yinxu zhi jingguo" (A Report of the Excavation of Shang Ruins in Anyang, the Institute of History and Philology) in *Fu Sinian quanji*, iv. Based on the investigation, Fu wrote an article discussing the new methods used in archeology: "Kaoguxue de xinfangfa" (New Methods in Archaeology), in *Fu Sinian quanji*, IV: 267–88 & 289–99.

39. Hu Shi, for example, told Gu Jiegang that "now my thinking has changed. I do not doubt antiquity any longer. I believe the authenticity of ancient Chinese history." Quoted in Liu Qiyu, *Gu Jiegang xueshu* (A Critique of Gu Jiegang's Scholarship) (Beijing: 1985), 262. In 1933, the institute started another archaeological project in Chengziya of Shandong Province. Fu announced that the new project was to probe the scope of the Shang Dynasty and to test the hypothesis whether Chinese civilization had been influenced by the sea. See "Chengziya xu" (Preface to Chengziya), *Fu Sinian quanji*, III: 206–11.

40. In fact, though Fu was interested in unearthed sources, his own study remained in the realm of textual criticism and comparison if we look at his major publications at the time.

41. When Yao returned to China and took a position as history professor at Beida, he was received in a meeting chaired by Hu Shi, then the dean of the School of Arts. In his introductory remarks, Hu especially mentioned to students and colleagues that Yao had received a long and solid German historical training, which left a strong impression on the audience. Tao Xisheng, "Yao Congwu xiansheng lei," in *Yao Congwu xiansheng aisilu* (Memories of Yao Congwu) (Taipei: 1971), 98.

42. For more information about Otto Franke and Erich Haenisch, see Mechthild Leutner's "Sinologie in Berlin: Die Durchsetzung einer wissenschaftlichen Disziplin zur Erschliessung und zum Verständnis Chinas," in which she discusses their careers, in *Berlin und China: Dreihundert Jahre wechselvolle Beziehungen*, ed. Kuo Heng-yü (Berlin: 1987), 44–46; 49–50.

43. Yao Congwu, "Guoshi kuodai mianyan de yidian kanfa," *Yao Congwu* (Taipei: 1979), 231–58. For a discussion of Otto Franke's view of Chinese history, see Mechthild Leutner's "Otto Frankes Konzeptionen zur Chinesischen Geschichte," *Deutsch-Chinesische Beziehungen von 19. Jahrhundert bis zur Gegenwart*, ed. Kuo Heng-yü and Mechthild Leutner (Munich: 1991), 183–208.

44. Wang Deyi, "Yao Congwu xiansheng nianbiao," *Yao Congwu xiansheng jinian lunwenji*, (Taipei: 1971), 11.

45. *Meng-ta Pei-lu und Hei-ta Shih-lueh, Chinesische Gesandtenberichte uber die fruehen Mongolen 1221 und 1237, nach Vorarbeiten von Erich Haenisch und Yao Tsung-wu*, ed. Peter Olbricht und Elisabeth Pinks (Wiesbaden: 1980). The translators write that Yao translated a part of the two books in the 1930s; see xvii.

46. See Du Weiyan, "Yao Congwu shi yu lishi fangfalun" (Professor Yao Congwu and Historical Methodology), in *Yao Congwu xiansheng aisilu* (Memories of Yao Congwu) (Taipei: 1971), 81–85.

47. "Shuo shiliao de jieshi" (On Interpretations of Historical Sources), *Yao Congwu xiansheng quanji* (The complete works of Yao Congwu) (Taipei: 1971–1982), I: 33–37.

48. In my recent trips to Taiwan University, where Yao spent his later years, I interviewed a few of his assistants and students. They all remember vividly Yao's approach to teaching the course on historical methodology.

49. Quoted from *Ding Wenjiang de zhuanji* (Biography of Ding Wenjiang) (Taipei: 1986), 136.

50. A detailed study of the *Duli pinglun* is Chen Yishen's *Duli pinglun de minzhu sixiang* (The Democratic Ideas of the Independent Critique) (Taipei: 1989).

51. See Fu Lecheng, *Fu Mengzhen xiansheng nianpu* (Chronological Biography of Fu Sinian) (Taipei: 1964), 50.

52. For the origins of Qing evidential scholarship, see Liang Qichao, *Intellectual Trends in the Ch'ing Period*, trans. Immanuel Hsu (Cambridge, Mass.: 1959), and Benjamin Elman, *From Philosophy to Philology: Intellectual and Social Aspects of Change in Late Imperial China* (Cambridge, Mass.: 1984). About the political conservatism in Rankean historiography, see Iggers, *The German Conception of History*, 63–89. A more radical view is shown in Peter Burke's article "Ranke the Reactionary" (*Syracuse Scholar*, 9:1 [1988]: 25–30), in which he charges that Rankean historiography reversed the sociocultural trend in European historical writing before the nineteenth century.

53. This is Dirlik's main argument in his *Revolution and History*, 1–18.

7

Transfer and Interaction

France and Francophone African Historiography

Matthias Middell

A frican historiography provides perhaps the best illustration of the contradictory processes that characterize history writing in the second half of the twentieth century: nationalization and internationalization. By "nationalization" I mean the use of historical narratives to bolster and stabilize so-called nation-building as well as the organization of a state- and nation-centered framework of institutions to promote historical research.[1] By "internationalization" I mean the participation in the international congresses and the publication of international studies that bring together historians from different countries. This also includes processes of cultural transfer that result from the collaboration of mixed academic staffs of Africans, Europeans, and Americans at African universities.[2] It also involves multicultural groups editing works such as the UNESCO's "General History of Africa" as well as the North American and European experiences of African scholars at some point during their careers.[3] These two processes are the decisive characteristics not only of African but also of all world historiography since 1900.[4]

However, in the last decade a third process has emerged, namely, the breakdown of larger national narratives into the histories of subnational or ethnic groups, as illustrated by the examples of Yugoslavia and Rwanda. Africa has not been exempted from the general pattern and thus has been part and parcel of global developments in historical scholarship.[5] What makes African historiography unique is that its very contradictory tendencies are concentrated within a short period of about forty years, or two or three academic generations, following the period of decolonization. In Europe, the phases of nationalization took much longer. Africa's place in world history and in today's balance of economic and political power influences its historians' self-understanding and self-assessment of their situation in comparison to Western colleagues. The greater importance of ethnicity in Africa as an interpretative framework for contemporary and historical conflicts is a consequence of the instability of the nation-state paradigm as constructed on the African continent.

The historical research on anglophone Africa written by British, Dutch, German, and North American historians is extensive.[6] In this chapter, however, I focus on the often underestimated relationship between French and francophone historiography written outside of France.[7] Here, I concentrate on the relationship between French historiography and the various forms of conceptualizing, writing, and teaching history in French-speaking African countries. It is difficult to present these in the same way as traditional topics in the history of history. Let me begin by naming four of the difficulties I have encountered.

First, at its core, is that writing history is a matter of language. During the French colonial and postcolonial eras a strong link existed among intellectuals from several African and European countries. France was not the only French-speaking country involved. Until 1960 French-speaking Belgian colonial historiography had a great impact on the formation of Congolese historiography. When Belgian academic institutions were confronted with decolonization, however, an entire interpretative edifice collapsed and an entire generation of scholars disappeared.[8] Although it is the most significant one for our purposes, Belgium itself is not the only example. In the former Belgian colonies, the Belgian academic system and, in particular, the structure of the University of Louvain played a prominent role.[9]

In reality, the concept of *Francophonia* is a very complex; it is not simply a language community or a union of states belonging to different political worlds yet culturally connected.[10] It has to be emphasized that Francophonia is not merely France's *chasse-gardées* or the area of its linguistic, political, and cultural reach.[11] The effects of the so-called francophone cultures in, for example, Africa on the so-called metropoles in Europe can clearly be seen in the suburbs of Paris, Marseilles, or Lyon, as well as in the corridors of the Bibliothèque Nationale or of the Ecole des Hautes Etudes en Sciences Sociales. Through the use of French as the official language the humanities in France—especially in the age of the renewal of cultural history and increased interest in ethnological and anthropological approaches—take advantage of the many-sided relationships with those countries that are culturally close to France. This advantage, however, is all too often exemplified by paradigms that are denigrating to the self-understanding of African historians.[12] It also is frequently interpreted by them as a desperate attempt to maintain an anachronistic hegemony.[13]

The second difficulty is that, when looking at the relationship between African and French historiography, one quickly realizes that French students of Africa are not very representative of historical writing in general. Basil Davidson discovered the same in the case of English-speaking Africa, and one can find similar quotations in, for example, Henri Brunschwig's histories of Africa. In 1976 Brunschwig wrote, with noted frustration, that the small number of French historians working on African topics can be explained by their reduced chances to embark on an academic career within a profession concerned primarily with the national heritage.[14] A consequence of this state of affairs was that these historians formed cartels around a small number of research centers and *écoles doctorales* (graduate programs). Although the same names appear repeatedly on the covers of French books on African history, they are absent from the discussions of the more general problems of modern history and historiography. The differences between the development of historiography in anglophone and francophone African countries can thus be explained by differences in institutionalization. Whereas U.S. universities have reacted in a more-or-less efficient way to attract students by creating new curricula when demand arises, the French system, with only a few chairs in African history and the presence of older colonial paradigms, was unable to respond to the needs of the new African academic historiography.[15]

But even outside the core historiography, in ethnological fields, it was difficult to connect the newer methodologies to materials coming from fieldwork in Africa. Structuralism in the French anthropological research focused interest only on traditional societies in Africa and legitimated historians interested in the dynamics of modernization.[16]

The third difficulty: Francophone historiography on Africa is a strange phenomenon because of the itinerant academics who define themselves as African historians. To make the confusion complete, they hand out their business cards written in both English and French and listing addresses on two or three continents.[17] Where are the limits of French-speaking historiography on Africa, and where do we locate its relationship to French historiography?

In the face of such mutual interaction the African case is hardly a model of linear influences in modernizing African historiography. Rather than impose a general scheme of modernization, it makes more sense to use the concept of the cultural transfer, which examines those elements that are picked up by the receiving culture and adapted for its own purposes as a result of deficits in its culture. However, we cannot dismiss the pressure that the West has exerted on African historiography to adopt the professionalization and institutionalization that have emerged in the second half of the nineteenth century in central and western Europe and in the United States. This pressure is stronger in the French-speaking countries then in other parts of Africa, because France has produced very specific institutional types in the humanities dating back to the reforms of the Directory and Napoleon.[18]

But it is not the colonial origin of academic institutionalization that was decisive. The career system at the West African universities of francophone countries follows a more-or-less uniform system of *concours* that a candidate must pass through in order to obtain a position. The mechanisms of selection are regulated internationally, by expert opinions within the Conseil africaine et malgache de l'Enseignement supérieure (CAMES).[19] In this way, African state authorities cannot manipulate recruitment for the universities and colleges, while ties to the specifically French patterns of academic institutionalization are simultaneously cemented.

Yet the processes of cultural transfer are mutual. The emergence of nationalist historiography in the 1960s can be understood as the application of a European pattern to a situation in which national coherence was to be created by the construction of mythical national communities.[20] The imitation of such a pattern, which had been particularly successful in Europe during the nineteenth century, has influenced many areas of African historiography ever since. However, it has produced hardly any satisfactory results.[21] Two problems stood in the way of the immediate competition between nation-states[22] as a primary scheme of identification as found in Europe. First, the current and historic relationship of Africa to the other continents was more important to the historical identity of Africans than their individual national histories. This can be seen with regard to the European-African-American triangle of slave trade or the postcolonial world, with its economic order of core and periphery. However, Anglophonia, Francophonia, and Lusophonia, as well as the Arabic north of Africa, created transnational communities that competed with the national paradigm. It was, above all, Francophonia's negritude that tried to react to this contradiction and was, at the same time in France and in other parts of the francophone world, further developed and used to promote very different identity constructions.[23] The other problem was the discordance of state borders or privileged areas for mass migration with those communities that sought to establish their identities by ethnic standards.[24] The conflict in Rwanda in the 1990s has made dramatically clear the extent to which explanatory patterns are formed in Europe—this time those of the strong ethnic differences and social distinctions between the Hutu and the Tutsi—and how they have been used to create antagonisms between social and cultural groups that then lead ultimately to genocide.[25] However, the "ethnicization" of parts of African history, as reflected today in the abandonment of political history and the great syntheses of national history that the first post-liberation historians worked toward, has also become evident by an increase in cultural approaches to history in the historiography in Africa in Europe and North America.[26] The list of such trends could be continued. Altogether, a picture of a cultural transfer emerges from which both sides receive something and "appropriate," in a very specific way, the developments that take place in each other's culture.[27]

The fourth is that the lack of knowledge of African languages has prevented me from gaining access to material that would otherwise aid my understanding of this problem. But even for materials in English or French, access has grown worse in recent years. The difficulty in finding the newer editions of historical textbooks from French-speaking African countries in the Bibliothèque Nationale is significant, as is the fact that the last bibliography compiled by the department of African studies at the Ecole des Hautes Etudes appeared in 1991. Accompanying the bibliography, which includes theses, monographs, and articles by French academics on African topics, was a statement that the bibliography no longer would be funded by the Ecole and the French Ministry of Culture. However, in 1995 Cathérine Coquery-Vidrovitch coedited a new publication that offers an overview of recent graduate papers, theses, and other forthcoming books by African historians.[28] Despite the great deal of published materials and surveys that reflect the development in special fields of African history, the question of transcultural relationships does not figure prominently.[29]

The title of this chapter assumes a relationship between French and French-speaking African historiography. Jürgen Osterhammel has posited a universal distribution of Western historiographical patterns as manifested in history journals, history departments at colleges and universities, and professional historian associations.[30] Thus, we must bear in mind both the nationalization of historiographies and the worldwide dispersion of Western values, patterns, and institutions of scholarly, research-oriented history writing. These contradictory processes have overlapped throughout the twentieth century. Whereas national historiograhies were established in Europe, North and South America, and Japan during the Enlightenment and the construction of nation-states, they also were developed through cultural interaction into one increasingly international historiography. In contrast, the former colonies of European states in Africa have developed their own national idea of history as a specific remake of the Whig interpretation of history.[31]

The idea of independent historical writing as favored by many African historians of the first generation after liberation was at the same time necessary and problematic. As Benjamin Ogot wrote in 1976: "Political independence could only have meaning if it was accompanied by historical independence."[32] But also, as Caroline Neale points out in a critical essay on African historiography from 1960 to 1980, "the new history sought to turn colonial history on its head . . . it was the older version upside down, with many of its faults intact."[33] Proving that the black man "lived not only in pre-literate tribal societies, but was right there in all the major events of 'world history' "[34] leads to a process of reselection of historical facts against the older colonial version. It also reveals a nationalist perspective that has accepted the value system of Western nineteenth-century history writing, whereby the West took the first steps toward progress centuries before the Africans did. Rulers supporting centralization and the creation of powerful political systems were evaluated highly in this type of history written in the 1960s. As a result, society was necessarily underestimating society when compared to the importance of the state. Decentralization and segmentation in this perspective were seen as negative aspects of the precolonial period in African history, and the slave trade occasionally is even presented as a positive phenomenon in overcoming segmentation. One can imagine that this sort of historiography, enthusiastic as it was, could not easily follow the other ways Western historical writing was evolving, for example, toward social history and, later, some sort of cultural and intellectual history that allows the very sorts of questions about intercultural exchange—the export and import of ideas and social patterns—posed in this chapter.

My point here is that after a period of colonial historiography (where for the first time, as Osterhammel emphasizes, we find an interest in autonomous historical development in African countries from the late 1930s, in France as well as in Britain even if the French professional historians were not so active as their British colleagues were[35]), there was a phase of a broader interest reflected in a growing number of publications and a professional institution-building.[36] It also could be seen in contradiction between a Western opening to internationalization as the new form of universalistic standards of professionalization, on the one hand, and the African efforts to nationalize their historiographies, on the other. This contradiction isolates the *africanistes-historiens* in France and elsewhere from the other constituents of Western historiographical fields—even if they felt this only on their return from field studies and teaching efforts in African universities in the mid-1970s. There was a remarkable growth of production on African history by African historians, by experts in African studies or people engaged in the broader conceptualized area studies. The number of items using the terms Africa or African in their titles in the *Bibliographie de France* increased, for example, from nineteen each in 1939 and 1945 to fifty-seven in 1961, seventy-seven in 1970, and to ninety-two five years later—that is, within thirty years five times more articles and books appeared on the general subject of Africa.

But this does not mean there was a link to the other developments within the system of French historiography or an overwhelming influence of Braudelian arguments or methods of other, now third-generation members of the Annales school on this new field of historical writing.[37] Of course, there exist intellectual relationships in the macro- or world history perspective between Braudel[38] and some African historians.[39] Otherwise, we can find links, for example, in the discussion on the importance of the slave trade for European, African, and American economies and societies.[40] That is not to deny that there were shorter bridges to the traditional forms, such as political, military, and other state-related history writing, but in France those ever-existing forms of historiography were more marginalized in the public mind than in Germany, Britain, or the United States. Thus, at least in part we can explain the marginalization of African history among the French historians by methodological orientation as well.[41]

The second assumption made in the chapter title is that special relationships should exist as created by the cultural consequences of colonialism, and realized for a long time by the use of the same language, that is, French, as the language of administration and higher learning. However, not only was language influential, but also crucial was the special patterns of the French university system (as we can see from the existence of the Ecole normale superieur in the French-speaking African countries). Although there was a general discourse of liberation with a very strong accent on liberation from cultural neocolonialism, those forms established or re-created by anticolonialist African leaders in the 1960s showed us that there is a permanent French influence in these countries on the organization and the presentation of knowledge, including historical knowledge. This allows French-speaking students and scholars from the francophone African countries to integrate faster than others into the French university system. If we look at French universities and the rate of Africans studying there, we will see that the numbers in different fields have been growing since 1960. A remarkable difference can be noted between the 1960s and 1970s, on the one hand, and the following decades, on the other: The political liberation from colonial status was followed almost immediately by the enthusiastic growth of so-called national institutions of higher learning in the African countries. People began their studies at these colleges, studied for three years, and went on to Paris or elsewhere in France for another two or three years to take their doctorates. Then they returned to their home countries to start a ''national'' career as administrators, businessmen, or even historians. Twenty years later the situation has completely changed: Now more and more freshmen come to France directly after high school and try to study not only for a first degree but to stay for a longer period of time.

With the founding of Francophonia, an organization established by non-French French-speaking political leaders of Senegal, Nigeria, Tunisia, and Quebec, this dependence of one part of the African system on post-secondary learning was both altered and reinforced. One example may be found in the activities of Agence de coopération culturelle et technique (ACCT), founded at a meeting in Dakar in 1989. This organization's activities, including historical ones, are based in France. Television programs broadcast throughout Africa are produced in France, even though they are created by Africans. The Ecole international de Bordeaux in Talence, with approximately 2,000 students (1992–1993) and as many as 10,000 during the last twenty years, demonstrates that the production of degrees for Africans means in part traveling to the former colonial power. However, the program to save African cultural heritage, which was adopted at the Liège meeting of the ACCT, focused on the development of African museums, the teaching of museum studies for Africans and Asians, and disseminating knowledge about Africa's historical heritage by printing catalogs and books. The program was an absolute failure, because so little money was invested outside France. Exceptions were the university institute at Niamey, the Senghor University in Alexandria, and the one scholarly book on a historical topic published with the support of ACCT.[42] Only in the area of textbooks do we notice a greater leap forward: ACCT supported an *Encyclopédie Afrique jeune* with one volume on *Les grandes dates de l'histoire africaine*, 30,000 copies of which were distributed in every French-speaking African and Asian country.[43]

The end of the Mobutu regime in 1997 dramatically showed that a special relationship still exists between France and the French-speaking African countries, although this common world is rapidly vanishing in the face of English-speaking globalization.[44] The discourse on Francophonia in France reveals more doubts than ideas about how to counter this development.[45] French efforts to form a French-speaking *mondialisation* with 400 million people living in the Francophonia, a type of second-level globalization, have so far been more of a defensive reaction than a program aimed at the future. Moreover, French financial support for this cause is decreasing and the concept of regionalization is centered on such countries as Central Africa and Vietnam or the Canadian province of Quebec, which have been in economic trouble for a number of years.

In his essay "Western Knowledge and the Non-European World," Jürgen Osterhammel presents a convincing description of the period from 1830 to 1930–1960. He writes that there was not so much interaction but a colonial historiography often written by amateurs (teachers, administrators, and members of the army staff). In the period from the 1930s on, the production of works of history was in some cases more self-reflected and open to possible cultural interactions between colonial Africa and European civilizations.

Two types of approaches were used to understand the development of African history writing from the early 1960s to the early 1980s. In a first period, the dominance of nationalistic points of view is very clear and there is a rich literature that describes this process. In a second period inside this phase we can see a process of professionalization in most of the African historiographies within a theoretically framework of more or less Marxist-influenced ideas. But the shift from the first, more nationalistic and/or autonomous period, to the second period was different in the northern, eastern, and western regions of Africa.

Until the late 1950s North African history was written almost exclusively as a history of events, an *histoire événementielle*, an approach that was applied to other parts of Africa as well. But in 1964 Charles-André Julien, with the aid of Pierre Renouvin, published his *Histoire de l'Algérie contemporaine*, which gave rise to several studies on the history of North Africa. These works took advantage of the methodologies being used at the time by the Annales historians. A combination of young French historians from a postcolonial generation and academics from African countries who were earning their degrees in Paris, renewed the field of African studies and set new professional standards.[46] The trauma of the war in Algeria created strong feelings in France that what was being lost were not merely colonies but an integral part of France itself.[47] Current events stimulated the work of historians on every aspect of the debate.[48] Decolonization has also had a profound impact on the structure of research institutions through the movement of archives, libraries, and special collections to France as well as the creation of chairs dedicated to the history of the Maghrib.[49]

In the Maghrib itself we can see a very early shift of the historians from nationalist concepts to more Marxist concepts with the integration in a developing field of Marxist discussion in the France of the 1950s and early 1960s. Some of the historians from Tunis or Algiers followed in the footsteps of the Annales school. Yet direct connections existed among the enormous role that was played by history in opposing colonialism, history's emphasis of national heroes, and mass movements against colonial power. This historiography oriented on "the nation" also finds expression in the use of Arabic as a form of cultural emancipation from French domination. The Marxist approach, in contrast, was strong in the field of analyses of imperialism and economic suppression in the colonial times, whereas the older forms of historiography, such as the publication of historical sources and the hermeneutic approaches, failed in this period. Between 1946 and 1961 the production of historical knowledge in French on the Maghrib more than trebled and did so again between 1961 and 1976. Compared to the production of histories of other African countries, French-speaking historians demonstrated a strong interest in North Africa.

Developments in sub-Saharan French-speaking countries contrasted very sharply those in the anglophone countries, especially on the east coast of the continent: Here, intellectuals, who were seen as societal elites and who were shaped by the system of Ecole normales, were more familiar with the French academic framework. They did not confront a society that rejected the West as their anglophone counterparts in East Africa did. Thus, differences among African countries depend on some extent on when the first concepts of a postcolonial history of Africa were formulated: Historians in the countries that had formerly belonged to the British Empire reacted to the idea of Africa as a world without history by emphasizing the old traditions of centralized African states. But here "nationalists affirmed the kind of past which imperialists had denied— there was no significant shift of perspective," as the Indian author Narayanan pointed out in comparing the similarity of developments in Asia and Africa.[50] This concept of a return to the perennial African potential in state- and nation-building supports the idea of military resistance to colonialism and of keeping the state's central position as the most important liberation issue.[51] After a decade of controversy, some authors articulated a Marxist perspective that there was more than an Africa–Western contradiction in this interpretation: "The tendency of recent African historiography to celebrate the rise of states is evidence that it is being written almost exclusively from the point of view of Africa's present ruling class."[52]

In the francophone countries, the concept of negritude, which was born in the literature of the 1930s but only later became important in shaping politics and contemporary history, concentrated less on "the state" and more on "natural leadership ability" in the African society. Here a cultural identity was created in a different possibility of Africans and Europeans to interact with nature. At its core a racial concept, negritude served to undermine the self-consciousness of former colonial history and reflected the search for another identity. Perhaps it was the more self-confident way of an elite in these countries to reflect their own ambiguous situation: shaped in France and for a certain time even accepted there as "black French," they were now looking for possibilities to translate this cultural capital into leadership in their own countries at the time of emancipation.

After liberation both of these ideas became problematic: the state administrations run by Africans were unable to overcome underdevelopment quickly enough to convince the people that traditions really worked, and the negritude position could not explain why these absolutely different cultures had to have the same governing institutions as state, administration, army, and so forth, as the former colonial power.

Responding to the needs of historical legitimation in contemporary politics, African intellectuals found Marxism increasingly attractive. On the themes of underdevelopment, exploitation in an international context, and the solidarity of the workers in all countries, uniting to go forward to a more or less socialist revolution, Marxism represented an interesting framework within which to integrate modern history. One cannot overlook the broad interaction of a lively institutionalized intellectual scene—for some time as bipolar as it was attractive—even when criticized today as an evolutionary modernist or nationalist paradigm born in the West. The professionalization both of Africanist historiography in France and of French-speaking historiography in African countries cannot be understood without the Marxist impact of people such as the geographer Suret-Canale, and the historians Coquery-Vidrovitch and Henri Brunschwig, who, even though they may not have been Marxists, were open to Marxist approaches. African historians were attracted not only by the political tone of emancipation from underdevelopment and imperialist exploitation with their partial disassociation from "Western traditions," but also by the search for a global interpretation of African society that suggested that older reductionist concepts could be overcome. But whereas the Marxist-oriented area studies in the United States focused on theories of underdevelopment and the idea of a parallel emancipation of African Americans, French Marxism concentrated more on Western themes and methods as structuralism and cultural hegemony. It was again also question of language: Whereas the French discussion for a long time was self-reflective and had only a loose connection to the Italian debate, African historians, even from French-speaking countries, were more open-minded and familiar with the Anglo-American debates and the contributions of English-speaking Dutch and Scandinavian historians on their topic than their French counterparts.

In sum, for about fifteen years, Marxism was the theoretical framework in the common discussion of historians from France and from French-speaking countries in Africa. Marxist historiography was less a closed ideology and more a language that allowed connections to be made among the different discourses in the West and in young African nation-states that were searching for a history adapted to the needs of modernization and integration. For more than a decade, strategies of emancipation in the West, in the East, and in the South have converged. Marxism provided very different communities of historians with the categories and intellectual tools that led them to think they could share the same discourse. A holistic interpretation of society and of an evolutionist concept, emphasizing revolutionary change as a possibility for historical subjects to deal with the hard structures of society, has led to a "common understanding." This description may seem overly generalized, but in this way Marxism has been functioning as a common language in looking for a compromise between different cultural traditions, historiographical approaches, and political interests.[53]

On the level of actual historical writing, this use of Marxist language benefited social history and its political counterpart, the *histoire événementielle*. The pattern of the Annales school of the 1960s fits more or less perfectly into these preferences.[54] In the political circumstances of the late 1970s the attraction of Marxian language decreased and a redefinition of methodological premises in French-speaking African historiography took place. What had been a vehicle of professionalization in history writing was now increasingly seen as a dogmatic prison. After the impact on synchronization of the historical approaches in the West and in Africa, history as a writing vehicle is now in danger of dissynchronization.

During decolonization the number of institutions that taught or researched African history increased in France, with three chairs being founded at Paris in 1960–1961; some specialized research centers being created generally in the Midi with good archives and collections taken from the national archives of the former colonies,[55] and with the founding of the *Journal of African History* in 1960 and the transformation of the former *Revue d'Histoire des Colonies* into the *Revue Française d'Histoire d'Outre-Mer* in 1958. As a result, academic production of historical studies on Africa multiplied between 1960 and 1975. This attracted students from such French-speaking countries as M'Bokolo from Zaire, who today is *directeur d'études* at the Ecole des Hautes Etudes en Sciences Sociales and the author of a history of Africa published by the Association des universités partiellement ou entierement de langue francaise–Université de reseaux d'expression francaise, another institution of the Francophonia.[56] This first generation of scholars from African countries, writing history as African historians within the framework of French academia, are represented by Mutamba Makombo, also from Zaire, with his doctoral dissertation on "Le Congo belge 1940 to 1960" (1978); Adalbert Owona on Camerunian national consciousness; Luc Garcia on the French conquest of Dahomey; and Clement Koudessa Lokossou on press and colonial administration between 1894 and 1960.[57]

There was no comparable acceleration of interest in area studies as was the case in the United States. French experts on Africa were so few that in 1972 they were concentrated in only one Parisian network, a group of advanced graduate students (*école doctorale*) at the EHESS and at the Sorbonne.

Yet even if the French institutional framework persisted at the same level as the 1960s, the situation changed dramatically during the late 1970s. Scholars from Africa introduced their intellectual interests into the French academic discourse. The general shift away from socioeconomic interpretations of political facts to a more cultural approach also influenced African self-interpretation. Of course, the period also witnessed numerous economic and political difficulties in many African countries.

In the 1980s different tendencies emerged in North Africa, such as the growing political importance of Islam as a means of independent development and as a basis for an independent historical culture. In an area where ten or twenty years ago interactions between French historiography and African intellectuals were exceptionally numerous, now the relationship is negligible.[58] The historians Mostefa Lacheraf and Abdelkader Djeghloul have looked for Arabic sources, such as Ibn Khaldoun, when rejecting a French version of his world history as a degenerated version of his thinking. Khaldoun is the author of an influential theory of decadence and is often presented as a founder of an Arabian non-Western historical scholarship. His work has been defended against European interpretations that are viewed seeking permanent underdevelopment in the Third World. Thus, a concerted effort to reinforce the intellectual links to France by non-Islamic historians may be contrasted with an open break with the idea of transcultural historiography within the Islamic movement.

In the context of research on sub-Saharan Africa, African historians teaching at Parisian colleges now emphasize multiculturalism and not just the French-influenced character of the societies in their home countries. They are trained in Western research methods and spend long hours in the archives in France, Zaire, or Senegal doing archival-based work. They apply the methods of cultural historians, not in terms of negritude but with a cultural and sociological analysis that authors, such as M'Bokolo, see as aiding a multiethnic, multilingual, and thus multicultural society, or on the specific character of the African economy with a larger informal sector and the ways of integrating into a globalizing world.[59] Here is a historical approach that seems to reflect the ideas of comparative historical sociology but at the same time that integrates elements of postmodern thinking on cultural differences in a very pragmatic sense.[60] The familiarity with French discussions and some theories presented in the United States as of French origin should not be overlooked.

More recently, African francophone historiography has been devoted to relatively narrow topics. The trend parallels the West's shift away from grand theory and narrative in light of postmodernism and toward a certain Afro-pessimism.[61] The decline of Marxist and modernization theories highlights similar developments in both the West and the South, in addition to effects of the internationalization and interdisciplinarity of contemporary historiography. Tendencies within Africa have much to do the profound crisis of the system of education on the African continent. Whereas universities had benefited from relatively large investments in the 1960s and 1970s, which were accompanied by a move to replace older elites, the situation has deteriorated since the beginning of the 1980s. The rapid growth in the number of institutions of higher education, and the concomitant increase in the student population, was founded on the belief that access to general education would yield a trained class that would have ample career opportunities in postcolonial societies. By the 1980s this development was no longer sustainable. African states reacted to the various financial crises and to the saturation of the academic job market by selectively granting university admission and by limiting support for poorer students. It is almost inevitable that this pragmatic reform in education policy, which was economically and socially necessary but was carried through in a particularly rigid way due to World Bank and International Monetary Fund pressures, created its own social and political problems in turn. University reforms heightened social tensions as access to higher education was greatly differentiated by social class and region.[62] Graduation from institutions of higher learning, even though no longer fulfilling the promises of the immediate postliberation era, still offered better chances to enter civil service and the middle class. But these tendencies led African scholars to a more internationalized career and to the discovery that even in France the educational market is under enormous pressure.

CONCLUSION

It would be hard to speculate on the outcome of these very contradictory tendencies at work in African historiography. The writing of history develops rather slowly and gives rise to both optimistic and pessimistic viewpoints. But an overview of developments since the 1960s seems to indicate that the relationship to France has been of considerable importance to historians from French-speaking countries in Africa. The presence of African scholars teaching African history at French universities today only reinforces this point. However, the interest of French historians in Africa—aside from a small minority of specialists—has not increased over the past two or three decades. Interest still is limited to a narrow circle of experts and has had hardly any impact on general historical debates. Part of the problem lies in the structure of the French system of higher education, whereby research centers and postgraduate studies continue to be separated from the masses of university students—despite all of the reform efforts.

The emphasis on multicultural integration of African history by historians in Africa, which has partly replaced nationalist concepts of historical interpretation and concepts such as negritude, has loosened the ties between French and francophone African historiography. This, in turn, offers a chance for a more intellectually balanced relationship, in spite of profound economic inequality. Instead, in Africa as well as in Europe and North America, historical studies have entered into new arrangements with cultural studies and anthropology, which look for the ambiguities rather than the certainties in the relationship between the "us" and the "others." But there also is the problem of an essentialist interpretation of cultural differences, bearing with it the danger of an ethnic overinterpretation of history and its use or abuse in political and military conflicts. It is difficult to predict which of the two trends will prevail in the end. Yet there is a chance that future African historical studies will be perceived in a transcultural perspective and noticed by others. Thus, the relationship between the history of France and that of francophone Africa has not come to an end but has been based on new foundations. This next part of the story certainly cannot be told only as a French–French-speaking African one.

NOTES

1. There is a large literature on this aspect of the African development in historical writing and research. See, for example, Bogumil Jewsiewicki and David Newbury, eds., *African Historigraphies: What History for Which Africa?* (Beverly Hills, Calif.: 1986).

2. For further information on the popularity of the paradigm of cultural transfers, as recently formulated in the French-German context of intercultural history, see Katharina Middell and Matthias Middell, "Forschungen zum Kulturtransfer: Frankreich und Deutschland," *Grenzgänge: Beiträge zu einer modernen Romanistik* 1, no. 2 (1994): 107–22.

3. On the effects, see Steven Feierman, "African Histories and the Dissolution of World History," in *Africa and the Disciplines: The Contributions of Research in Africa to the Social Sciences and Humanities*, ed. Robert H. Bates (Chicago: 1993), 167–212.

4. The best overall is Jeremy Bentley et al., eds., *Companion to Historiography* (London: 1997).

5. Albert Wirtz, "Klio in Afrika: Geschichtslosigkeit als historisches Problem," *Geschichte in Wissenschaft und Unterricht* 34, no. 2 (1983): 98–108.

6. Anthony Kirk-Greene, ed., *The Emergence of African History at British Universities: An Autobiographical Approach* (Oxford: 1995); Toyin Falola, ed., *African Historiography: Essays in Honour of Jacob Ade Ajyi* (London: 1993), emphasizes the different academic schools in African historiography and the main fields of actual research such as oral history, religious and church history, socioeconomic analy-

ses of trade and slavery, the more cultural approaches on education, and the history of intellectuals.

7. For a first attempt to formulate an overview of the last three or four decades, see Marc Michel, "Défense et illustrations de l'historiographie française de l'Afrique noire (ca. 1960–1995)," *Revue Française d'Histoire Outre-Mer*, 84 (1997): 83–92.

8. John Stengers, "Belgian Historiography Since 1945," in *Reappraisals in Overseas History*, ed. P. C. Emmers and H. L. Weeseling (Leiden: 1979), 161–81.

9. See, for example, the description in Ndaywel E. Nziem, "La Formation des historiens africains à la Faculté des Lettres au Zaire (1963–1975)," *Likundoli (Lumumbashi)*, ser. c, 1, no. 2 (1976): 1–42. It was only after 1976 that the academic staff of the Université Officielle du Congo, founded in 1956, was "Africanized."

10. On this topic from an African perspective, see, for example, Kazadi Nzole, *L'Afrique afro-francophone* (Paris: 1991); Sélim Abou and Katia Haddad, eds., *Une francophonie differentielle* (Paris: 1994).

11. There is a permanent interest in the phenomena of Francophonia and of the relationships between Africa and Europe leading to a rich bibliography from which we take here only some of the recent examples: Daniel C. Bach and Anthony A. Kirk-Greene, eds., *Etats et sociétés en Afrique francophone* (Paris: 1993); William I. Zartman, ed., *Europe and Africa: The New Phase* (Boulder, Colo.: 1993). Serge Michailof, ed., *France et l'Afrique: Vade-mecum pour un nouveau voyage* (Paris: 1993); Gintte Adamson and Jean Marc Gouanvic, eds., *Francophonie plurielle* (Quebec: 1995); Janos Riesz, *Französisch in Afrika: Herrschaft durch Sprache: Studien zu den frankophonen Literaturen ausserhalb Europas* (Frankfurt am Main: 1998).

12. On this in a more general sense, see Adam Jones, "Kolonialherrschaft und Geschichtsbewusstsein," *Historische Zeitschrift* 250, no. 1 (1990): 73–92.

13. For a short English-written review of the development in France before and after 1945, emphasizing the influences of Charles-André Jullien, Jean-René Suret-Canale, and Henri Brunschwig, see Cathérine Coquery-Vidrovitch, "Changes in African Historical Studies," in *African Studies Since 1945*, ed. Christopher Fyfe (London: 1976), 200–8. For the wide discussion in France on colonial ideology, see Henri Brunschwig, *Mythes et réalités de l'impérialisme colonial* (Paris: 1960); Raoul Girardet, *L'idée coloniale en France* (1972; reprint, Paris: 1978).

14. Henri Brunschwig, "French Historiography Since 1945 Concerning Black Africa," in *Reappraisals in Overseas History*, ed. P. C. Emmers and H. L. Weeseling (Leiden: 1979), 84–97.

15. François Leimdorfer, *Discours acaddémique et coloniasation: Thèmes de recherche sur l'Algérie pendant la période coloniale* (Paris: 1992).

16. See Claude Lévi-Strauss, "L'anthropologie sociale devant l'Histoire," *Annales E.S.C.* 15 (1960): 635. In the opposite sense, see the arguments in Georges Balandier, *Anthropologie politique* (Paris: 1967) and *Sens et Puissance* (Paris: 1971). What we cannot ignore is the fact that only a minority of French historians and anthropologists has escaped the structuralist scheme. Some examples are described by Coquery-Vidrovitch, "Changes in African Historical Studies," 204.

17. The multilingualism of the elites and of some parts of the population in general in African societies leads some of the Francophonia-experts to the alarm-

ing question, "L'Afrique noire peut-elle encore parler français?" (title of a publication from P. Dumont). For the actual research on the ability to write and to read French in the officially French-speaking countries, see Robert Chaudenson, *La Francophonie: représentations, réalités, perspectives* (Aix-en-Provence: 1991).

18. Victor Karady, "De Napoléon à Duruy: les origines et la naissance de l'université contemporaine," in *Histoire des Universités en France*, ed. Jacques Verger (Paris: 1986), 261ff.; George Weisz, *The Emergence of Modern Universities in France, 1863–1914* (Princeton, N.J.: 1983).

19. An exception is Cameroon, which has both a French and an English colonial past and has been a member of both organized Francophonia and of the Commonwealth. I appreciate the most valuable hints concerning the specific university regulations in the Cameroons that were supplied by David Simo from the University of Yaoundé I.

20. On the newer interpretation of the nationalist movement and the role the historiography plays, see the excellent overview by Dieter Langewiesche, "Nation, Nationalismus, Nationalstaat: Forschungsstand und Forschungsperspektiven," *Neue Politische Literatur* 40 (1995): 190–236.

21. Leonhard Harding, *Einführung in das Studium der Afrikanischen Geschichte* (Münster: 1992); Manfred Kossok and Matthias Middell, "Nationale Frage und soziale Bewegungen in den Transformationsprozessen der Neuzeit 1500–1850," *Comparativ* 3, no. 3 (1993): 9–42.

22. Jean-Yves Guiomar, "Vaterland—Staat—Nation," *Comparativ* 3, no. 5 (1993): 118–32.

23. Richard Werbner, *Postcolonial Identities in Africa* (London: 1996); Kwasi Wiredu, *Cultural Universals and Particulars. An African Perspective* (Bloomington, Ind.: 1996).

24. Okwudiba Nuoli, "Tribalismus oder Ethnizität: Ideologie gegen Wissenschaft," in *Das Afrika der Afrikaner. Gesellschaft und Kultur Afrika*, ed. Rüdiger Jestel (Frankfurt am Main: 1982), 97–116; Georg Elwert, "Nationalismus und Ethnizität: Über die Bildung von Wir-Gruppen," *Kölner Zeitschrift für Soziologie und Sozialpsychologie* 41 (1989): 440–53; Renate Kreile, "Politisierung von Ethnizität in Afrika," *Aus Politik und Zeitgeschichte: Beilage zu Das Parlament* B 9 (1997): 12–18.

25. Leonhard Harding, ed., *Ruanda – der Weg zum Völkermord: Vorgeschichte, Verlauf, Deutung* (Münster: 1998).

26. See the literature described by Andreas Eckert, "Grundprobleme und Forschungsfelder in der neueren afrikanischen Geschichte, *Neue Politische Literatur* 42 (1997): 48–69; see also the very convincing remarks by Sally Falk Moore, *Anthropology and Africa: Changing Perspectives on a Changing Scene* (Charlottesville, Va.: 1994), on Western upward trends in anthropology on the basis of materials from African studies.

27. The protests against the way African history is taught in French universities are one of the signs that today this process is really active and mutual. See Charles Didier Gondoal, "La crise de la formation en histoire africaine en France, vue par les étudiants africains," *Politique africaine* 65 (1997): 132–39.

28. Cathérine Coquery-Vidrovitch and Claude Chanson-Jabeur, eds., *L'Histoire africaine en Afrique: Recensement analytique des travaux universitaires inédits soutenues*

dans les universités francophones d'Afrique noire (Paris: 1995). See also Cathérine Coquery-Vidrovitch, Odile Goerg, and Hervé Tenoux, eds., *Des historiens africains en Afrique: Logiques du passé et dynamiques actuelles* (Paris: 1998).

29. Christopher Fyfe, ed., *African Studies Since 1945: A Tribute to Basil Davidson* (London: 1976); Caroline Neale, *Writing "Independent" History: African Historiography, 1960–1980* (Westport, Conn.: 1985). From an African viewpoint, see Benjamin Ogot, "Three Decades of Historical Studies in East Africa, 1949–1977," *Kenya Historical Review* 6, nos. 1–2 (1978): 25ff.; A. Temu and B. Swai, *Historians and African History: A Critique: Post-Colonial Historiography Examined* (London: 1981).

30. See the two articles of Jürgen Osterhammel, "Westliches Wissen und die Geschichte nichteuropäischer Zivilisationen" and "Einige Tendenzen der Epoche," in *Geschichtsdiskurs*, vol. 4, *Krisenbewusstsein, Katastrophenerfahrungen und Innovationen 1880–1945*, ed. Wolfgang Küttler, Jörn Rüsen, and Ernst Schulin (Frankfurt am Main: 1997), 307–13, 393–98. On the processes of internationalization of institutional patterns, see Lutz Raphael, "Organisational Frameworks of University Life and Their Impact on Historiographical Practice," *KVHAA Konferenser* 37 (1996): 151–67.

31. H. Butterfield, *The Whig Interpretation of History* (Hamrondsworth, U.K.: 1931).

32. Benjamin Ogot, "Towards a History of Kenya," *Kenya Historical Review* 4 (1976): 1.

33. Neale, *Writing "Independent" History*, 4.

34. O. Patterson, "Rethinking Black History," *Harvard Educational Review* 41, no. 3 (1971): 305.

35. Osterhammel, "Westliches Wissen und die Geschichte," 309. Further details in Brunschwig, *French Historiography Since 1945*, 84–86. Brunschwig is more skeptical than Osterhammel and underlines the break after World War II: "When we consider the period in question—that prior to 1945—the number of professional historians then concerned with the history of Africa, can be counted on one hand. . . . Typically . . . the concern is with the *French* in Africa, not with the peoples already there and fated to put up with their presence" (p. 86). The journals of professional historians have remained indifferent to black Africa with only one article dealing with Africa in the *Annales E.S.C.* before the late 1950s. It was Brunschwig who represented the new interest with two articles in the prestigious French academic journal, *Le monde à l'heure de la décolonisation* (1957), and *Histoire, passé et frustration en Afrique noire* (1962).

36. It has to be considered that the experience of the French organizing the resistance movement of France Libre since 1942 for a large part in African territories plays a certain role encouraging publications on African topics.

37. There is an abundant literature on the Annales school. See, for an overview, Lutz Raphael, *Die Erben von Bloch und Febvre: "Annales"-Geschichtsschreibung und "nouvelle histoire" in Frankreich 1945–1980* (Stuttgart: 1994), and the bibliography and the introduction in Matthias Middell and Steffen Sammler, eds., *Alles Gewordene hat Geschichte: Die Schule der Annales in ihren Texten* (Leipzig: 1994), 7–39, 356–71.

38. Fernand Braudel, ed., *Le monde de Jacques Cartier: L'aventure au XVIe siècle* (Paris: 1984).

39. Braudel commented on the approach of Ki-Zerbo as one of his own academic school: "Ki-Zerbo est des nôtres." See "Introduction" to J. Ki-Zerbo, ed., *Histoire de l'Afrique noire. D'Hier à Demain* [1972] (Paris: 1978).

40. Frédéric Mauro, *L'expansion européenne 1600–1860* (Paris: 1964); Pierre Chaunu, *L'expansion européene du XIIe au XVIe siècle* (Paris: 1969); Robert Cornevin and Marianne Cornevin, *La France et les Français outre-mer* (Paris: 1990).

41. Perhaps the most influential books on African history in French are Cathérine Coquery-Vidrovitch and Henri Moniot, *L'Afrique noire de 1800 à nos jours* (Paris: 1974), and H. Deschamps, ed., *Histoire générale de l'Afrique noire*, 2 vols. (Paris: 1970–1971). See also the remarks on Africa in Fernand Braudel, *Civilisation matérielle, Economie et Capitalisme Xve–XVIIIe siècle*, 3 vols. (Paris: 1979).

42. "Miroir du passé: grandes fresques du Niger," in Agence de coopération et technique, ed., *Rapport d'activité 1992–1993* (Paris: 1994), 47–55. Compare Agence de coopération et technique, ed., *Rapport d'activité 1992–1993* (Paris: 1994), 49–50.

43. *Miroir du passé*, 53.

44. For the specific French way to deal with globalizing tendencies, see Zaki Laidi, *Mailaise dans la mondialisation* (Paris: 1997), and Olivier Dollfus, *La mondialisation* (Paris: 1997).

45. Zaki Laidi, ed., *Géopolitique du sens* (Paris: 1998).

46. For Tunisia, see Jean Ganiage, *Les Origines du protectorat français en Tunisie 1861–1881* (Paris: 1959), and Jean Poncet, *La colonisation et l'agriculture européennes en Tunisie depuis 1881: Etudes de géographie historique et économique* (Paris: 1961); for Algeria, see XavierYacono, *La Coloniasation des plaines du Cheliff*, 2 vols. (Algiers: 1956), André Nouschi, *Le Nationalisme algérien* (Paris: 1962), and Charles R. Ageron, *Les Européens à Casablance au XIXe siècle* (Paris: 1955); *Les Algériens musulmans et la France 1871–1919*, 2 vols. (Paris: 1968); for Morocco, see Jean-Louis Miège, *Le Maroc et l'Europe*, 4 vols. (Paris: 1961–1963).

47. On the situation of the educational system in Algeria before liberation, see Hartmut Elsenhans, *Frankreichs Algerienkrieg 1954–1962: Entkolonisierungsversuch einer kapitalistischen Metropole: Zum Zusammenbruch der Kolonialreiche* (Munich: 1974), 114ff. In 1950 the number of Algerian students numbered only 436, whereas 4,316 Europeans dominated Algiers University. The idea of assimilation by cultural integration was failing in Algeria not only because of differences in the ability to mobilize Arabic origins but also, and above all, because the racism of the French was stronger and more explicit in a situation of confrontation than in l'Afrique noire.

48. Jean-Louis Miège, "Historiography of the Maghrib," in Emmers and Wesseling, *Reappraisals in Overseas History*, 70–71.

49. For further information on the archives and research centers at Aix-en-Provence, Lyon, Toulouse, Tours, and Tunis, Algiers, and Rabat, see Miège, "Historiography of the Maghrib," 72.

50. Cited in Neale, *Writing "Independent" History*, 126.

51. See, for example, Roland Oliver and Anthony Atmore, *The African Middle Ages 1400–1800* (Cambridge, Mass.: 1981), 29. The same authors argued in 1967 that the resistance to colonial power is legitimated by its foundation in modern thinking toward the nation and not toward the tribes. *Africa Since 1800* (Cambridge, Mass.: 1967), 158.

182 *Middell*

52. C. C. Wrigley, "Historicism in Africa: Slavery and State Formation," *African Affairs*, 70, no. 279 (1971): 123. See also C. Ake, "The Congruence of Political Economies and Ideologies in Africa," in P. Gutkind and I. Wallerstein, eds., *The Political Economy of Contemporary Africa* (Beverly Hills, Calif.: 1976), 204–11. It is evident from these very few quotations that African historiography in the mind of the majority of American authors is English-speaking African historiography.

53. Here we mention for the first time the case of South Africa that was included in the African historiographical discourse by the writings of exiled Marxists in the 1980s: Christopher Saunders, *Writing History: South Africa's Urban Past and Other Essays* (Pretoria: 1992), 71–80.

54. Emphasizing in a critical way the shift from the Braudelian era to the 1970s: François Dosse, *L'histoire en miettes: Des 'Annales' à la "nouvelle histoire"* (Paris: 1987); Hervé Coutau-Bégarie, *Le phénomène nouvelle histoire: Grandeur et décadence de l'école des Annales*, 2nd ed. (Paris: 1989).

55. On the precipitate transportation of archive materials from Alger to France in the moment of armistice in 1962 and on the destruction of the campus library with more than 400,000 volumes by the Organization of African States, see the bitter remarks of Mostefa Lacheraf in his interview in *La semaine d'emigration* (July 7, 1983): 205–39.

56. Elikia M'Bokolo, *Afrique Noire: Histoire et Civilisations*, 2 vols. (Paris: 1992).

57. Henri Brunschwig, "French Historiography Since 1945 Concerning Black Africa," in Emmers and Wesseling, *Reappraisals in Overseas History*, 94.

58. Mostefa Lacheraf and Abdelkader Djeghloul, *Histoire, culture et société* (Paris: 1986).

59. Robert Kappel, "Informalität als Normalität—Anmerkungen zu einem vernachlässigten Thema," *Comparativ* 6, no. 4 (1996): 97–119; J. F. Bayart, *L'état en Afrique: Las politique du ventre* (Paris: 1989); S. Ellis and Y.-A. Fauré, eds., *Entreprises et entrepreneurs africains* (Paris: 1995).

60. David Simo, ed., *La politique du developpement à la croisée des chemins: Le facteur culturel* (Yaoundé: 1998).

61. Michel Levallois, "Actualité de l'afro-pessimisme," *Afrique contemporaine* 179 (1996): 3–18; Megan Vaughan, "Colonial Discourse Theory and African History, or Has Postmodernism Passed By Us," *Social Dynamics* 20, no. 2 (1994): 1–23.

62. See, for example, the detailed description in Yann Lebeau, *Etudiants et campus du Nigeria* (Paris: 1997).

8

The Historical Discipline in the United States

Following the German Model?

Gabriele Lingelbach

The institutionalization, "disciplinization," and standardization of the U.S. historical science during the second half of the nineteenth century were embedded in the broader process of the reform of U.S. colleges and universities at that time. Until well into the 1860s most colleges in the United States were poorly funded institutions dependent on denominational sponsorship.[1] Expansion of knowledge through research was not their purpose. Instead, they offered a single uniform curriculum that consisted mainly of Latin, Greek, rhetoric, and mathematics. Students did not have the option of choosing their own plan of study. During the lessons, teachers read textbook passages aloud and asked students to memorize them. The aims of the curriculum were the development of the mind and the inculcation of morals and behavioral discipline.

In the second half of the nineteenth century, college reform became a persistent issue that either changed slowly but steadily the structures of existing colleges, or led to the creation of new ones. It is very often said that this change was inspired and heavily influenced by the model of the German university.[2] The emerging graduate schools with their new educational techniques—that is, lectures and seminars—were especially to have reproduced the German characteristics. We are told that the new insistence on research, the introduction of the doctoral thesis, and the emphasis on academic freedom of teaching and learning (*Lehr- und Lern-freiheit*) in the form of the elective system, and other elements of reform drew heavily from German precedents. However, the hypothesis that U.S. graduate schools were exact copies of German universities would be an exaggeration. It is recognized that the institution of the German unsalaried university lecturer (*Privatdozent*) as well as the German *Habilitation* found no counterparts in the United States. Similarly, the distinction between undergraduate and graduate education in the United States found no parallel in Germany. Of course, U.S. university professors did not become civil servants (*Beamte*), and the German practice of academic self-government had great difficulties in taking roots on the other side of the Atlantic. It is clear that U.S. university reformers borrowed selectively from Germany and adapted those institutions they chose to emulate to their own needs.[3] This chapter's task will be to explore the influence, if there was in fact one, of different features of the German historical science on historians in their efforts to implant their field of study in U.S. colleges and universities—a process that took place approximately one generation after its equivalent in Germany. Did U.S. historians draw from German "models" when they tried to institutionalize, professionalize, and standardize the U.S. historical discipline?

The answer to this question has three parts: some preliminary remarks on the concept of "model"; an investigation of the possible ways and means of transmission by which the U.S. historical discipline may have imported features of its German counterpart; and a differentiation between several fields in which an orientation on a German "model" may have taken place. In this third part, it is necessary to distinguish between historiography on the one side and the institutional structures on the other side.

The notion of the "model" is often used without precision in the secondary literature, but using it carries with it some dangers: It implies that there was something like *the* German historical discipline in the nineteenth century. But this was definitely not the case. A uniform, static German historical science did not exist. During the period when we may expect some orientation by Americans toward the German historical science, the latter was undergoing a process of change. Significant differences existed between those German historians whose lectures were heard by the first U.S. students coming to Germany in the 1850s, those of the so-called Prussian School some twenty years later, and those of the so-called Ranke-Renaissance in the 1890s.[4] Even within one generation of historians, there was no uniformity. For example, if an American in the 1890s heard a lecture or read a book of Karl Lamprecht or of Erich Marcks, clearly he was exposed to totally different methodological conceptions of history. A long tradition of competing and even antagonizing historical methodologies or philosophies existed in Germany. The historiography as well as the forms and contents of instruction varied from one professor to the next. The structures of seminars or lectures were different, too, from university to university. In addition, research institutions, for example in Prussia and Bavaria, were distinct from one another. The federalism of the German Empire was reflected in the plurality and diversity of its historical scientific institutions. The long tradition of competing approaches in historiography also undermines any attempt to draw a unified picture of the German historical science.[5]

This consideration makes a differentiated analysis of the processes of cultural transfer and reception unavoidable. Thus, we will turn our attention to the possible ways in which different features of the German historical science may have become known in the United States before looking more closely at the different elements of the U.S. case, where imported structures may have played a role.

One obvious and perhaps the most important means for Americans to inform themselves about the German historical science was to travel to and to study in Germany. At least 9,000 U.S. students matriculated in German universities between 1820 and the outbreak of World War I.[6] The exact number of those who studied history during their stay is not known. But of those historians who received a university professorship in history during the 1880s and 1890s in the United States, roughly 50 percent underwent a historical apprenticeship in Germany. To name only a few of them in chronological order: Andrew D. White, Charles K. Adams, John W. Burgess, Herbert B. Adams, Albert B. Hart, Charles H. Haskins, and W. E. B. Dubois. Undeniably it was a great part of the rising elite of academic historians who had traveled to European shores. Some of these—but not all—officially stated in their later lives how much they owed to their German experience.

On closer inspection, however, some of the shine of the so-called model starts to fade. After they had returned home, some of the U.S. historians officially acknowledged their indebtedness toward their German teachers, but this gratitude was rarely reflected in their private correspondence, where they almost never alluded to their student days in Germany. Some of these travelers even went so far as to make public their negative impressions of their German experience. They found rather harsh words for their professors and the German university system. At the end of the 1880s at the latest, many of the reports sent home and also the published articles were not panegyric at all. In other words, critical voices multiplied at a time when historical science in the United States had already achieved its first successes in becoming an institutionalized and recognized discipline. Exemplary of this critical attitude was Claude H. Van Tyne's 1897 description of a German lecture:

> The room is crowded with students and a horrible odor of beer. Several of
> these ardent admirers of science have in hand the remnant of a sausage or

sandwich. . . . Fifteen minutes, a bell tinkles, the door bursts open and like a
Jack-out-of-the-box in pops a snuffing, ill-dressed, nervous but fat old gentleman who dives into the box, and turning with a jerk, screams "Meine Her-
ren." . . . Now is all still. For three-fourths of an hour the professor's arms
fly excitedly, his voice rises to the highest pitch and descends to mere mut-
terings as he becomes lost in his subject. The pine box has become an abyss
of learning from which are extracted inexhaustible stores of the dry bones of
knowledge. Suddenly the bell tinkles. The gyrations cease, the shrill voice is
hushed . . . , and the professor rushes out encouraged in his flight by a wild
stamping of feet. Now this is funny once, but when it is repeated in exactly
the same manner at every lecture . . . it becomes a most monotonous
comedy.[7]

The experiences and impressions of these future U.S. historians in Germany were, for the most part, rather superficial. On average, they stayed
only two semesters in Germany, and their first months were devoted to
struggling with a foreign language most of them could not understand or
speak when they embarked on the steamer for Europe. Consequently,
only a few could profit from the first lectures they heard in Germany.
Scarce also was any contact with German students: Foreign students preferred housing with each other and spending their free time in club-
houses of the U.S. student colonies.[8] Many Americans had a rather
negative impression of their German fellow students, who they sometimes described as beer drinking, smoking, and dueling slackers. Only
few visiting students had personal contacts with German university professors who could have given them insight into the university system. In
addition, there were only a few Americans who studied intensively in
Germany. Most changed their alma mater at least once, and semesters
spent at universities were only part of a longer grand tour that also led
them to a study at the Sorbonne in Paris, to the classical monuments in
Italy, and to travel elsewhere in Europe. For others, meanwhile, the purpose of their sojourn was not the search for knowledge, but rather the
advancement of their careers. Thus Henry E. Scott replied in 1883 to the
remarks of his friend Albert B. Hart regarding the value of a German
Ph.D.:

I quite agree with you that a German degree is "a certificate recognized
everywhere among educated men"; and it would certainly be a great help to
you or to me in securing a good position in the United States.[9]

Depending on when, where, what, with whom, how long, how intensive,
and with which intentions apprentice American historians studied at
German universities, they could have developed completely different
notions of the "German historical science." Only a few stayed long

enough and studied intensively enough to come into close contact with German realities. A uniform image of the German historical science— even if this uniformity had existed—could not have resulted from these travels. The knowledge assembled during these stays about the methodology and institutions was in most cases therefore rather superficial.

In addition to personal experiences, publications about the German university system from a variety of sources represented a second, albeit limited, means by which U.S. historians informed themselves about Germany.[10] But most of these reports did not concentrate specifically on the historical science. Only a few publications, for example, such as those by the young U.S. historians Charles K. Adams, Herbert B. Adams, and Fred M. Fling, offered some relevant insights.[11] The translation of an essay by the Belgian historian Paul Frédéricq also presented information about how history was taught and written in Germany.[12] Nevertheless, on the whole, these reports were rare and most of them discussed not only Germany, but included descriptions of historical studies in France as well. They were also not often published in the central organs of the discipline. In the *American Historical Review* (AHR), Charles H. Haskins dedicated an article to opportunities for U.S. students of history in France, but no such contribution in the journal discussed German academic history.[13] Except Leopold von Ranke, German historians were almost never the subject of articles or monographs written by Americans. Properly speaking, it was only the German historical seminar that deserved more of their attention.

U.S. publications about institutional structures of the historical science or about historiography often made allusions to Germany, but these remarks were normally rather superficial and almost always only fragmentary. These scattered references to the German historical science could not effectively inform U.S. historians about how history was taught, researched, and written in Germany. U.S. historians could well have talked about and discussed their German counterparts and thus contributed to the spread of information, but that is rather unlikely. The regional fragmentation of the U.S. university system precluded frequent face-to-face contacts, and—to reiterate—the private correspondence of U.S. historians indicates that the German historical science was not an oft-discussed theme.

Americans could also have informed themselves about German historiography—this is the third and allegedly most obvious possibility—by reading the works of the scholars themselves. But how easy was it to get access to the works of German historians in the United States? In most cases, it is impossible to reconstruct the content of private collections of individual U.S. historians, and a systematic study of the purchases of German historical books by U.S. university libraries has not yet been undertaken. We do know, however, that several possessed a considerable amount of German publications in that field. The library at Cornell University holds the Andrew D. White collection of German books, which he had bought during his stays in Germany. At the beginning of the 1880s, Johns Hopkins University purchased the entire private library of the Swiss professor of constitutional and international law and representative of the historical paradigm in legal studies (*Historische Rechtsschule*), Johannes Caspar Bluntschli.[14] After the death of Ranke, Syracuse University bought his collection, and Yale purchased the private library of Robert von Mohl, another German professor of constitutional law. At least historians who worked at these universities had the opportunity to read German historians.[15]

As not all U.S. historians mastered the German tongue, it is worthwhile to determine how many German historical works were translated into English.[16] The list of German historical books available in English is not very long, and most of these translations were issued by British rather than U.S. publishers.[17] Such surveys as Arnold Heeren's *History of the Political System in Europe*, Karl Rotteck's *General History of the World*, Leopold von Ranke's *History of the Reformation in Germany*, which was the only book of Ranke to be translated in the United States and not in England, Theodor Mommsen's *Rome from Earliest Times*, and Heinrich von Sybel's *Founding of the German Empire* were published in English by Americans. Though an English version of Karl Lamprecht's *What Is History?* was also released in the United States, that of Droysen's *Historik* did not appear until 1893, and Bernheim's famous *Lehrbuch der historischen Methode* (Introduction to the Historical Method) was never translated. All in all, the list of German historical monographs to which U.S. scholars had access is not very impressive, a fact which calls into question the degree to which U.S. historians read German history books.

Visits by German historians to the United States represent a fourth means by which Americans could have learned about the German historical science. Some German scholars did travel to the United States in the nineteenth century. Indeed, Kuno Francke taught German cultural history for decades at Harvard. Hermann von Holst was, however, the only German academic with a doctoral degree in history to receive a chair at a U.S. university in the last quarter of the nineteenth century, and he didn't arrive in the United States until 1892. Because the structures of the U.S. historical science had by that time already been institutionalized, U.S. historians no longer found it necessary even to pay lip service to the German "model." While the impact of von Holst at the University of Chicago is difficult to determine, the fact that he stayed only for about seven years suggests that he did not revolutionize its history department.[18] The same can be said of those German historians who came to the United States when Harvard and Columbia universities created their exchange programs with German universities at the beginning of the twentieth century, among them Hermann Oncken, Erich Marcks, and Eduard Meyer.[19] These international contacts had no great impact because they were contaminated by growing international tensions. France and Germany considered the United States a battlefield for competing cultural and educational policies (*Kultur- und Wissenschaftspolitik*), which they understood as an extension of foreign policy. U.S. academic audiences realized that German professors, rather than concentrating on so-called objective, scientific historical investigation, were using their posts for the dissemination of propaganda in light of the coming war.

The different means by which information about the German practice of historical science could have been transmitted to U.S. scholars were less effective than it has often been supposed. The conditions discussed above impaired cultural transfer from Germany to the United States in the field of historical science. Nevertheless, the question of the degree to which U.S. historians actually adopted elements of German historical practice in the second half of the nineteenth century remains to be explored. This task is best separated into two fields: First, what were the methodological orientations of U.S. historians and what subjects did they prefer to address in their writings? Second, did U.S. institutional structures replicate elements that could be found in Germany?

The methodological orientations of the "scientific historians" differed in many substantial points from those of the German historicists. U.S. historians seriously misinterpreted German *Historismus* (historicism).[20] At the end of the nineteenth century, U.S. historians were—to say the least—not very interested in the methodological and epistemological problems of their discipline. Most of them were not very conscious of the premises that underlay their historiography. In rare cases of methodological reasoning, they emphasized only that remaining close to the sources was the sine qua non of historical writing: "No accurate history can be written which does not spring from the sources."[21] The establishment of the facts was the main task of historiography. The followers of the law-in-history school practiced this factualism. This school held that historical scientific research could discover through induction the laws and principles that determine historical development. On the other hand, however, were those historians who no longer shared this positivistic conviction but who also subscribed to the view that it was possible to look at the facts of history with the same detachment as natural scientists looked at their objects of study. For almost all academic U.S. historians in the second half of the century, objectivity was attainable through a critical analysis of the sources. They thought that this way of historical science was invented and practiced in Germany and that it was incarnated by Leopold von Ranke. Edward G. Bourne wrote in 1896:

The increase of positive historical knowledge, the elaboration of sound historical method, the enlargement of the range of historical evidence . . . [t]o these immense changes no one contributed so much as Leopold von Ranke. . . . [H]e resolved in his works to avoid all imaginary and ficticious [sic] elements and to stick strictly to the facts.[22]

Herbert B. Adams added:

Ranke . . . determined to hold strictly to the facts, to preach no sermon, to point no moral, to adorn no tale, but to tell the simple historic truth. His sole ambition was to narrate things as they really were, *wie es eigentlich gewesen*. Truth and objectivity were Ranke's highest aims.[23]

Most U.S. historians took Ranke for precisely what he was not: a protagonist of nonphilosophical empiricism.[24] Neither did they recognize the reaction against the philosophy and historiography of the Enlightenment that characterized Ranke's thinking, nor did they notice the impact of neo-Kantianism on German historical scholarship. They therefore did not adopt the distinction between the *Geisteswissenschaften* (humanities) and *Naturwissenschaften* (natural sciences). On the contrary, they often drew a parallel between the laboratory and the historical seminar: "Libraries and archives are for the historian what laboratories and nature are to the students of natural science."[25] The spiritualization of power that characterized Ranke's conception of the state also escaped their attention. On the whole, German historicism was coarsely misinterpreted by U.S. historians and often limited to mere techniques of research. They claimed to take out of the historicist paradigm what could legitimate their scholarship and thereby raise the prestige of their young discipline, even if it was not in this paradigm at all.[26] The emphasis on sources and objectivity also allowed these academics to distance themselves from those amateurs who practiced the historian's craft as a leisure activity. Furthermore, the late standardization of the discipline in the United States in comparison with Germany also helps to explain the importance of the natural sciences in the methodological convictions of U.S. historians. While historicism developed during the preindustrial phase of German history, in which the natural sciences exercised little influence on everyday life, the United States in the second half of the nineteenth century was undergoing rapid change fuelled by technological advances and scientific discoveries.

If Americans did not copy the epistemological orientations of traditional German historians, did they at least imitate their thematical predilections? In other words, did they put their emphasis on political and institutional developments as did the majority of German academic historians? To answer this question, it is necessary to distinguish between the different branches of history. Because U.S. historians of antiquity and the

Middle Ages could not afford to travel as often as they may have wished, they depended on research done by European historians. They relied heavily on the hundreds of critical editions of ancient and medieval sources that were dominated by German scholarship and were therefore inclined to emulate their German colleagues. In his work on Greek history, William S. Ferguson drew on Droysen; and the Egyptologist James H. Breasted made no secret of his proximity to the views of Eduard Meyer.[27]

Judging from the literature ancient historians and medievalists cited in their works, and that which they recommended as basic readings to their students, it is nevertheless clear that German historical scholarship enjoyed no monopoly of influence. French and English historians also marked the field. In his *Manual of Historical Literature*, a bibliography of important historical works in all subfields of the discipline that was first published in 1882, Charles K. Adams listed thirty-one books for those who wanted to study the general history of antiquity.[28] Of these, six were written by Germans, three by Frenchmen, and twenty by Englishmen. Even in the field in which Germans were particularly active—Roman history—Adams's reading suggestions included two books of Niebuhr and one of Mommsen, along with J. J. Ampère's *Histoire Romaine*, Victor Duruy's *Histoire des Romains*, Jules Michelet's *Histoire romaine*, and Henri Taine's *Essai sur Tite-Live*. When it came to the question of translating a standard work on European medieval history, George B. Adams of Yale did not choose a German work, but those of two Frenchmen: Victor Duruy and Gabriel Monod. Dana C. Munro listed French authors in English translation in the references of his canonical work on medieval history, but not a single German work.[29]

Historians focusing on antiquity and the Middle Ages were, however, a minority in the United States. At least until the end of the nineteenth century, specialization in subfields was not advanced enough to allow more than a handful of U.S. historians to concentrate on remote eras. Contemporary European history was also neglected by U.S. historians.[30] There was no reason to compete with allegedly superior European, especially German, historians, and their ethos required them to rely on sources. The documents necessary to write European history were, of course, not available in the United States. Most U.S. historians dedicated themselves, then, to U.S. history. In this field, there was almost no reason to fall back on German historians.[31] Young historians could find a huge amount of as yet undiscovered documents, and they were confronted with vast areas of virtually unknown territory. To be sure, there already existed a long tradition of American writings on the nation's history, but the new generation tried subtly to dissociate themselves from those earlier U.S. historians, whom they reproached for having written in too "literary" a style and not having worked scientifically enough—meaning not close enough to the sources. This younger generation tried to emphasize specialized professional skills by writing monographs about restricted topics rather than the large syntheses that had been characteristic of the generation of "gentlemen historians."

In the 1870s and 1880s, these young academic historians and those who aspired to a doctoral degree often concentrated on local history, because they could find the unknown source material they needed in the archives and collections of local and state historical societies.[32] As did most German academic historicists, these Americans treated mainly the development of political institutions, occasionally discussing economic and educational institutions as well, but they were not necessarily imitating their German counterparts. One should not neglect the internal origins of their focus on institutions, which represented the historical continuity that U.S. scholars wanted to emphasize. The ideology of conservative, antirevolutionary evolutionism found a fitting subject of inquiry in the development of slowly but continuously reforming structures.[33] It should not be forgotten that many U.S. historians were committed to the Civil Service Reform movement. To these scholars, the study of history was a preparation for the study of politics and government as well as for the resolution of contemporary problems. Thus Andrew D. White wrote in 1885:

> This is an epoch of historical studies. It is a matter of fact . . . that whereas in the last century state problems and world problems were as a rule solved by philosophy . . . this century such problems are studied most frequently in the light of history.[34]

In the United States the disciplines of history and political science were close to each other, as both played roles of advising policymakers.[35] By emphasizing continuity and the slow reform of institutions, historians wanted to show the way in which political and social problems should be solved. U.S. historians, who enjoyed little influence on contemporary politics, envied the more prominent political role played by their German colleagues, especially those of the Prussian School. There were exceptions, such as Andrew D. White, but U.S. historians could not, for the most part, contribute to the shaping and guidance of policy, like a Treitschke or a Sybel did in Germany. They were restricted to indirect efforts through educating an emerging political and journalistic elite to protect the United States from revolutionary or dilettante politics and to be aware of its rights and—more importantly—of its duties. These aspiring journalists had the task of influencing the as yet uneducated masses and of propagating reformism.[36] The cause for the emphasis on institutional history was therefore less an imitation of German historiography than the product of methodological standards and an ideology specific to elitist historians living in a democratic political culture.

After having analyzed the impact of German historicism on the methodological and thematic orientations of U.S. historians, I discuss the institutions that were created for the historical science in the second half of the nineteenth century. They were crucial for the development of the historical discipline because they functioned "as a mould that tacitly forms persons and capacities to fit the routines of the discipline and thus asserts continuity and stability in the discipline."[37] Yet, in spite of its importance, historians have not yet studied in depth the institutionalization process of the historical science in the United States.[38]

As it is not possible in this chapter to treat the whole range of structures emerging in the second half of the nineteenth century, it is necessary to concentrate on at least a few of them. Here it is convenient to distinguish between those institutions created inside universities and those that were independent of university infrastructures. Unquestionably, the historical science took root in U.S. colleges and universities rather late compared to its counterpart in Germany. Harvard created the first professorship in history in 1838, but other colleges did not follow this example.[39] Until 1870, college curricula normally did not incorporate history as a distinguished field of study.[40] In the 1880s the situation changed. In 1884, one could count twenty full-time teachers of history in the 400 institutions of higher learning in the United States.[41] Only ten years later, there existed already a hundred professorships in history; the structures of U.S. historical science were in place. It was the task of this generation of recently hired history professors to organize and shape the institutions of their discipline within universities and to form their own way of practicing their science.

If one looks at the lectures and seminars that these historians started, it becomes clear that they differed greatly from their predecessors. Most of this younger generation did not fall back on the recitation method but rather gave their own lectures and thus introduced originality and creativity into their teaching.[42] Nevertheless, these presentations differed in many points from what was said to be the distinguishing features of German historical instruction.[43] Most of the history lectures at U.S. universities were mere surveys on a rather elementary level and were presented in a very didactical manner. For the most part, these professors did not offer newly acquired results of their own or their colleagues' research, nor did they treat in a sophisticated way special points of history. This approach could have been a reaction against the highly specialized lectures many of them heard when they were in Germany and later criticized in their writings. But it is more likely that this distinguishing characteristic of U.S. historical instruction derived from the fact that their main aim was the preparation of students for their frequent examinations.

The main task of American history professors was to teach their students facts. The students had to reproduce the facts at least twice a year in examinations, which helped to standardize the historical discipline by selecting what had to be known. For that purpose, American history professors also wrote short lecture outlines for distribution to students at the beginning of the semester. These syllabi contained the summary of each lesson and the titles of those books that had to be read in preparation for each lecture. Students could often find in these syllabi examination questions from the previous year as well. Such features were not to be found in German instruction. The demanding examination system not only reduced the academic freedom of teaching (*Lehrfreiheit*), but also the freedom of learning (*Lernfreiheit*). In contrast to their German colleagues, U.S. students could not choose independently which classes they wanted to attend. Most colleges suggested or even required special lectures for freshmen and also occasionally for sophomores, juniors, and seniors. The students' liberty to choose was therefore much more limited in the United States than in Germany, where examinations were held only at the end of the average four years of study. Embedded in this teaching style is a notion about U.S. students—namely, that they were not independent, responsible, self-actuating people, but that they were rather young, imperfect adolescents incapable of coping with absolute academic freedom. The average student, who was admittedly younger than the average German one, had to be guided and disciplined.

Meanwhile, historical seminars were the place where the historical practice and professional habit were actually learned.[44] As previously stated, the historical seminar was the structure most often referred to when U.S. historians wrote about German historical science. These references were almost all positive. Thus wrote Charles K. Adams in 1889:

> At the present day there is no thoroughly good teaching of history anywhere
> in the world that is not founded on that careful, exact, and minute examina-
> tion of sources which was originally instituted . . . by the German seminar
> system.[45]

Charles K. Adams also claimed to have been the first U.S. historian to introduce the seminar in the United States, sometime between 1869 to 1871 (the sources are contradictory in this case).[46] He designed his course as follows: First, he determined the general theme of the semester. Next, he distributed questions that the students were to research on their own in the library. Adams also gave them printed copies of annotated bibliographies directed to their research areas. After the students presented the written results of their research in class, a discussion followed. Adams claimed to have imported these teaching methods from Germany: "Observation in the seminaries of Leipzig and Berlin had convinced me that even advanced undergraduates could use the methods of the German seminar with great profit."[47]

It is virtually impossible to assess the degree to which Adams's seminar actually resembled those he had attended during his stay in Germany. His personal papers are all lost, and his writings do not contain a detailed account of his German experiences. Furthermore, imitations of "the" German seminar were not possible, because a standardized way of organizing a seminar in Germany did not exist.[48] One valid generalization about German seminars, however, is that they were, in contrast to Adams's seminar in Ann Arbor, Michigan, directed toward advanced students. Consequently, Adams employed a more didactic method of instruction, and his students did not conduct original research. This evaluation is reflected in the comments of a participant in Adams's seminar:

> I question whether it is quite true to say that he [C. K. Adams] introduced the seminary method of instruction into this country. It should be rather called emancipation from the textbook and independent work along the line of topics. It certainly was not, in any sense of the word, the seminary method as it has been understood in Germany.[49]

Henry Adams introduced his own historical seminar at Harvard in the 1870s. He had not been trained as a professional historian when he began to discuss Anglo-Saxon law with his students at Harvard by criticizing the work of Sir Henry Maine. He assigned a chapter of Maine's history of Anglo-Saxon law to his students and required them to test Maine's arguments against primary sources. Some of the student's results were even published. Though Henry Adams's seminar at Harvard was more research-oriented than that of Charles K. Adams,[50] Henry Adams was probably not attempting to imitate the German historical seminar. His impressions of the German university system were so negative that he gave up the idea of studying there intensively after a short while and without having participated in classes.[51]

Johns Hopkins University (JHU) in Baltimore inaugurated its own variant of the seminar method.[52] Austin Scott, who had previously studied in Leipzig, presided over his first historical seminar at JHU in 1876–1877 and labeled it "Sources of American History." Between six and eight students participated. Scott was the "secretary" of the "gentleman historian" George Bancroft. Scott assigned questions as subjects for his students' primary research. Bancroft himself often read and commented on these papers, and it is possible that he used some of the results in his *History of the United States.*

At the beginning of the 1880s, Herbert B. Adams returned from Germany with a German Ph.D. and took charge of the seminar. While Scott had concentrated on constitutional history, Adams focussed on institutional history. This change was inspired by the experiences of Adams in Germany: "The idea was the outgrowth of a special interest in municipal history, first quickened in a seminary at Heidelberg, thence transplanted to Baltimore."[53] Adams also assigned separate topics to his students and gave them references to various standard works. The students had to present a paper to be discussed during the lessons. Some of his graduate students were urged to do their research in the existing archives, which meant with the help of unpublished sources. This seminar produced original work and contributed to the extension of knowledge. Its results were published in the *Johns Hopkins University Studies in Historical and Political Science*, founded in 1886. This regular seminar of Adams overlapped with the Historical and Political Science Association of JHU that was founded in 1877 and that held monthly or biweekly meetings.[54] Here, invited guests as well as the more advanced students read papers, and sometimes reviews of books were presented. Yet, because of a lack of student interest, Adams's attempt in 1883 to teach students how to examine documents critically failed after a single year. He had more success with the organization of an institutionalized seminarium with its own library, its own rooms, and even the beginnings of an anthropological museum and a statistical bureau.[55]

In some respects, Herbert B. Adams came close to what was said to be a research-centered German seminar, especially because he worked with graduate students. But even this ardent admirer of German historical scholarship said of himself: "From these German professors [Stark, Erdmannsdörfer, Bluntschli] he learned the seminary method of instruction which he later adapted in Baltimore to the needs of American students."[56] His institution was no blind imitation, not one to copy what he had seen in Germany, but an adaptation to U.S. needs.

In the 1880s and 1890s, historical seminars were introduced in almost all of the main universities in the United States. Their shape differed from case to case, from professor to professor, as did those that were inaugurated in the 1870s. There is one commonality that stands out: Many professors compared their seminars with the laboratories of natural scientists. U.S. historians tried to attain the same reputation for scientific rigor that was already attributed to their colleagues in the biology or chemistry departments. The seminar was a means to prove the scientific seriousness of the emerging historical discipline, and it was attractive to U.S. historians because it helped to standardize their discipline. Furthermore, the seminars could be seen as cooperative efforts to extend historical knowledge and to accumulate historical facts that would serve as bricks for the scientific, objective synthesis of U.S. history to be written by the following generation of historians. It needs to be emphasized that the impact of "the" German historical seminar, which, as already stated, did not really exist, on "the" U.S. equivalent must be analyzed on an individual basis. U.S. seminars differed greatly from each other, and in each case, the impact, if there was one, of the German "model" took a different shape. There were, of course, U.S. historians who attempted to imitate what they had seen in Germany or what they had been told about a German seminar. These professors were, however, compelled to take into consideration the institutional structures within which they worked and thus to adapt their conceptions of a "German" seminar to existing circumstances. And there were certainly cases where seminars were founded with no allusion whatsoever to their German counterparts.

Two institutions independent of university affiliation had a crucial impact on the way history was researched and written in the United States in the second half of the nineteenth century. Both the American Historical Association (AHA) and the *American Historical Review* (AHR) helped to codify the scholarly discourse among historians and channeled trends of historical research. The AHA was founded in 1884, several years before its German counterpart, the Deutscher Historikerverband.[57] Nonetheless, the AHA drew on European and especially German examples. At the 1891 annual meeting of the AHA, J. Franklin Jameson presented a paper addressing "The Expenditures of Foreign Governments in Behalf of History."[58] Jameson summarized the funding given by the German imperial government to the *Monumenta Germaniae Historica* (*MGH*) and the Archaeological Institute and its activities in Rome and Athens. He also discussed the financial support of the Prussian government for the state archives, the Historical-Philosophical Class of the Prussian Academy, and their publications, such as the *Corpus Inscriptionum Latinarum*. Jameson also mentioned subsidies for the Historical Institute in Rome, the *Monumenta Borussica*, and so on. The state-sponsored collection of sources MGH had already been introduced at the first meeting of the AHA in 1884 in the hopes of securing public funds for a similar project in the United States.[59] But the AHA and its Historical Manuscript Commission received only a small contribution from the government. As a result, they managed to publish only a few original documents in their annual reports. When Americans deplored the disastrous situation of their governmental archives, they referred to well-organized holdings in Germany.[60] When the AHA proselytized for a reform of history instruction in schools, they pointed to the German gymnasium.[61] German institutional practices were, in short, strategically used as a point of reference by the AHA in its appeals for reform or for public financing of the discipline's infrastructure.

The historical reviews, on the other hand, were less inclined to refer to German "models." In the early nineteenth century, the first attempts to create such journals came from numerous local historical societies. Their amateur historians had almost no contact with German historiography. The *AHR*, founded in 1895, represented the first attempt independent of university sponsorship to organize a nationwide historical review emphasizing "scientific standards."[62] One of the founders, the Englishman Henry M. Stephens, cited the German *Historische Zeitschrift* (*HZ*) as an example influencing his own journal, but only after the French *Revue Historique* (*RH*) and alongside the *English Historical Review* (*EHR*).[63] J. Franklin Jameson later wrote about the founders of the *AHR*:

> They were readers of the Historische Zeitschrift . . . and of the Revue Histori-
> que . . . which most of them probably regarded as the best model of what an
> historical journal should be.[64]

There were even some features of the *HZ* that met with disapproval of U.S. historians. For example, reviewers were urged to be less harsh in their critiques of colleagues than German historians in the *HZ*: "No one wishes . . . to emulate the controversial manner of the Germans."[65] In its structure, the *AHR* distinguished itself in its first editions from its European predecessors. As did the *RH* but neither the *HZ* nor the *EHR*, the *AHR* published sources. On the other hand, the *AHR* did not offer the type of systematic bibliography found in the pages of the *RH*. The European equivalents of the *AHR* served as models for the founders of the latter journal, but the *HZ* was not more privileged in this respect than the *RH* and *EHR*. German historiography was also not a preferred subject of analysis for the reviewers of the *AHR*. Of the 487 critical reviews written for the first five volumes of the *AHR*, only fifteen of the books reviewed were published in Germany, but forty-five were published in France and ninety-nine in Great Britain.[66]

U.S. historians were well aware that European researchers were better equipped than they were. They often pointed at those "models" in a strategic way, for example, to appeal for more government sponsoring of projects. But U.S. historians did not imitate slavishly the European structures. Not all European institutions found counterparts on U.S. soil. To a certain extent, this was because the state did not play such a central role in organizing and financing the necessary infrastructure, as was the case, for example, in Germany or France. In terms of the German influence on U.S. historians, when the latter referred to European examples, they also claimed English and especially French institutions as good prototypes.

CONCLUSION

The influence of the "German model" in the U.S. historical discipline was less pervasive than has often been claimed. The means through which U.S. historians could have imported methodological and institutional features of the German historical science were not viable in many respects. The reception process was affected by a low level of intensity and by selective and partially inaccurate perceptions on the part of the U.S. historians. Institutional structures survived the transatlantic journey in relatively better condition than methodological, philosophical, and epistemological concepts. The specific adaptation of these scholarly fragments imported from Germany into U.S. institutional structures varied according to location, personalities, timing, and intentions. To determine their actual "influence," a contextualized, individualized consideration that also takes into account the contributions of French and English structures is absolutely necessary.

Unquestionably, the "myth" of an objective, scientific, factualistic German historical discipline and knowledge about its high level of institutionalization, professionalization, and governmental sponsoring had an impact on U.S. historians. Their actual efforts to build and standardize their discipline were conditioned, however, by the local circumstances in which these scholars were working. The fact that the historical discipline was institutionalized and standardized comparatively late and under different historical and cultural conditions than its German counterpart therefore impeded the import of features of the German historical science into the United States.

NOTES

Special thanks go to Gregory Caplan, who helped with the English version of this chapter.

1. The history of U.S. colleges and universities is the subject of many substantial works. The standard work is Laurence Veysey, *The Emergence of the American University* (Chicago: 1965).

2. On the influence of the Germany university system on U.S. reform efforts, see, among others, John A. Walz, *German Influence in American Education and Culture* (Philadelphia: 1936), and Edward Shils, "Die Beziehungen zwischen deutschen und amerikanischen Universitäten," in *Deutschlands Weg in die Moderne: Politik, Gesellschaft und Kultur im 19. Jahrhundert*, ed. Wolfgang Hardtwig et al. (Munich: 1993), 185–200.

3. See Lenore O'Boyle, "Learning for Its Own Sake: The German University As Nineteenth-Century Model," *Comparative Studies in Society and History* 25 (1983):

3–25; Nathan Reingold, "Graduate School and Doctoral Degree: European Models and American Realities," in *Scientific Colonialism: A Cross-Cultural Comparison*, ed. Nathan Reingold and Marc Rothenberg (Washington, D.C.: 1987), 129–49.

4. The difference between Ranke's historicism, the so-called Prussian School, and the so-called Ranke Renaissance is treated by, among others, Friedrich Jaeger and Jörn Rüsen, *Geschichte des Historismus* (Munich: 1992).

5. The often-used "model" concept does not admit the difference between active influence and active reception. The German historical "guild" first showed an interest at the end of the nineteenth century in exporting (in competition with France) its research methods and scholarship and thus became active in cultural politics on the international stage. This happened at a time when U.S. historians explicitly started to distance themselves from their German colleagues.

6. This number is cited in Karl Diehl, *Americans and German Scholarship, 1770– 1870* (New Haven, Conn.: 1978), 50.

7. Claude H. Van Tyne, "In Heidelberg's Famed University: An American Student's Interesting Experience," *Detroit Free Press*, January 16, 1897.

8. See, for example, Daniel B. Shumway, "The American Students of the University of Göttingen," *German-American Annals* 8 (1910): 171–254; John T. Krumpelman, "The American Students at Heidelberg University 1830–1870," *Jahrbuch für Amerikastudien* 14 (1969): 167–84; Paul G. Buchloh and Walter T. Rix, *The American Colony of Göttingen: Historical and Other Data Collected Between the Years 1855 and 1888* (Göttingen: 1976); Konrad H. Jarausch, "American Students in Germany, 1815–1914: The Structure of German and U.S. Matriculants at Göttingen University," in *German Influences on Education in the United States to 1917*, ed. Henry Geitz et al. (New York: 1995), 195–211.

9. Henry E. Scott to Albert B. Hart, January 21, 1883, Albert Bushnell Hart papers, Harvard University Archives, HUG 4448.5, box "Correspondence— Personal."

10. See, for example, Charles P. Taft, *The German University and the American College: An Essay Delivered Before the Cincinnati Literary Club, January 7, 1871* (Cincinnati, Ohio: 1871); James Morgan Hart, *German Universities: A Narrative of Personal Experience* (New York: 1874).

11. Charles K. Adams, "Recent Historical Works in the Colleges and Universities of Europe and America," *Annual Report of the American Historical Association, 1889*, 19–42; Herbert B. Adams, "From Germany," *Amherst Student*, May 16, 1874: 66; May 30, 1874: 75; October 31, 1874: 137; November 14, 1874: 146; Herbert B. Adams, "New Methods of Study in History," *Johns Hopkins University Studies in Historical and Political Science* 2 (1884): 25–137; Fred M. Fling, "The German Historical Seminar," *Academy* 4 (1889): 129–39.

12. Paul Frédéricq, "The Study of History in Germany and France," *Johns Hopkins University Studies in Historical and Political Science* 8 (1890): 195–346.

13. Charles H. Haskins, "Opportunities for American Students of History at Paris," *American Historical Review* 3 (1898): 418–30.

14. An analysis of the accession books of the Johns Hopkins library produced the following results: In 1876, the first year that a large quantity of books was purchased, more than a third of the 1,726 works from all fields were German. The

following year, a fifth of the books acquired were German, but the percentage climbed to almost 50 percent in 1878. Among the more than 2,000 acquisitions resulting from the incorporation of the Bluntschli Library in 1883 are numerous standard works by German historians. The accession books are located in the Special Collections of the Milton S. Eisenhower Library, Johns Hopkins University.

15. The question of whether they in fact did it will be treated below.

16. For a list of German works translated into English, see Bayard Q. Morgan, *A Critical Bibliography of German Literature in English Translation, 148 –1927,* 2nd ed. (New York: 1965).

17. See Richard S. Barnes, "German Influence on American Historical Studies 1884–1914," Ph.D. dissertation, Yale University, 1953.

18. Jörg Nagler, "A Mediator between Two Historical Worlds: Hermann Eduard von Holst and the University of Chicago," in Henry Geitz et al., eds., *German Influences on Education,* 257–74.

19. Bernhard vom Brocke, "Der deutsch-amerikanische Professorenaustausch: Preussische Wissenschaftspolitik, internationale Wissenschaftsbeziehungen und die Anfänge einer deutschen auswärtigen Kulturpolitik vor dem Ersten Weltkrieg," *Zeitschrift für Kulturaustausch* 31 (1981): 128–82.

20. Georg G. Iggers, "The Image of Ranke in American and German Historical Thought," *History and Theory* 2 (1962): 17–40; Dorothy Ross, "On the Misunderstanding of Ranke and the Origins of the Historical Profession in America," in *Leopold von Ranke and the Shaping of the Historical Discipline,* ed. Georg G. Iggers and James M. Powell (Syracuse, N.Y.: 1990), 154–69.

21. Albert B. Hart, "Editor's Introduction to the Series," in *The American Nation: A History. From Original Sources by Associated Scholars,* ed. Albert B. Hart, 28 vols. (New York: 1904–1918), 1: xvi.

22. Edward G. Bourne, "Leopold von Ranke," *Annual Report of the American Historical Association, 1896,* 67, 71.

23. Herbert B. Adams, "Leopold von Ranke," *Papers of the American Historical Association* 3 (1888): 105.

24. Peter Novick also expresses this view in *That Noble Dream: The "Objectivity Question" and the American Historical Profession* (Cambridge, Mass.: 1988), 28. Richard S. Barnes even calls Ranke a "man of straw" who was instrumentalized by U.S. historians for their own interests, in Barnes, *German Influence,* 90.

25. H. Adams, "Leopold von Ranke," 108.

26. In some respects, dominant conceptions of historical methodology in the United States, especially those of the law-in-history-school, are more reminiscent of Karl Lamprecht—with whom many Americans studied—than the historicism of Ranke and the second generation of his disciples, the so-called neo-Rankeans.

27. E. Christian Kopff, "William Scott Ferguson," in *American Historians, 1866–1912,* ed. Clyde N. Wilson (Detroit: 1986), 92–97; William J. Murnane, "James Henry Breasted," in Wilson, *American Historians,* 53–64.

28. Charles K. Adams, *A Manual of Historical Literature* (New York: 1882).

29. Dana C. Munro, *A History of the Middle Ages* (New York: 1902). Hans Rudolf Guggisberg discusses the American medievalists in his *Das europäische Mittelalter im amerikanischen Geschichtsdenken des 19. und 20. Jahrhunderts* (Basel: 1964).

30. Of the approximately 400 articles that appeared in the _American Historical Review_ before 1915, only eight treated European history after 1815. Figures cited in J. Franklin Jameson, "The _American Historical Review_, 1895–1920," _American Historical Review_ 26 (1920): 17.

31. Von Holst was the only one to have treated U.S. history according to allegedly scientific standards in his _The Constitutional and Political History of the United States_, 8 vols. (Chicago: 1876–1892).

32. The increasing mobility of U.S. historians in an ever stronger academic market counteracted this concentration on local history.

33. The scientific historians of the first generation took the claim of continuity so far that they attempted, through the use of the Teutonic Germ Theory, to place the origins of U.S. democratic and liberal institutions to the Teutonic tribes. This effort to trace a racial kinship between Germany and the United States was popular in the 1880s but was increasingly rejected in the 1890s. The "Imperial School" around Herbert L. Osgood, Charles M. Andrews, and others then investigated mainly the English background of U.S. colonial history. It is worthy of note that the connection of U.S. and English history occurred at a time when the foreign affairs of the German Empire were undercutting U.S. sympathies for Germany.

34. Andrew D. White, "On Studies in General History and the History of Civilization," _Papers of the American Historical Association_ 1 (1885): 69.

35. The disciplinary unity of "historico-politics" disintegrated at the turn of the turn of the century. See Dorothy Ross, _The Origins of American Social Science_ (Cambridge, Mass.: 1991), 257–300.

36. See Jurgen Herbst, _The German Historical School in the American Scholarship. A Study in the Transfer of Culture_ (Ithaca, N.Y.: 1965), 161–202. It could be supposed that some former historians with activist inclinations switched to the social sciences. For example, Albert B. Hart and John W. Burgess tended increasingly toward political science, and Albion W. Small transferred to the young discipline of sociology. The advisory role of historians became more important during the imperialistic phase of U.S. foreign policy. Historians sat on the commission appointed by President Cleveland that dealt with the Venezuelan boundary controversy. They were also active in the peace negotiations following World War I. See Jonathan M. Nielson, _American Historians in War and Peace: Patriotism, Diplomacy, and the Paris Peace Conference 1919_ (Dubuque, Iowa: 1994).

37. Lutz Raphael, "Organisational Frameworks of University Life and Their Impact on Historiographical Practice," in _History-Making: The Intellectual and Social Formation of a Discipline_, ed. Rolf Torstendahl and Irmline Veit-Brause (Stockholm: 1996), 151.

38. See Gabriele Lingelbach, _Die Institutionalisierung der Geschichtswissenschaft in Frankreich und den USA von den 1860er Jahren bis zum Beginn des 20. Jahrhunderts_ (Göttingen: forthcoming).

39. See Ephraim Emerton, "History 1838–1929," in _The Development of Harvard University Since the Inauguration of President Eliot, 1869–1929_, ed. Samuel E. Morison (Cambridge, Mass.: 1930), 150–77; Robert A. McCaughey, "The Transformation of American Life: Harvard University, 1821–1892," _Perspectives in American History_ 8 (1974): 239–332.

40. See the first three chapters of Oliver M. Keels, "The Beginnings of Modern Curricula of History in American Colleges and Universities," Ph.D. dissertation, Indiana University, 1983.

41. Figures cited in John Higham, *History: Professional Scholarship in America*, new ed. (Baltimore: 1983), 4.

42. Not all of the U.S. historians who had studied in Germany discarded the old forms of historical instruction with which they had become familiar during their college years in the United States. Specifically, several professors continued to use textbooks. The example of Andrew D. White at the University of Michigan in the 1850s and 1860s can be cited here. See Ruth Bordin, *Andrew Dickson White: Teacher of History* (Ann Arbor, Mich.: 1958).

43. Charles K. Adams,for example, had the following image of German lectures: "In the lecture-room he [the student] will find that the work done by the professor has for the highest object the opening of avenues of research and the guiding of the student in certain methods of thought and investigation" (Charles K. Adams, "On Methods of Teaching History," in *Methods of Teaching History*, ed. G. Stanley Hall [Boston: 1883], 175–76).

44. See Walter P. Webb, "The Historical Seminar: Its Outer Shell and Its Inner Spirit," *Mississippi Valley Historical Review* 42 (1955): 3–23.

45. C. Adams, "Recent Historical Work," 37.

46. See James Turner and Paul Bernard, "The Prussian Road to University? German Models and the University of Michigan, 1837–c. 1895," in *Intellectual History and Academic Culture at the University of Michigan: Fresh Explorations*, ed. Margaret A. Lourie (Ann Arbor, Mich.: 1989), 9–37.

47. C. Adams, "Recent Historical Work," 25.

48. *Seminarium* in nineteenth-century German had two potential meanings. It could signify a semiautonomous department inside or even outside the university. Classes for advanced students were held in this type of *seminarium*, which usually would have its own library in which students wrote their theses or did original research. Conversely, it could mean a weekly colloquium of advanced students who were introduced by their professor to scientific research techniques. Even this introduction could have been organized in different ways: by learning how to decipher original documents, by going to the antiquity collection of a nearby museum and analyzing an ancient inscription, or by shaping a student's presented paper, which would be commented on by the professor or discussed by the entire class.

49. Lucy M. Salmon, as cited in Charles Forster Smith, *Charles Kendall Adams: A Life-Sketch* (Madison, Wis.: 1924), 17.

50. See Deborah L. Haines, "Scientific History As a Teaching Method: The Formative Years," *Journal of American History* 63 (1976–1977): 892–912.

51. Henry Adams, *The Education of Henry Adams: An Autobiography* (Boston: 1918), 75–76.

52. See Herbert B. Adams, "Special Methods of Historical Study As Pursued at the Johns Hopkins University and at Smith College," in Hall, *Methods of Teaching History*, 149–69.

53. H. Adams, "New Methods of Study in History," 101.

54. See Marvin E. Gettleman, "Introduction," in *The Johns Hopkins University Seminary of History and Politics: The Records of an American Educational Institution, 1877–1912*, ed. Marvin E. Gettleman, 2 vols. (New York: 1986), 1: 3–82.

55. Herbert B. Adams, "Seminary Libraries and University Extension," *Johns Hopkins University Studies in Historical and Political Science* 5 (1887): 443–69.

56. Herbert B. Adams, "Autobiographical Sketch," 6, Adams papers, Milton S. Eisenhower Library, Special Collections, JHU, box 32.

57. A short discussion of the early years of the AHA can be found in J. Franklin Jameson, "Early Days of the American Historical Association," *American Historical Review* 40 (1934): 1–9.

58. Franklin J. Jameson, "The Expenditures of Foreign Governments in Behalf of History," *Annual Report of the American Historical Association, 1891*, 33–61.

59. This report was compiled by Kuno Francke; see Herbert B. Adams, "Secretary's Report of the Organization and Proceedings, Saratoga, September 9–10, 1884," *Papers of the American Historical Association* 1 (1886): 31–32.

60. See Arthur S. Link, "The American Historical Association 1884–1984: Retrospect and Prospect," *American Historical Review* 90 (1985): 1–17, esp. 11.

61. This statement refers only to the decades before 1900. Thereafter, however, the reformers had more self-confidence and thus pointed less to European or German "models"; see Hartmut Lehmann, "Deutsche Geschichtswissenschaft als Vorbild. Eine Untersuchung der American Historical Association über den Geschichtsunterricht an deutschen Gymnasien in den Jahren 1896–98," in *Aus Reichsgeschichte und nordischer Geschichte*, ed. Horst Fuhrmann et al. (Stuttgart: 1972), 384–96.

62. See Gabriele Lingelbach, "Die *American Historical Review*. Gründung und Entwicklung einer geschichtswissenschaftlichen Institution," in *Historische Zeitschriften im internationalen Vergleich*, ed. Matthias Middell (Leipzig: 1999), 33–62.

63. Henry M. Stephens to J. Franklin Jameson, February 17, 1895, Jameson papers, Library of Congress, Manuscript Division, box 51.

64. Jameson, "The *American Historical Review*," 2.

65. Jameson, "The *American Historical Review*," 13.

66. These figures may inform us also about the actual reading practice of U.S. historians at the end of the nineteenth century. On the rare engagement of U.S. historians with German history, see Fritz Stern, "German History in America, 1884–1914," *Central European History* 19 (1986): 131–63.

9

🎋

The Politics of the
Republic of Learning

International Scientific Congresses in Europe, the Pacific Rim, and Latin America

Eckhardt Fuchs

The internationalization of science and scientific institutions is a product of nineteenth-century Europe. Cross-boundary scientific contacts
existed long before the nineteenth century, and scientific cosmopolitanism has a long tradition in Europe. However, the technological and
economic developments of the Industrial Revolution and the internationalization of political life, beginning with the Congress of Vienna, were the
events that created the necessary conditions for the scientific internationalism that emerged in the mid-nineteenth century. It also resulted from
changes within the scientific process itself and was characterized above
all by intensified scientific contacts across borders. The need for general
coordination, standardization, and institutionalized exchange of the rapidly growing volume of research, the necessity for international cooperation on large-scale projects, and the need for exchanging current research
results led to new forms of international scientific relations.[1]

The establishment of international scientific congresses became
extremely important in the process of scientific internationalization. Not
only did they offer a regular meeting place where scientists could share

their most recent findings, but they also frequently provided the occasion for the establishment of international scientific organizations. It was at these congresses that an international community of scholars was created. The dimension of this form of international scientific cooperation becomes apparent when one looks at the trend in the number of international congresses being held. The first two congresses were held in 1798 in Gotha and Paris, but the real surge did not come until after 1850.[2] Five congresses took place in 1857 and ten in 1865. In 1889, when the World's Fair was held in Paris, the number reached 111. The quantitative high points of the congress movement prior to World War I were in 1900 (World's Fair in Paris), 1910, and 1913, with 232, 258, and 237 meetings, respectively.[3] In short, the number of congresses quintupled in the two decades between 1880 and 1900.[4] Whereas an average of ten congresses a year took place between 1860 and 1869, the number grew to 135 in the first decade of the new century, and to 230 between 1910 and 1913.[5]

In this essay I will analyze the character of scientific internationalism between 1850 and 1920 by way of comparing different types of scientific congresses in three geographical and cultural areas: Europe, the Pacific Rim, and Latin America. In the case of Europe, the international congresses of historians and orientalists are treated (part one and two). The orientalists were selected as a case study in addition to the historians because, in the course of the professionalization of European historical science, the non-European world fell outside the focus of a nationally oriented historiography; along with philology and archeology, it became the subject of a peripheral discipline: oriental studies. Oriental studies, therefore, represents an ideal discipline for examining the geographical and cultural expansion of the international scientific community because its very subject matter is transcultural.[6] In the third and fourth parts, I will look at scientific internationalism outside Europe and investigate the Pan-Pacific and Pan-American scientific congresses. In contrast to Europe, international congresses in these regions did not start on a disciplinary basis but began as enterprises of scientific institutions that embraced many of the natural sciences and the humanities.

In all sections I focus on four issues: first, the origins and structures of the congresses; second, the scientific ethos of the international community of scholars; third, the geographical realm and cultural boundaries of the congresses; and fourth, the political goals and limitations of the congresses. In discussing these topics I also hope to show the shift of the geographical center of scientific internationalism from Europe toward the United States during and after the outbreak of World War I, a war that led ultimately to the collapse of international scientific cooperation between European countries. I argue that, despite the expansion of the geographical scope of international scientific cooperation, neither the political, non-scientific implications underlying the congresses, nor the conception of science itself differed from those of the European, prewar congresses. At the same time, however, these congresses provided a forum in which a specific regional and cultural self-awareness could be articulated in the context of major political developments such as the Pan-American and Pan-Pacific movements.[7]

EUROPE: THE INTERNATIONAL
CONGRESSES OF HISTORIANS

When one looks at the development of international congresses of historians in relation to the general history of congresses, one cannot say either that historians were taken over "relatively late" by the congress wave, nor that the historian congresses beginning in 1898 were a "typical example" of the "new practice of organizing international scientific congresses."[8] Chronologically, history congresses followed those in such disciplines as astronomy, geography, archeology, geology, and psychology, but among the humanities they came before philosophy and sociology. Even physics congresses came later, and the mathematicians met only one year before the historians.

As with other international congresses—compare the role of A. Quetelets in the statisticians' congresses and that of A. Kekulés for the chemists[9]—the establishment of history congresses was based initially on private efforts, in this case by de Maulde, a Frenchman interested in history.[10] As chairman of a national society, the Société d'Histoire Diplomatique, founded in 1886, he had an existing organization at his disposal.[11] However, in contrast to developments in most of the other sciences, this organization was outside the ranks of professional historians. Thus, the impetus for establishing international meetings of historians did not come from history professors, but de Maulde's proposal did arouse their interest. Despite the difficulties involved in organizing the first congresses in Paris in 1900, Rome in 1903, and Berlin in 1908, the initial response of the established brotherhood was one of approval. German historian Georg von Below, in his evaluation of the inaugural congress, urged that the endeavor be continued, though he expected nothing more from these international meetings than personal contacts and making of presentations, which hardly permitted any real progress for (national) historiography.[12]

However, resistance to the congresses was voiced early, as well. The proposal of French historians at the 1903 congress in Rome that the next meeting be held in Berlin in 1908 met with little sympathy from historians there. Supporters of the idea included Adolf von Harnack, probably the most ardent scientific internationalist, classical philologist von Wilamow-itz-Moellendorf, and legal historian von Gierke. Others, however, complained that such a congress would bear little scientific fruit. Their complaint was probably not entirely unjustified judging from the preceding congresses. The influence of political and national conflicts on historiography, argued the skeptics, left little room for consensus in the scientific discussion. The majority of historians had a nationalist orientation and a corresponding tendency to distance themselves from new perspectives in historiography, such as those represented by the appearance of Henry Berr in Paris (which was, after all, a congress of comparative historiography) or in Rome by a turning away from historical idealism toward a scientistic conception of history. The congress took place in Berlin anyway, not because these reservations were laid to rest, but because the German historians realized that refusal would be seen as an act of international rudeness and they feared losing their opportunity to influence the form and content of the congresses.[13] It was therefore matters of politics and science policy, rather than purely scientific factors, that convinced the Berlin historians of the necessity of the congress, at which they did not even deliver a plenary address. The French, too, started showing less interest in the congresses. While they were well represented in Rome, they sent only a few delegates to Berlin and London.

The study of history began to be professionalized in Europe as an academic discipline, with its main focus on national history. This did not require international cooperation. Indeed, the historiography of foreign historians regarding one's own national history was often either disregarded or rejected as incompetent. It is no wonder, then, that the first international history congresses were more social than scientific events, at which the exchange of new historical findings was of secondary concern.

A look at the participants and subjects of the first congresses shows that non-European historiography was a marginal phenomenon, as table 9.1 indicates. Additionally, no congress took place outside of Europe.

Whereas the inaugural congress of 1898 was held under the banner of traditional European diplomatic history, the eight sections of the following congress in Paris bore the motto of comparative historiography.[14] However, non-European issues were discussed only in the section on comparative legal history, in which numerous missionaries and colonists participated. Legal history was regarded as a political tool of European colonial policy, for example, in the training of colonial officials.[15] Overall, however, as Villari emphasized in his inaugural address at the Rome congress, the congresses were oriented toward a concept of history that went beyond traditional methodology, allowing national-centered historiogra-

Table 9.1   International Congresses of Historians

Congresses	Registered participants			
	Africa	*Asia/Australia*	*Latin America*	*Total participants*
The Hague 1898	1	3	1	360
1. Paris 1900	3	5/1	18	864
2. Rome 1903	7	3/1	3	2060
3. Berlin 1908	7	5	1	1042
4. London 1913	—	—	—	680
5. Brussels 1923	5	8	—	999

Note: The compilation is based on data in Erdmann, *Die Ökumene der Historiker*, 468ff.

phy to be placed in a broader context of world history. It went without saying, however, that this was restricted to European peoples.[16]

In 1908 in Berlin, a section on the history of the Orient was added to the program for the first time. In 1913 in London, it was expanded to "Oriental History with Egyptology." However, even these two congresses had a strongly national orientation biased toward the host country. Nevertheless, in England, the leading colonial power, Section IV on "Modern History" had a subsection dealing with colonial policies of the major European powers and the United States. Section IX, "Related and Auxiliary Sciences," had a subsection on "Ethnology, Historical Geography, Topography, and Local History," in which nine papers on non-European subjects were given.[17] However, no non-European scholars spoke in these sections either.

Both the Berlin and London congresses had a strict scientific orientation. Political factors played a much smaller role in these congresses than in those of other disciplines, as we shall see below. The emphasis on a scientific understanding that aimed at complete "truth"[18] was inconsistent with political optimism. Although James Bryce, in his inaugural address at the London congress, stressed the responsibility of the historian to serve the cause of peace,[19] the participants made no pledge to promote international understanding. The French had been quite reserved in Berlin and in London, and also did not appear to be particularly interested in this political component of the congresses. Although the specter of the coming war was not directly palpable in London, no "entente cordiale" was reached between the historians. The congresses hardly served as a tool of international friendship, as had been hoped by U.S. historian John Franklin Jameson who, as we shall see below, played a decisive role in reorganizing the international community of historians after the war.[20]

EUROPE: THE INTERNATIONAL
CONGRESSES OF ORIENTALISTS

Long before historians gathered in 1898 for their first international congress, the orientalists had begun to move toward consensus on an international level regarding the fundamental principles of their discipline and
the most recent research findings. The first international congress of orientalists was convened in Paris on the initiative of the French in 1873.[21] It
began with French Japan scholars under the leadership of Léon de Rosny,
a professor at the École spéciale des langues orientales, and was initially
conceived as a congress of Japan researchers, but three of the eight days of
the congress were set aside for the discussion of general issues in oriental
studies. At the same time, it was proposed that a second orientalist congress be held in the future.[22] Indeed, the second orientalist congress took
place just one year later in London under the leadership of Samuel Birch,
an Egyptologist and director of the classical art collection at the British
Museum. Official delegates were sent from nineteen countries and the
French colonies, and a total of 206 scholars registered. Nineteen scholars
came from non-Western countries, and fourteen representatives attended
from Algeria and the French colonies.[23] The subsequent congresses took
place at three-year intervals. The eighth congress in Stockholm and Christiana in 1889 was the climax up to that point in terms of registration,
duration, and quality.[24]

The programs at the different congresses reflected geographical expansion in areas of research and the associated fragmentation of the discipline. The London congress in 1874 was divided into six sections: Semitic,
Turanian, Aryan, Hamitic, archeological, and ethnological. As expressed
by Birch in his inaugural address, this congress was still devoted almost
exclusively to the discovery, deciphering, and translation of the oriental
languages. At this point, the discipline of oriental studies was still defined
purely as linguistics and was just on the verge of developing into a more
historically oriented field of study.[25] Archeology was a prerequisite for
oriental philology but in the minds of the orientalists themselves it functioned only as a tool in philology and not as its own subdiscipline.[26]

The seven sections in Florence covered an extensive geographic area.[27]
Five sections took place in Leyden and Vienna (a Semitic section, divided
into Arabic and the literature of Islam, on the one hand, and the remaining Semitic languages on the other; an Aryan and a Malayan-Polynesian
section; a section for Central and Eastern Asia; and a section on Africa/
Egypt), whereas the London conference with ten sections and the London
statutory conference with twenty-two sections reflected the increasing
specialization of orientalists.[28] The main addition to the body of congresses after 1891 was the section titled "Interaction between Orient and

Occident."[29] The founding of the International Association for the Exploration of Central and Eastern Asia at Rome in 1899 began the formation of international specialist associations within the field of oriental studies.

From the beginning, the orientalists debated vigorously the scientific and political purposes of their congresses. The oriental scholars themselves felt that in the context of nineteenth-century scientific development oriental studies "have contributed more than any other branch of scientific research to change, to purify, to clear, and intensify the intellectual atmosphere of Europe, and to widen our horizon in all that pertains to the science of man, in history, philology, theology, and philosophy."[30] This self-consciousness and the belief in a European intellectual community, however, did not necessarily lead to close international cooperation. Whereas German scholars of American studies, for example, felt that the value of this "roving international assembly" lay "not only in the facilitation of personal relationships between scholars from various countries but largely in the distribution of printed proceedings," German orientalists appeared more skeptical.[31] For example, Dillmann, the president of the Fifth International Congress of Orientalists in Berlin in 1881, certified that the congresses produced neither scientific innovation nor decisions related to science policy, and certainly no new discoveries. Even the scientific discussion was usually unsatisfying, he claimed, due to inadequate time and often to the rather arbitrary composition of participant groups. He concluded that:

> Indeed, our intent in these congresses cannot be the direct advancement of science; rather their real significance lies in their international character, in the congregation of men from the widest variety of nations for a common purpose. Science naturally is . . . international: A light that goes on in one country cannot be hidden; rather, it shines into the other countries as well. Anyone who neglects to seek researchers from abroad is often cheating himself out of the best help. All the nations of Europe have contributed to the scientific wealth that we now enjoy.[32]

The international character per se applies particularly to those sciences whose objects of study are so far removed from one's own land and so large that they can be studied only in collaboration with others. This, according to Dillmann, applied above all to oriental studies, geography, ethnology, and anthropology. These also were the disciplines that played a pioneering role in the establishment of the congress movement. Overall, in the words of one German report on the London meeting in 1874, the congresses were seen as "a powerful, influential educational tool that, protected from unilateralism, expands one's horizons, abolishes prejudices, and is unbelievably stimulating."[33] Dillmann, however, doubted the claim made by Max Müller in 1874 that the most important reasons for the international congresses were to provide status reports and guidelines for future research and to give the world a sense of oriental studies.[34]

This question about the scientific purpose of oriental studies, between practical science and "la science pour la science," sparked vehement debates and finally led to a schism of the congresses in 1891. In violation of the bylaws, the congress in Stockholm/Christiana in 1889 failed to determine the next congress site. Therefore, on the petition of Albrecht Weber of Germany, a provisional organizing committee composed of the presidents of past congresses was appointed. This committee selected Oxford as the next congress site. This met with bitter resistance by the French and English, who were unrepresented in this "emeritus meeting."[35] The French, in particular, viewed the provisional committee as an enterprise dominated by Germans, especially because the founder and first president of the congress of orientalists, de Rosny, was not invited to be a member of the committee.

The French national committee, with the concurrence of the English orientalists, called for the ninth congress to be held in London in 1891. In London, a proper organizing committee was constituted under the honorary chairmanship of Sir Henry C. Rawlinson.[36] A consensus among the French national committee, Rawlinson's committee, and the Stockholm committee was met, and the congress was set for London in 1892 under the chairmanship of Max Müller. However, part of the London organizing committee followed through with the original plan, holding a separate congress, the so-called Statutory Congress, in London in 1891. This division between a faction supported by the original organizer of the congresses, de Rosny, and a scholars' faction also affected the subsequent tenth congress, which took place in 1892 as a Statutory Congress in Madrid and in 1894 as a "normal" congress in Geneva.

The conflict involved more than purely statutory problems, however. A significant point of contention was the effort of some scholars to give the congresses a purely scientific character, that is, to exclude laypersons and other congress guests from the meetings and to restrict the social component, which had by far overshadowed the scientific element in Stockholm and Christiana.[37] The Germans, in particular, had spoken out in favor of professionalization and centralizing control. This sort of attempt to redefine the character of the congress without consulting the French was guaranteed to create an uproar, quite apart from any substantive disagreements.[38] The German initiative was therefore countered with the Statutory Congress, which had been promoted since October 1889 by the French national committee, citing the congress founders of 1874.

For the organizer of the Statutory Congress, G. W. Leitner, the secession was "a battle to maintain the independence of 'our open republic of oriental letters' against an attempt to transform it into a closed or official oligarchy, a monopoly for a few professors and government officials."[39] Leitner opposed a permanent and limited orientalist council, opting instead for establishing the International Assembly of Orientalists, which would decide on the site and structure of the congresses.[40] Representing more than a hundred members of this international assembly, Leitner sought to defend "the principles of our Republic of Oriental Letters."[41] He felt that the congress should be open to all, whether or not they belonged to the scholarly class.[42] Leitner referred here—as had Müller a quarter century before—to the connection between science and life.[43] However, whereas Müller had accepted this division as a given but envisioned the utilization of science in practical life, Leitner questioned the exclusivity of science and thereby of scholars themselves.

Leitner's criticism was ignored. The German Oriental Studies Society (Deutsche Morgenländische Gesellschaft) and German orientalists in general boycotted the Statutory Congress.[44] The consensus of the leading orientalists at the eleventh congress in Paris in 1897 showed, moreover, that the scholars unanimously agreed in principle that they should meet in the future as a purely scholarly society. The disputed point regarding organization of the congresses was made binding in a new bylaw.[45]

In looking at the geographical origin of the congress participants and the cultural perspective of European academics, it becomes evident that although the orientalists had close ties to non-European cultures and societies, they mostly considered them pure research objects. Leitner, the main figure of the Statutory Congresses, was one of the few orientalists who criticized the Eurocentrism and colonial perspective of European academics:

> No; oriental learning is worth saving, not because it gives a reputation to some of its professors, in whose hands the living East is killed, so that a conjectural East may be evolved by them; but because, when its treasures are revealed, as they will be if the process of Europeanizing the East is retarded, every branch of thought or action will be benefited, and every thinking man or woman will derive comfort or instruction from the invaluable lessons of its philosophy.[46]

Müller, one of the leading orientalists of the second half of the nineteenth century, also saw his discipline as a bridge between Orient and Occident. For him, oriental studies had lifted the millennia-old curtain between East and West and had reunited the two. The orientalists, therefore, did not fail to appreciate the accomplishments of ancient oriental cultures and their superiority to pre-Hellenic Europe.

> We no longer say vaguely and poetically say *Ex Oriente Lux*, but we know that all the most vital elements of our knowledge and civilisation—our lan-

guages, our alphabets, our figures, our weights and measures, our art, our religion, our traditions, our very nursery stories, came to us from the East; and we must confess that but for the rays of Eastern light, whether Aryan or Semitic or Hamitic, that called forth the hidden germs of the dark and dreary West, Europe, now the very light of the world, might have remained forever a barren and forgotten promontory of the primeval Asiatic continent.[47]

As sincere an acknowledgment as this was of the great ancient oriental culture, it also contained an equally clear claim, based on Europe's advanced development, to the "oriental treasure." Orientalists behaved in this regard like soldiers for the "reconquest of the Eastern world," with the attitude that "the East is ours, we are its heirs and claim by right our share in its inheritance."[48] From the superiority of the ancient orient and its multitudinous influences on Europe is derived a European claim of inheritance, a claim that justifies the scientific exploration and exploitation of oriental lands.

In general, the postulated international scientific community was based on a hegemonic understanding of civilization that was never intended to include more than the so-called civilized peoples. The German Minister von Gossler enunciated this at the Seventh International Congress of Americanists in Berlin in 1888: "Only by the cooperation of all sciences and all civilized peoples [can] we understand the new world as it was when it came into contact with the old world, and as it had developed up to that point."[49] This held true for the orientalists as well. European scholars took for granted the exclusion of non-European peoples from the international scientific community, in part because the development and status of modern knowledge was seen as being purely the result of European science. Non-European scientific traditions were either unacknowledged or dismissed as marginal. Of course, there were other voices as well, as when Müller singled out the establishment of a new school of Sanskrit researchers in India who, trained by European scholars, "have already become most formidable rivals to our own scholars." For him, collaboration with Indian scholars on an equal basis was an obvious principle: "They work for us, as we work for them."[50] A decade later, at the ninth congress in London, Müller, as president of the congress, assessed its tasks as follows:

> Now what we who are assembled here are aiming at, what may be called our real raison d'être, is to bring the East, which seems so far from us, so distant from us, nay, often so strange and indifferent to many of us, as near as possible—near to our thoughts, near to our hearts.[51]

Müller wanted to overcome the boundaries between Occident and Orient by means of oriental studies.

This perspective, however, was not the rule, and the oriental participants were often treated not as scholars of equal stature, but as exotic creatures. Albrecht Weber reported something of the sort from Stockholm:

> The orientalist congresses to date have served purely scientific purposes. It is lovely if the Orient itself appears and speaks to them as a decoration and ornament. However, if the scientific character is not to suffer, they must not be used as a kind of . . . exhibition.[52]

The congresses must not be allowed to sink to the level of "gatherings of orientals and oriental travelers," he said. With a racist undertone, he added:

> Not a trace of real intelligence was to be found in all those Islamic faces, for all the cleverness that emanated from them. . . . Rather, it was a decidedly embarrassing feeling for the other participants in the congress to see themselves on the same level as—or even overshadowed by—men who, as was revealed during the subsequent proceedings in the sections, were absolute nothings from a scientific point of view.[53]

The few non-European scholars who communicated with the Western academic world thus were not recognized as equal partners. Their writings and participation at international congresses were seen as evidence of "how grateful these people are for what we have done for them, how they gather around the font of science on the arm of their occidental guides and are already helping with joint research projects." Not *ex oriente lux* but *orienti reddenda lux* was the motto of the orientalists.[54]

Without a doubt, oriental studies in Europe are unthinkable without the political interest that was taken in them and the resultant large-scale governmental support. Of course, it was stressed repeatedly that internationalism ruled out nationalistic competitiveness: "In the realm of science, in the striving for truth, there are no competitors, only collaborators."[55] However, the unremitting conflict over the language of the congress illustrates the fact that these were arenas not only of scientific rivalry, but of national rivalry as well. According to the bylaws, only French and the language of the host country were permissible as official languages, but in fact presentations could also be made in English, German, Italian, or oriental languages. Because the use of French predominated, however, the Germans in particular attempted to propagate their language and always celebrated it as a victory when official guests or participants delivered their speeches in German.[56] The selection of congress sites was also frequently beset with nationalistic motives. For example,

French delegates rejected Berlin as the site of the third congress of orientalists for political reasons.[57]

The close collaboration between oriental studies and politics would cause the discipline to flourish but would also lead it into exploitation by national and imperial interests. The internationalism postulated by the orientalists was subject to certain limitations of culture and national politics, which demonstrated that the ideal of a harmonious international society of scholars did not coincide with reality.

The example of Germany illustrates the extent to which scientific research and political interests coincided. In Germany alone, the number of oriental professorships rose from fifteen to thirty-four between 1810 and 1881, and numerous international excavations were organized and financed, laying the foundation for the oriental collections in German museums. It is no coincidence that oriental studies experienced a great boom in Germany at the end of the nineteenth century.[58] "We Germans as a people are excluded from any direct contact with the Orient, we have no colonial possessions, no spot of oriental earth that we can call our own . . . we have no traditions which point us toward the Orient." These unfavorable external circumstances, says Dillmann, did not prevent the boom in oriental studies: "It was purely and simply the fervor for research, the thirst for knowledge, the drive to learn, which brought that about."[59] This perspective masks the political function that the German government attached to its support of oriental studies. Due to its lack of a colonial empire, Germany was at a particular disadvantage in this discipline compared to England and France, and was attempting to catch up. International power politics and German science policy coincided. "We still have no noteworthy share in the treasures of Nineveh and Babylon," Dillmann noted as one of the deficits of oriental studies in Germany.[60] It was not only scientific interest leading European scientists to India, the Near East, Persia, Arabia, and Africa. It also was the missionary spirit that allowed scientists to act as cultural diplomats propagating "European refinement" worldwide.[61]

The high political value attached to the orientalist congresses is evident in the number of official delegates that the different nations sent, as compared to other international scientific congresses. The governments offered financial support to the delegates and subsidized their travel costs. The congresses were generally held under the patronage of the host country's government or royal family, and official invitations were made through diplomatic channels.[62] Governments sent official delegates who, as in the case of the Germans, were expected to act as a cohesive bloc in representing German interests.[63] The scholars had always considered participation in the congresses to be a national duty, and the national angle was used as an argument to encourage the German government to provide financial support. Orientalists supported colonial policies as a "cultural mission" of their countries and, like the German Albrecht Weber, for example, also supported further colonization of the Orient by the major powers. Weber called for all Muslim peoples to "come as soon as possible under the guardianship of European governments," for "present-day Islam has no further cultural mission to fulfill."[64]

THE PAN-PACIFIC SCIENTIFIC CONGRESSES

Compared with European scientific internationalism, attempts to expand the international scientific community into non-European regions have received little attention to date. Worth noting in this regard are the scientific congresses, however rare, that met in Asia and Africa.[65] For example, the first International Congress of the Studies of the Further East met in Hanoi, Tonkin, in 1902 on the initiative of the École française d'Extrême-Orient. A conference of orientalists that was not initiated in Europe was held in Simla, India, in 1911. This conference debated both the establishment of the Central Institute of Oriental Studies in Calcutta and the possibility of convening an international congress of orientalists in India in 1912. The participants in Simla discussed the specifics of such an international meeting as a response to their dissatisfaction with the low level of Indian participants in the European congresses and the rejection of Calcutta as the next congress site by the delegates to the orientalist congress in Copenhagen in 1908. In order to convince Europeans to undertake the trip, the congress was to be limited to Indian studies.[66] This idea ultimately could not be implemented, and the sixteenth International Congress of Orientalists took place in Athens in 1912. The proposal made there that the next congress be held in Cairo was rejected by the delegates.[67]

An enterprise by Hawaii and the United States, centered around international scientific cooperation in the study of the Pacific, met with more success, however. In 1898 Charles R. Bishop, founder of the Bernice P. Bishop Museum in Honolulu, formulated plans for Pacific studies. Expeditions to the Mariana Islands and the South Pacific took place at the beginning of the new century. In 1907 the Pacific Science Institution was founded in Honolulu by the zoologist William A. Bryan Jr., later professor at the College of Hawaii, with the goal of studying the Pacific Ocean and using the scientific findings for the advancement of humankind.[68]

This internationalism, undiminished even by the U.S. annexation of Hawaii in 1898, found its institutional expression in the Pan-Pacific Union, founded by Alexander H. Ford in 1917. Ford, who came to the Pacific island as a journalist in 1907, built this institution on the model of the Pan-American Union, with which he had worked in close collaboration.[69] Under the doctrine of "Patriotism of the Pacific," the primary goal of the Pan-Pacific Union was to promote mutual cultural understanding among Pacific peoples as a guarantee of peaceful coexistence. Ford's idea of holding international congresses to create this "international brotherhood" coincided with Bryan's efforts toward scientific exploration of the Pacific.[70]

U.S. scientists on the mainland also began to take an interest in the Pacific region. Harvard geographer William M. Davis was one of the first scholars to call for scientific exploration of the Pacific. He attended the Australian meeting of the British Association for the Advancement of Science in 1914, where he promoted Pacific studies. Two years later, Davis organized the Symposium on Pacific Exploration at the annual meeting of the National Academy of Sciences, where he presented his plans for systematic scientific exploration of the Pacific in the postwar period.[71]

At the same time another group of U.S. scientists, including William E. Ritter, of the Scripps Institution for Biological Research, and Barton W. Evermann, director of the California Academy of Sciences, addressed exploration of the Pacific within the American Association for the Advancement of Science (AAAS). They discussed the subject at the annual conference of the AAAS in 1915 and at the three subsequent annual meetings of the newly established Pacific Division of the American Association for the Advancement of Science.[72] Ritter also played a significant role in a 1918 conference on international relations held on the occasion of the fiftieth anniversary of the University of California. Among other things, this conference also addressed Pacific issues.

In 1915 in San Francisco, where the Panama-Pacific Historical Congress was held on the occasion of the Panama-Pacific International Exposition, Davis met John Campbell Miriam, a paleontologist and later director of the Carnegie Institution in Washington, D.C., who proposed merging East Coast and West Coast initiatives. In 1916 Miriam and Davis took up the leadership of the Committee on Pacific Exploration of the National Academy of Sciences; its task was to coordinate U.S. research on the Pacific and initiate international collaboration. At a meeting of the committee in New York, which included Herbert E. Gregory, a professor at Yale University and director of the Bishop Museum in Honolulu, it was decided that a scientific congress would be organized in Honolulu.[73] Gregory had visited Australia and New Zealand in 1916 and solicited international cooperation there. He was later named director of the Committee on Pacific Investigations, as the Committee for Pacific Exploration was renamed after the war. In 1920 this committee became part of the Division of Foreign Relations of the National Research Council. It was one of the chief organizers, along with the Pan-Pacific Union and the Pacific Science Institution, of the first Pan-Pacific Science Congress, which took place in Honolulu in 1920.[74]

Whereas the congress in Honolulu was still experimental, the subsequent congresses in 1923 in Melbourne/Sydney, in 1926 in Tokyo, in 1929 in Batavia/Bandoeng, and in 1935 in Victoria/Vancouver attracted more participants and covered a wider range of scientific subjects.[75] Whereas eleven sections were organized in Melbourne, a variety of scientific problems was handled in Tokyo within three divisions: a physical division, a biological division, and a joint division.[76]

The objective of the Honolulu congress was "to outline scientific problems of the Pacific Ocean region and to suggest methods for their resolution, to make a critical inventory of existing knowledge, and to devise plans for future studies."[77] Unlike previous international scientific congresses, the conference in Honolulu was a meeting of individual scientists without official representation from governments or governmental institutions. As the first informal meeting, its purpose was to discuss the possibilities and scope of international cooperation. To this end, a special Symposium on Means and Methods of Cooperation addressed cooperation not only between Pacific nations in the areas of collecting, research, and publication, but also between various disciplines.[78] The representatives from seven countries ultimately agreed that, given the immense scope of scientific exploration of the Pacific, the congress should be established as a permanent institution to be held at regular three-year intervals.[79]

The conferences did not escape the risk, as in the case of the orientalist congresses, of the social component becoming so strong that it hindered scientific work more than it promoted it. For example, Gregory reported on the Tokyo congress:

> To a degree heretofore unknown in international scientific gatherings, this congress was a national event, participated in by the imperial family, government officials, educators, business men, financiers, farmers and school children. In the true sense of the word, the overseas visitors were honored guests of the nation. So obvious was the feeling of goodwill that the congress seemed to be a group of friends gathered to discuss science rather than scientists welcomed to a delightful country.[80]

Aside from the first congress, the Pacific Science Congresses—like the European prewar congresses—were characterized by governmental involvement. (See table 9.2.) They were convened and carried out by the National Research Council of the host country and took place under government patronage.[81] Ford had already seen his interest in developing Hawaii as the center of international cooperation on the Pacific impaired

Table 9.2 The Pan-Pacific Science Congresses

Congress	Participants (total)	Participants (USA)	Foreign participants (number of countries)
1. Honolulu 1920	99	33	23 (7)
2. Sydney/Melbourne 1923	1,294	17	80 (15)
3. Tokyo 1926	>300	56	194 (21)
4. Batavia/Bandoeng 1929	275	26	169
5. Victoria/Vancouver 1933	409	101	129 (17)

Note: Data vary considerably, and congress documentation also does not provide conclusive answers regarding exact participant counts. I am basing these figures on H. M. Tory, "History of the Pacific Science Association," in *Proceedings of the Fifth Pacific Science Congress. Held under the Auspices of the National Research Council of Canada and through the Generosity of the Government of Canada* (Victoria: 1933), 52ff.

by the involvement of the National Research Council, particularly in organizing the first congress. In his opinion, the council acted "dishonorably" in establishing the Committee on Pacific Investigations.[82] Therefore, the Pan-Pacific Scientific Research Council was established in Honolulu in 1921 on his initiative; its intent was to guarantee the Pan-Pacific Union control over scientific cooperation among the Pacific nations, over financing of research projects, and over the Pacific congresses, thereby curbing the influence of the National Research Council.[83] Despite the preliminary work by the Pan-Pacific Union and the Pacific Scientific Institution, the convening of the first congress was primarily a U.S. effort. The organization, programming, and implementation were in the hands of the Committee on Pacific Investigations.[84] Ford's fears of a takeover of Pacific studies by the United States therefore were not entirely unjustified. In fact, Davis himself had announced in 1916 that his plan for exploring the Pacific could be carried out only by Americans, "to whom the scientific conquest of the Pacific may make strong appeal."[85]

It was not without reason that even U.S. scientists warned the National Research Council to stay behind the scenes in its involvement. However, Ford was soon forced to acknowledge that his ambitious plans could not be carried out without U.S. support.[86] U.S. initiatives quickly led to the establishment of close relationships with scientific institutions in Canada, Japan, the Philippines, Australia, and New Zealand. In addition, the Committee on Pacific Investigations conducted the preliminary negotiations in 1921–1922 with the appropriate scientific and governmental institutions, which were decisive in convening the second congress.[87] At the second Pan-Pacific Scientific Congress in Melbourne/Sydney in 1923, a decision was made to establish the Pacific Science Association, which was eventually founded at the fourth congress in Tokyo in 1926. Its members represented fourteen of the countries participating in the congress.[88] Article 2 of the association's constitution sets forth its two main objectives:

(a) To initiate and promote cooperation in the study of scientific problems relating to the Pacific region, more particularly those affecting the prosperity and well-being of Pacific peoples; (b) To strengthen the bonds of peace among Pacific peoples by promoting a feeling of brotherhood among the scientists of all the Pacific countries.[89]

The association also served as the main organizer of the congresses.

It is impressive how, after World War I—an event that revealed as merely an illusion the idea of an international, peace-loving scientific community in Europe—scientists again gathered under precisely the same ethos. The peaceful and egalitarian cooperation, of which the warring European nations were no longer believed capable, became a reality in the Pacific region. The president of the congress in Melbourne, Sir David Orme Masson, made it clear in his inaugural address that the underlying motive of the congress was to maintain the "peace of nations." Other speakers called for "cultural alliances" and "alliances between nations based on intellectual co-operation but working through mutual respect and mutual confidence."[90] Three years later, the Japanese National Research Council referred to the association being founded as a "family of groups of people, every member of this family being equally eager to promote the creed of truth and Humanity and enjoying an equal privilege."[91]

THE PAN-AMERICAN SCIENTIFIC CONGRESSES

In contrast to the Pan-Pacific Scientific Congresses, the initiative for the establishment of Latin American scientific cooperation came not from a U.S. initiative but from the Sociedad Científica Argentina. The beginnings of the Latin American congress movement can be traced to a proposal in 1878 by the society's founder, Estanislao S. Zeballos, that a Congreso Científico Internacional Sud-Americano be held on the occasion of the tricentennial of the founding of Buenos Aires in 1880. This proposal was initially met with great skepticism. However, Zeballos referred in his petition to the European and U.S. congress movement and the participation of Argentinean scholars therein: "Organized with a permanent character like those in the United States and in Europe, sessions are held frequently, for example every other year, and are announced to the scientific world through the programs." At the same time, he saw these scientific congresses as part of the general movement toward moral advancement of the world. "Why do we not finally join the movement for moral progress of the civilized world?"[92] It was just as important to him, however, to popularize the congress idea in South America and establish a forum for

South American scientific cooperation. It was no accident that he proposed "Orígin del hombre Americano" as the theme of the congress.

The Sociedad Científica Argentina did not manage to hold the first Congreso científico latino americano in the Argentinean capital until 1898. This congress, the occasion for which was the twenty-fifth anniversary of the founding of the Sociedad Científica Argentina, was the first in a long series of South American scientific congresses held at regular intervals.[93] The next two congresses took place in 1901 in Montevideo and in 1905 in Rio de Janeiro. In 1908, at the fourth meeting in Santiago de Chile, all twenty-one South American republics took part for the first time. This conference also expanded its scope to the entire American continent by inviting the United States. The inclusion of the "Saxon Americans" in the Latin American congresses and the associated renaming of the congress, which became the Pan-American Scientific Congress, symbolized the abandonment of ethnically defined membership in the South American scientific community.[94] This also marked the transition from a national undertaking, initiated by a local institution, to an international scientific forum.

Whereas the Pacific Scientific Congresses encompassed only the natural sciences, the Latin American congresses included social sciences, engineering, medicine, and pedagogy from the very beginning. The broad subject range of the first congresses, however, quickly led organizers to realize that the congresses should be tightened and should concentrate on concrete scientific problems of particular interest to Latin American countries. Therefore, the organizing committee for the 1908 congress in Chile decided to focus on issues of law, ethnology, archeology, linguistics, and medicine. It is no surprise, then, that 21 percent of the participants in 1899 were professors, 20 percent were legal professionals, 18 percent were engineers, and 17 percent were medical professionals.[95] The concentration on specific themes did not reduce the number of presentations made. The number increased from 121, 202, and 120 at the first three congresses, respectively, to 742 in Santiago. Although the organizers of the subsequent congress in Washington, D.C., sought a similar thematic restriction, this philosophy did not prevail beyond Chile.[96]

As with the Pacific Science Congresses, the scientific value here is difficult to measure. One indicator, however, is the number of resolutions the congresses approved dealing with long-term international research projects or institutions. For example, the 1916 congress in Washington, D.C., approved forty-nine resolutions in all branches of science, including many proposals regarding jurisdiction for international arbitration as well as motions to adopt the metric system, to form a Department of Education within the Pan-American Union, and to establish a Pan-American

Intellectual Union as an umbrella organization for a planned Pan-American University Union, Pan-American Library Union, and Pan-American Archeological Union. (See table 9.3.)

The congresses were announced by the governments of the host countries and invitations were issued through diplomatic channels. The participant list therefore was composed of official delegates from the participating countries, delegates from scientific institutions, and individual scholars. The Pan-American Scientific Congresses reflected a new South American self-confidence that not only showed the world what the continent could accomplish in many fields of science, but also demonstrated the cohesiveness of the western hemisphere.[97] As with the European prewar congresses, however, the scientific meetings were also seen as a peacekeeping tool for international relations. For example, the U.S. delegate in Santiago de Chile, Leo S. Rowe, stressed precisely this motive, in addition to the necessity for international scientific collaboration in pursuit of human progress:

> For this reason it has such a psychological significance for international relations. I am convinced that it will be by scientists that we remove the last relics of the epoch when the terms stranger and enemy were synonym.[98]

Seven years later in Washington, D.C., this factor was still primary. The goal was not only scientific exchange; personal encounters were intended to form a foundation for peaceful and harmonious cooperation in the future.[99]

This political spin was also discernable in the relationship between the scientific congresses and their political counterpart, the Pan-American Union. The Commercial Bureau of the American Republics was founded in 1890 and renamed the International Bureau of the American Republics in 1902. In 1910 it was renamed the Pan-American Union.[100] This institution pursued, at least in the political and economic arenas, the same interests as the Pan-American Scientific Congresses, namely, promoting collaboration between the countries of the Americas. Elihu Root, the U.S.

Table 9.3   The Pan-American Scientific Congresses

Congress	Number of participants	Number of countries involved	Number of sections
1. Buenos Aires 1898	552	12	4
2. Montevideo 1901	839	11	9
3. Rio de Janeiro 1905	863	17	10
4. Santiago de Chile 1908–1909	2,238	21	9
5. Washington, D.C. 1915–1916	>2,500	21	9

secretary of state, made the following remarks in this spirit to the U.S. delegates at the Pan-American Scientific Congress in 1908:

> Many of the matters that will be discussed, according to the programme of this conference, are matters which while there discussed in their purely scientific aspects, will be later discussed on the political side before the next Pan-American conference, to be held in Buenos Aires in 1910.[101]

The Pan-American Union showed great interest in international cultural collaboration and supported scientific endeavors.[102] There was coordination between the union and the congresses, and it was the union that proposed Mexico City as the site for the eighth American Scientific Congress. In 1928 the Pan-American Union established its Division of Intellectual Cooperation.

The scientists, too, were in favor of cooperation between the two institutions. For example, the Pan-American Scientific Congress in Santiago in 1909 proposed that the International Bureau of the American Republics establish a section of U.S. bibliography.[103] As early as 1898 in Buenos Aires, delegates discussed holding a Latin American congress on geography and history and to establish a federation of geographic societies. The sixth Pan-American Scientific Congress in Lima in 1924 took up the proposal again, and the International American Conference in Havana in 1928 finally decided to establish the Pan-American Institute of Geography and History.[104]

The great political value that the Americans placed on these scientific congresses is made clear by the formation of a special delegation for the 1908–1909 congress, for example, which had political tasks in addition to representing the U.S. scientific community. Root appealed to the delegates as follows:

> My own judgement would be that as you go solely as delegates to a scientific congress, where there is no diplomatic function whatever, you should call in, as far as possible, the other delegates from the United States, without any reference as to whether you go representing the Government of the United States or whether you go representing this or that or the other university. Of course, if you do that, you will form a general organization, which will elect its own officers and adopt its own methods of organization, you bearing in mind your relations to the Government of the United States.[105]

The U.S. delegates had several preparatory meetings in Washington, D.C., and, after their arrival in Chile more than a month before the Congress began, enjoyed privileges comparable to those of a state delegation: They were received by the Chilean president and representatives of numerous governmental and scientific institutions, among other things.

The transformation of these congresses into a symbol of unity for the Americas, which began in Santiago and extended far beyond the boundaries of science, and the usurpation of this scientific stage by the United States for political purposes, were completed in Washington, where the fifth congress in 1915 called for the establishment of Pan-Americanism in the western hemisphere.[106] The congress, initially planned for 1912, had to be postponed for three years due to various organizational difficulties, and ultimately took place while World War I was raging in Europe. The congress was organized in close collaboration with the Pan-American Union, which celebrated its twenty-fifth anniversary in 1915, and with the U.S. government. Largely because of the war in Europe, interest was focused not on scientific themes but rather on international law, a section led by James Brown Scott, secretary of the Carnegie Endowment for International Peace.[107]

In light of the war in Europe, Glen Levin Swiggett, assistant secretary general of the congress, stated the political mission of the congress in a circular letter to the U.S. press, saying that the establishment of Pan-Americanism was the fulfillment of the dreams of James Monroe and Simón Bolivar—namely, the creation of a "new world-group" in the context of a "new internationalism." For Swiggett, the task of this new Pan-American group of young nations was to repair the political, economic, and intellectual destruction caused by the war. This, let there be no doubt, was to be done under the leadership of the United States. Swiggett designated the Washington, D.C., headquarters of the Pan-American Union as the "Capitol of Pan-America."[108]

The inauguration of a new, peaceful "Republic of America," based on justice and freedom from European domination under the banner of Pan-Americanism, was also the basic tenor of the inaugural addresses by U.S. Vice President Thomas R. Marshall and Secretary of State Robert Lansing: "The Monroe doctrine is a national policy of the United States; Pan-Americanism is an international policy of the Americas."[109] The American scientific congresses thus aimed to serve as the cradle, after the war, for a new international scientific community that would include Europe. This dream was not fulfilled because the Europeans established a new international scientific system on their own continent and were not willing to turn over their leadership claims to other, non-European efforts by former colonial lands. However, Pan-Americanism was to remain the guiding political principle behind the American congress movement, not least due to the strong influence of the United States. For instance, the chairman of the U.S. delegation to the sixth congress in Lima in 1924 proclaimed: "This congress expresses, better than any other assembly, the true spirit of Pan-Americanism."[110]

The South American republics followed the U.S. banner. The internationalist doctrine of Pan-Americanism, integrated by the United States into the South American liberation tradition, appeared to overshadow the fear of U.S. imperialism on the southern continent. This is illustrated in the Chilean ambassador's welcoming address in 1915:

> Thus the Monroe doctrine might have seemed a threat so long as it was only a right and an obligation on the part of the United States. Generalized as a derivation from the Pan-American policy, supported by all the republics on the continent as a common force and a common defense, it has become a solid tie of union, a guarantee, a bulwark for our democracies.[111]

Overcoming the isolation of the nations of the Americas, the call for continental solidarity, and the creation of a single identity for both Americas, namely an "American" identity, therefore became the leitmotifs in a congress movement intended to ring in a new epoch of intellectual cooperation in the Americas.[112]

CONCLUSION: SCIENTIFIC CONGRESSES AND THE POLITICS OF SCIENTIFIC INTERNATIONALISM

In comparing the congress movement in all three regions along the four issues discussed in the introduction, it becomes evident that the greatest similarities can be found in their origins, structure, and scientific ethos. Except for the historians, a general need for international cooperation led to the initiatives by scholars to establish frequent scientific congresses in order to exchange the latest research findings and to establish international projects. The importance of the congresses was generally seen in their scientific character. Despite debates about the practical value of their disciplines, less among scientists than among the orientalists, scholars agreed that their meetings also had to serve public needs. Differences in time and scope should not be overlooked, however. Whereas in Europe the congress movement began after the middle of the nineteenth century, the first congresses in Latin America and the Pacific took place near the turn of the century. The scientific themes in the Pacific and Latin American cases did not focus on individual areas of science as was customary with their European counterparts. Rather, a broad range of scientific disciplines was covered. The unanimity in language, namely English, was considered a major advantage for communication that prevented nationalist resentments. However, it also symbolized the leadership of the United States in the Pacific and Latin American congress movements, whereas in Europe the unresolved question of the official congress language highlighted the different nationalistic ambitions for scientific (and cultural) hegemony.

The case studies also show that, despite the expansion of the geographical scope of international cooperation, this internationalism did not become global. The three regions did not cooperate with each other and excluded scholars of other areas and cultures. The internationalism of the Pacific and Latin American scientific congresses was bound to their geographical roots but was never intended to reach beyond geographical boundaries. In the case of the Pacific congresses, for instance, only scientists from countries that belonged to the Pacific region or owned territory there could be members of the association or participate in the congresses.[113] The Pacific science congresses were not convened to discuss purely scientific problems; rather, they always dealt with practical applications for the advancement of the Pacific region. The program included no general scientific questions, only those dealing with the Pacific.

By contrast, the European idea of scientific internationalism was not restricted to the European continent. It was an idea, however, that meant a global scientific hegemony that excluded non-Western science. With very few exceptions, non-European countries did not host congresses. Representatives of non-Western countries were present only in very small numbers at the congresses, if at all, and were usually from Japan. One of the most prominent examples of this limitation to Western science is the International Congress of Arts and Science, held during the World's Fair in St. Louis in 1904. Portrayed by its organizers as a meeting of the world's leading scientists, the congress was supposed to reflect the status quo of international science. However, both the subjects addressed and the origins of the participants made it clear that this congress by no means represented a worldwide scientific community. Its structure and scientific conceptions were Eurocentric and ignored non-European scholars and perspectives.[114]

The history of the congresses shows that these scientific meetings did not take place in a political vacuum. In Europe the internationalization process unfolded in a state of tension between nationalism and cosmopolitanism, coinciding as it did with the heyday of national science and nationalistic thought. The congresses often remained subject to nationalistic and hegemonic concerns, and the governments of the major powers used the sciences too much as a political tool in their international and foreign cultural policy.[115] The scientific congresses therefore provided a stage on which political differences could be discussed under the aegis of science. The selection of congress sites and the establishment of international institutions in specific fields were guided not only by scientific criteria but by political motives as well. More than a few scientific congresses were convened by government initiative or sponsored by the state.

However, the scholars also considered themselves part of an "international republic of scholars." The objective of this imagined community was not only the exchange and dissemination of scientific findings but also the peaceful assembly of an international community of scholars and researchers intended to promote understanding among nations. This optimism conceals the fact that one important function of the congresses was for each nation to display its own scientific acumen, frequently with claims of superiority. The scholar representing a scientific institution considered himself a representative of his nation and culture. Although the congresses were organized by national bodies composed primarily of government officials and scholars, the official invitations usually came from the respective diplomatic missions. Governments often appointed their representatives to the congresses. As a result, the internationalization of science occurred against the backdrop of nationalist competition over hegemonic cultural claims. This included an actual desired cultural transfer, using scientific transformers, that would allow a kind of export of one's own culture and specific national traits. The internationalism of a cosmopolitan republic of scholars was defined in hegemonic terms and remained limited to Europe before World War I.[116]

The idea of internationalism did not collapse with the outbreak of World War I. Of course, scientific collaboration among the European countries stopped, but it did not prevent similar initiatives outside of Europe.[117] It was precisely this idea that was a decisive motive for establishing a non-European scientific system during and after World War I, when Europe lost its claim to leadership of international science in the eyes of non-European scientists. The "occidental people," in particular, saw in the inauguration of their congresses a possibility for preventing war and violence.[118] The war for them was evidence not of the collapse of the ideal of peaceful international scientific cooperation but of the very practicability of such an ideal under a new ethos, a "cooperation which has united the East and the West and the North and the South into one heart and soul as well as in mind."[119] This was destined to remain an ideal, for even the non-European internationalization movement was based on political preconditions.

As shown by the heavy involvement and dominance of the United States, internationalization of the East did not take place independently of the West. It was based on Western models of science and institutionalization. There was a widespread respect for European science outside of Europe. The originality of the Pan-Pacific and Pan-American congresses did not signify a complete detachment from the European international science movement,[120] but neither the Pan-Pacific Scientific Congress nor the American Scientific Congress had contact with the European-dominated congresses of oriental and American studies.[121] Both of these institutions, therefore, allowed the voices of non-European scientists to be heard in the international republic of scholars, thus laying the groundwork for the creation of a non-European scientific identity.

The only link among all three regions was the United States. Americans were involved in the prewar European congress movement and were the main force in establishing the Pan-Pacific and Pan-American Scientific Congresses. They also were very much engaged in reorganizing the European scientific community after the end of the war. U.S. astrophysicist George Ellery Hale at the National Research Council of the National Academy of Sciences in Washington, D.C., took a leading role in working for resumption of international scientific relations and establishment of the International Research Council.[122] U.S. historians, notably John Franklin Jameson, Waldo G. Leland, and James T. Shotwell, were among the main actors in revitalizing international cooperation among historians. Jameson, who had been director of the Carnegie Endowment and publisher of *American Historical Review* since 1905, had spoken out even before the war for the establishment of an international society of historians. He continued his efforts during the war and, in 1919, tried to convince European historians to convene an international congress of historians. Jameson's efforts ultimately led to the first postwar conference in Brussels in 1923, and to the founding of the Comité International des Sciences Historiques (CISH) in Geneva in 1926.[123]

World War I led not only to the breakup of European scientific internationalism but also to serious shifts within the system and changes in its institutional structure. The restoration of the European-Atlantic international scientific community and the creation of new international scientific institutions were accompanied in Europe by nationalist and political resentments. This can be seen both in the establishment of large institutions, such as the International Research Council and the Union Académique Internationale in Brussels in 1919, and in the futile efforts to revitalize the international community of historians on an equal footing.[124] Despite U.S. initiatives to reestablish the European scientific community, and although the National Academy of Sciences in Washington, D.C., provided considerable impetus to establish postwar scientific institutions in Europe, the implementation was almost exclusively in the hands of the French and the Belgians.[125]

Considering the variety of political, cultural, and scientific motives and the long-term results of U.S. involvement in international science during and after the war, the scientific center began shifting from Europe to the United States. Whereas the Americans played a major role in the European scientific community in the 1920s they also became increasingly engaged in the Latin American and Pacific regions. This global scientific engagement reached far beyond scientific congresses and is too complex to be investigated in this paper, but it led in the following decades to its replacement of Europe as the world's scientific center. This replacement, however, neither changed the ethos nor the politics of science, nor did it go behind a Eurocentric worldview.

NOTES

I would like to thank Sally E. Robertson for the translation of this text and Lucius G. Eldredge, executive secretary of the Bernice P. Bishop Museum of Honolulu, for providing me with publications from the museum.

1. See Anne Rasmussen, *L'Internationale Scientifique (1890–1914)* (Paris: 1995); F. S. L. Lyons, *Internationalism in Europe 1815–1914* (Leyden: 1963), 299; P. S. Reinsch, "International Unions and Their Administration," *American Journal of International Law* 1 (1907): 617–18; Georges P. Speeckaert, *Les 1978 Organisations Internationales fondées depuis le Congrès de Vienne. Liste chronologique* (Brussels: 1957).

2. See Maurice P. Crosland, "The Congress on Definitive Metric Standards, 1798/99: The First International Scientific Congress?" *Isis* 60 (1969): 226–31. On the first astronomers' congress, see Peter Brosche, "Gotha 1798. Vorder- und Hintergründe des ersten Astronomen-Kongresses," *Photorin: Mitteilungen der Lichtenberg-Gesellschaft* 5 (1982): 38–59.

3. Rasmussen speaks of 242 congresses. See Anne Rasmussen, "Les Congrès internationaux liés aux Expositions universelles de Paris (1867–1900)," *Mil Neuf Cent. revue d'Histoire Intellectuelle* 7 (1989): 23.

4. See the data in *Les congrès internationaux de 1681 à 1899* (Brussels: 1960), *Les congrès internationaux de 1900 à 1919* (Brussels: 1964), 51. The overviews presented there include all international meetings. See, also, Eckhardt Fuchs, "Wissenschaft, Kongreßbewegung und Weltausstellungen: Zu den Anfängen der Wissenschaftsinternationale vor dem Ersten Weltkrieg," *Comparativ* 6, no. 5/6 (1996): 156–77; Brigitte Schröder-Gudehus, "Internationale Kongresse und die Organisation der Wissenschaft: Ein Blick auf die Jahrhundertwende," in *Nachdenken über Geschichte. Beiträge aus der Ökumene der Historiker*, ed. H. Bockman and K. Jörgensen (Neumünster: 1991), 247–55.

5. Detailed statistical data on the congresses can be found in C. Tapia, and J. Taieb, "Conférences et Congrès Internationaux de 1815 à 1913," *Relations Internationales* 5 (1976): 11–35; C. Tapia, *Colloques et Sociétés. La Régulation Sociale* (Lille: 1981), 39ff., 45ff.

6. This logic led to the desire to consider international Americanist congresses as well, which developed at the same time as the orientalist congresses. This field had to be omitted for space reasons.

7. This chapter will not address Africa, since it did not develop international scientific cooperation in the period under consideration here. The Pan-Africanism that developed near the turn of the century with the first Pan-African Congress, and that was convened in 1900 by Henry Sylvester Williams of Trinidad, was a purely political movement unaccompanied by scientific cooperation. The next

Pan-African Congresses took place in London in 1919, Paris in 1921, Lisbon in 1923, and New York in 1927, with significant involvement by W. E. B. DuBois. See Imanuel Geiss, *Panafrikanismus. Zur Geschichte der Dekolonisation* (Frankfurt am Main: 1968), chaps. II.2, II.4.

8. Schröder-Gudehus, "Internationale Kongresse," 247; Gerhard A. Ritter, "Motive und Organisationsformen der internationalen Wissenschaftsbeziehungen und die Anfänge einer auswärtigen Kulturpolitik im deutschen Kaiserreich vor dem Ersten Weltkrieg," in *Studien zur Geschichte Englands und der deutsch-britischen Beziehungen*, ed. Lothar Kettenacker, Manfred Schlenke, and Hellmut Seier (Munich: 1981), 154 and note 12, 175.

9. See Eric Brian, "Y a-t-il un objet Congrès? Le cas du Congrès international de statistique (1853–1876)," *Mil Neuf Cent. Revue d'Histoire Intellectuelle* 7 (1989): 9–22; B. Bensaude-Vincent, "Karlsruhe, septembre 1860: l'atome en congrès," *Relations Internationales* 62 (1990): 149–69.

10. For details, see Karl Dietrich Erdmann, *Die Ökumene der Historiker. Geschichte der Internationalen Historikerkongresse und des Comité International des Sciences Historiques* (Göttingen: 1987). On the beginnings, see especially pp. 18–28.

11. On the Société d'Histoire Diplomatique, see *Revue d'Histoire diplomatique* 1 (1887): 5ff.

12. See G. v. B. [Georg v. Below], "Vermischtes," *Historische Zeitschrift* 82 (1899): 185–87, here 186.

13. See Geheimes Staatsarchiv Preußischer Kulturbesitz, Rep. 76, Vc, sect. 1, Tit. 11, pt. VI, no. 13, vol. 1.

14. See *Exposition Universelle Internationale de 1900. Congrès International d'Histoire Comparée. Tenu à Paris du 23 au 28 Juillet 1900. Procès-Verbaux Sommaires* (Paris: 1901).

15. *Annales internationales d'histoire. Congrès de Paris 1900*, vol. 2 (Paris: 1900).

16. See *Atti del Congresso Internazionale die Scienze Storiche (Roma, 1–9 Aprile 1903)*, vol. 1, *Parte Generale* (Rome: 1907) 97ff.

17. See *International Congress of Historical Studies. London, April 3rd to 9th, 1913. Pamphlet C. List of Readers*, 16, 22.

18. This is how the president of the Paris Congress of 1909, Henri Houssaye, described the goal of historiography: "La vérité, toute la vérité, rien que la vérité." In *Annales Internationales d'Histoire. Congrès de Paris 1900*, vol. 1 (Paris: 1901), 6.

19. See *Presidential Address by the Right Hon. James Bryce with Suppl. Remarks by A.W. Ward* (Oxford: 1913). International Congress of Historical Studies, London, 1913.

20. See *American Historical Review* 18 (1912–1913): 691.

21. By the time World War I had begun, sixteen international orientalist congresses had been held. In addition to the 1873 congress in Paris, congresses were held in London in 1874; St. Petersburg, 1876; Florence, 1878; Berlin, 1881; Leyden, 1883; Vienna, 1886; Stockholm/Christiana, 1889; London, 1891–1892; Lisbon, 1892–Geneva 1894; Paris, 1897; Rome, 1899; Hamburg, 1902; Algiers, 1905; Copenhagen, 1908; and Athens, 1912.

22. *Congrès International des Orientalistes. 1re Circulaire* (January 7, 1873).

23. One each from Ceylon, Egypt, Mauritius, San Salvador, and Turkestan; two

from Turkey; four from India; and eight from Japan. However, the participant lists given in the congress materials should be used with caution since many representatives of non-European countries were of European origin, and since many scholars registered for the congress but did not attend. For example, Lepsius and Steinthal announced the congress in Berlin by saying: "It is not necessary to appear in Paris in order to participate in the congress. As with other international congresses, one may register as a member and thereby obtain the right to all printed matter from the congress." ["Zur Theilnahme an dem Congress ist das Erscheinen in Paris nicht nothwendig. Wie auch sonst bei internationalen Kongressen kann man sich als Mitglied einzeichnen und erhält dadurch das Anrecht auf sämmtliche Druckwerke des Kongresses."] See *Congrès International des Orientalistes: Compte-Rendu de la Première Session: Paris 1873*, vol. 2 (Paris: 1876), 96.

24. The congress took place in the capitals of both Sweden and Norway, since the two were united in personal union under the Swedish crown and, given the royal patronage of the congress, there was a desire to avoid tensions. A total of 715 scholars participated, including 515 from abroad. These included one each from Abyssinia, Brazil, and Colombia; two from Siam; three from Japan; four from Persia; seven from Egypt; eleven from India; and twenty-eight from Turkey. See *Liste des Membres Inscrits du VIIe Congrès International des Orientalistes à Stockholm et à Christiania. 2–13 Sept. 1889* (Stockholm: 1889).

25. For a German perspective on the transition to a historically oriented discipline, see Carl H. Becker, "Der Islam im Rahmen einer allgemeinen Kulturgeschichte," in *Islamstudien. Vom Werden und Wesen der islamischen Welt*, ed. Carl H. Becker, vol. 1 (1924; reprint, Hildesheim: 1967), 24–39. On Becker, see Josef van Ess, "From Wellhausen to Becker: The Emergence of *Kulturgeschichte* in Islamic Studies," in *Islamic Studies: A Tradition and its Problems*, ed. Malcolm H. Kerr (Malibu: 1980), 27–51.

26. "President's Address," in *Report of the Proceedings of the Second International Congress of Orientalists, Held in London, 1874* (London: 1874), 4.

27. The seven sections were: Africa settentrionale; Semitica antica, Elbraico e Assiriologia; Arabica; Studii Indo-Europei ed Iranici; Studii Indiani; Altaica; Chinese, Indo-Chinese e Tibetana e Yamatologica.

28. The ten sections at the London conference were: Indian; Aryan; Semitic (Babylonian and Assyrian, general); Persian and Turkish; China, Central Asia, and the Far East; Egypt and Africa; Australasia and Oceania; anthropological and mythological; geographical; and Archaic Greece. See *Ninth International Congress of Orientalists. September 1892. Order of Proceedings for Saturday, September 12th; Transactions of the Ninth International Congress of Orientalists. Held in London, 5th to 12th September 1892* (London: 1893). The twenty-two sections are found in "The Statutory Ninth International Congress of Orientalists," *Asiatic Quarterly Review* 11, no. 3 (1891): 104. Sections were added on sinology, Japanese, relations with orientals, and oriental art. Since the organization of the congress was in the hands of the host country's organizing committee, the structure of the meetings changed from congress to congress. For example, there were twelve sections in Rome in 1899, seven in Copenhagen in 1908, and eleven in Athens in 1912.

29. The purpose of this section was both to conduct systematic research into

relations between the two hemispheres and to help "[make] the union of orient and occident 'in the peaceful edifice' a reality." See K. Krumbacher, "Über den Zweck und die allgemeine Bedeutung der Sektion 'Wechselwirkungen zwischen Orient und Okkzident,'" in *Verhandlungen des XIII. Internationalen Orientalisten-Kongresses. Hamburg September 1902* (Leyden: 1904), 357.

30. "Max Müller's Address," in *Report of the Proceedings of the Second International Congress of Orientalists*, 18–19.

31. W. Reiss to the German Foreign Ministry, March 27, 1888, Bundesarchiv Potsdam, *Auswärtiges Amt*, no. 37459.

32. ["In der That nicht auf die unmittelbare Förderung der Wissenschaft kann das Absehen bei diesen unseren Congressen gerichtet sein, sondern ihre eigentliche Bedeutung haben sie in dem Zusammenschluss der Männer verschiedenster Nationen zu einem gemeinsamen Zweck, in ihrem internationalen Charakter. International . . . ist die Wissenschaft an sich: ein Licht, das in einem Lande aufgegangen ist, kann sich nicht verbergen, sondern scheint hinein in die anderen; wer um den Erwerb der Mitarbeiter im Ausland sich nicht kümmert, beraubt sich oft der besten Hülfe; zu dem wissenschaftliche Besitz, dessen wir uns jetzt erfreuen, haben alle Nationen Europa's beigetragen."] *Verhandlungen des Fünften Internationalen Orientalisten-Congresses. Gehalten zu Berlin im September 1881. Ersther Teil. Bericht über die Verhandlungen* (Berlin: 1881), 31.

33. ["ein mächtiges, tief wirkendes Bildungsmittel, das vor Einseitigkeiten schützt, den Gesichtskreis erweitert, Vorurtheile abschleift und unglaublich anregt . . ."] "Report of September 26, 1874, on the Congress of Orientalists in London," by Rudolf Krehl, professor and head librarian of the University of Leipzig, to the Cultural Ministry of Saxony, in *Sächsisches Hauptstaatsarchiv*, Ministerium für Volksbildung, no. 10270, vol. 3.

34. "It seems to me that the real and permanent use of these scientific gatherings is twofold: (1). They enable us to take stock, to compare notes, to see where we are, and to find out where we ought to be going. (2). They give us an opportunity, from time to time, to tell the world where we are, what we have been doing for the world, and what, in return, we expect the world to do for us." See "Max Müller's Address," 18. Of course, personal contact with friends and colleagues was also an important component of the congresses for Müller. See *The Life and Letters of The Right Honourable Friedrich Max Müller* (London: 1902), 1: 493, 2: 110.

35. The committee consisted of the four presidents of the congresses in Vienna, Leyden, Berlin, and Stockholm/Christiana who were still living.

36. An overview of the debate is given in Albrecht Weber, *Quousque Tandem? Der Achte Internationale Orientalisten-Congress; und der Neunte? Eine Zusammenstellung* (Berlin: 1891). See also, "The Basis of the Statutory Ninth Congress of 1891," in *Asiatic Quarterly Review* 11, no. 3 (1891): 12–13; *The Times of India*, May 14, 1891, 4.

37. "The libations to Bacchus far exceeded the offerings to Minerva." "Programme of the Ninth International Congress of Orientalists," *Asiatic Quarterly Review* 11, no. 3 (1891): 7.

38. The selection of Max Müller, a native German, as president of the congress may have been another reason that the congress was rejected by the statutory fac-

tion. In a letter of May 2, 1892, Müller asked Renan to participate in the congress: "I have to act as President, and an ill-natured report has been spread that French scholars could not attend a Congress presided over by a German" (*The Life and Letters of The Right Honourable Friedrich Max Müller,* 2: 298).

39. ["um einen Kampf zur Erhaltung der Unabhängigkeit 'unserer offenen Republik der orientalischen Wissenschaft' gegenüber dem Versuch, dieselbe in eine geschlossene oder officielle Oligarchie, in ein Monopol für ein paar Professoren und Beamte zu verwandeln."] See *Münchner Allgemeine Zeitung,* April 8, 1891, insert.

40. "Dr. Leitner's Report to the Members as Organizing Secretary," August 31, 1891. "The Statutory Ninth International Congress of Orientalists," *Asiatic Quarterly Review* 11, no. 3 (1891): 99–101.

41. "The Ninth International Congress of Orientalists of 1891," *Asiatic Quarterly Review* 11, no. 3 (1891): 2.

42. "Programme of the Ninth International Congress of Orientalists," *Asiatic Quarterly Review* 11, no. 3 (1891): 5–6.

43. "Max Müller's Address," 18–19.

44. See, among others, Rudolf Krehl to the Cultural Ministry of Saxony, February 15, 1891, *Sächsisches Hauptstaatsarchiv,* Ministerium für Volksbildung, no. 10270, vol. 3. English orientalists also belonged to the scholars' faction and determined its objective: "What we chiefly want are *Oriental scholars,* that is to say, men who have proved themselves able to handle their own spade, and who have worked in the sweat of their brow in disinterring the treasures of Oriental literature" (Max Müller, "Inaugural Address," in *Transactions of the Ninth International Congress of Orientalists. Held in London, 5th to 12th September 1892* [London: 1893], 6).

45. *Actes du Onzième Congrès Internationale des Orientalistes. Paris 1897* (Paris: 1899), xvff.

46. "Programme of the Ninth International Congress of Orientalists," 6.

47. "Max Müller's Address," 18–19.

48. "Max Müller's Address," 18–19.

49. ["So finden Sie . . . ein volles Verständnis dafür, dass nur durch das Zusammenwirken aller Wissenschaften und aller Kulturvölker die neue Welt, wie sie war, als sie mit der alten Welt in Berührung kam, und wie sie sich bis dahen entwickelt hatte, begriffen werden kann."] *Compte-Rendu du Congrès International des Americanists. 7e session. Berlin 1888* (Berlin: 1888), 33.

50. "Max Müller's Address," 20–21. The recognized Indian Sanskrit scholar Bhandarkar took part as early as 1886 in Vienna, after having been given an honorary doctorate by the University of Göttingen.

51. Müller, "Inaugural Address," 7.

52. ["Die Orientalisten-Congresse sind bisher rein wissenschaftlichen Zwecken dienstbar gewesen. Es ist ganz schön, wenn bei ihnen als *Schmuck und Zierrath* auch der Orient selbst zu Worte und zur Erscheinung kommt. Wenn aber der wissenschaftliche Charakter derselben nicht leiden soll, dürfen sie nicht zu einer Art Schaustellung . . . benutzt werden."] Weber, *Quousque Tandem* (emphasis added).

53. ["Nicht die Spur von wirklicher Intelligenz war in allen diesen islami-

tischen Gesichtern, bei aller Schlauheit, die sich darin ausprägte, zu finden. . . . Für die übrigen Mitglieder des Congresses dagegen war es entschieden ein peinliches Gefühl, sich mit Männern auf gleicher Stufe, ja diese sogar im Vordergrunde, zu sehen, die, wie sich bei den späteren Verhandlungen in den Sectionen ergab, vom Standpunkt der Wissenschaft aus reine Nullitäten waren."] Weber, *Quousque Tandem*, 5.

54. *Verhandlungen des Fünften Internationalen Orientalisten-Congresses, 1881,* 39–40.

55. ["Im Reiche der Wissenschaft, im Streben nach Wahrheit giebt es nicht Nebenbuhler, nur Mitarbeiter."] *Proceedings of the Fifth International Congress of Orientalists, Verhandlungen des Fünften Internationalen Orientalisten-Congresses. Gehalten zu Berlin im September 1881. Erster Theil. Bericht uber die Verhandlungen* (Berlin: 1881), 26–27. On the subject of "harmony" between the scholars based on "common principles," "common purposes," and "common sympathies," see also "Max Müller's Address," 18. At the Leyden congress in 1883, the hope was expressed, "que lors de la prochaine réunion de Congrès tous les membres se retrouveront et continueront ces traditions du sympathie et de confraternité scientifique." See "Der sechste internationale Orientalisten-Congress," *National-Zeitung,* October 19, 1883.

56. "The congress of American studies scholars which has been meeting here since the 9th of this month offers an opportunity to show German science and the German spirit of research in a favorable light since the numerous and excellent presentations by German scholars, combined with the fact that even most of the Swedish scholars are presenting their papers in German, place the German element very prominently in the foreground" ("Report to von Caprivi of August 7, 1894," in Bundesarchiv Potsdam, *Auswärtiges Amt,* no. 37460). See also the report of Albrecht Weber on the Stockholm congress, in Weber, *Quousque Tandem.*

57. See Krehl, "Report of September 26, 1874, on the Congress of Orientalists in London." On the French-German conflicts, see also Ernst Windisch, the report of October 7, 1883, on the congress in Leyden, in Sächsisches Hauptstaatsarchiv, Ministerium für Volksbildung, no. 10270, vol. 3.

58. See Suzanne L. Marchand, *Down from Olympus: Archeology and Philhellenism in Germany, 1750–1970* (Princeton, N.J.: 1996), chap. 6; Johannes Renger, "Die Geschichte der Altorientalistik und der vorderasiatischen Archäologie in Berlin von 1875 bis 1945," in *Berlin und die Antike,* ed. Willmuth Arenhövel and Christa Schreiber, 2 vols. (Berlin: 1979), 2: 151–92. For a general overview see Johann Fück, *Die arabischen Studien in Europa bis in den Anfang des 20. Jahrhunderts* (Leipzig: 1955); Edward W. Said, *Orientalism* (London: 1978); François Charette, "Orientalisme et histoire des sciences: l'historiographie européenne des sciences islamiques et hindoues, 1784–1900," master's thesis, Université de Montréal, 1995. For accounts from the time, see Enno Littmann, *Der deutsche Beitrag zur Wissenschaft vom Vorderen Orient* (Stuttgart: 1942); Eduard Meyer, "Fünfundzwanzig Jahre Deutsche Orient-Gesellschaft," *Mitteilungen der Deutschen Orient-Gesellschaft zu Berlin* 62 (1923): 1–25.

59. ["Wir Deutsche als Volk sind abgeschlossen von jeder directen Berührung mit dem Morgenland, haben keinen Colonialbesitz, kein Fleckchen morgenlän-

discher Erde, das wir unser eigen nennen könnten . . . wir haben keine Traditionen, die uns nach dem Orient hinweisen . . . Es war einzig und allein die Forschungslust, der Wissensdurst, der Erkenntnistrieb, der das bewirkt hat."] *Verhandlungen des Fünften Internationalen Orientalisten-Congresses, 1881,* 35. Dillmann likewise appealed somewhat later to the "German colleagues who live only for their service to science" ["nur im Dienste der Wissenschaft lebenden deutschen Collegen"] *Verhandlungen des Fünften Internationalen Orientalisten-Congresses, 1881,* 37.

60. ["Noch haben wir keinen nennenswerthen Beuteantheil an den Schätzen Ninive's und Babylon's."] *Verhandlungen des Fünften Internationalen Orientalisten-Congresses, 1881,* 37.

61. See Lewis Pyenson, *Cultural Imperialism and Exact Sciences: German Expansions Overseas, 1900–1930* (New York: 1985); Lewis Pyenson, *Civilizing Mission. Exact Sciences and French Overseas Expansion, 1830–1940* (Baltimore, Md.: 1993). Pyenson suggests a general cross-national analytical model of cultural imperialism in his "Pure Learning and Political Economy: Science and European Expansion in the Age of Imperialism," in *New Trends in the History of Science: Proceedings of a Conference Held at the University of Utrecht,* ed. R. P. W. Visser, H. J. M. Bos, L. C. Palm, and H. A. M. Snelders (Amsterdam: 1989), 274ff. For a German view of the time, see the two essays by Carl H. Becker, "Der Islam und die Kolonialisierung Afrikas" and "Ist der Islam eine Gefahr für unsere Kolonien?" in *Islamstudien: vom Werden und Wesen der islamischen Welt,* ed. Carl H. Becker, 2 vols. (Leipzig: 1932), 2: 187–210, 156–86.

62. See W. Reiss and A. Bastian to Bismarck, December 15, 1887, Bundesarchiv Potsdam, *Auswärtiges Amt,* no. 37459. The thirteenth Congress of Orientalists, held in New York at the American Museum of Natural History in October 1902, was not sponsored by the U.S. government, but the international invitations were sent out by the U.S. State Department. See U.S. Embassy in Berlin to the German Foreign Ministry, December 26, 1901, Bundesarchiv Potsdam, *Auswärtiges Amt,* no. 37460.

63. See Rosen, German Delegate in Tangier, to the Culture Ministry of Saxony, October 6, 1907, regarding the fifteenth Congress of Orientalists in 1908 in Copenhagen, *Sächsisches Hauptstaatsarchiv,* Ministerium für Volksbildung, no. 10273, vol. 9.

64. [". . . daß alle islamitischen Völker 'möglichst bald unter die Tutel europäischer Regierungen kommen mögen,' denn "der jetzige Islam hat keine Cultur-Mission mehr zu erfüllen."] Weber, *Quousque Tandem,* 4.

65. Noteworthy are a social sciences congress held in Melbourne in 1880 on the occasion of the World's Fair, the fourteenth Congress of Orientalists in Algiers in 1905, the eleventh Congress of Americanists in Mexico in 1895, and the seventeenth Congress of Americanists in Buenos Aires in 1912. The proposal made in Stockholm in 1889 that the ninth Congress of Orientalists be held in Cairo was rejected by the participants.

66. *The Conference of Orientalists Including Museums and Archaeology: Conference Held at Simla, July 1911* (Simla: 1911), 66–67. Reference is made here to one reason for the minimal participation of Indians in the European congresses: "It is only in

case they happen to be in Europe on leave that they can arrange to attend. They have to wait till their retirement from the service."

67. Report of May 8, 1912, on the orientalist congress in Athens by August Fischer and Heinrich Zimmern to the Culture Ministry of Saxony, in Sächsisches Hauptstaatsarchiv, Ministerium für Volksbildung, no. 10273, vol. 10. The reason cited was that "the (Muslim) scholars of Cairo seem to offer no guarantee that a congress organized by them would be on the *highest scientific niveau*" (emphasis added).

68. Herbert P. Gregory, "The Pacific Science Congress," *Scientific Monthly* 9 (1924): 272–73.

69. "In Washington, D.C., the Pan-American Union has acted as the big brother to the Pan-Pacific Union." The former provided space at the Carnegie Institution and helped in obtaining appropriations. See "The Pan-Pacific Union," *Bulletin of the Pan-Pacific Union*, no. 19 (May 1921): 10.

70. For details on the early history of the Pacific congresses, see Philip F. Rehbock, "Organizing Pacific Science: Local and International Origins of the Pacific Science Association," in *Nature in its Greatest Extent. Western Science in the Pacific*, ed. Roy MacLeod and Philip F. Rehbock (Honolulu: 1988), 195–221; "The Pan-Pacific Union," 9–11. An early Pan-Pacific Congress had taken place in 1911 and led to establishment of the Hands-around-the-Pacific Club, the precursor to the Pan-Pacific Union. See "The Pan-Pacific Research Council," *Bulletin of the Pan-Pacific Union*, no. 17 (March 1921): 10. Honolulu was also selected as the union's headquarters due to its geographical location "at the very crossroads of the Pacific." For a general account, see A. P. Elkin, *Pacific Science Association: Its History and Role in International Cooperation*, Bernice P. Bishop Museum Special Publication 48 (Honolulu: 1961). Relevant material can also be found in *Report on the Pacific Science Association*, Bernice P. Bishop Museum Special Publication 41, prepared by the Secretariat of the Pacific Science Council (Honolulu: 1951).

71. William M. Davis, "The Exploration of the Pacific," *Proceedings of the National Academy of Sciences* 2 (1916): 391–94.

72. See "The American Association for the Advancement of Science. Pasadena Meeting of the Pacific Division," *Science* 49 (May 23, 1919): 483–87.

73. This was suggested by A. G. Mayor of the Carnegie Institution. See Gregory, "The Pacific Science Congress," 5–6; Rehbock, "Organizing Pacific Science," 198, 204ff. The proposal at the conference of 1918 that a further conference be convened in Japan after the end of the war was apparently never realized. For details, see "Minutes of the Meeting of the Committee on Pacific Investigations, June 9, 1921," in National Academy of Sciences Archives, NAS 1919–1939, Foreign Relations: Committee on Pacific Investigations, 1921–1931, Meetings: Minutes. For general information, see also the notes of E. C. Andrews, chief of the geological survey, Sydney, "The Pan-Pacific Congress of 1923. Its Origin and Objects," in National Academy of Sciences Archives, NAS 1919–1939, International Congresses, Pan-Pacific Science: Second, Melbourne & Sydney: Origin and Objects, Andrews, E. C.

74. On the preparations for this congress, see Herbert E. Gregory, "Introduction," *Proceedings of the First Pan-Pacific Scientific Conference: Under the Auspices of*

the Pan-Pacific Union. Honolulu, Hawaii, August 2 to 20, 1920, Bernice P. Bishop Museum, Special Publication No. 7, Part I. (Honolulu: 1921), iiiff; "Resolutions and Recommendations of the Pan-Pacific Science Congress Called by the Pan-Pacific Union and Held in Honolulu in August 1920," *Journal of the Pan-Pacific Institution* 1 (1926): 3–7. The official title of the conference was the First Pan-Pacific Scientific Conference of the Commercial and Educational Congress.

75. On the second congress, see "Resolutions Adopted at the Australian Meeting of the Pacific Science Congress," *Science* 58 (1923): 502–3. See also *Proceedings of the Pan-Pacific Science Congress, Australia, 1923. Held Under the Auspices of The Australian National Research Council and Through the Generosity of The Commonwealth and State Governments,* ed. Gerald Lightfoot, vol. 1 (Melbourne: n.d.).

76. Melbourne: agriculture; anthropology and ethnology; botany; entomology; forestry; geodesy and geophysics; geography and oceanography; geology, hygiene; veterinary science; and zoology. Within the three divisions in Tokyo, eleven sections met on the subjects of astronomy, radio waves, meteorology, terrestrial magnetism, seismology, architecture, geology, geography, botany, zoology, fishery, agriculture, anthropology, ethnology, medicine, and hygiene.

77. Gregory, "Introduction," v. See also Albert L. Barrows, "Pacific Science Congresses, March 25, 1935," National Academy of Sciences Archives, NAS 1919–1939, Foreign Relations: International Congresses, Pacific Science: Activities and Histories, 1924–1938, 2.

78. "Symposium on Means and Methods of Cooperation," *Proceedings of the First Pan-Pacific Scientific Conference,* pt. 3: 895–919.

79. *Proceedings of the First Pan-Pacific Scientific Conference,* pt. 1: 27. Australia, Canada, China, Japan, New Zealand, Peru, and the United States sent representatives.

80. Herbert E. Gregory, "Pacific Science Association," *Science* 65 (April 8, 1927): 358.

81. Gregory writes in his memorandum: "The conference [of 1920] demonstrated that the task of gathering desired information is beyond the strength of single institutions, that cooperation is the only feasible method, and that some much needed information can be procured only by governmental agencies." Gregory was referring primarily to the inclusion of the navy in scientific research projects. Herbert E. Gregory, "Memorandum for the Secretary of the Navy of January 13, 1922," in National Academy of Sciences Archives, NAS 1919–1939, Foreign Relations: Committee on Pacific Investigations, 1921–1924, General, 2.

82. Herbert E. Gregory to Albert L. Barrows, secretary of the Division of Foreign Relations of the NRC, August 2, 1921, in National Academy of Sciences Archives, NAS 1919–1939, Foreign Relations: Committee on Pacific Investigations, 1921/22, Relations with Pan-Pacific Union.

83. See "The Pan-Pacific Scientific Research Council," 9–11. See also C. H. Edmondson, professor of biology, University of Hawaii, to Herbert E. Gregory, August 2, 1921, National Academy of Sciences Archives, NAS 1919–1939, Foreign Relations: Committee on Pacific Investigations, 1921/22, Relations with Pan-Pacific Union. In 1924 the Pan-Pacific Research Foundation was founded to serve as a research institute for Pacific and other foreign scientists. See "The Pan-Pacific

Research Institution," *Bulletin of the Pan-Pacific Union,* no. 62 (December 1924): 3–9.

84. "The Honolulu meeting was a child of the American National Research Council." "Objects and Organization of the Pan-Pacific Science Congresses," in *Proceedings of the Pan-Pacific Science Congress. Australia 1923. Held Under the Auspices of The Australian National Research Council and Through the Generosity of The Commonwealth and State Governments,* ed. Gerald Lightfoot, vol. 1 (Melbourne: n.d.), 1590. The U.S. institutions that were significantly involved, in addition to the National Research Council, were the Bernice B. Bishop Museum of Honolulu, the Carnegie Institution, the American Museum of Natural History, and the California Academy of Sciences. See Gregory, "Memorandum for the Secretary of the Navy of January 13, 1922."

85. Davis, "The Exploration of the Pacific," 394.

86. On the relationship between the National Research Council and the Pan-Pacific Union, see "Minutes of the Meeting of the Committee on Pacific Investigations, June 9, 1921." The United States contributed $9,000 to the financing of the first congress, Hawaii contributed $6,000, and the Pan-Pacific Union contributed about $18,000. "The Pan-Pacific Scientific Research Council," 9; "The Pan-Pacific Union," 9; Barrows, "Pacific Science Congresses," 9. Ford envisioned the establishment of a Pan-Pacific League of Nations, with Hawaii as "The Hague of the Pacific." See "The Pan-Pacific League of Nations," *Bulletin of the Pan-Pacific Union,* no. 21 (July 1921): 7; Alexander H. Ford, "A Pan-Pacific League of Nations," *Bulletin of the Pan-Pacific Union,* no. 31 (May 1922): 13–15; "A Hague of the Pacific," *Bulletin of the Pan-Pacific Union,* no. 65 (June 1925): 3–6.

87. "Second Pan-Pacific Science Congress, Introductory Note," in National Academy of Sciences Archives, NAS 1919–1939, Foreign Relations: International Congresses, Pan-Pacific Science: Second, Melbourne & Sydney: General; see, also, National Academy of Sciences Archives, NAS 1919–1939, Foreign Relations: International Congresses, Pan-Pacific Science: Melbourne & Sydney: Proposed. Also found there are the lists of those to whom letters were mailed concerning cooperation in Pacific investigation, and the corresponding replies.

88. These were Australia, Canada, China, France, Great Britain, Hawaii, Indo-China, Japan, Netherlands, Netherlands Indies, New Zealand, Philippine Islands, United States, and Union of Soviet Socialist Republics. These "countries" included colonies. On the highly politicized debates about which colonies would receive the status of a "country" for purposes of international scientific unions of the International Research Council in the 1920s, see Pyenson, *Civilizing Mission,* 146f.

89. See *Proceedings of the Pan-Pacific Science Congress, Australia, 1923,* 39; The National Research Council of Japan, ed., *Proceedings of the Third Pan-Pacific Science Congress. Tokyo. October 30th–November 11th, 1926. Held under the Auspices of the National Research Council of Japan and through the Generosity of the Imperial Japanese Government,* vol. 1 (Tokyo: 1928), 98ff.

90. See *Proceedings of the Pan-Pacific Science Congress, Australia, 1923,* 17, 27.

91. Joji Sakurai, Imperial University of Tokyo and National Research Council of Japan, to T. W. Vaughan, National Research Council, March 28, 1914, National

Academy of Sciences Archives, NAS 1919–1939, Foreign Relations: International Relations: International Organizations, Pacific Science Association: Formation, 1924–1926.

92. ["Organiszados con carácter permanente, como acontece en Estados-Unidos y en Europa, celebra sesiones periódicas, cada dos años verbigracia, que son anunciadeas al mundo científico por medio de los programas." "¿Por qué no nos hemos de asociar una vez al fin, al movimiento de los progresos morales del mundo civilizado?"] Estanislao S. Zeballos, *Congreso Científico Internacional Sud-Americano* (Buenos Aires: 1878), 4.

93. The society was founded in 1872. In addition to publishing the "Annales," it had organized a scientific–technical exhibition in 1875–1876 and initiated an expedition to the Andes. See *Sociedad científica Argentina. Congreso Científico Intern-acional Americano* (Buenos Aires: 1910), 7.

94. This and the subsequent Pan-American Congresses in 1915–1916 in Washington, D.C., and in 1924–1925 in Lima were initially counted as the first three Pan-American Scientific Congresses. It was decided in Lima to include the Congreso científico latino americano in the count. Lima was thereafter counted as the sixth congress. See *Report of the Delegates of the United States of America to the Third Pan American Scientific Congress. Held at Lima, Peru. December 20, 1924 to January 6, 1925* (Washington, D.C.: 1925). In addition to this series, another "Congreso científico internacional americano" took place in 1910 in Buenos Aires on the occasion of the hundredth anniversary of the Mayo-Revolution. See *Sociedad científica Argentina. Congreso Científico Internacional Americano. Buenos Aires 1910*. European scholars also took part in this congress.

95. *Cuarto Congreso Científico (1.° Pan-Americano). Reseña General por Eduardo Poíríer, Secretario General del mismo Congreso* (Santiago de Chile: 1915), 2.

96. The sixth Pan-American Scientific Congress took place in Lima in 1924–1925, where the future congresses were renamed the American Scientific Congress. San Jose was planned as the site of the seventh congress in 1929. This plan could not be carried out due to the economic crisis, so the Pan-American Union Board of Directors suggested Mexico for 1932. The congress finally took place in Mexico City in 1935. On the occasion of the fiftieth anniversary of the founding of the Pan-American Union, the eighth American Scientific Congress was convened in Washington, D.C., in 1940. See *Septimo Congreso Científico Americano. General Information on the Seventh American Scientific Congress* (Mexico City: 1931), 3f.; *Proceedings of the Eighth American Scientific Congress. Held in Washington. May 10–18, 1940. Under the Auspices of the United States of America*, vol. 1 (Washington, D.C.: 1941), 9f. In addition to the American Scientific Congresses, international specialist congresses were also held. For example, the Pan-American Medical Congress met eight times between 1893 and 1908; in 1916, an American Congress of Social Science was held in Tucumán and an American Congress of Bibliography and History and Book Fair was held in Buenos Aires. In 1922, the first International Congress of History of America took place in Rio de Janeiro, followed four years later by the second International Congress of History and Geography in Asuncion.

97. "Up to now, we have only assimilated the intellectual achievements of the

Orient and of Europe, and it is time to pay our tribute to the world with our own original scientific results in order to improve the conditions of the people in the future. . . . By frequent congresses we achieve the formation of an American league." ["Hasta ahora, solo hemos asimilado los productos de la intelectualidad del Oriente y de la Europa y es tiempo ya de pagar al mundo nuestro tributo, con resultantes científicas originales, que mejoren las cindiciones del hombre del provenir . . . llegomos en sucesivos congresos, á la formación de una liga americana."] See *Segunda Reunión del Congreso Científico Latino Americano. Celebrada en Montevideo del 20 al 31 de Marzo de 1901*, vol. 1 (Montevideo: 1901).

98. ["Por esta razón tiene él un significado psicológico tan grande para las relaciones internacionales. Estoy convencido que por intermedio de los hombres de ciencia es como vamos a llegar a destuir los últimos resabios de la época en la cual las palabras extranjero y enemigo eran casi sinónimas."] *Cuarto Congreso Científico (1.° Pan-Americano)*, 72.

99. *Second Pan American Scientific Congress. Held in the City of Washington in the United States of America. December 27, 1915–January 8, 1916. The Final Act and Interpretative Commentary Thereon. Prepared by James Brown Scott*, vol. II (Washington, D.C.: 1916), 44f.

100. Since 1970, the organization has been called the General Secretariat of the Organization of the American States. Up until the time of World War II, the Pan-American Union had held eight International American Conferences: Washington, D.C., 1889–1890; Mexico, 1901–1902; Rio de Janeiro, 1906; Buenos Aires, 1910; Santiago de Chile, 1923; Havana, 1928; Montevideo, 1933; and Lima, 1938. For a perspective of that time on the first conferences, see Robert Büchi, *Die Geschichte der Pan-Amerikanischen Bewegung mit besonderer Berücksichtigung ihrer völkerrechtlichen Bedeutung* (Breslau: 1914); Alfred H. Fried, *Panamerika. Entwicklung, Umfang und Bedeutung der panamerikanischen Bewegung (1810–1910)* (Berlin: 1910).

101. *Report of the Delegates of the United States to the Pan-American Scientific Congress. Held at Santiago, Chile. December 25, 1908, to January 5, 1909* (Washington, D.C.: 1909), 7. He meant the fourth International American Conference in Buenos Aires in 1910.

102. The International American Congresses approved corresponding resolutions, for example, the Convention on the Practice of the Learned Professions and a Convention on the Literary Exchange in 1901–1902 in Mexico, and an exchange of students and professors in Buenos Aires in 1910. Beginning with the congress in Chile in 1923, intellectual cooperation was recognized as an important pillar of intra-American relations. In 1938, a third of all resolutions dealt with intellectual cooperation. See *Evolution of the Pan American Movement*, vol. 4, *Inter-American Cultural Cooperation* (Washington, D.C.: 1942), 26.

103. *Report of the Delegates of the United States to the Pan-American Scientific Congress, 1909*, 12. The proposal involved establishing national bibliographic agencies. See *Conferencias Internacionales Americana 1889–1936* (Washington, D.C.: 1938), 202.

104. *The Pan American Institute of Geography and History. Its Creation, Development, and Current Program. 1929–1954*, PAIGH Publication No. 180 (Mexico: 1954), 21f. An initial Pan-American Geographical Congress had taken place in Rio de Janeiro in 1914.

105. *Report of the Delegates of the United States to the Pan-American Scientific Congress, 1909*, 8.

106. See Robert N. Seidel, "Progressive Pan Americanism: Development and United States Policy Towards South America, 1906–1931," Ph.D. dissertation, Cornell University, 1973.

107. *Second Pan-American Scientific Congress. Held in Washington in the United States of America. December 27, 1915–January 8, 1916. The Report of the Secretary General. Prepared by John Barret and Glen Levin Swiggett* (Washington, D.C.: 1917), 11f, 30. The other eight sections were anthropology; astronomy, meteorology, and seismology; conservation of natural sources, agriculture, irrigation, and forestry; education; mining and metallurgy, economic geology, and applied chemistry; transportation, commerce, finance, and taxation; engineering; and public health and medical science.

108. Glen Levin Swiggett, "Circular Letter to the Press," in *Second Pan American Scientific Congress, Report of the Secretary General*, 31ff.

109. "Address of Welcome on Behalf of the United States Given by Hon. Thomas R. Marshall, Vice President of the United States," in *Second Pan American Scientific Congress, Report of the Secretary General*, 51ff; "Address of Welcome on Behalf of the Department of State by Hon. Robert Lansing, Secretary of State," in *Second Pan American Scientific Congress, Report of the Secretary General*, 55ff, quote on 57.

110. "Address of the Chairman of the Delegation of the United States, Dr. L. S. Rowe, at the Inaugural Session of the Congress," in *Report of the Delegates of the United States of America to the Third Pan American Scientific Congress. Held at Lima, Peru. December 20, 1924, to January 6, 1925* (Washington, D.C.: 1925), appendix C.

111. "Address of the President of the Congress, the Ambassador of Chile," in *Second Pan-American Scientific Congress, Report of the Secretary General*, 63.

212. *Report of the Delegates of the United States to the Pan-American Scientific Congress, 1909*, 13; appendix C.

113. "Art. 3—Those countries, dominions, colonies, territories or dependencies lying within or bordering the Pacific ocean, and those countries having dominions, colonies, territories, or dependencies in the Pacific region and interested in the above object, shall be eligible for admission to the Association." See constitution of the Pacific Science Association that was adopted at the third Pan-Pacific Science Congress in Tokyo. *Proceedings of the Third Pan-Pacific Scientific Congress, Tokyo, October 30–November 11, 1926. Held under the auspices of The National Research Council of Japan and Through the Generosity of the Imperial Japanese Government*. Ed. National Research Council of Japan (Tokyo: 1926), 98. Repr. in Elkin, *Pacific Science Association*, 75.

114. See Howard J. Rogers, ed., *Congress of Arts and Science. Universal Exposition, St. Louis, 1904*, vol. 1 (St. Louis, Mo.: 1905). Of the 105 representatives from sixteen countries, only five (aside from Canadians) came from non-European countries: four from Japan and one from Mexico.

115. There has been detailed research on this point in recent years as concerns German cultural policy. For example, see Kurt Düwell, *Deutschlands auswärtige Kulturpolitik, 1918–1932. Grundlinien und Dokumente* (Cologne: 1976); Rüdiger v. Bruch, *Weltpolitik als Kulturmission. Auswärtige Kulturpolitik und Bildungsbürgertum*

in Deutschland am Vorabend des Ersten Weltkrieges (Paderborn: 1982); Gerhard A. Ritter, "Motive und Organisationsformen der internationalen Wissenschaftsbeziehungen und die Anfänge einer auswärtigen Kulturpolitik im deutschen Kaiserreich vor dem Ersten Weltkrieg," in *Studien zur Geschichte Englands und der deutsch-britischen Beziehungen*, ed. Lothar Kettenacker, Manfred Schlenke, and Hellmut Seier (Munich: 1981), 153–83; Bernhard v. Brocke, "Internationale Wissenschaftsbeziehungen und die Anfänge einer deutschen auswärtigen Kulturpolitik: Der Professorenaustausch mit Nordamerika," in *Wissenschaftsgeschichte und Wissenschaftspolitik im Industriezeitalter. Das "System Althoff" in historischer Perspektive*, ed. Bernhard v. Brocke (Hildesheim: 1991), 185–242; Ragnhild Fiebig-von Hase, "Die politische Funktionalisierung von Kultur: der sogenannte 'deutsch-amerikanische' Professorenaustausch von 1904–1914," in *Zwei Wege in die Moderne. Aspekte der deutsch-amerikanischen Beziehungen 1900–1918*, ed. Ragnhild Fiebig-von Hase and Jürgen Heideking (Trier: 1998), 45–88.

116. From the perspective of the history of the discipline of history of science, see Lewis Pyenson, "The Ideology of Western Rationality: History of Science and the European Civilizing Mission," *Science and Education* 2 (1993): 329–43; Lewis Pyenson, "Prerogatives of European Intellect: Historians of Science and the Promotion of Western Civilization," *History of Science* 31 (1993): 289–315.

117. Details on this can be found in Jürgen von Ungern-Sternberg and Wolfgang von Ungern Sternberg, *Der Aufruf an die Kulturwelt: das Manifest der 93 und die Anfänge der Kriegspropaganda im Ersten Weltkrieg; mit einer Dokumentation* (Stuttgart: 1996); Bernhard v. Brocke, " 'Wissenschaft und Militarismus.' Der Aufruf der 93 'An die Kulturwelt!' und der Zusammenbruch der internationalen Gelehrtenrepublik im Ersten Weltkrieg," in *Wilamowitz nach 50 Jahren*, ed. W. M. Calder 3rd, H. Flasher, and T. Lindken (Darmstadt: 1985), 649–716.

118. Herbert E. Gregory, "Responses to Delegates," in *Proceedings of the Third Pan-Pacific Scientific Congress*, 130.

119. Joji Sakurai, "President's Banquet," in *Proceedings of the Third Pan-Pacific Scientific Congress*, 128.

120. For example, see proposal of collaboration with the International Research Council that had already been made at the first Pan-Pacific Scientific Congress. See *Proceedings of the First Pan-Pacific Scientific Conference*, 27.

121. The first international congress of American studies met in Nancy in 1875 at the instigation of the Societé Américaine de France. The later meetings took place in: Luxembourg, 1877; Brussels, 1879; Madrid, 1881; Copenhagen, 1883; Turin, 1886; Berlin, 1888; Paris, 1890; Huelva, Spain, 1892; Stockholm, 1894; Mexico City, 1895; Paris, 1900; New York, 1902; Stuttgart, 1904; Quebec, 1906; Vienna, 1908; Buenos Aires, 1910; London, 1912; Washington, D.C., 1915.

122. On Hale, see Daniel J. Kevles, " 'Into Hostile Political Camps': The Reorganisation of International Science in World War I," *Isis* 62 (1971): 47–60. Documentation on the international involvement of the National Academy of Sciences can be found in National Academy of Sciences Archives, NAS, 1914–1918, International Relations.

123. See Jameson to Woodward, May 24, 1918, in *An Historian's World*, ed. Elizabeth Donnan and L. F. Stock (Philadelphia: 1956), 223; also Erdmann, *Die Ökumene*

der Historiker, 102ff, 137 ff. The first postwar congress of orientalists, the seventeenth, did not take place until 1928, in Oxford.

124. Among others, see Brigitte Schröder-Gudehus, "Deutsche Wissenschaft und internationale Zusammenarbeit 1914–1928. Ein Beitrag zum Studium kultureller Beziehungen in politischen Krisenzeiten," thesis, Geneva, 1966, 90ff; Paul Forman, "Scientific Internationalism and the Weimar Physicists: The Ideology and Its Manipulation in Germany after World War I," *Isis* 64 (1973): 150–80; Frank Greenaway, *Science International: A History of the International Council of Scientific Unions* (Cambridge, Mass.: 1996); A. G. Cock, "Chauvinism and Internationalism in Science: The International Research Council, 1919–1926," *Notes and Records of the Royal Society of London* 37 (1983): 249–88.

125. See Kevles, " 'Into Hostile Political Camps'," 47–60. Documentation on the international involvement of the National Academy of Sciences can be found in National Academy of Sciences Archives, NAS, 1914–1918, International Relations.

Part III

BEYOND EUROCENTRISM: THE POLITICS OF HISTORY IN A GLOBAL AGE

10

History without a Center?

Reflections on Eurocentrism

Arif Dirlik

To raise the question of how to center, or de-center, history in the current intellectual climate is to invite, almost automatically, the question of Eurocentrism, which seems to be on everyone's minds these days, including the contributors to this volume. How to rescue history from the Eurocentrism that has dominated it for the past two centuries is an important question, and not just an academic one. The question may not be new, and may even be misleading in a variety of ways, as I suggest below. However, it has acquired renewed vigor and persuasiveness as the hegemony of a European, and subsequently American, conception of globality recedes before alternative claims to the globe, or to significant portions of it, that are accompanied by demands for writing the past non-Eurocentrically, which includes the revival of pre-Eurocentric histories. Within Europe and North America, Eurocentrism, understood additionally in terms of white male domination, finds itself challenged by women, peoples of color, and indigenous peoples who demand the rewriting of history so that they may be written into it in full recognition of their historical presence. Politics globally and identity politics more locally unite to call for alternatives to Eurocentrism, which has come to overshadow other questions concerning history in both historical and cultural studies.

Interestingly, these calls from outside of history as a discipline gain more of a hearing presently because of developments in the study of the past, which, for all its Eurocentrism, has produced results that render untenable further sustenance of Eurocentric consciousness and para-

digms. As William H. McNeill, a distinguished student of "world history,"[1] remarked:

> The expansion of readily available information has been spectacular, and
> academic historians can no longer, as they did in my youth, remain cheer-
> fully indifferent to what happened among the four-fifths of humankind that
> did not inhabit Western Europe and the United States. This strikes me as an
> obvious advance, even at the price of cacophonous confusion.[2]

The only thing that seems to be clearly audible in this cacophony, we
might add, is the call for overcoming Eurocentrism. How to do so is the
source of the confusion. The problem, however, may involve more than
confusion over technical problems of writing non-Eurocentric histories,
or even conflicting ideologies, but may be a product rather of a contradiction in the very issue of Eurocentrism. Such a contradiction is indicated
by the chapters in this book, which point in two nearly opposite directions. On the one hand, there is an urge on the part of most of the authors
to overcome Eurocentrism in the conceptualization and writing of history.
On the other hand, however, the chapters indicate that it may be impossible to comprehend history in the various societies discussed without reference to its origins in modern Europe. Intellectual and cultural values
expressive of Eurocentrism are no longer confined to Europeans and
North Americans, but are a fundamental part of the experience of modernity, lodged in the consciousness of all who have been participants in
modernity globally. History is very much part of this consciousness. Nicholas Dirks has referred to history as "a sign of the modern."[3] The particularly modern experience of the relationship between the past, the present
and the future pervades consciousness even in those societies where
modernity may remain an incomplete project, or that may claim alternative modernities of one kind or another. Not only the conceptualization
but even the practice of history in widely divergent societies has been
shaped in the encounter with modernity by paradigms and practices that
have their origins in an earlier Eurocentric rewriting of the past. This is to
suggest not identity but commonality in the experience and the organization of the past. If Eurocentrism is an intractable problem, it is because
the peculiar modern European consciousness of the past—spatially no
less than temporally—is now a common legacy of modernity.

Overcoming Eurocentrism, therefore, requires first that we consider the
location of Eurocentrism, which is by no means self-evident. This is the
question that I take up below. I would like to suggest that the issue, ultimately, is not one or another way of "centering" history, but rather the
status of history as a way of knowing the past and the present. To complicate matters, the very desire to rescue history from Eurocentrism is entan-

gled in the history of Eurocentrism, and a politics that may serve
conservative and even retrograde causes as readily as it may contribute to
progressive global visions.

THE LOCATION OF EUROCENTRISM

If Eurocentrism could be overcome by bringing Europe's many "others"
into history, or even by a recognition of historicity to "peoples without
history," as McNeill's statement suggests, then our times could be celebrated as heralding a new, post-Eurocentric age. It seems, at least within
a U.S. context, that all one needs to be admitted into history is to ask for
it, and sometimes even that is not necessary, for it is possible to be
included in history these days without even knowing it. It is possible even
to challenge "the view that American people shared a precious and
unique 'Western civilization' with parts of Europe" on the grounds that
"the historical heritages of every people of the earth are of equal value,
even if, or especially if they were mistreated by European imperialists in
the recent past."[4]

The crowding of history, and a recognition in at least some quarters
that the crowds have a right to be there, not only de-centers "Western
civilization," but calls into question the temporalities of a Eurocentric
conceptualization of the world, where the particular historical trajectory
of Euro-American societies served as a teleology worldwide in marking
time. It was this teleology, empowered by claims to the present as well as
the future, that provided the yardstick for determining stagnation in history as well as exclusion from it. There is certainly a widespread feeling
presently that since different historical heritages have equal claims on history, the future, too, is up for grabs—at least among the societies that now
make their own claims to the center. At its extreme, the criticism of a
Euro-American teleology, in its bourgeois as well as Marxist formulations, takes the form of denying to Europe and North America a significant part in history, portraying them as unwanted intruders who
managed for a brief while to hijack time, as they had colonized space.

Probably few of us would agree that any of this signals the imminent
demise of Eurocentrism. We may feel more critically self-conscious, or
even guiltier, than in the past about excluding others from history, and
do our best to adopt world or global history perspectives that not only
enable us to accommodate as many peoples and perspectives as technically possible, but help us transcend our own parochialisms; at the
extreme, we may even deny to Europe (and North America) a special
place in the shaping of history. And yet none of this alleviates a sense of
unease that Eurocentrism persists against all efforts to overcome it. It

seems often enough that the very preoccupation with Eurocentrism perpetuates it by endlessly returning attention to Euro-America. No matter
how hard we try to de-center, recenter or "ex-center"[5] history, Eurocentrism persists as a frame of reference. Critics of Eurocentrism inspired by
cultural studies spend more time on what Euro-American writers and
theorists have had to say about the rest of the world than they do speaking of the societies at hand, which further displaces the latter from the
historian's attention. Aside from area specialists who long have sought
to bring the societies they study to the center of their disciplines (with
considerable irony, given the origins of area studies in a Eurocentric paradigm of the world, of which more below), so-called world or global historians are particularly prominent in our day in efforts to open history to
others, and to search for explanations that eschew the centrality of Euro-
America to historical development. As Raymond Grew, a sympathetic
critic, observes, however, the "central question" of most world history
writing is still "to explain why European civilization outshone all others."[6] Inclusion of others in history is by no means inconsistent with a
Eurocentric teleology. Grew also writes:

> World history offers the framework for a continuous narrative, one that starts
> with the pulse of civilization beating to the rhythm of riparian agriculture
> along the Tigris and Euphrates, then moves through the classical world and
> across two millennia until Europe's power and influence extend across the
> globe. The civilizations not in this direct line, however much admired, are
> presented initially as separate stories but differ most from the main narrative
> in always coming to an end, each giving way to the next until all become part
> of the world the West has won.[7]

Beyond textbook histories, influential works by both Francis Fukuyama
and David Landes have in recent years, respectively, reaffirmed Euro-
American political models as "the end of history," and Euro-America as
the dynamic force of the last millennium.[8] Landes's work in particular is
addressed to critics of Eurocentrism, whom he lambastes as bad historians, "Europhobes" and "anti-intellectuals." He also argues against
"multicultural, globalist, egalitarian history" to affirm the centrality of
"Western civilization and its diffusion" to historical progress over the last
millennium.[9] His explicitly critical stance against anti-Eurocentrists is an
indication that Eurocentrism is not merely a residue of past habits (as
might be the case with world history textbooks), but continues to function
as an important component of thinking about the past.

   If inclusion of others in history does not in and of itself negate Eurocentrism, neither does the repudiation of a Eurocentric teleology, as is evident in the case of Samuel Huntington's "Clash of Civilizations," which

is not a historical work per se, but freely draws upon history.[10] What is relevant about Huntington's argument in the present context is his disavowal of the "West" as either the end of history, or a model to be emulated by other "civilizations," which retain immutable characteristics against all historical change. Under the circumstances, "the concept of a universal civilization helps justify Western cultural dominance of other societies and the need for those societies to ape Western practices and institutions."[11] Huntington's world, too, is "multicultural" but, unlike in liberal versions of multiculturalism, he views it not as a product of but as an insurmountable obstacle to globalization; civilizations in this view will go their separate ways in the foreseeable future. What qualifies his argument as Eurocentric is neither exclusion of other societies from history, nor their subjection to a Eurocentric teleology, but his normative evaluation of the "West," with its unique values—from democracy to human rights—which others simply will not get.

To reiterate what I said previously, Eurocentrism persists not just as a residue of the past. These various reaffirmations of Eurocentrism are as much a response to contemporary circumstances as the repudiation of Eurocentrism. There is little in this persistence of Eurocentrism that is surprising. After all, if history is important in the construction of identity, there should be nothing unexpected about the centering of history around a real or imagined identity. Much of the current discussion of history in relationship to identity seeks to abolish identity by denying to it a center, by stressing the fluidity or instability of identity, or its constructedness and inventedness, which issues in the replacement of settled with hybrid identities, and of centers by borderlands. However appealing this dethroning of identity may be under current circumstances (more in some societies than in others, and more for some groups in those societies), it does not, as Lewis Wurgaft argues, abolish the concern for identity per se.[12] In fact, one of the ironies of the current ferment over identity is its simultaneous questioning of the possibility of stable identities and its demand for the recognition of identities suppressed in the past, which in the realm of history takes the form of demands for the recognition of the historical presence of those groups that earlier had been left out of history. Globally, the questioning of civilizational, cultural, or national identity coincides with the reaffirmation of such identities. What we seem to have presently is not the abolition of centers, but the crowding of the center to history by proliferating claims to it, on the one hand, and a proliferation of centers, on the other.

It is silly under the circumstances to expect that a reflexive awareness of Eurocentrism should lead, therefore, to abolition of a Europe or U.S.-centered history. This is especially the case if we recognize that European and U.S. power still dominates the world, and the economic, social, political, and cultural products of Europe and the United States continue to play a transformative role globally. One may not like the way world histories are written presently, or the way a Landes or Huntington deals with the relationship between culture and history, but that is no reason for rejecting offhand the issues that they raise.

My goal here, however, is not to justify the Eurocentrism of these works, but to return, through these explicit reaffirmations of Eurocentrism, to the question at hand: the location of Eurocentrism. What these works reveal is that the inclusion of others in history, or even the repudiation of Eurocentric teleology, does not suffice to exhaust the question of Eurocentrism. In fact, the persistence of Eurocentrism, in spite of inclusiveness and a multidirectional approach to history, reveals that there may be something quite misleading about the problem of Eurocentrism framed in those terms—especially if we recall that there is little that is new in Euro-American historiographies about either inclusiveness or the recognition of civilizational diversity. Eurocentrism goes much deeper. Kerwin Klein reminds us that even anti-Eurocentrism in some of its versions may be very much part of a Western tradition.[13]

The distinguishing feature of Eurocentrism is not its exclusiveness, which is common to all ethnocentrisms, but rather the reverse: its inclusiveness. When I stated previously that it is possible to be included in history without even knowing it, I was not being flippant. From books to television, and now the Internet, peoples of the world, their cultural practices, and their experiences are inventoried, organized, and recorded into history in ways that are mostly beyond their imagination and control—unless they are participants in the activity. It is this activity, and its organizing principles, that at the most fundamental level constitute Eurocentrism. Since this activity coincided in its origins with a new scientific classification and explanation of the world, moreover, it claims both access to truths that are not available to the people so classified themselves, and priority over *their* self-perceptions and perceptions of the world. History, along with other social sciences systematized in the nineteenth century, articulates a new mastery over the world. This history is no longer a history of states, or the church, or of moral exemplars that serves the present by offering to it the mirror of the past. It is a history that takes entire societies and the whole world in all its aspects as its domain, and seeks to classify and explain them holistically and systematically. History as we know it—with its truth claims based on its methods, with its spatial and temporal assumptions, its units of analysis, and its analytical categories—is ultimately the most fundamental location of Eurocentrism. This is not to say that there is only one way of doing history, that history (or Eurocentrism) is free of contradictions, or that it is itself immune to historicity. Quite the contrary, as I will argue below. The very claim to universality, and the effort to encompass the world as a whole, generates its own contradictions. Efforts to resolve these contradictions, however, are circumscribed by their own context in history, and intensify its domination of modern consciousness.

To rehearse a few well-known facts, historically, Eurocentrism as we confront it now is the product of an unprecedented urge and effort to organize the knowledge of the world, including other ways of knowing, into one systematic whole. Appearing at the origins of European modernity, both the urge and the effort still characterize our present. Throughout the centuries peoples other than Europeans have come to participate in the effort, but it is still Euro-Americans—by now, most prominently, the Americans of the United States—who are driven by the urge, and disseminate it across the globe. The participation of others, on the other hand, does not signal the dissolution of Eurocentrism, but their incorporation in a Eurocentric modernity.

The urge to inventory the world is visible already in the *Travels of Marco Polo*, which reads in many of its parts as a mapping of the world, and a catalog of its peoples and commodities. The inventorying of both the natural and the human worlds intensifies with overseas explorations. Daniel Boorstin has documented that the inventories included not only what Europeans observed of the world, but also what others knew of it; in other words, European knowledge grew also by incorporating local knowledge.[14] By the eighteenth century both the accumulation and the organization of this new knowledge became more systematic, issuing in the nineteenth century in the social sciences of which we are heirs. McNeill writes that:

A flood of information about the Americas and other formerly unknown parts of the earth assaulted European consciousness . . . European learning reaffirmed (or at least paid lip service to) Christian truths, explored new fields of knowledge, accumulated more and more information about the past, and about far parts of the earth, and dodged the question of how to fit all the new data together. This remained the case until the eighteenth century when radical efforts to organize empirical knowledge systematically (stimulated partly by Newton's spectacular success in physics and astronomy) began to meet with apparent success in such fields as botany. . . . In these same centuries, the Chinese, Moslem and Indian traditions of learning were far more successful in resisting challenge from without, improving upon the Europeans by refusing to pay attention to new and discrepant information. When a few self-styled "Enlightened" thinkers, located mainly in France, began to abandon the inherited Christian framework of knowledge entirely, guardians of inherited truth in Asia were not impressed. Instead, serious efforts to come to grips with what eventually became undeniably superior European knowledge and skills were delayed until almost our own time.[15]

This remarkable passage, coming from the most prominent "world historian" of our times, is noteworthy for dodging the question of agency, of which I will say more below, but it illustrates cogently the point here: that the accumulation of knowledge is central to distinguishing European from other civilizations in the modern world. In this development, history played the part of cataloging human societies and reordering the past in order to account for their diversity. Before societies could be assigned their places in this new order, or excluded from it for being without history, they first had to be included in the new account of the past.

This accumulation of knowledge, and its organization, became not just the context but also the formative moment of Eurocentrism. It is curious that critics of Eurocentrism have little to say about these well-known developments, which could come out of any textbook on Western civilization or world history; or perhaps it is not very curious, for that very reason: that this account of developments has a Eurocentric sound to it. The price to be paid for ignoring these developments, however, is to endow the concept of Eurocentrism with a transparency that it does not have, mostly by dehistoricizing it.

In 1970 John Elliott argued that it was the discovery of human societies around the globe that forced a revision of the past, and ultimately inspired a new narrative that placed Europe at the center and the end of history.[16] It matters little, I think, whether a sense of Eurocenteredness or European (Christian) superiority preceded these developments. Such a sense, possibly a universal feature of all ethnocentrisms, does not suffice to distinguish Eurocentrism as a historical phenomenon. Neither does it help to explain why the "centering" of history emerges as a problem in the first place. We may observe from our contemporary perspective that Eurocentrism and Sinocentrism, to take just two examples, coexisted for centuries blissfully unaware of their respective claims to the center of the world, because in an ideological sense, if not *just* an ideological sense, they inhabited different "worlds," as did most of the populations inhabiting the globe. I will say more on this question below with reference to contemporary world historiography; suffice it to say here that it was their incorporation into a single world that was to raise the question of the center that, needless to say, persists to our day.

The consequence in a European perspective, at least in the long run, was the disappearance of the outside. The "wild" men and curious peoples outside of Europe were now brought within the boundaries of Europe,[17] calling forth a new narrative that ordered "civilizations" as well as the "timeless" others in a new temporal hierarchy. History itself became possible only in relationship to other civilizations "vegetating in the teeth of time," to cite a well-known phrase of Marx's, or in relation to these timeless others, which in the nineteenth century would become the domain of anthropology. Eurocentrism and history, in other words, coincided in their emergence. We might add to them the new spatialization of the world, which was a condition of their emergence. When by 1768 James Cook had completed his explorations of the Pacific, Europeans could claim a new global vision to which there was no outside; the task that remained was to explore regions that remained in the interstitial shadows of this new world. As they mapped and named this world, so they assigned its inhabitants into natural and temporal categories, newly designed to account for the diversity of the world. This global vision was the justification ultimately for the hubris toward other peoples and their knowledge—that Europeans could know them and their knowledge better than they did as they could claim a global oversight. What was suppressed in the process was the possibility of other ways of knowing the world—and the past.

We need to be cautious here not to reify either Europe or Eurocentrism, but to view them in their historicity. Eurocentrism in contemporary discourse is understood primarily in its relationship to the rest of the world. It was equally important, as Samir Amin has argued, in the invention of Europe. Amin has argued convincingly that it was the discovery of a world crowded with peoples that in the end culminated in the invention of a European tradition, that continues to inform textbook accounts such as the one quoted previously. Medieval Europeans, Amin suggests, had much more in common with their contemporaries outside of Europe than they did with their predecessors or their successors on the continent. It was modern Europe that invented a linear history that proceeded from origins in Greece and Rome, through the medieval period, to the modern.[18] Europe itself had to be invented as Europeans reinvented the world. What was suppressed in the process was the part European expansion, and European appropriation of other knowledge, played in the formation of Europe. A product of these developments, history, was rendered into their cause.

The argument is highly suggestive in pointing to a fundamental contradiction within Eurocentrism: the abolition of the outside by bringing the world within Europe, while at the same time insisting on an outside in the invention of Europe; Europe unique, but universal, to recall the claim to which Huntington objects. Eurocentrism as a vision directed within as much as without calls attention to other possible contradictions as well: that the claims to universality may have led to contestations over its meaning within a Europe that experienced fragmentation into nation-states even as a secular vision emerged of Europe as a whole vis-à-vis the outside. The problems of Eurocentrism on a global scale that we encounter today, in other words, may have been played out first on a European scale, pointing to the possibility that due to its internal contradictions,

Eurocentrism must remain an unfinished project, because its very claims to universality, its very efforts to contain the outside by bringing it within, generate new particularities that refuse to be so contained. The particularities may be marked by the Eurocentrism of their origins, however, complicating the location and meaning of Eurocentrism.

Parallels between intra-European relations and European relations with the outside world in the emergence of Eurocentrism are revealing in more ways than one. I do not wish, in historicizing Eurocentrism, to assign causal priority to developments internal to Europe as a continent versus European interactions with others beyond the continent, as the two were part of the same process (the separation of the two in many ways is crucial to, and characteristic of the Eurocentrism–anti-Eurocentrism debate). Fernand Braudel, employing world system analysis, has argued that the formation of Europe from the eleventh century on was very much entangled in the relations of various European societies with one another *and* with the outside world.[19] As Amin would suggest, there was no clear delineation early on of an inside and an outside to Europe. The "wild men" inhabited the interstices of European societies, as they inhabited the world outside of Europe, which should make us wonder if, say, in spite of assumptions of a common world of Christianity, to a Venetian in the twelfth century the colonization of locations within Europe differed substantially as political or ideological projects from colonization of locations outside of Europe.

I raise this question for two reasons. First is to underline the reification of the idea of "Europe" that informs dehistoricized uses of the term Eurocentrism by its critics no less than by its defenders. Such reification suppresses the fact that the invention either of Europe or of Eurocentrism was not a "European" project per se, but the product of initiatives that emanated from shifting locations within Europe temporally, in which the collaboration between states and capital played a dynamic part, as Giovanni Arrighi has analyzed recently, and which was accompanied by intense conflict between various European states.[20] Class and gender status played an important part in determining participation in these projects, as well as the distribution of their rewards and punishments. There were, in other words, close parallels between colonization at home and abroad. The paradigm of colonialism may have much to tell us about state-building projects, especially with the emergence of the nation-state: in the state monopolization of the instruments of violence, in the use for the control of the population of new techniques of surveillance and inventory, and in the efforts to create homogeneous national cultures that erased local differences, to cite some of the most important.[21] Most relevant for purposes here may be the erasure of local knowledge, whether place-based or women's knowledge, as feminist critics of science have argued. Scholars in recent years also have pointed to parallels between the "civilizing mission" of imperial states in the colonies and the "civilizing mission" they employed with regard to women and the working classes at home.[22]

The second reason is to complicate further the relationship between Eurocentrism and history. Here, too, history had a crucial role to play, but with rather different results for its boundaries, identified in this context with the nation, which may be the reason for the close association between history and the emergence of the nation-state: to absorb into one narrative diverse local histories, to order the latter in temporal hierarchies that presupposed the nation as the center and the end of history, and to erase "alternatives" to history that did not fit with the teleology of the nation. History conceived in terms of the nation is not necessarily inconsistent with universalism; at the very least it renders the nation into the medium for the articulation of universal ideals, raising the possibility of national claims to universality, which is no longer to be taken for granted as it serves now as the grounds for contestation between a variety of national claims. State-building and nation-making within Europe were subject to much contestation and conflict both between and within states, and so were the ideologies that articulated them, including history.

Assertions of universal history were accompanied by contending claims to the center, and to the spirit of universality; F. W. Hegel, whose name comes up regularly in discussions of Eurocentrism, was not simply a European philosopher but also a German one, who held forth Germanic claims to universality. On the other hand, J. G. Herder, also an Enlightenment product whose name does not come up very often, insisted on locating universality in the characteristics particular to each nation that derived from different historical (and geographical) legacies. The neglect of Herder in contemporary discussions of Eurocentrism is rather surprising (and, perhaps, revealing). While Herder was a product of the Enlightenment in his universalism, and may have introduced a linear history of Europe (from Babylon to his present) by the back door, the editor of the English edition of his historical reflections, Frank E. Manuel, in 1968, wrote in very contemporary sounding words that:

> Herder, the outstanding representative of a new German philosophical history that ran counter to the French current of linear, rationalist progression, altered the traditional historical perspective and the universe of historical discourse in a revolutionary manner. . . . Reading the French philosophical histories from Turgot through Comte, one is still impressed with their fundamental Eurocentrism, and the finiteness, even narrowness, of their historical appreciation of "otherness." Herder believed in the individuality of each *Volk*, or agglomeration of people, wherever and whenever it had appeared and its equivalent (or almost equivalent) status in the history of mankind.[23]

The relationship between nation, history, and Eurocentrism is important for at least three reasons. First, Eurocentrism is not an undifferentiated term, but should be qualified in terms of the ways in which it has been expressed through different national articulations. Most relevant in this context may be its complication during the last two centuries by the emergence of states that are the products of the European diaspora, most notably, the United States, whose relationship to Europe is immensely complicated; the United States is a product of European colonialism, and its image in European eyes would seem to vary over time from a degenerate version of Europe, at one extreme, to a cultural colonizer of Europe at the other. On the U.S. side, the practice of Eurocentrism is complicated by simultaneous assertions of American "exceptionalism." It is this complicated relationship that accounts for my use of the term "Euro-America" in this discussion, by which I seek to convey both a unity and a difference. At any rate, given the complex relationship between the United States and Europe, it seems too simplistic to endow them with a common outlook toward the world that may be encompassed by the term "Eurocentrism." Such a qualification, needless to say, should be applicable also to differences between European societies. The goal here is not to abolish Eurocentrism, but to make it more precise.

Second, the stress on the nation is necessary because while history conceived in terms of the nation contradicts the notion of a universal history or, therefore, an undifferentiated Eurocentrism—in its emergence within the context of a European history with its universalistic assumptions—the nation-form itself is endowed with universal relevance and legitimacy. The nation, and history written around the nation, may be the most cogent articulations of the contradictions of a universalism that generates its own particularisms. At the same time, given its entanglement in the history of a Eurocentric universalism, the nation-form serves as a prime location for Eurocentrism, and a medium for its global diffusion.

Finally, the nation is important because the particular composition of the nation shapes the understanding of the problematic of Eurocentrism, and means to overcoming it. As I noted in my introductory paragraph, within the particular context of the United States, for example, the question of Eurocentrism is tied in with other issues—such as gender, race, and ethnicity—which once again abolishes the distinction between the inside and the outside. The writing of non-Eurocentric histories globally becomes indistinguishable under the circumstances from writing histories free of white male domination. There is little reason to assume that this version of Eurocentrism points to the way the problem of Eurocentrism is understood globally, least of all in non–Euro-American societies that have been the historical objects of a universalist Eurocentrism.

One more dimension needs to be added to these considerations of the location of Eurocentrism, most importantly to question the domination by a geographical or spatial bias of both the issue of Eurocentrism, and of the problem of de-centering history. To speak of Europe or of the nation as locations for history and, therefore, Eurocentrism, is to remain in largely spatial, or spatially identifiable, categories. But what of categories that are not spatial per se, or spatial only in a metaphorical sense, in the sense, say, of social and political spaces? Class, gender, race, ethnicity, religion, and culture, among others, are such categories. These categories, which cut across national and even continental boundaries, have provided alternative ways of centering history since the nineteenth century, often in explicit opposition to notions of Europe or the nation. Could they nevertheless serve as locations for Eurocentrism, and media for its dissemination, since they, too, are entangled in the history of Europe, and have been introduced into other histories through the agency of European historiography? Each one of them, moreover, has been proposed at different times and by different people as candidates around which to rewrite the history of the world.

Where class is concerned, the verdict seems to be clear; critics of Eurocentrism these days readily include Marxist historiography among the perpetrators of Eurocentrism. This may well be the case, but could not the same be said of histories written around those other categories, which equally are products of European historiography and social science, very much rooted in Euro-American categories cataloging of the world, and its theorization? It seems to me that separating these categories out of considerations of Eurocentrism is informed by the limited understanding of Eurocentrism against which I have argued above: on the basis of absences and exclusions from Eurocentric histories. However, viewed from the perspective I have suggested above—that is, Eurocentrism as a principle for reordering the world's evidence and reorganizing the past—they are very much complicit in a Eurocentric conceptualization of the world, as the world in its historical unfolding called forth new categories for its comprehension. That much of the opposition to Eurocentrism these days is conducted in the name or with the aid of such categories does not prove that they stand in opposition to Eurocentrism. On the contrary, the employment of such categories may be an indication of the depth to which even opposition to Eurocentrism is by now entangled within a Eurocentric conception of the world.

This is the final question I raise with regard to the location of Eurocentrism. Is there an outside to Eurocentrism in our day? Is Eurocentrism just a European or American thing, or is it part of a consciousness that is by now global? The answer seems obvious: Eurocentrism is internal to societies worldwide, if not explicitly, then in the internalization of history, of its spatial and temporal assumptions, and its categories. Eurocentrism is crucial to understanding the spatialities and temporalities of modernity, not just in Euro-America but globally, from at least the nineteenth century. The spatial conceptualizations around which we have organized history, from nations to areas to continents and oceans to the Three Worlds and beyond to globalization, are in a fundamental sense implicated in a Eurocentric modernity. Even more fundamental may be the reworking of temporalities by a Eurocentric conceptualization of the world, which in the end has come to serve as the temporality around which to rewrite the pasts of widely different societies. For the last century, but especially since World War II, Eurocentrism has been the informing principle in the constructions of history, not just in Euro-American historiographies, but in the spatial and temporal assumptions of dominant historiographies worldwide. Euro-Americans conquered the world; renamed places; rearranged economies, societies, and politics; and erased or drove to the margins premodern ways of knowing space, time, and many other things as well. In the process, they universalized history in their self-image in an unprecedented manner. Euro-Americans did not do all this themselves, however, but with the participation and complicity of those in other societies who perceived in Eurocentric history and its categories new ways of grasping the present and the past, and resolving the problems inherited from the past, or thrown up by the challenges of the present. There may still be peoples untouched by history, but they are fewer and more marginal by the day.

A further, perhaps even more profound, consequence of the global internalization of Eurocentrism is that Eurocentric history provides the medium through which societies around the globe know one another. This is partly a matter of the continued economic, political, and cultural power of Euro-America that enables the historians of European and U.S. societies to play an intermediary role in the organization and practice of history everywhere. But more fundamental are the conceptualizations of space and time that are the legacies of the last few centuries of Euro-American domination of the world, as I will argue in the next section, with the consequence that the Euro-American writing of the world, and of its past, mediates the comprehension of the world globally. This raises the question of whether there could be, say, a Chinese or Indian history of the world that is not mediated by Eurocentrism? Probably not, is the likely answer. To the extent that the Chinese may be interested in Indian conceptions of the past, or even in Indian history, that interest would seem to lie primarily in placing China and India within a history, the standards of which have been laid down already in Eurocentric temporalities.[24] Even if Euro-America were to be taken out of history, so that history could be written around non–Euro-American societies, and their interactions, the spatial and temporal legacies of Eurocentrism would still be there, as those societies as they now exist are themselves the products historically and conceptually of the Euro-American writing of the world.

The internalization of Eurocentrism in non–Euro-American societies has even created an ironic situation where they appear as the perpetrators of Eurocentrism when Euro-Americans are in the process of renouncing it. The situation is also revealing of the hegemonic implications of a globalized world history. A 1998 report on the status of world-history writing in China observes (to the astonishment of its author, Dorothea A. L. Martin) that contrary to what one might expect (we are not told who shares in the expectation—presumably all "westerners"), Chinese historians continue to write modern world history around the history of capitalism, and, it follows for Martin, a Eurocentric paradigm. This, to Martin, is, of course, a product of the continued domination of Chinese historical thinking by the "ideological framework" of "a European-centered, Marxist-imbued world history."[25] The irony that Chinese should perpetuate Eurocentrism when Euro-Americans have already liberated their thinking from it escapes Martin. So does the patronizing conclusion that this is due to the domination of Chinese thinking by ideology (in contrast, presumably, to our scientific approaches), which perpetuates the hegemonic attitudes of an earlier day. No wonder that Martin can also state that the large place given to Chinese history (autonomously of world history) in school curricula issues "from an ethnocentric view not unfamiliar to Western historians. China's self-perception as *Zhongguo*, or the Middle Kingdom, is well known."[26] Not only does Martin erase Chinese historians as contemporaries, instead of questioning her own version of world history, but she also proceeds to erase Chinese history by falling back on the authority of long-standing cliches in the "Western" historiography of China. Aside from the fact that this Chinese "self-perception" has its own history, other societies, too, teach their national histories separately from world history, and give it a large place, which has more to do with nationalist education in the modern world than some Chinese "ethnocentrism."

I turn to the question of agency that I raised previously with reference to the quotation from McNeill. McNeill states there that "a flood of information . . . assaulted European consciousness," without telling the reader where this information came from, as if it simply rained down on Europeans from the skies above. It is also curious that the quotation seems to privilege Chinese, Moslems, and Indians for their ability to resist this "assault," for which, however, they seem also to have paid a price when confronted later on with Europeans with their "undeniably superior knowledge." The argument seems convoluted, possibly because it seeks in words to escape Eurocentrism while reaffirming its ultimate victory. The contradiction may characterize a great deal of current anti-Eurocentrist arguments. The immediate question it raises, however, is whether

Eurocentrism may be grasped without reference to the structures of power that propelled it globally. It is a question that is ignored in most discussions of Eurocentrism that treat it as simply an intellectual or cultural issue. Indeed, to even raise the question opens one to the charge of Eurocentrism. Nevertheless, the question needs to be raised not only because it is relevant to grasping the global victory of Eurocentrism in the midst of its renunciations at the level of culture, but also because it enables a critique of the contradictions that characterize currently popular globalist alternatives to Eurocentrism. It is to this question that I turn below.

POWER, CAPITALISM, AND THE
QUESTION OF EUROCENTRISM

Eurocentrism as an intellectual, cultural, and historiographical issue is very real, as it is a historical legacy of the present that needs to be confronted in order to address very real problems of the present. Is it also possible that preoccupation with Eurocentrism as a cultural issue may serve as a distraction from those problems?

Even though we are not always very careful to specify what we mean when we employ the term "history," we are all aware that the term carries two broad meanings: history as something that happened in the past, and history as something that historians do. The conflation of the two meanings is the source of much confusion in debates concerning the past, where what may be debates among historians, or competition between different constructions of the past, appear as competition between the truths presented by the past to which the historian serves merely as a mouthpiece. How to center history, in other words, is simultaneously a problem of how historians compete to center one or another interpretation of the past. When such interpretations are of immediate ideological and cultural significance, the past itself may be a casualty of such competitions over the center.

Discussions over Eurocentrism these days pay scant attention to the fact that such competition itself, especially where it relates to the history of the world as a whole, is itself a very modern problem. How to produce systematic coherence out of the incoherence of the many pasts of the world is one aspect of the problem. The other aspect, with even more serious consequences, is establishing the dominance of history by reformulating as history diverse ways of conceiving the past that were at odds with the spatial and temporal teleologies of modernity—in other words, erasing diversity by containing widely different narratives within a single dominant narrative. As Ashis Nandy writes:

> The historical mode may be the dominant mode of constructing the past in most parts of the globe but it certainly is not the most popular mode of doing so. The dominance is derived from the links the idea of history has established with the modern nation-state, the secular worldview, the Baconian concept of scientific rationality, nineteenth-century theories of progress, and, in recent decades, development.[27]

As the "historical mode of constructing the past" has been globalized, so has the competition over the center. I later return to the complex implications of Nandy's statement. Suffice it to say here that even where a Eurocentric teleology is renounced, a teleology of history persists, and that may represent the ultimate global victory of Eurocentrism—through the agency of history. The claims we hear these days to the twenty-first century (that it will be a Chinese century, an Asia–Pacific century, or even a Turkish century) would have been unimaginable before the globalization of history.

This presents the professional historian with particularly severe problems, which may be the reason that, while historians have been quite vociferous in the critique of Eurocentrism, the critique has been rather limited. The professional historian would seem to be condemned to serve as a carrier of Eurocentrism for two reasons, both of them professional. First, the professional historian must address the problems of the past, as formulated by earlier historians. To the extent that the problems we address also leave their mark on the solutions we offer, even those that are directed against past solutions, the Eurocentric historiography of the past of necessity lives on through the anti-Eurocentrism of the present.[28] The other, even more insurmountable problem is the problem of history itself, for to observe that history is the most fundamental medium of Eurocentrism is in effect to call for the abolition of history and, with it, of the historian.

Whether this is feasible or even desirable is a question I will take up in the conclusion. The concern I would like to raise here is simpler: the silence of historians over the conditions of their own undertaking.[29] Much of the discussion of Eurocentrism these days takes place as if it were merely a cultural or a historiographical question, without reference to its context in structures of power, or the historians' relationship to those structures and the new ideological orientations that they produce or call for. Only a rare "globalizer" of history is willing to concede that much of the debate over Eurocentrism these days is "largely a Western debate," and that "globalization is a continuation of the Modernization project."[30] Even there, the author hopes that when others are included, it will be a global project with the potential for overcoming Eurocentrism, rather than considering that such a global history, as postmodernism in general, may serve to further consolidate the cultural hegemony of the modernization project.

It is the relationship of the question of Eurocentrism to this modernization project, and the problematic of modernity, that I will consider here. The argument I offer may be stated simply: Eurocentrism as a historical phenomenon is not to be understood without reference to the structures of power Euro-America produced over the last five centuries, that in turn produced Eurocentrism, globalized its effects, and universalized its historical claims. Those structures of power include the economic (capitalism, *capitalist* property relations, markets and modes of production, imperialism, and so on); the political (a system of nation-states, and the nation-form, most importantly, new organizations to handle problems presented by such a reordering of the world, new legal forms, and so forth); the social (production of classes, genders, races, ethnicities, religious forms, as well as the push toward individual-based social forms); and cultural (including new conceptions of space and time, new ideas of the good life, and a new developmentalist conception of the life-world). The list is woefully inadequate, and the categorizations themselves are admittedly problematic, but it suffices to indicate the intractability of the problem of Eurocentrism, which is my major purpose here.

A culturalist appreciation of Eurocentrism that proceeds from a quite productive assertion of the autonomy of culture to an obscurantist isolation of culture and discourses from questions of political economy, and even renders culture into a privileged site that has priority over other aspects of life, may end up only with a dehistoricized, desocialized understanding of Eurocentrism that does not even come close to acknowledging the problems it presents. Does capitalism, regardless of the possibility of "different cultures of capitalism," nevertheless serve as an agent not just of new economic forms but also of certain fundamental values emanating from Euro-America? Does nationalism, as Partha Chatterjee argues, have imbedded in its "thematic" the most fundamental assumptions of a Euro-American orientalism?[31] Does the very existence of certain forms of media, even apart from their content, introduce new values into everyday life globally? What may be said of "material" agencies as the carriers of Eurocentrism may be observed in reverse of the ways in which cultural constructs of Eurocentrism may acquire the power of material forces. Does it matter at some point that the current mapping of the world was a Euro-American construct, when that mapping is internalized by others, and shapes the goals and boundaries of life-activity? Especially crucial in this regard is the ideology of developmentalism, on which I will say more below.

There seems to be some anxiety in contemporary thinking that to raise anew the question of these structures is to open the way to some kind of "functionalism" that once again reduces social phenomena to a few of its elements.[32] Let us leave aside the question that culturalist functionalism may be as much a functionalism as any other. To recognize a multiplicity of phenomena that coincide historically and appear in structural and structuring relationships of one kind or another requires neither a reduction of those phenomena to one or more of their numbers, nor that we ignore the relationships of contradiction between them—that in effect serve to undermine efforts to functionalize the structure. In fact, it is these relationships, in their totality and particularity as well as their functionality and contradictoriness, that enable a coherent grasp of differences in history, not self-referential localized differences that "result in an utter particularism in which history becomes a meaningless jumble of stories with no connection to each other"[33]—as in contemporary postcolonialist alternatives with their repudiation of totalities in favor of localized encounters, or, in quite the opposite fashion, in the deterritorialized totalities that have no clear spatial and temporal referents, as in the globalist alternatives.[34]

The complexity of Eurocentrism becomes even more daunting if we note that Eurocentrism, as we have it now, is hardly a Euro-American phenomenon. Much of what we associate with Eurocentrism is now internal to societies worldwide, so that to speak of "Europe and its others" itself appears as an oxymoronic distraction. Legacies of Euro-America are everywhere, from global structures to daily economic practices, from state formations to household practices, from ideologies of development to cultures of consumption, from feminism to the centering in politics of race and ethnicity. Ashis Nandy, as did Franz Fanon in an earlier day, locates them in the psyches of "Europe's others."[35] They are also in the ways we think the world, from theorizations about society to thinking about history. Even where claims are made these days to premodern and, therefore, pre-"historical" ways of knowing, they fail to convince because their own efforts to refute a modernist historicism are conditioned by a self-consciousness about their own historicity. Equally unconvincing are arguments that seek to deny Eurocentrism by pointing out that these legacies have been assimilated into local contexts, which overlooks that the issue is not homogenization but transformation; the assimilators are also assimilated in the very process of assimilation. How would we write the world without the legacies of Eurocentric mappings? Writing the world, no less than anti-Eurocentrism itself, may be incomprehensible without reference to those same legacies. If today we find it impossible to think the world without reference to classes, genders, and so forth, premoderns (and maybe even pre-postmoderns) would have been surprised that identities are negotiable, as one negotiates commodities in the marketplace.

The recognition of the pervasiveness of Eurocentrism in its various dimensions in many ways reveals the limitations of a preoccupation with "Europe and its others." That juxtaposition may still make sense with reference to the past, when a separation could be assumed between Europeans and others, which would play an important part both in the construction of others, and in the construction of Eurocentrism. At present, when more than ever the others are most visible in their relocations to older colonial centers, they have, so to speak, come home. As a Euro-American modernity long has been internalized in the rest of the world, the rest of the world has now entered the interior of Euro-America physically and intellectually—which, not surprisingly, is also the prime location for the concern with Eurocentrism. Preoccupation with "Europe and its others" seems under the circumstances a distraction from the confrontation of the victory of Eurocentrism, which is evident above all in the rendering of Euro-America and its many products into objects of desire globally.[36]

The contemporary concern with Eurocentric constructions of the other, interestingly (and with some irony), seems to provide endless occasion for speaking about Euro-America, perpetuating the Eurocentrism it would formally repudiate—which may be the form this desire takes among intellectuals. At the risk of simple-minded psychologizing, anti-Eurocentrism strikes me above all as the mirror image of this desire, not so much as a negative compensation for it but rather as a demand for admission of non–Euro-American cultural elements into the interior of a world that has been shaped already by its historical legacy in a Eurocentric modernity. What, after all, is multiculturalism that calls for the recognition of cultural relics or heritages without challenging the structures of power that are the products of Euro-American domination of the world, and imbued through and through with its values? These same circumstances may have something to tell us about why globalism and postcolonialism, in their very contradictoriness, have caught the imagination of many as ways to deal with such a contemporary situation—even though in their different ways they may evade the most fundamental and pressing question: whether there is an outside to Eurocentrism in a world that has been worked over by the forces of modernity.

If Eurocentrism as understood as a cultural phenomenon is insufficient as a critique of Euro-American domination of the world, which was hardly just a "discursive" domination but has been imbedded in structures of power, the power of Eurocentrism itself is not to be grasped without reference to these same structures. This is not to say that culture and discourses are insignificant, but only to reiterate that they are insufficient as explanations of the world; the separation of culture and discourse into realms apart from the material is itself very modern. For the same reason, to argue for a reconnection of culture and discourse to the materiality of everyday life is not to argue for a return to an earlier privileging of political economy, but rather to open up new ways of thinking the connection under contemporary circumstances—which implies also rethinking the connections that were repudiated under the regime of modernity. Eurocentric modernity then appears as one way of connecting modes of living and cultures, rather than as establishing a "scientific" and, therefore, forever valid, causal relationship between the two.

The problem, as a historical problem, then is to inquire why Eurocentric ways of representing this relationship have acquired such power. Eurocentrists may suggest that it is the power of Euro-American cultures. I would like to suggest here that it is power that dynamizes the claims of culture; contrary to tendencies in some versions of cultural studies that conflate power and culture until they become indistinguishable, it is important to distinguish the two so as to enable a more historical treatment of the relationship. The issue here is not one of ethical judgment or choice. The issue rather is ethical domination. And cultural domination is hardly its own justification. Neither Eurocentrism, nor the contemporary challenges to it, may be understood without reference to elements outside of the strictly cultural—which, needless to say, raises significant questions about what we mean by the cultural.

To recognize Eurocentrism as a historical phenomenon it is necessary to view it within the context of other instances of domination, of which Eurocentrism was neither the first instance nor is likely to be the last. Such a historical perspective may also provide clues for a more thoroughgoing critique of power and domination than is currently available.

Eurocentrism is a complex term that disguises all manner of struggles within Euro-America over the meanings of "Europe" and "modernity," but most importantly, that Eurocentrism was the product of a historical process, if not itself a historical process, that is inextricable from the invention of Europe's "others." While at the level of power there may be little question that by the end of the nineteenth century Euro-Americans had more or less conquered the whole world, and proceeded to produce ideological legitimations for the conquest, as a cultural orientation Eurocentrism itself is a hindsight invention of the Europe–other binary, not the other way around, as Samir Amin pointed out. Cliches about Enlightenment rationalism, unilinear histories, and so on that are quite common these days in the critiques of Eurocentrism overlook the ways in which historical processes mediated the understanding of such ideological products within a Euro-American context. Euro-America itself is still within this historical process of invention. Globalism, explicitly, and postmodernism and postcolonialism, inadvertently, may well be constituents of this process in its contemporary phase.

Without the power of capitalism, and all the structural innovations that accompanied it in political, social and cultural, and military organization, Eurocentrism might have been just another ethnocentrism. It is rather remarkable in an age of proliferating ethnocentrisms such as ours that so little attention should be paid to ethnocentrism as a legacy not just of Eurocentrism (although that may have contributed to it in significant ways), but as a condition of the world at the origins of modernity, more often than not expressing the centrality in a variety of "world-systems" of the cultural assumptions of those who dominated those world-systems. This may be stating the obvious, but it needs to be stated nevertheless since considerations of political correctness have led to a shyness about criticism of ethnocentrisms other than the Euro-American (or blatantly murderous expressions of it in such places as Bosnia, Rwanda, or Turkey). Spheres of cultural hegemony that more or less coincided with economic and political domination have been present all along, defining a "Chinese" world, an "Islamic" world, "Arabic" and "Indic" worlds, to name just a few.[37] In spite of real or imagined hegemonies over vast territories, however, none of these worlds were in the end able to match Eurocentrism in reach or transformative power. The statement may seem foolhardy when the end of history is not yet in sight; what seems safe to say is that if these other cultural hegemonies are ever globalized and universalized in the same manner as Eurocentrism, it will be on the basis of a world globalized and universalized through Eurocentrism, and in their articulations to this new world. Efforts are being made to discover an early "modernity" in East and Southeast Asia, but it did not occur to anyone in those regions to even raise the question of modernity until modernity had been established as a principle of history. Similarly, East Asian societies may claim a "Confucian" heritage that explains their recent success in capitalism, but this Confucian heritage is one that has been reinterpreted by the very requirements of capitalism.

Eurocentrism is the one centrism that historically has encompassed the globe and reached levels of life that were not even of much concern to its competitors; it revolutionized lives around the globe, relocated societies in new spaces, and transformed their historical trajectories—to the point where it makes no sense to speak of history without reference to Eurocentrism. There may have been no shortage of "cultural hybridities" earlier; what is interesting and compelling about Eurocentrism is that by the time its globalizing aspirations neared (for they could never be reached) their geographical boundaries, Eurocentrism was to become a constituent of most people's hybridities—which is not to be said of any of the other centrisms, which were regionally limited and historically unstable. This also helps to explain the fixation with Euro-America globally. As I noted above, Chinese, Indians, and others may care little about one another, but they are all focused on Eurocentrism one way or another in the definition of their various identities—and the yardsticks they use in placing themselves, and one another, in history.

The question is, then, what accounts for this power? The Eurocentric answer is clear enough: the superiority of Euro-American values. It is an answer that is convincing only to Eurocentrists themselves.[38] It is also the cultural level at which most critiques of Eurocentrism proceed, and run into dead ends. The problem with the culturalist critique of Eurocentrism is not only that it provides no explanation for the hegemony of Eurocentrism, in contrast to other centrisms, but that it is also for the same reason incapable of addressing normative questions of value. The values of the dominant (such as human rights) are not prima facie undesirable because of the fact of domination, just as the values of the dominated are not to be legitimated simply by recourse to arguments of cultural difference. If capitalism is as much an agent of Eurocentrism as the advocacy of human rights, it does not make much sense to laud the entry into capitalism of other societies while also collaborating in their abuse of human rights on the grounds of cultural difference. The conflict between history and value is nowhere better illustrated in the historicist (culturalist) affirmations of difference, which then proceed nevertheless to discover in these different societies civil societies, and so on, without any awareness that the latter might be products of Eurocentric teleologies, imbedded in the very terms themselves, that contradict the notions of difference.

I suggest here that such contradictions are products of the isolation of cultural questions from those of political economy. Eurocentrism was globalized not due to any inherent virtue of Euro-American values, but because those values were stamped on activities of various kinds that insinuated themselves into existing practices (such as trade), proved to be welcome to certain groups in non–Euro-American societies, or, when there was resistance to them, were enforced on the world by the power of arms. In other words, the globalization and universalization of Eurocentrism would have been inconceivable without the dynamism it acquired through capitalism, imperialism, and cultural domination. As Karl Marx observed in the middle of the nineteenth century, capitalism, in drawing the world together in its operations, created a world history out of many local histories. One may reject Marx's own teleological prejudice toward the homogenization of the world, but that does not diminish the significance of what he had to say about the relationship between capitalism and the globalization of history. The world history that Euro-Americans created is an absent presence of all history. And that world history, now in the guise of globality, is inextricably entangled with the history of capitalism.

It is remarkable, then, that there should be a tendency in various realms of intellectual activity in recent years to erase the role of capitalism in history on the grounds that it is a perpetuation of Eurocentrism to speak of capitalism as the formative moment of modern history. We may suggest to the contrary that without an account of the relationship between Eurocentrism and the enormous power of capitalism that enabled Euro-American expansion, the criticism of Eurocentrism not only may perpetuate Eurocentrism in new guises, but also disguise the ways in which globalism itself is imbued with a Eurocentric worldview. The preoccupation with Eurocentrism pervades not just cultural studies but the rewriting of history, most visibly in efforts to produce a new "world history" that is immune to the Eurocentrism of past histories, which overlooks that the urge to produce world history may itself be a Euro-American preoccupation that perpetuates earlier hegemonies in a new guise. I am quite sympathetic to the epistemological concerns of world or global history proponents, namely, to overcome the restrictions of nation-based histories. There is nothing objectionable either about "putting Europe in its place" historically. However, the representation of Eurocentrism as emphasis on the historical role of modern capitalism promises not only to erase the distinctiveness of modern history, but also to eliminate the capitalist mode of production as a distinct mode with its own forms of production and consumption, oppression and exploitation, and ideology. This is the case with Andre Gunder Frank's "5,000 year world-system," which, in the name of erasing Eurocentrism, universalizes and naturalizes capitalist development in much the same fashion as classical economics—that is, by making it into the fate of humankind, rather than the conjunctural product of a particular history. Gunder Frank does not explain either why a China- or Asia-centered history constitutes more of a world history than a Euro-American-centered one. Most seriously, the naturalization of capitalism historically also undermines the possibility of perceiving other alternatives in history, as the only alternatives it allows are alternative capitalisms.[39] As William Green writes of current repudiations of Eurocentrism, with specific reference to Frank:

> Too many contemporary Western scholars are obsessed about Eurocentrism. Eurocentrism takes many forms. It is ironic that some of the most dedicated historical materialists, scholars like Andre Gunder Frank, are quick to condemn Eurocentrism in others. Barraclough considered such sturdy materialism to be a decidedly Western (one might say, European) orientation to the past. He wondered whether world history written from an Asian perspective would not be substantially less materialist. I do as well.[40]

Probably not any more, we might add, but Green is correct in pointing to the ultimately Eurocentric assumptions on history that pervade much of discussion of world and global histories. What he has to say of Frank may be applicable also to other efforts to discover "world-systems" or "global-isms" in the past that do *not* clearly distinguish their claims about the premodern past from the globalizing and universalizing consequences of the modern world-system. To state that human beings have had relations with one another since their origins is to make a trivial point that merely restates an evolutionary or diffusionist view of history, while offering lit-tle more than conventional textbook accounts. That societies were inter-linked with relations of trade, religion, migrations, or war is hardly fresh historical news, deriving their novelty mostly from an insistence on claims to break with Eurocentric accounts of the past. These relationships are still with us, but they carry a very different meaning within the con-text of the modern world-system than they did in the past. That the past needs to be periodized in terms of one or more of these relationships is innocuous at best, as is evident in the haphazardness of the premises that inform such periodization, which fall far short of the theoretical rigor made possible by the unification of the globe with capitalism.[41] This itself may be viewed as an assertion of history against (Eurocentric) theory—that different periods in the past may be subject to different criteria of systematization.[42] Such a claim is not inconsistent with theory, and affirms, rather than negates, the unprecedented consequences of moder-nity. It also makes one wonder if a weak, undertheorized, and unself-con-scious Eurocentrism is preferable to a rigorously historicized one.

Such claims overlook that it was the Eurocentric urge to comprehend the past in its totality that was responsible in the first place for inquiry into those questions. They also overlook that this shift of emphasis to "world" or "global" history de-centers not only Europe, but other socie-ties as well, more often than not by reviving reified notions of those socie-ties that are imbedded in modern historiography, as is evident most prominently in the frequent use of the term "cross-cultural" or "cross-civilizational" in describing encounters and relationships of one kind or another. The conflation of "center" and "boundary" in such usage is made possible by assumptions of homogeneity in such societies, so that the center and the surface may be used interchangeably (as, for instance, in Eurocentrism or Sinocentrism). Rather than examine how those rela-tionships may have produced those societies in interaction with local practices, their existence as whole "societies" or "cultures" (rather than realms of political control, often with vague boundaries) is taken for granted. This may make it easier to produce a "world" or "global" his-tory, but only at the cost of perpetuating a mapping of the world that is a product of the urge to catalog the world in Eurocentric historiography. It is not clear why this is any more of a "world" history than histories that examine totalities from the ground up in various locations—except for the urge to discover the origins of the present somewhere in the past, which continues to colonize the past with the questions of the present, in the process erasing other ways of examining the past. The relationship to the present, albeit of a different and more revealing kind, is most evident in the case of "world" or "global" historians who insist on the "policy" implications of "world history."[43]

A commitment to world or global history does not necessarily erase Euro-American ethnocentrism either, as in the case I cited above of Martin's report on world history writing in China. The author's statements on Chinese historians provoke immediate questions—"Whose ethnocentrism" and "whose ideology"—but those questions may not be as important as the underlying hegemonic assumptions in much of the discussion on globalization, including the globalization of history. World history as an undertaking is not to be held responsible for this kind of obscurantism, but its possible hegemonic implications are a reminder nevertheless of the need for intellectual vigilance in an undertaking that is highly vulnerable to producing the opposite of what it intends.

One necessary caution is to distinguish Eurocentrism from recognition of the historical role that Euro-America, empowered by capitalism, played in the shaping of the modern world; the rejection of the former does not necessitate the rejection of the latter, which may be accomplished only at the cost of a disavowal of history. Such disavowal also deprives "world" and "global" historians of a critical consciousness of the entanglement of their own undertaking in the history of European modernity. As Raymond Grew writes:

> World history can . . . be seen as a natural product of modern ideas and experience, including the impact of imperialism (and the need to explain, justify, or criticize it), the related spread of capitalism and commerce (understood as both the product of history and also an engine of change); and the fascination with technology which stimulated attempts to predict the future in visions both utopian and nightmarish. There was a direct line from Jules Verne to H. G. Wells and the historical theories of Jacques Ellul, James Burnham, and Roderick Seidenberg. The world such historians wrote about was European and North American, but the outcomes they predicted were global.[44]

The world contemporary "global" historians write about may be global, we may add, but the origins of what they write are European and North American.

A further consequence of these strenuous efforts to take Europe out of history is the disavowal of the part that imperialism and subjection of the world played in the globalization of capitalist modernity.[45] One of the most remarkable pieties of our times is that to speak of oppression is to erase the subjectivities of the oppressed, which does not seem to realize that not to speak of oppression, but still operate within the teleologies of modernist categories, is to return the responsibility for oppression to its victims.[46] Alternatively, it is to make a mockery of any notion of resistance to oppression, by identifying resistance with any kind of deviation from "normalcy." The result, in either case, is the evasion of any significant, and historically determined, notion of politics by turning all such encounters into instances of cultural politics. What is also remarkable is the resonance between the political conclusions of contemporary culturalism with the culturalism of an earlier modernizationism: that what is at issue is not politics or political economy but culture.

Samuel Huntington's works to which we have referred already provide a blatant example of the dangers implicit in the new culturalism. Huntington's views on "civilizations," his approach to the question of culture, and the conclusions he draws are diametrically opposed to those of globalism. He reifies civilizations into culturally homogeneous and spatially mappable entities, insists on drawing impassable boundaries between them, and proposes a fortress Euro-America to defend Western civilization against the intrusion of unmodernizable and unassimilable others. What is remarkable about his views is his disavowal of the "West's" involvement in other civilization areas. His is a conception of the contemporary world that divides the world into several "civilization" areas, where each hegemonic power should be responsible for the achievement of order in its area. Huntington sustains this remarkable view of the world by refraining from serious analysis of the structures of political economy (does not even say if fortress Euro-America is to withdraw its transnational corporations from the rest of the world), by taking out of the definition of culture any element of material culture, by confounding ethnicity, culture, race, and civilization, by questioning the significance of the nation, by an erasure of the legacies of colonialism, and an insistence that whatever has happened in other societies has happened as a consequence of their indigenous values and cultures, and, at the most general level, by a disavowal of history. His divisions of the world are a far cry from the insistence in globalism and postmodernism on the abolition of boundaries, rejections of cultural reification, and negotiations of cultural identity. However, his reinstatement of the power of indigenous "cultures," understood not in terms of nations but "civilizations," his erasure of colonialism and the reinstatement of persistent native subjectivities, his obliviousness to questions of political economy, and his disavowal of modernity's history resonate with globalist and postmodernist arguments. This is not to suggest that they are identical, therefore, or even operate out of the same paradigm (Huntington's is a paradigm of top-down order), but that they are contemporaneous. There may be a world of difference between the bounded ethnocentrism of Huntington's vision of the world and the multiculturalist pluralisms of globalism and post-modernism, but they are at one in foregrounding ethnicity to mystify the transnational structures of unequal power that are their context.

Recognition of Eurocentrism as a historical phenomenon, which differs from other centrisms in terms of the totalizing structures that served as its agencies, returns us to the question that I raised above. If Eurocentrism globalized a certain ethnocentrism, and rendered it into a universal para-digm, is there then an outside to Eurocentrism? An outside to Eurocen-trism may be found in places untouched and marginalized by it, which are fewer by the day, or it may be found in its contradictions, which proliferate daily. The universalization of Eurocentrism must itself be understood in terms of the ways in which Euro-American values were interpellated into the structures of societies worldwide, transforming their political, social, and economic relations, but not homogenizing them, or assimilating them to the structures and values of Eurocentrism. Questions of homogenization versus heterogenization, sameness and dif-ference, and assimilation and differentiation are in many ways mislead-ing questions, for they confound what are historical processes with the apportionments of identity into ahistorical, static categories. As I under-stand it here, the universalization of Eurocentric practices and values through the Euro-American conquest of the world implies merely the dis-lodging of societies from their historical trajectories before Europe on to new trajectories, without any implication of uniformity, for the very uni-versalization of Eurocentrism has bred new kinds of struggles over his-tory, which continue in the present. It also implies, however, at least in my understanding, that these struggles took place increasingly on ter-rains that, however different from one another, now included Euro-American power of one kind or another as their dynamic constituents. That, I believe, distinguishes what we might want to describe as a moder-nity defined by Euro-America from earlier forms of domination, which were regionally, politically, and socially limited by the technological, organizational, and ideological limits of domination. Sinocentrism, how-ever effective in East and Southeast Asia, was nevertheless limited to those regions.

Eurocentrism as compared to earlier "centrisms" is universal in three senses. First is the omnipresence globally of the institutions and cultures of a Euro-American modernity. While the effects of this modernity may not be uniformly or equally visible on all the surface implied by global, it is nevertheless everywhere forcing widely different peoples into parallel historical trajectories (which, I stress, does not imply identity). Second, it is universal in the sense that Eurocentrism may be diffused through the agencies of non–Euro-Americans, which underlines the importance of a structural appreciation of Eurocentrism. And, finally, while Eurocentrism may not be universal in the sense that it permits no outside, it is nevertheless the case that it has become increasingly impossible to imagine outsides to it, if by outside we understand places outside of the reach of Euro-American practices. It is not that there are no outsides, but that those outsides must of necessity be conceived of as post-Eurocentric, as products of contradictions generated by the dialectic between a globalizing Euro-America, and places that struggle against such globalization. What this implies is a common history, which of necessity provides the point of departure even for imagining outsides or alternatives to Eurocentrism. Eurocentrism, in other words, is not to be challenged by questioning the values that emanate from Euro-America. It requires challenging values and structures that are already part of a global legacy.

To affirm the historical role that Eurocentrism has played in shaping the world is not to endow it with normative power, but to recognize the powerful ways in which it continues to shape the world, ways that are not going to disappear with willful acts of cultural negation. One aspect of Eurocentrism that has infused both earlier revolutionary ideologies and the accommodationist alternatives of the present, seems to me to be particularly important, perhaps more important for the historian than for others because it is complicit in the imagination of temporalities: this is the ideology of development, what we might call developmentalism. The notion that development is as natural to humanity as air and water is one that is imbedded deeply in contemporary consciousness globally, and yet development as an idea is a relatively recent one in human history.[47] Development as a discourse is imbedded not just in the realm of ideology, but also in the institutional structures that are fundamental to the globalization of capital. Neither is it any longer a "Western" idea, as it has become a measure globally of the past, the present, and the future. When the Chinese claim that the twenty-first century will be a Chinese century, it is development discourse that justifies the claim. The failure to question development discourse, as if it had little to do with the globalization of Eurocentrism, is one of the most fatal failings of current criticisms of Eurocentrism, which renders them vulnerable to the arguments of a David Landes, for example, who recognizes clearly the relationship between Eurocentrism and development. It is also not very surprising, in light of this failure, that world or global histories offered as alternatives to Eurocentric history should in actuality contribute to further the hegemony of Eurocentrism by extending the premises of development discourse over the entirety of the past.

CONCLUDING REMARKS:
ALTERNATIVES TO HISTORY

Much of what passes as anti-Eurocentrism in contemporary historiography is Eurocentrism by other means—not due to ill will or ideological
duplicity on the part of the historians, but because of a failure to look for
Eurocentrism where it is really imbedded; not in exclusions of others or
Eurocentric teleologies, but within history as an undertaking. While the
effort to be inclusive, and the recognition of multidirectionality to history,
are by no means insignificant, they are not to be confused with the abandonment of Eurocentrism. A thoroughgoing critique of Eurocentrism
must confront history as its most fundamental expression. And if history
is a "sign of the modern," as Nicholas Dirks observes, the confrontation
of history requires also a confrontation of modernity, which is no longer
just a European or an American project.

In his *Cultural Imperialism,* John Tomlinson argues that opposition to
Euro-American cultural imperialism may be meaningless because it does
not make much sense to speak of imperialism when the products of Euro-
American culture are voluntarily accepted in societies that are supposedly the victims of such imperialism.[48] In a similar vein, Ashis Nandy
writes with reference to history that:

> Historical Consciousness now owns the globe. Even in societies known as
> ahistorical, timeless, or eternal—India for example—the politically powerful
> now live in and with history. Ahistoricity survives at the peripheries and
> interstices of such societies. Though millions of people continue to stay out-
> side history, millions have . . . dutifully migrated to the empire of history to
> become its loyal subjects. The historical worldview is now triumphant glob-
> ally; the ahistoricals have become the dissenting minority.[49]

Nandy is not alone in arguing that confronting Eurocentrism requires
ultimately a confrontation of history and the project of modernity as a
whole. A similar, and even more uncompromising argument has been
offered recently by the distinguished Amerindian historian, Vine Deloria
Jr., who likewise perceives history as part of the constellation of "white"
values, knowledge, and power that must be rejected in toto.[50] The questioning of history is not restricted to antimodernist Third World or indigenous intellectuals. Immanuel Wallerstein, whose own formulations on
capitalism have contributed significantly to ideas of global or world history, sees the only way out of Eurocentrism as "unthinking social science," and William McNeill, in spite of his commitment to scientific
history, moves at least part way in a similar direction in conceding that
"an adequate world history must take respectful account of the older,
competing worldviews."[51]

A thoroughgoing critique of Eurocentrism leads inescapably to a conclusion that the project of overcoming Eurocentrism calls not for alternative histories but, in Nandy's words, *alternatives to history*—and, by implication, *alternatives to modernity*. It requires not only a repudiation of history as the only possible or the most desirable way of knowing the past, but also a questioning of the epistemologies of modernity, to which history is fundamental. And since these epistemologies are no longer just Euro-American, the critique of Eurocentrism must encompass other histories as well, which may be formally anti-Eurocentric, but still are informed by assumptions that are Euro-American in origin, most importantly a developmentalist historical vision. In Vinay Lal's eloquent and impassioned words:

> In a world where the most radical theories are sold on the market, and revolutions are managed by financiers and corporate executives, the abandonment of history may well be the only heresy that remains to us, for that defiance is nothing other than the defiance of the categories of knowledge which have become the most effective and insidious means of oppressing humankind today.[52]

It is only when Eurocentrism is confronted at this fundamental level that the real difficulties of overcoming it become apparent. If history as epistemology is entangled in the history of our times, is it possible to repudiate the epistemology without disavowing the history? I realize that the question itself is historicist, which is revealing of the difficulties it presents. What justifies it is my sense that the search for "alternatives to history" may contribute to the avoidance of certain crucial questions as much as the search for a "globalized" history. Whether we wish to "unthink" social science, or conceive of "alternatives to history," is it possible nevertheless to accomplish those tasks without thinking through the very categories that are by now an inextricable part of the ways in which we think the world; its past, present, and future? Must any such effort, in other words, of necessity be posthistorical—not just in the sense of overcoming history, but more importantly in the sense of being indelibly marked by historical ways of thinking? Lal's statement that "the abandonment of history may well be the only heresy that remains to us" may be read also as a confession of despair occasioned by imprisonment in history.

There are normative questions as well. Nandy observes with reference to the importance of history to radical criticism, that "as long as the nonhistorical modes thrived, history remained viable as a baseline for radical social criticism. That is perhaps why the great dissenters of the nineteenth century [such as Karl Marx] were the most aggressively historical."[53] Does this critical role of history disappear, as he suggests, once historical con-

sciousness has achieved global hegemony? Nonhistorical ways of thinking are important for the deconstruction of this hegemony, but do such
ways of thinking, even if they were recoverable, lead automatically to
desirable social ends? Especially at a time of ethnocentric revivals, it is
important to distinguish critical from oppressive conceptions of "alternatives to history," which distinction itself is inescapably posthistorical. Do
"alternatives to history" include revivals of native pasts, which claim
authenticity even though they are clearly informed by modern conceptions of national, ethnic, or religious purity, often with fascist overtones?
Is history still necessary to the deconstruction of such claims that dissolve
all manner of native oppressive practices into homogenized cultural identities of one kind or another, which then serve to justify inherited oppressions, and produce new oppressions of their own? Do categories such as
gender and class have a role to play in bringing to the surface such ine-
qualities and oppressions, even though they may be marked by their
Eurocentric origins? History is to be opposed for erasing alternative ways
of thinking the past, but does it still have a critical role to play when
oppressive practices of the past, reinforced or mediated by those of
modernity, are still very much part of our world? Perhaps most importantly, history, released from its servitude to the ideology of development, may have a crucial part to play in deconstructing that ideology by
exposing *its* historicity, and rescuing from the shadows of the past other
ways of thinking life.[54]

It may be necessary under the circumstances to concede that history is
very much part of the constitution of our world, and direct it to goals that
are egalitarian and democratic, that serve the purposes of life at the everyday level rather than the abstractions of development. Too much concern
with centering or de-centering history at the level of ethnicities, nations,
civilizations, religions, trade and development, and so on nourish such
abstraction. The stories that historians tell at that level are stories of
power. But there are other stories as well, stories that people tell with
everyday life at their center, that serve to assert democratic and egalitarian
demands against power. It seems to me that even the reintegration of
human life with the natural, which is one of the most important issues of
the new ferment over history, is best achieved at that level.

This is not a call for avoiding totalities in the name of places, but rather
a plea for attention to another location from which to view totalities,
which may be indispensable to any democratic conception of history. On
one hand, global vantage points reveal human existence in all its diversity
and unity, but also are driven by an urge to contain diversity in narrative
totalities that erase both nonhistorical ways of apprehending life and the
"little" narratives that sustain it. This is the predicament of history as we
have known and practiced it. On the other hand are places, the locations

for everyday life, where people tell stories that are intimately linked with the necessities of existence and survival against the abstract demands of states and capital. But places are themselves vulnerable to parochialism, and legacies of different kinds of inequality and oppression, the recognition and alleviation of which may be impossible without the help of history. The challenge to history presently is not globalization, which has always been basic to its constitution, but how to accommodate the global and the place-based in simultaneous mutuality.

NOTES

This chapter was written while I was a fellow at the Netherlands Institute for Advanced Studies in the Humanities and Social Sciences. I thank my colleagues at the institute, Rogers Hollingsworth and Reinhart Koselleck, its rector, H. L. Wesseling, as well as Eckhardt Fuchs, Roxann Prazniak, and Marilyn Young for their comments and encouragement.

1. I put this term in quotation marks when I refer to "world history" as an approach, in order to distinguish it from references to the history of the world. The distinction is necessary for two reasons. First, "world history" as an approach does not necessarily cover the history of the world as a whole, which most "world" or "global" historians concede readily. Second, it is my opinion that much of history is world history, even when the focus may be narrow, and an author does not necessarily identify him/herself with the approach so designated.

2. William H. McNeill, "History and the Scientific World View," *History and Theory* 37, no. 1 (February 1998): 7.

3. Nicholas Dirks, "History As a Sign of the Modern," *Public Culture* 2, no. 2 (1990): 25–32

4. McNeill, "History and the Scientific World View," 6.

5. This term is Janet Lippman Abu-Lughod's. See "The World-System Perspective in the Construction of Economic History," *History and Theory* 34, no. 2 (1995): 94–95.

6. Raymond Grew, "Paul Costello, *World Historians and Their Goals: Twentieth Century Answers to Modernism*" [rev. art.], *History and Theory* 34, no. 4 (1995): 372.

7. Grew, "Paul Costello," 371.

8. Francis Fukuyama, *The End of History and the Last Man* (New York: 1992), and David S. Landes, *The Wealth and Poverty of Nations: Why Some Are So Rich and Some So Poor* (New York: 1998).

9. Landes, *Wealth and Poverty*, 513.

10. Samuel P. Huntington, "The Clash of Civilizations?" *Foreign Affairs* (Summer 1992): 22–49; "The West Unique, Not Universal," *Foreign Affairs* (November–December 1996): 28–46; and Samuel P. Huntington, *The Clash of Civilizations and the Remaking of World Order* (New York: 1996).

11. Huntington, *Clash of Civilizations*, 66.

12. Lewis D. Wurgaft, "Identity in World History: A Postmodern Perspective," *History and Theory* 34, no. 2 (1995): 67–85.

13. Kerwin Lee Klein, "In Search of Narrative Mastery: Postmodernism and the People without History," *History and Theory* 34, no. 4 (1995): 275–98.

14. Daniel J. Boorstin, *The Discoverers* (New York: 1983).

15. William H. McNeill, "The Changing Shape of World History," *History and Theory* 34, no. 2 (1995): 10.

16. John H. Elliott, *The Old World and the New 1492–1650* (Cambridge, UK: 1970).

17. This argument has been inspired by Hayden White, who has written of the implications for the European psyche of the internalization of the "wild man." See Hayden White, "The Forms of Wildness: Archaeology of an Idea," in Hayden White, *Tropics of Discourse: Essays in Cultural Criticism* (Baltimore, Md.: 1978), 150–82.

18. Samir Amin, *Eurocentrism*, trans. Russell Moore (New York: 1983).

19. Fernand Braudel, *Civilization and Capitalism, 15th to 18th Century*, 3 vols., trans. Sian Reynolds (New York: 1984), esp. vol. 3, *The Perspective of the World*.

20. Giovanni Arrighi, *The Long Twentieth Century: Money, Power and the Origins of Our Times* (London: 1994).

21. For the use of the paradigm of colonialism in the analysis of nation-building, in a more positive sense than here, see Eugen Weber, *Peasants into Frenchmen: The Modernization of Rural France, 1870–1914* (Stanford, Calif.: 1976).

22. Susan Thorne, " 'The Conversion of Englishmen and the Conversion of the World Inseparable': Missionary Imperialism and the Language of Class," in *Tensions of Empire: Colonial Cultures in a Bourgeois World*, ed. Frederick Cooper and Ann Laura Stoller (Berkeley, Calif.: 1997), 238–62.

23. Frank E. Manuel, "Editor's Introduction," in Johann Gottfried von Herder, *Reflections on the Philosophy of the History of Mankind*, abridged and introd. Frank E. Manuel (Chicago: 1968), xiv–xvi.

24. An example of this historicization of China and India is to be found in an influential book by Liang Shuming, which arranged historically Chinese, Indian, and Western civilizations, each with its defining civilizational characteristic, so that the past belonged to India, the present to the West, and the future to China. See Liang Shuming, *Dongxi wenhua ji qi zhexue* (Eastern and Western cultures and their philosophies) (n.p., 1921). This kind of thinking persists, and not just in China. Little comment is needed on views of "less advanced" or "primitive" societies. In light of what I say below, it is important to note that Liang's book was pre-Marxist. For a similar preoccupation with the "West" on the part of Indians, see Vinay Lal, "Discipline and Authority," *Futures* 29, no. 10 (1997): 993–94.

25. Dorothea A. L. Martin, "World History in China," *World History Bulletin* 14, no. 1 (Spring 1998): 6.

26. Martin, "World History in China," 8.

27. Ashis Nandy, "History's Forgotten Doubles," *History and Theory* 34, no. 2 (1995): 44.

28. For an example of how the past of a field creates problems for efforts to overcome the limitations of the past, see H. L. Wesseling, "Overseas History, 1945–1995," in H. L. Wesseling, *Imperialism and Colonialism: Essays on the History*

of European Expansion (Westport, Conn.: 1997), 140–97. Here, Wesseling discusses the contradictions created for "overseas history" by its origins in "imperial history." A note may be in order here in light of what I have to say of "world" and "global" history. Interestingly, the most visible and prominent proponents of these fields are historians of Europe, some of whom are in the process of reinventing themselves as "world" or "global" historians. The critique of Eurocentrism is hardly new, viewed from "Third World" perspectives. In spite of the origins of "area studies" in a very Eurocentric mapping of the world, area studies specialists, especially those of a radical orientation, long have been critics of Eurocentrism, usually through Marxist or Marxist-inspired perspectives, which include "world-systems analysis," associated with the names of Immanuel Wallerstein, Samir Amin, Andre Gunder Frank (in a previous incarnation), and so forth, who played an important part in the creation of "world" or "global" histories, albeit radically critical ones. Area studies specialists also drew for their critiques of Eurocentrism on historians from the societies of their specializations; in other words, their "conversations" included other than Euro-Americans. That these earlier critiques are now labeled "Eurocentric" may be revealing of the politics at work in the repudiation of Eurocentrism. That multiculturalism within a modernization/globalization paradigm has replaced earlier critiques based on cultural imperialism should not occasion much surprise, when it is clear that "Third World" societies have given up on radical alternatives to bourgeois modernization, instead turning to a reassertion of "native values" within a common context of globalization. With the decline of radicalism in "Third World" societies, which earlier empowered radical critiques of Eurocentrism, there seems to be some indication that those area studies specialists who participate in contemporary critiques of Eurocentrism are drawn to a type of "world" or "global" history that is closer to the globalizing and postcolonial urges of the present. The victory is a victory not just of modernization, but of liberal, even conservative, versions of it, minus earlier assumptions of a Eurocentric teleology, which is what globalization is.

29. For a refreshing exception that examines the question of the historian's place in both historiographical and political perspective, see Alfred W. Crosby, "The Past and Present of Environmental History," *American Historical Review* 100, no. 4 (October 1995): 1177–89.

30. Bruce Mazlish, "Global History in a Postmodernist Era?" in *Conceptualizing Global History*, ed. Bruce Mazlish and Ralph Buultjens (Boulder, Colo.: 1993), 117, 120.

31. Partha Chatterjee, *Nationalist Thought and the Colonial World: A Derivative Discourse* (Minneapolis: 1993)

32. In a rather ill-conceived essay, Stuart Hall brings a charge of ("primitive," as well as, "primeval") "functionalism" against this author (along with Robert Young). See Stuart Hall, "When Was 'the Postcolonial'? Thinking at the Limit," in *The Postcolonial Question: Common Skies Divided Horizons*, ed. Iain Chambers and Lidia Curti (New York: 1996). The charge does not call for comment, except to note that it is rather below the potential of such a distinguished cultural critic, to whose formulations I would myself acknowledge a debt. Rather than method-

ological problems of culturalism and functionalism, Hall's attack may have something to do with the post-Thatcherite turn in British Marxism.

33. Ken Armitage, "The 'Asiatic'/Tributary Mode of Production: State and Class in Chinese History," Ph.D. dissertation, Griffith University (Australia), 1997, 3.

34. For a more detailed discussion of the problem of history with regard to questions of postcolonialism and globalization, see Arif Dirlik, "Is There History After Eurocentrism: Globalism, Postcolonialism, and the Disavowal of History," *Cultural Critique* 42 (Spring 1999): 1–34.

35. Ashis Nandy, *The Intimate Enemy* (Oxford: 1983).

36. The relationship to Europe and Eurocentrism, needless to say, long have been issues in cultural and political debates in non-European societies, where Eurocentrism clearly carried positive connotations for reformers and revolutionaries of various kinds. For an example with reference to China in the 1980s, see Chen Xiaomei, *Occidentalism As a Counter-Discourse in Post-Mao China* (New York: 1995). Taking her cue from cultural developments in China in the post-Mao period, Chen upholds, "occidentalism," the mirror image of orientalism, while accusing critics of orientalism, such as Edward Said, of colonialist sins!

37. Contrary to some recent interpretations, I think it is safe to say that such empires as the Islamic and the Mongolian, which were unlike the Chinese or the Indic in extending beyond the boundaries of any single state-society, were nevertheless quite limited in their transformative power as compared to the ability of modern capitalism to enter every sphere of life. For arguments with regard to Islam, see Michael Adas, ed., *Islamic and European Expansion: The Forging of a Global Order* (Philadelphia: 1993).

38. Culture and values are important, for example, to David Landes's defense of Eurocentrism in the work cited previously.

39. Andre Gunder Frank, *ReOrient: Global Economy in the Asian Age* (Berkeley, Calif.: 1998), chap. 1. My analogy with "classical economics" pertains only to the conclusions to be drawn with regard to economic development. Otherwise Frank's analysis is informed both by Marxism and world-system analysis, of which he has long been a practitioner.

40. William A. Green, "Periodizing World History," *History and Theory* 34, no. 2 (1995): 111.

41. Jerry H. Bentley, "Cross-Cultural Interaction and Periodization in World History," *American Historical Review* 101, no. 3 (June 1996): 749–70. See also the response by Patrick Manning, "The Problem of Interactions in World History," *American Historical Review* 101, no. 3 (June 1996): 771–82. Manning's essay also mentions the issue of the use of "culture" in such analyses, which I take up below. For the question of theory in periodization, see Green, "Periodizing World History."

42. Examples of such an approach are available in Roxann Prazniak, *Dialogues Across Civilizations: Sketches in World History from the European and Chinese Experiences* (Boulder, Colo.: 1996), and R. Bin Wong, *China Transformed: Historical Change and the Limits of European Experience* (Ithaca, N.Y.: 1998). These authors focus on thematic comparisons that take into account different perceptions in different

contexts of similar problems that are also sensitive to historical changes that call for different uses of theoretical insights at different times in history. Above all, they are sensitive to normative developmentalist biases.

43. Bruce Mazlish, "An Introduction to Global History," in *Conceptualizing Global History*, ed. Bruce Mazlish and Ralph Buultjens (Boulder, Colo.: 1993), 20. For a "softer" claim to policy relevance, see McNeill, "The Changing Shape of World History," 26. See also the critical and thoughtful essay on the limits of "global history" by Raymond Grew, "On the Prospect of Global History," in Mazlish and Buultjens, eds., *Conceptualizing Global History*, 227–49.

44. Grew, "Review Essay," 373.

45. See, for example, Michael Geyer and Charles Bright, "World History in a Global Age," *American Historical Review* 100, no. 4 (Oct. 1995): 1043, 1045–46. In Bright and Geyer's account, "interactions," "indigenous causes," and "autonomous trajectories of development" replace what used to be imperialism, domination and unequal exchange, because there was no "prime mover at work" (1046). The authors in this case draw freely on the insights of postcolonial criticism. Obviously, with diasporas and borderlands replacing nations, and identities dissolving into "hybridities," it is difficult to tell who the dominant and the dominated may have been.

46. I am referring here to certain kinds of writing that assume categorical teleologies, and then proceed to judge other peoples for having failed to live up to them. An example of this kind of teleology, on the issue of class, is Dipesh Chakrabarty, *Rethinking Working Class History* (Princeton, N.J.: 1989). Equally prominent are writings on feminism. There has been an almost concerted writing attacking the condition of women in China, which not only ignores what Chinese women might or might not want, but also has encouraged attacks on the socialist program for women, which has certainly accomplished a great deal for women, more than anytime earlier. It is interesting that feminists who attack the socialist program for what it has failed to achieve are often oblivious to what socialism has achieved, because it has not achieved what they think ought to have been achieved. This is not to say that women's questions should be reduced to what is of concern to women under socialism, but that women under socialism or under precapitalism may have a great deal to teach women who have discovered their "womanness" under capitalism and, regardless of what they may claim, are conditioned in their feminism by the mode of production that is their context.

47. Arturo Escobar, *Encountering Development: The Making and Unmaking of the Third World* (Princeton, N.J.: 1994), and Gilbert Rist, *The History of Development: From Western Origins to Global Faith*, trans. Patrick Camiller (London: 1997)

48. John Tomlinson, *Cultural Imperialism: An Introduction* (Baltimore, Md.: 1991).

49. Nandy, "History's Forgotten Doubles," 46.

50. Vine Deloria Jr., *Red Earth, White Lies: Native Americans and the Myth of Scientific Fact* (New York: 1995).

51. Immanuel Wallerstein, *Unthinking Social Science: The Limits of Nineteenth Century Paradigms* (Cambridge, Mass.: 1991), and McNeill, "History and the Scientific Worldview," 13. McNeill, of course, does not say what might happen to these worldviews when they are brought within the domain of "scientific" history.

52. Vinay Lal, "History and the Possibilities of Emancipation: Some Lessons from India," *Journal of the Indian Council of Philosophical Research* (June 1996): 130.

53. Nandy, "History's Forgotten Doubles," 46.

54. The importance of this crucial project is demonstrated in works such as Rist, *The History of Development,* and Escobar, *Encountering Development.*

11

Africa and the Construction of a Grand Narrative in World History

Maghan Keita

Africa is no vast island separated by an immense ocean from other portions of the globe, and cut off through the ages from the men who have made and influenced the destinies of mankind. She has been closely connected, as both source and nourisher, with some of the most potent influences which have affected for good the history of the world.

—Edward Wilmot Blyden, 1880

I am challenging Authority.[1]
A narrative of Africa in the world? An analytical narrative of Africa in the world? The advent of modern world history is, in part, response to national and regional conflicts, and global crises. As such, it is a commendable exercise. Its limitations, however, are rooted in its grounding, if Gilbert Allardyce's reading of the history of world history is correct.[2] Allardyce reminds us that world history came into being as a subject of academic discourse as a derivative of the "Western Civilization" course. That course was an attempt to globalize U.S. historical vision during and after World War I. The course allowed U.S. intellectuals to provide clarity as to where the United States fit within the space of "world culture."[3] At a time that even in historical hindsight seemed quite grave, this was an

exercise that sought to tie an isolationist United States to Europe, and in so doing create the "West" in very much the way in which we understand it today. The West, in some ways, was depicted as a world unto itself—a world defined by its "Greco-Roman heritage" and its "Judeo-Christian moorings." It was and is the world that Edward Said has so ably critiqued in terms of "orientalism." Yet it was also a world that desired an expanded, albeit limited, vision itself. That vision was key to the construction of a cultural unity based on a historically rendered world. At the time, such a vision could offer a way out of regionalized crises, or, at the very least, the basis for uniting against a common foe.

Clearly, however, as both Allardyce and Lawrence Levine indicate, the United States and the Western world had been primed for this type of world history. As Levine puts it, the U.S. enterprise of higher education had been firmly committed to a European paradigm that saw classical civilization as its base. The "classical" base of this type of civilizational study was not unique. The process of attempting to construct a history of the world was historical.

An element of what the modern exploration of world history attempted to do for us was to expand the "world" per se. Building on globalized notions of a "Christian" world or worlds, modern historians conceded— some even propagated—a world of Islam. The most modern of secularized definitions provided expansive terminology that spoke of the "Eurasian" and "Afro-Eurasian" worlds. To my way of thinking, all these conceptualizations involved new and critical ways of contemplating the world that might have inclusive repercussions.

These repercussions were also indicative of the ways in which the writing of world history might be guided by the biases of the historians and their histories. By example, it is clear that the Chinese knew a history of the world that was guided by their own sensitivities regarding its center: China. The Japanese knew the world as well from a particular vantage, as the place where the "world began": Japan, the land of the rising sun. For the sake of speculation, how many other peoples and cultures developed perspectives of the world and their place and space in it? What might their perspectives tell us of the world at large and how might those perceptions help us to fashion histories of it? These questions and others are part of the extended legacy—the repercussions of the development of modern world history.

THE CHALLENGE

Africa and the world; the world and Africa. In 1946, W. E. B. DuBois attempted such a project in *The World and Africa*. He subtitled his work,

An Inquiry into the Part Which Africa Has Played in World History. It is a reminder of how critical a part Africa has played in human history past and present, and how impossible it is to forget this and rightly explain the present plight of mankind.[4] His is a point we need to revisit, to admit and to privilege Africa in the new writings of world history. Not as a "historical 'entitlement program,' " as Andre Gunder Frank has put it,[5] but as a challenge to existing historiographies and epistemologies. It is to question, as DuBois pointed out, how world history might be constructed without Africa. Such a challenge would open up notions like William McNeill's "Eurasia" or Marshall Hodgson's "Afro-Eurasia."[6] It should position us to entertain questions concerning the possible interpretations of such concepts.

We are forced to ask questions because we live in a modern age dominated by Enlightenment constructions. We are subject to racialized historiographies and epistemologies. This racialization has posed a serious impediment to any consideration of Africa in the history of the world.

Consider the fourteenth-century, Catalonian map of Africa.[7] Center it on a globe as its cartographers intended. Allow it to rotate counter-clockwise, as if against time—certainly against convention. Place this against some of the most recent historical and historiographic backdrops of the world: Jerry Bentley's *Old World Encounters*, Janet Abu-Lughod's *Before European Hegemony*, Philip Curtin's *Cross-Cultural Trade in World History*, and Alfred Crosby's *The Columbian Exchange*. In their very specific and innovative approaches to human movement and interaction, where is Africa? How is it represented? What is its agency? How is its partnership in the construction of the worlds in question illustrated in ways that might be consonant with DuBois's earlier inquiry? If not, why not? How would the acknowledgment of Africa change our writing of history and our construction of knowledge?

THE HISTORIOGRAPHIC ISSUE: THE ABSENCE OF AFRICA IN THE WORLD

The questions Africa poses for world history and its construction merit historiographic analysis. We need to inquire into the development of history as a "modern" and "professional" field, and the implications of that professionalization. The particulars of the professionalization of history have direct impact on the construction and legitimation of world history as a field. They also tell us what we might expect vis-à-vis the inclusion of Africa in such a project.

The field of history emerged as an activity of amateurs. The science of the Enlightenment gave rise to the notion that there might be a scientific way of doing history; that history might be bounded and defined by its own scientific methodology. Such a bounding and definition would confer legitimacy and discipline (in all senses of the word) on a field that had been, until then, regarded the preserve of gentlemen of leisure. Without regard for their social status, history would remain the purview of amateurs unless it was prescribed by science. That prescription could come only at the hands of professionals. Two characteristics defined this approach. The first was the question of what constitutes history. The second centered on who may or may not write history.[8] The answers to these questions and others was reiterated in the conclusion that history must be constructed by professionals guided by a "scientific methodology."

The late–nineteenth-, early–twentieth-century reification of history as a discipline also witnessed the possibilities for the professionalization of world history, or, more precisely, the possibilities for rendering a history of the world in a modern, more professional manner. As such, history assumed global proportions as well. It could be conceived of as a critical tool in the ordering of the social relations that would help to guide both the construction of nations as well as the rights, rites, and roles of the unfolding imperial project of the modern world.[9] History became crucial by the nineteenth century as an essential component of the project of race/nation/empire.[10] The histories emerging from the nineteenth century onward, whether written by Europeans or not, were decidedly Eurocentric. Within this context works centering on the construction of race and nation in resistance to empire appeared.[11] Yet even where they wished to privilege non-European, and specific African forms, the historiographic choices made by this latter group of historians were predetermined by an epistemology that equated the professional discourse in which they wished to enter with the scientific processes for the construction of that discourse, all of which were designed to make the discourse modern.

In the rational tones of professional history, how could "uncivilized" space (read "unmodern" and "unscientific" space) have history? Whatever history might be given to such a space could come only through the racialized notions of the imperial nation. How could Africa possibly have history? If we were to read history backward and then forward, empire—that is the achievement of empire outside Africa—becomes synonymous with "civilization" and "culture." It is this notion that is carried forward by some of the most renowned of contemporary world historians, including Marshal Hodgson, William McNeill, and Fernand Braudel. Their work represents the juggernaut of "civilizational studies." Theirs is clearly the study of imperial formation as civilization. As such we must recognize that their treatments are informed by racialized historiography and epistemology.

Fernand Braudel's monumental three-volume work, *Civilization and Capitalism, 15th–18th Century*, (Berkeley, Calif.: 1992) embraces the civilizational mode and serves as the path for many world historians. Yet his treatment of Africa is ambiguous, at times dismissive. Where there are signs of African agency, Braudel glosses over them to take us back to his main premise: the world Europe made.

Braudel's position here is important, because it is one that is extended by the omission and repudiation of Africa by authors such as Abu-Lughod. Clearly, however, the work of neither can stand unchallenged critically in the light of historical analyses of "Black Africa" for Braudel's fifteenth century or Abu-Lughod's "long thirteenth century." These analyses not only tie Africa to the construction of a world political economy for the periods in question, but they also pose at least two attendant issues in relation to those ties. The first centers on the extensive, integral, and more than likely inextricable ways in which Africa was linked to that political economy—North to South, East to West. The second centers on historiographic and epistemological issues: questions concerning the reading and re-reading of the primary and secondary sources on these eras.

One rationale for Braudel's position might be found in William McNeill's reasoning for the neglect of Africa in *The Rise of the West*. In the *Journal of World History*, McNeill argued that his treatment of Africa was, indeed, an oversight, as the scholarship of the past twenty-five years has revealed a far more complex interplay of peoples and cultures than was accessible when he wrote *The Rise of the West*. Having justified Africa's absence historiographically, McNeill adds the epistemological rejoinder that the study of the "history" of Africa does not fit the body of knowledge constructed by the civilizational paradigm; yet sub-Saharan Africa never became the seat of a major civilization, and the continent remained peripheral to the rest of the world, down to and including our own age.[12] McNeill allows for some expansion in his exposition on Eurasia. For Braudel, however, it remains the world Europe made. Africa is "peripheral to the rest of the world."[13]

My historiographic and epistemological concerns are encapsulated herein. The world for Braudel is constructed from a body of knowledge that actively denies Africa and its participation in the world. According to Mudimbe, this is the body of knowledge from which was "invented the savage" Africa. It is the same body of knowledge that limits contemporary world historians today.[14] What are the lapses in the current historiography? Take the narrow chronological band Braudel addresses—the fifteenth through the eighteenth centuries—then pose questions about the two consequential phenomena that would allow Africa a global presence: cities and empires. What is it we find, and what is it they do in Africa?

At the close of the fifteenth century, the state of Songhai reached its zenith. Successor to the states of Ghana and Mali, larger than all of western Europe combined, it would last another century in this form before it succumbed to the invasions of the Moroccans and internal strife. Even then it would retain its identity through the absorption and assimilation of its invaders. Until the close of the nineteenth century, it remained the Pashalik of Timbuktu in name only.[15] One question to these data must be "why?"; another must be "what are the implications, and how might they relate to the construction of a world historiography?" The fundamental issue concerning Songhai imperialism and the subsequent imperialism of the Moroccans is political-economic. They are actions that govern the construction of the imperial structures, and like all others, they revolve around the power to secure and/or deny access to resources within a given geopolitical sphere. Taking note of this we might ask: If Songhai is imperial—if it is an empire—then is it representative of the "civilizations" that privilege the histories of McNeill, Hodgson, and Braudel?

One of the prime indicators overlooked by Braudel and others was the conduct of commerce within this sphere. Even if the works of Susan and Roderick McIntosh, Ivor Wilks, Nehemia Levtzion, Ann McDougall, Robin Lawless, David Hull, Graham Connah, and many, many others[16] were not available fifteen or twenty-five years ago, what about the primary sources from which they draw?[17] What would a quick reference to Henri Pirenne and the debate over his thesis reveal? How might Robert Lopez's sources aid us? Contemporary histories like those of Bentley's *Old World Encounters* and Abu-Lughod's *Before European Hegemony* help to illustrate this problem.

Philip Curtin praises Bentley's volume as a "careful," "accurate and well written" work. It is the "carefulness," the caution of the work, which gives me pause. In his carefulness and caution Bentley fails to bring out the possibilities of African participation and the participation of an African diaspora in the history of the world Bentley wishes to construct.[18] For instance, Bentley might have entertained the reciprocity of movement that must have occurred along the "silk roads." This would have meant referencing Egypt, Nubia, and Carthage as African states and recognizing their participation in such trade. Here Bentley's *entré* might begin with a broader discussion of "commercial networks that progressively linked the Middle East, Egypt, Persia, and even northwestern India." He might have expanded on the "sea lanes" that "linked" East Africa to Indian Ocean trade, and through this provided a series of rich and stimulating questions that would have further enhanced his theme of "old world encounters."

This broadened field of vision might have led Bentley further down "silk roads" upon which Xerxes's "30,000 black horses"—his Ethiopian cavalry—and his other African auxiliaries might have been encountered.

Rome's trade in African goods all the way to China might have given pause for speculation. The relations to be had between the basilus of Ethiopia and his Christian brother in Byzantium, or Cosmas's record of his voyages, would have (and could and do) provide the animation to explore what might be entailed here in the construction of a wider world.[19] Africa would be enjoined in a discourse that moved beyond the conventional notions of Africa north and south of the Sahara.

The caution that Bentley displays in *Encounters* precludes a "post-classical" world where a true Afro-Eurasian dynamism shapes political, economic and cultural devices for the era in question and for those to come. In the conventional shaping, there can be no anticipation of Antar or the "Black Crows." We are unable to contemplate the full implications of Jahiz's indictment of contemporary Islamic theology and its possible racialization from tenth century Baghdad. Nor can we comprehend why a huge section of the Persian population in the tenth century would choose to call themselves "African" ("Zanj") and then participate in more than a decade of revolution against the caliphate.[20]

Here we might engage Abu-Lughod's *Before European Hegemony*. Such an engagement should be contextualized by one question: How does one construct a history of the dominant trade networks of the world from 1250 to 1350 C.E., in an era "before European hegemony," and omit Africa? Abu-Lughod consults the same primary sources available to Hodgson, McNeill, and Braudel. The European focus of the work employs sources used by Pirenne or Lopez—sources found in Arabic for the most part. Again, both sets of sources force the question: How does one presume a system of pre-European trade networks that excludes the trans-Saharan and the Swahili networks?

Abu-Lughod argues that she excludes the East African zone, even though it was well "integrated" and "intense" in terms of its Indian Ocean–Persian Gulf commerce, because "its geographic reach was relatively limited" and "African merchants were largely local and African goods seldom made their way to China or Europe."[21] Should we assume that West Africa is excluded for the same reasons in spite of what the evidence says to us? A reading of Pirenne and Lopez with copies of Levtzion, Connah, Hull, Saad, McDougall, and others nearby might be of great aid in answering these questions. From the outset they imply that it is impossible to structure the kind of world history that Abu-Lughod seeks to write without the inclusion of Africa.

Abu-Lughod's work is bound by the same conventions of historiography and epistemology as those who precede her. She is unable to envision an Africa that is a global player in her long thirteenth century. So what should historians make of Catalonian maps? Why do Norman kings and Roman popes commission geographies and histories of these spaces? Why are Africa's fabled cities spoken of in places as distant as Baghdad or Al-Andalus? For Abu-Lughod, there are no caravans moving from cities across the desert to Sahel, linking spaces north and south, east and west, Africa with Europe, Africa with the heartlands of Islam and beyond. The trans-Saharan trade and its networks are fictive devices, in her analysis. The Swahili ports have no function. Africa has no spaces to be crossed or acknowledged for any reason. Africa is an obstacle around which one must find passage.[22] Africa has no place in this history of the world.

Writing in Andre Gunter Frank and Barry K. Gills's *The World System*, Immanuel Wallerstein provides a fairly succinct and cogent explanation of his concept of "world-systems" theory and how it differs from the "world-system" approach offered by Frank, Gills, and others. In short, Wallerstein sees a distinct break in the formation of world political economies that marks the definitive emergence of capitalism and heralds the beginning of the modern age. It is this "modern age," capitalist dynamic that has characterized Wallerstein's work on world history, particularly that concerning Africa and the world. The dynamics for Wallerstein revolve around capitalist expansion, the relations between core and periphery, and the ways in which capitalist expansion as a global phenomenon has led to unprecedented development for some, and striking levels of underdevelopment for most others.[23]

Wallerstein's work in world history has little to say of African agency, given that its organizing principles center on the rise of capitalist imperialism. It says nothing of Africa as a precapitalist entity except in the most oblique manner, by way of clarifying Wallerstein's world-systems thesis. The oblique implication centers on the possibility of Africans and others participating in a type of capitalist accumulation that was distinct from Wallerstein's modern definition in that modern capitalist accumulation is prefixed by the term "ceaseless."[24]

Wallerstein and Frank and company were fellow travelers at one time. The point of divergence centers on a hyphen and a single "s." The two, however, hold significant implications for theorizing the construction of the world and its history. Whereas Wallerstein sees distinct shifts in modes of production and accumulation, Frank argues that there has been no such thing. For Frank, what has been witnessed in the evolution of capitalism is just that: the evolution of the world-system itself. It is an evolution that is without distinct and well-defined junctures in its own development, an evolution marked by the continual presence of the "antedated" alongside the "modern."

However, even the *longue duree* espoused in Frank's work is inadequate in bringing Africa into the picture as an equal player. The work that he and Gills edited, with its promising and provocative subtitle ("Five Hundred Years or Five Thousand?") still embraces debate, as they put it, on how to write the history of "the 'old' Afro-Eurasian world system." This is a system whose conceptual basis had little or nothing to do with what might be determined as Africa "proper" by the most generous of definitions. In fact, the global community that the work embraces celebrates a "fertile crescent" dynamic—the Mesopotamian/Arab/Islamic heartland motif—and then drifts further East in anticipation of Frank's latest work. That work provides an even more marked decoupling of the systems debate and world historiography from Africa itself.[25]

This is in large part my reading of Frank's *ReOrient*. In spite of Frank's aggressive attacks on Eurocentrism, in spite of his call for a long view of world history, the oppositional thinking of the Enlightenment still reigns. The world is still divided between the "Orient" and the "Occident." Where it is "black" and "white," the "black" is largely dismissed. There is little or no Africa in the new Frank. In fact, in light of the subtitle, one might be forced to ask whether Frank's volume signals the need to write a world history in the "African Age"?[26]

The question appears almost ridiculous. And it would be, if not for the fact that the most recent works by the most prominent authors on world history still pretend that Africa is nonexistent. Frank's treatment of Africa in *ReOrient* is peripheral and sporadic. He has also dismissed theoretical issues that attempt to place Africa within a global discourse. Frank has conventionally identified Afrocentrism as "ideological," and as such useless.[27]

Afrocentrism has no nuance for Frank. He has reduced more than a century of intellectual activity to caricature. In the most immediate sense he has dismissed such intellectuals as Carter G. Woodson, DuBois, William Leo Hansberry, and Frank M. Snowden, because they argued that Africa has a place in the world. In 1998, Frank's *ReOrient* is devastating as an illustration of the epistemological and historiographic issues framing this debate. Frank has brought into stark relief what he believes constitutes knowledge, and who has the right to engage in the construction of knowledge. He reaffirms the conventions on what is history and who might be a historian.[28]

In both Frank and Wallerstein, we find the most progressive and the most conventional aspects of the construction of world history. Their treatments of world history imply that "systems theory" is broad enough to encompass a number of thematic devices without difficulty. However, there is some real discomfort in recognizing alternative epistemologies and different ways of knowing, seeing, reading, and writing world history.

In brief, the world historiography of both Alfred W. Crosby Jr. and Philip Curtin can be characterized as falling within the parameters of systems theory if only because their discrete themes encompass global dynamics that might be regarded as systemic. The Crosby work has looked at systematic patterns of biological and cultural migration associated primarily with European expansion. Both his *Columbian Exchange* and *Ecological Imperialism* focus on Europe's biological and cultural impact on the world and its construction. And while the works are thoroughly innovative in terms of their approach and subject matter, they still decidedly center on Europe.[29] One of the major surprises of *Columbian Exchange* is that, in spite of Braudel's statement that Europe could not have developed the New World without Africa and Africans, the two hardly fit into Crosby's narrative.

Although some might take issue with Curtin's statement that "Sub-Saharan Africa remained isolated from the main currents of world trade far longer than most of the rest of the Afro-Eurasian landmass,"[30] *Cross-Cultural Trade* may mark the first real post-1970s attempt to place Africa thematically within the context of the world. The work is still bound by some of the same conceptual limitations that characterize the other works discussed here. Chiefly, there is an inability to fully integrate Africa into the world, a tendency illustrated by the initiating clause: "sub-Saharan Africa." The image conjured up for readers is still one of an Africa separated from the rest of the world by a real and impenetrable barrier precluding its participation and mandating its isolation.

This image is underscored when Curtin writes of sub-Saharan Africa's "three coasts," the Sahara, the Indian Ocean, and the Atlantic Ocean, and when he speaks of the commercial and cultural activities occurring there as transitory and without reciprocity. What is omitted is African movement and participation in the establishment of communities, cultures, and patterns of international trade, which are crucial to our understanding of the world. The "sub-Saharan" designation also leads the reader to assume that Africa above the Sahara is not Africa, since in Braudelian terms it is "white." I am not convinced that Curtin fully satisfies the terms for Africa in a global exchange if he is content making the northern coast of this Africa the Sahara rather than the Mediterranean. Much evidence shows that this needs rethinking.

The integration of Africa and its commercial networks, and the ways in which those networks respond to and interact with the rest of the world, are the most critical needs of Curtin's work. Without them, he has provided the basis for others to speculate on the implications of his thesis and the ways in which they further illustrate Africa's links with the world at large as a historical actor. This is no mean task, however; it is an indication of the work ahead.[31]

EPISTEMOLOGY: THE CONSTRUCTION OF KNOWLEDGE AND THE CONTEXTUALIZATION OF HISTORY

Marshall Hodgson wrote of the "precommitments" that shape historical discourse. Valentine Mudimbe speaks of the "presuppositions" of a discourse, dominated by certain ways of knowing that construct and subjugate "a world submitted to its memory." The discourses to which both speak are history and the construction of history within the context of an epistemology—a way of knowing—that recognizes no other ways of knowing. Thus, there are no other ways of reading or writing history, no other ways of contributing to the prescribed body of knowledge without conceding to its dictates.[32]

The way of knowing that contextualizes the construction of world history/memory is dominated by a memory/history of an expansive, imperialistic Europe. The epistemology, the history, the Europe, and the "memories" they are designed to invoke are products of the Enlightenment. These products provide rationalization for who and what we have become through the present. This is a memory/history dedicated to the articulation of race/nation/empire—an "empire" that may now be translated as several separate and seemingly disparate "hegemonies." Frank and Allardyce's terminology is still operative, however. The epistemological context of our notion of the world, and our writing about it, are still decidedly Eurocentric.[33] The epistemology is oppositional. It is dialectic. It is racialized.

Let me return to Andre Gunder Frank's injunction on Afrocentrism. Frank's recognition of Eurocentrism as a crucial problem, his dismissal of Afrocentrism, and the Afrocentric argument itself, are elements of racialized discourse. It is a discourse that Afrocentrism does not make new. It is indicative of the sentiments of very many historians, a considerable number of whom write histories of the world.

In his dismissal of Afrocentrism, Frank evokes the work of Martin Bernal. Frank indicates an acceptance of Bernal's scholarship by placing it in opposition to whatever Frank characterizes as Afrocentric. He does so in this way: He writes of Bernal's reluctance at having his thesis used "apparently against the original intentions of the author to support the idea of Afrocentrism."[34] What Frank and so many others overlook in the epistemological debates is that Bernal has precedents, people of substance who have provided substantial ideas. They represent a historical antecedent to anything that he, Molefe Asante, or a host of other scholars might propose about Africa's place in the world.

The racial nature of the epistemological and historiographic discourse led Bernal to conclude that "only I could have made such claims" concerning Africa's role in the construction of the world.[35] Bernal's claims parallel those of Edward Said's, whose works receive some attention from Frank. Yet Frank, in addressing the writing of history and the ways in which it is contextualized, pays little attention to the ways in which Said's "demystifying of Eurocentrism" in his analysis of "orientalism" is profoundly similar to the Afrocentric works of the same vein, particularly those of Asante.[36]

Frank's foray into Afrocentrism, and his own orientalist bias, help to summarize his reading of Africa in world history. In fact the roots of Athens were much more embedded in Asia Minor, Persia, Central Asia, and other parts of Asia than in Egypt and Nubia.[37] Frank illustrates, possibly inadvertently, the epistemological context out of which so many world historians write. Even for the most progressive scholars there is an inability, or a reluctance, to escape the existing epistemological and historiographic paradigms.

There is also no real recognition that these paradigms are Enlightenment paradigms. They are the paradigms that impose structure, create modernity, and rationalize imperialism. These same paradigms have assisted in the construction of a racialized body of knowledge in the modern sense that focuses on the exclusion of Africa from historical discourse and the process of creating or adding to the existing body of knowledge. Frank, as the best of those whom he critiques, still regards Africa as a junior partner. The subordinate nature of the relationship is implied in the way in which he initiates his discussion of Africa by way of Bernal and Asante, and Afrocentrism, Egypt, Nubia, and Greece.

Frank's initiative on Africa in world space, however, points to another glaring epistemological feature shared by a good number of historians of the world and of Africa. The only Africa they seem to know is an Africa defined by modern space. For world historians, Africa's premodern presence is negligible, and its modern existence is characterized largely by colonization and modern imperialism. There is little regard for A. Adu Boahen's observation that the "colonial moment" was just an episode, "a mere episode," whose impact merits serious reconsideration, especially by scholars of Africa's colonial period.[38] This reconsideration must be made within the context of a much larger history of Africa, and an enlarged history of the world.

That reconsideration must also be made in light of the preoccupation of the majority of those Africanist scholars who have focused their overwhelming attention on a modern, post-Columbian Africa. Africa before this period has had relatively little appeal, and therefore little "history." In large part, Africanists have treated us to Trevor-Roper's injunction on the state (or lack thereof) of African history "before the coming of the Europeans."

It might be argued that scholars of Africa and its diaspora have just not weighed in on the issue of Africa and the world. Of course, again, careful examination of close to two centuries of the discourse that Frank criticizes proves otherwise. Joseph Miller considered the issue, in part, in his 1999 presidential address to the American Historical Association. Miller suggests that the serious engagement of African history by historians in other fields will have dramatic repercussions in both historiography and epistemology.[39] As Miller implies, those repercussions can be witnessed in the works of some Africanist scholars and their ideas concerning Africa and the world. Yet it bears repetition that these are intellectuals and ideas that up to now have been readily dismissed. However, the proofs that these ideas represent are key factors in the construction of other histories and other ways of knowing—particularly, other ways of knowing the world. In large part, the Afrocentric debate is a debate over world history, that is, Africa's place in the history of the world.

African American intellectuals early in the nineteenth century, along with African intellectuals at the century's end, formulated theses that were quite similar to Bernal's regarding Africa's place in the world. David Walker, Frederick Douglass, Edward Wilmot Blyden, George Washington Williams, C. C. Reindorf, and Samuel Johnson all created a formulation whose basic rule centered on Africa's role in the construction of the ancient world. Their history built up a body of knowledge and a way of knowing that contextualized their identities and those of peoples of African descent around the world.

Woodson, DuBois, Hansberry, and Snowden carried into the twentieth century refinements in the historiography and epistemology of Africa and the world. Their works would be reemphasized by African scholars and scholars of African descent who were representative of the Presence Africaine group in post–World War II Paris. The voices of Negritude—voices that deserve serious reappraisal—were also voices of historical, historiographic, and epistemological importance. The works of Leopold Sedar Senghor, Alouine Diop, Aime Cesar, Leon Gontran Damas, and, of course, Cheikh Anta Diop and Theophile Obenga underline the critical genealogy of a concept like Afrocentrism. These scholars and their works give Afrocentrism a vision and links that take it far beyond the United States and the twentieth century.

The extension of the debate and critique of Afrocentrism and Africa's place in the world by and among scholars of African descent are seen in the works of Colin Palmer on Africans in colonial Mexico and Paul Gilroy on the modern African diaspora and Afro-Europeans. Sidney Lemelle has weighed in with a critique of Afrocentrism itself, and Ann duCille considers the impact of Afrocentrism on poststructural, postmodern, postcolonial discourses.[40]

While all these works face the West and modernity, they are nonetheless critical in sparking questions that might arise if scholars interested in Africa and the African diaspora face the East and the North, and look "backward" beyond 1492. The impact that such a gaze might have for conceptualizing Africa in the world is seen in works like Hans Debrunner's encyclopedic *Presence and Prestige*, which engages the African presence in Europe from 1000 through 1917.[41]

The western and southern focus of the works of Africanist scholars are indicative of the limitations of the age in which we write. The scholars and their works are products of the Enlightenment. No matter the level of protest—as Kwame Appiah has observed in a commentary on Afrocentrism—there is a distinct level of Enlightenment bonding that has informed and shaped the intellectual sensibilities of all who write history.[42] To be sure, such shaping is not uniform. Its differing contexts create different content. However, the arguments, for the most part, are guided by the same suppositions. These suppositions speak to the same limitations of African agency in world history.

In general, these limitations can be described as stasis. That stasis is articulated in the assumed inability of Africans to move through time and space. It is an immobility that precludes African agency on a global level and is witnessed in historical treatments on Africa. This historical treatment focuses on post-1492 Africa and the "movement" of Africans to the "West." Pre-1492 movement seems problematic, in that it is hardly thought of and therefore unreported and unresearched. In many ways, this scholarship is trapped by the Enlightenment paradigm set by the Comte de Buffon. Having no plausible way to explain the "blacks" of New Guinea or "New Holland," de Buffon simply states that "no communication can ever be supposed to have taken place between Africa and the southern continent." Africans were assumed incapable of such an exercise.[43]

This is countered by the legacy of Afrocentric scholarship in the *longue durée* when it is considered seriously. Again, early African American and African scholars linked their myth-history to the East. Cheikh Anta Diop simply reemphasized this.[44] However, it takes little to realize, in spite of the volume and various types of documentation, that these notions have been summarily dismissed rather than queried and investigated.

Does this mean, however, that "Eurocentric" histories should be replaced by those that are "Afrocentric"? What then of "Asiocentric," or "Amerocentric," or "Pacific-centric" histories? What of thematic approaches to the history of the world? Clearly in the space of intellectual contention, no one set of theoretical premises should or can dominate *in pertuitam*. This fact I find most comfortable. I value the contention and the critical thought such contention might provoke. That thought allows for the possibility of generating new ways to see the world and ourselves. These new ways of "seeing" are, of course, new ways of knowing new epistemologies. In turn, these new epistemologies provide the context for doing new histories through the development of new ways of doing history (historiography). As yet, scholars of Africa and its diaspora may not have a coherent, concise, or clear articulation of global history, but their legacy and current intellectual activity suggest that they are not far from it.[45]

The writing of Africa in world history is an epistemological moment, and while it was not my intent to provide a critique of Afrocentrism, something should be said of the intellectual opportunities it provides in the construction of world history, and the scholastic paradigm it mirrors. In fact those paradigms are an indication of the shortcomings of the most prevalent of Afrocentrist theses and, of course, their Eurocentric counterparts.

Afrocentrism and Eurocentrism as they are conventionally understood are quite similar. Both are Enlightenment conceptualizations focused on the issue of "rationality" as a conceptual framework. Even in Leopold Sedar Senghor's "Negritude," the acceptance of "Negro spirituality" is argued in opposition to "European rationality," a sentiment that speaks to the emergence of "postdiscourse." Race in these instances has become the vehicle for various discourses plagued by the desire and the inability to rid themselves of both race and rationality as Enlightenment definitions.

The use of the same paradigmatic structures for resisting the construction of race, racism, and other oppressions can be seen in an examination of both Eurocentric and Afrocentric analyses from Negritude, through "Black Power," through the work of Molefe Asante and others on Afrocentrism. Within the context of a world shaped by the Enlightenment, these conceptualizations looked to the creation of new structures that illustrate their modernity in relation to the construction of alternate empires or "empires of culture."

The oppositional notions of Enlightenment rationality and the archetypal pairing of "black" and "white" are revisited in the conventions that surround Eurocentrism and Afrocentrism. These are in many ways mirror images. Yet with critical and imaginative thinking, Afrocentrism in particular may open the door to new historiographies and epistemologies in at least two ways. First, a close reading of Afrocentric theory acknowledges the validity of Eurocentrism to understand some construction of the world. That acknowledgment is made with the firm dictum that Eurocentrism cannot be assumed as universal in its analysis and description of the world's condition and its history.[46] By implication such a reading emphasizes as well that Afrocentrism cannot assume those proportions.

Second, a nuanced reading of Afrocentrism also acknowledges that there must exist ways of writing and knowing the history of the world that are different from both the dominating Afrocentric and Eurocentric paradigms. The question is how we can integrate best these ways of knowing and writing to engender, at the very least, a clearer picture of the history of the world and its participants. In this regard world history cannot be configured as one voice, or through one voice, or sometimes a chorus of voices. World historians must become cognizant of the many and different voices that illustrate the world. This recognition should compel the reader of world history to extrapolate from the examples of any given history.

Here the invocation of historical imagination implies that both the reader and the writer of world history think critically about processes and possibilities. Can there be a world history? No. But there certainly exist and will exist histories of the world. Their richness can only be compounded by a consideration of the role that Africa and African peoples have played in the construction of each variant.

The inclusion of Africa in the construction of world history will affect the ways in which the field is approached. At the very least, it could lead to a deracination of history. If historians were to evaluate the contributions of Africa on a world-scale, the evaluation would prove strikingly similar to that of other peoples. The similarities are only recognized if historians will allow themselves and Africans to cross geographic and temporal boundaries. As our writing of the history of the world now stands, this type of analysis is largely negated by historical conclusions drawn on the basis of race.

One result of this deracination may be a closer consideration of global historical devices in relation to class. Therefore, the inclusion of Africa in the construction of histories of the world dictates that historiography must engage new parameters. For example, the debates concerning the modern slave trade might be enhanced by identifying all of its beneficiaries. What are the implications of such identifications? What might they tell us, not only of class structure in Africa, but also of the ways in which certain class elements, including those in Africa, joined to construct the world as we now know it? What could such an analysis tell us about the process of colonization? Was it as ubiquitous as generally stated, or is there any room in which African agency might be discovered? And when it is discovered, what will it say of Africa's role in the construction, destruction, and deconstruction of the age of imperialism, of modernity, of its structures?

REWRITING NARRATIVES/
RETHINKING ANALYSES

The epistemological issues featured here ask not only what constitutes knowledge and how its context might be identified, but also who might produce knowledge. The most current epistemological and historiographic debates have reinforced conventional notions of who may and may not participate. This is done through the evocation of Afrocentrism as an allusory device to describe the narrowest, and for some, the most distasteful preoccupations on the subject. For those who hold these views there is little evidence that the questions inherent to the Afrocentric position, in their broadest sense, might be legitimate questions that should be entertained in the epistemological and historiographic debates.

This is a critical question for scholars concerned with epistemology and historiography and the construction of grand narratives in world history. In racialized epistemology and historiography there is a certain clarity as to what and who might be validated as producers of scholarship and as subjects of scholarship. Bernal gives an explicit answer when he refers to his preference to be listed among the "damn[ed] 'Negro intellectuals.' " These are intellectuals who, historically, have been "damned" from numerous quarters, yet whose work has been critical to restructuring the epistemological and historiographic debate.[47] They represent at least a century and a half of intellectual production that preceded Bernal. How is this, and will this be, addressed?

Can we honestly examine who and what these authors were and are and the ways in which they have contributed to who and what we believe ourselves to be? Can we recognize and then acknowledge their contributions to the construction of epistemology(ies), historiography(ies), and the history of the world? Will we be able to ascertain the ways in which they contribute to our understanding of the construction of world history? What do we, as world historians, do about black scholars and historians and their intellectual production?

Within the context of modernity the issue of the history of the world vis-à-vis Africa is profoundly tied to racialized epistemologies and historiographies. The questions and the answers posed by this epistemological and historiographic nexus have serious implications not only for understanding world history, but also for understanding who we are as "citizens of the world." The questions bear serious implications for refined, critical inquiry into the issues spurred by "poststructural," "postmodern," and "postcolonial" discourse. These issues are engaged if we simply ask how the modern world is explained and might be explained in light of Africa and of the globalism of "post"-discourses.[48]

One way to approach the "post"-discourses and their implications is to pursue their assumptions in the light of world history. One assumption of "post"-discourse, by definition, is that it follows the event that the prefix describes. What if the event is enjoined both before and as it unfolds? What does this say about the "subjects" that "post"-discourse wishes to engage and the nature of the discourse itself?

Let me explain this in two ways. First, the "post"-discourse assumes the "loss" of voice of the subject people within the prefixed events: that is, colonial peoples are heard only after colonization has ended. It is their voice, their "hearing," that defines the "postcolonial" moment. Second, this particular prefixing is indicative of the "regained" voice that seems only to occur after the event; in fact, it signals the event's closing and its end. What it ignores is the fact that the event is challenged immediately at its inception. So what does this say of the confluence of "pre," "current," and "post" moments and the histories they incite?

As I have indicated for Africa and Africans, entrance into the world generally has been regarded as a modern phenomenon. What happens to the histories of the world and the histories of Africa if that entry is charted well before the emergence of the modern era? What happens to the critiques of structure, modernity, and colonialism if one sees the impetus for enjoining and resisting them as both precedent to and coincident with them?

Return to Frank's dismissal of Afrocentrism and the fact that this dismissal epitomizes many conventional historians and histories far more conservative than Frank. Then take note of the way in which Frank diminishes Africa in the ancient period in terms of the construction of world history. Then revisit Bernal in light of his critics and a good deal of the primary source material. From the ancient through the medieval the primary sources construct a world in which Africa and Africans cannot be ignored. The African presence is even larger when the political nonsense of "black" and "white" and sub-Saharan and "hyper" Saharan Africa are properly contextualized.

We know Egypt and contend for it. Nubia/Kush/Ethiopia is/are speculative and dismissed because it is/they are African. Carthage? Carthage, reflective of the "modern" historiography on Egypt, is not seen as a part of Africa, though geographic, demographic, and primary sources argue otherwise. The imperial nature of these domains gives them prominence in the world. Who writes about Axum and the shift along the Rift up the Nile Valley to the Red Sea and Indian Ocean coast as part of a global phenomenon? Where is the position of this "Ethiopian" state in Indian and Pacific Ocean trade illustrated in the context of world history? What world history emphasizes that Axum was one among many in a flourishing East African trade nexus that fronted the Indian Ocean?

There are many ways to rewrite Africa and this early world history:

Rome, its provinces and its military, the religions of the Near East, the commerce of the East and the West. The same is true for the medieval and Renaissance periods as well. These possibilities defy the definitions of Africa and Africans provided by the structures of the modern world—the structures of colonialism. These possibilities and the histories that they invoke are the elements of historical consciousness used by various Africans as keys to their resistance to the structures of modern colonization.

These are parts of useable pasts that allowed some "Africans" parity in modern space. These pasts have allowed some peoples of African descent to shape their positions and the positions of their classes in the modern era. These pasts were injunctions of an history before the act that "post"-discourses describe and, indeed, before the histories that many histories of the world celebrate. These pasts were key to the resistance that ensued the very moment that the act of "modernity" commenced. Here the "post"-moment can be recognized by the very acts that challenge the structures of modernity and its colonialism at the instance of their inception. It becomes indicative of the fact that not all "subject" peoples are "subjugated."

So here the "regained" voices (Eric Wolf and others) are not voices regained at all. They are simply voices that the epistemologies and historiographies of modernity fail, and in many instances refuse, to hear. They are representative of historical activity that we have refused to see. Yet these are historical activities and voices that question our definition, order, and structure for this age and any we seek to describe as preceding it. These activities and these voices are key to the resistance to modern definition and its histories—including world history—and the driving force for serious reconsideration of how we might characterize the modern world and its history.

The act of considering Africa within the context of world history is laden with historiographic and epistemological consequences. It requires, as DuBois put it, "challenging authority."

NOTES

1. William Edward Burghardt DuBois, *The World and Africa* (1946; reprint, New York: 1992), viii.

2. Gilbert Allardyce, "Toward World History: American Historians and the Coming of the World History Course," *Journal of World History* 1 (1990): 23–76.

3. Lawrence Levine, *The Opening of the American Mind* (Boston: 1996), 57–60.

4. Levine, *Opening*, vii.

5. Andre Gunder Frank, "A Plea for World System History," *Journal of World History* 2 (1991): 3.

6. William McNeill, *The Rise of the West* (1963; reprint, Chicago: 1991). William

McNeill, "The Rise of the West After Twenty-Five Years," *Journal of World History* 1 (1990): 1–21; Marshall G. S. Hodgson, *Rethinking World History,* ed. Edmund Burke 3rd (Cambridge: 1993).

7. Basil Davidson, *African Kingdoms* (New York: 1980), 89.

8. Allardyce, "Toward World History," 23–25. In the discussion on who might write history—that is, who might be considered an historian—and what constituted history itself, the issue of race is central. One only need to consider the nature of historical study from the late nineteenth through the twentieth centuries and to apply that notion to the possibilities of black historians or histories of black folk themselves. The two are implausible for a number of reasons:

1. If (world) history is the domain of gentlemen of leisure, blacks are precluded.
2. If it is dominated by men of means who are by their very definition amateurs, there could be no professional black historians.
3. If black scholars were compelled to address issues that were critical to the advancement of their race, how could they indulge the frivolous exercise of historical inquiry?
4. If black folk were devoid of history, just what would black historians write?

This was the general tenor of the age of the professionalization of historical scholarship. It is revealed in large part in the work and letters of black scholars who were determined to write history. See Maghan Keita, *Race and the Writing of History: Riddling the Sphinx* (Oxford: 2000), 76–291.

9. See Frederick Teggart, *The Processes of History* (New Haven, Conn.: 1918) and *Rome and China; a Study of Correlations in Historical Events* (Berkeley, Calif.: 1939). Teggart's work refers to the quest for a "scientific" process of doing history—a product of Enlightenment thought—that, he concluded in 1939, was not only impossible, but also undesirable. Also see Frank, "Plea," and Allardyce, "Toward World History," 23–24. The real emphasis in these works is not the Enlightenment per se, but the work of the "children" of the Enlightenment and the ways in which Enlightenment principles have shaped the construction of history in relation to the concept of "science."

10. This notion of "race/nation/empire" seems best played out in Edward Said's *Orientalism* (New York: 1978) and *Culture and Imperialism* (New York: 1993); Valentine Y. Mudimbe's *The Invention of Africa: Gnosis, Philosophy, and the Order of Knowledge* (Bloomington, Ind.: 1988) and *The Idea of Africa* (Bloomington, Ind.: 1994). Anne McClintock's *Imperial Leather* (New York: 1995) introduces the issues of sexuality and gender into this construction.

11. H. G. Wells, *The Outline of History* (Garden City, N.Y.: 1920); Oswald Spengler, *The Decline of the West* (New York: 1926–1928); Arnold J. Toynbee, *A Study of History* (New York: 1947); Edward Wilmot Blyden et al., *The People of Africa* (New York: 1871); George Washington Williams, *History of the Negro Race in America 1619–1880* (New York: 1883); Jawaharlal Nehru, *Glimpses of World History* (New York: 1942).

12. McNeill, "25 Years," 7. On Braudel, see Fernand Braudel, *The Structures of Everyday Life,* vol. 1., trans. Sian Reynolds (1967; reprint, New York: 1979); Fernand Braudel, *The Wheels of Commerce,* vol. 2 (1979; New York: 1982); Fernand Braudel,

The Perspective of the World, vol. 3 (1979; reprint, New York: 1984). Braudel's "ambiguity" concerning Africa is expressed in the following way in volume 1, referring to Europe's westward expansion: "Without Africa it could not have developed the New World" (54). In volume 3, in the chapter "For and Against Europe: the Rest of the World," he writes that "Black Africa . . . has perhaps been too hastily dismissed as 'primitive' " (386). We might also note that the span of years between volumes 1 and 3 (twelve) should have given Braudel some pause in relation to the new syntheses on Africa that appeared in the intervening years.

13. Braudel, *Perspective*, 293–94.

14. Mudimbe, *Idea of Africa*, xii. This "savagery" is to be equated with an assumed inability to participate in the construction of the world and its history.

15. Elias Saad, *Social History of Timbuktu* (Cambridge, Mass.: 1983), Lansine Kaba, "Archers, Musketeers, and Mosquitoes: the Moroccan Invasion of the Sudan and the Songhai Resistance (1591–1612)," *Journal of African History* 22 (1981): 457–75; Lansine Kaba, "The Pen, the Sword, and the Crown: Islam and Revolution in Songhai, 1461–1493," *Journal of Africa History* 25 (1984): 241–56; Lansine Kaba, "Background to Change in West African Economic History: Songhai, 1492–1750," *Journal of African Studies* 4 (1977): 344–56; John O. Hunwick. "Religion and State in the Songhai Empire, 1464–1591," in I. M. Lewis, *Islam in Tropical Africa* (London: 1966), 296–315.

16. Nehemia Levtzion, "Rural and Urban Islam in West Africa: An Introductory Essay," in *Rural and Urban Islam in West Africa*, ed. Nehemia Levtzion (Boulder, Colo.: 1987), 1–20. Levtzion argues effectively that Islam was an urban phenomenon in its origins. As such, the urban character of the Western Sudan led itself to the cultivation of Islam in its cities long before the religion became ruralized. John Hunwick, *Shari'a in Songhai: the Replies of Al-Maghili to the Questions of Askia Al-Hajj Muhammad* (Oxford: 1985); Graham Connah, *African Civilizations: Precolonial Cities and States in Tropical Africa: An Archaeological Perspective* (Cambridge, Mass.: 1987); Richard Hull, *African Cities and Towns before the European Conquest* (New York: 1976); Susan Keech McIntosh, "A Reconsideration of Wangara/Palolus, Island of Gold," *Journal of African History* 22 (1981): 145–58; Roderick J. McIntosh, "Flood Plain Geomorphology and Human Occupation of the Upper Inland Delta of the Niger," *The Geographical Journal* 149 (1983): 182–201; Roderick J. and Susan K. McIntosh, "The Inland Niger Delta Before the Empire of Mali: Evidence from Jenne-Jeno," *Journal of African History* 22 (1981): 1–22.

17. Al-Idrisi, *Nuzhat al-mushtaq fi ikhtiraq al-afaq*; Al-Yaqubi, *Tarikh*; Nehemia Levtzion, "Ibn-Hawqal, the Cheque and Awdaghost," *Journal of African History* 9 (1968): 223–33; Al-Bakri, *Kitab al-masalik wa-'l-mamalik*; Ibn Khaldun, *Muqaddima*. These sources and others are readily available in *Corpus of Early Arabic Sources for West African History*, ed. Nehemia Levtzion and J. F. P. Hopkins (Cambridge, UK: 1981). Leo Africanus (Johannes Leo), *Geographical Historie of Africa* (1600; reprint, London: 1969).

18. For instance, Bentley's masterful opening, an examination of I Kings 10—the coming of the Queen of Sheba—centers on the conventional: Solomon. Solomon and his state are implicitly conferred historical legitimacy while those of the land of the Queen of Sheba are not. An interesting take on this that might have

given more depth and breadth to Bentley's suppositions on "old world encounters" would have included speculation on "Makeda," the Queen of Sheba, the wealth represented by the spaces from which she hailed, and the establishment of a political alliance that the Ethiopians claim as their *entre* into the Judeo-Christian world. Jerry H. Bentley, *Old World Encounters: Cross-cultural Contacts in Premodern Times* (New York: 1993). None of this is outside of what William McNeill proposes in his *Mythistory and Other Essays* (Chicago: 1986). However, Bentley's considerations of Africa in the space of world history have undergone important modification since the writing of *Old World Encounters*. Bentley writes that "there were definitely some African connections that I missed when writing *Old World Encounters*. Some things I have become aware of in the meantime and have tried to incorporate into more recent works." Personal correspondence, February 3, 1999.

19. Herodotus, *The Histories* (New Haven, Conn.: 1998); Frank M. Snowden, *Blacks in Antiquity* (Cambridge, 1979); Inidcopleuistes Cosmas, *Christian Topography* (London, 1897); Philip Snow, *Star Raft* (New York 1988).

20. See *The Life and Works of Jahiz*, ed. Charles Pella (Berkeley, Calif.: 1969). Al Tabari, *The Revolt of the Zanj*, trans. and an. David Waines (Albany, N.Y.: 1992).

21. Janet Abu-Lughod, *Before European Hegemony: The World System A.D. 1250–1350* (New York: 1989), 36.

22. Abu-Lughod, *Before European Hegemony*, 19, 121, 169, 188, 208, 243, 258. Out of eleven references made to Africa, seven deal with the issue of Africa's "circumnavigation" by peoples other than Africans.

23. Immanuel Wallerstein, "World System versus World-Systems," in *The World System*, ed. Andre Gunder Frank and Barry K. Gills (London: 1993), 292–96. Immanuel Wallerstein, *Africa and the Modern World* (Trenton, N.J.: 1986).

24. Wallerstein, "World System," 293.

25. Andre Gunder Frank and Barry K. Gills, "Rejoinder and Conclusions," in *The World System*, ed. Andre Gunder Frank and Barry K. Gills (London: 1993), 297–307. In light of Frank's most recent work, *ReOrient*, and his criticism of Philip Curtin in 1991, all this becomes much more interesting. Remarking on Philip D. Curtin's *Cross-Cultural Trade in World History* (Cambridge, Mass.: 1984), Frank stated that "Curtin . . . has not sought to pursue the African connection in Afro-Asia as far back in history as it may deserve." See Frank, "World System History," 8. There have been some recent and very interesting attempts to explain pre- and early modern Africa in terms of systems theory. Alice Willard's "Trade and Ideology in the Sahel: the Songhai from a World-Systems Perspective" (unpublished paper presented at the Annual African Studies Association, Chicago, November 1998) is one such attempt.

26. Andre Gunder Frank, *ReOrient. Global Economy in the Asian Age* (Berkeley, Calif.: 1998).

27. Frank, *ReOrient*, 339.

28. If these assertions seem too bold, readers should refer to David Levering Lewis's characterization of the writing of the young Du Bois in *The Negro* (1915; New York: Oxford University Press, 1970) as "a large building block in an Afrocentric historiography." This observation appears in an award-winning autobiography that has wide currency in conventional circles. Professor Lewis goes on to

state that this Afrocentric historiography has "achieved credibility" through the contemporary works of scholars such as Martin Bernal, Basil Davidson, and Cheikh Anta Diop. See David L. Lewis, *W. E. B. Du Bois: Biography of a Race* (New York: 1993), 359–60.

29. Alfred W. Crosby, *The Columbian Exchange: Biological and Cultural Consequences of 1492* (Westport, Conn.: 1972). Alfred W. Crosby, *Ecological Imperialism: The Biological Expansion of Europe, 900–1900* (Cambridge, Mass.: 1986).

30. Curtin, *Cross-Cultural Trade*, 15. The statement is contradicted by the evidence and argument Curtin provides in the chapters on "Africa: Incentives to Trade, Patterns of Competition," and "Africa: Traders and Trade Communities."

31. Mudimbe quotes T. Hodgkin in *Invention* as a way of referencing the need to rethink and rewrite Africa (1). Here, however, we need to be careful. It is possible to regard the chapters of Curtin's *Cross-Cultural Trade* as the opening foray of this "new historical form" in the field of world history. My only concern is that it is not extensive or integrative enough to satisfy the demands that Africa itself places on the construction of world history, even from a thematically contextualized approach such as trade.

32. Hodgson, *Rethinking World History*, xiv; Mudimbe, *Idea of Africa*, xii.

33. Allardyce, "Toward World History," 24–25, 57, 66–67. Frank, "World System History," 2–3. Also see McNeill's declaration of "intellectual imperialism" in "After Twenty-Five Years," 2.

34. Frank, *ReOrient*, 8. Obviously, Frank had not read Lewis's characterization of Bernal as an "Afrocentrist historiographer"; compare 56.

35. Bernal's comment can be weighed against the considerable tension around Diop's assertions, methodology, and credentials. The "critique" of Diop is very much in accord with Bernal's observations concerning the ways in which ideas that do not conform to convention are received. See Martin Bernal, "Black Athena and the APA," *Arethusa* (special issue, Fall 1989): 17–18, 20.

36. Frank, *ReOrient*, xxv, 8, 11, 276. Also see Ann DuCille, *Skin Trade* (Cambridge, Mass.: 1996), 123. Keita, *Race*, 313–16.

37. Frank, *ReOrient*, 8.

38. Albert Adu Boahen, *African Perspectives on Colonialism* (Baltimore, Md.: 1987), 94.

39. Joseph Miller, "Presidential Address: History and Africa/Africa and History," *American Historical Review* 104 (1999): 1.

40. Colin Palmer, *Human Cargoes: British Slave Trade to Spanish America, 1700–1793* (Urbana: University of Illinois Press, 1981); Colin Palmer, *Slaves of the White God: Blacks in Mexico* (Cambridge, Mass.: Harvard University Press, 1976); Sidney Lemelle, "The Politics of Cultural Existence: Pan-Africanism, Historical Materialism, and Afrocentricity," *Race and Class* 35 (1993): 94–105; Paul Gilroy, *Black Atlantic* (Cambridge, Mass.: Harvard University Press, 1993).

41. Hans Debrunner, *Presence and Prestige, Africans in Europe: A History of Africans in Europe before 1918* (Basel: 1979). Allison Blakely's *Russia and the Negro: Blacks in Russian History and Thought* (Washington, D.C.: 1986) is also a very useful source as well. Gretchen Gerzina's *Black London: Life Before Emancipation* (New Brunswick, N.J.: 1995) augments Gilroy's *Black Atlantic* arguments and the con-

struction of "Afro-Brits," while Paul Edwards's *The Early African Presence in the British Isles* (Edinburgh: 1990) provides an even longer view and more ways on which to speculate and then construct an African presence in medieval Britain. See also Allison Blakely, "Problems in Studying the Role of Blacks in Europe," *Perspectives* 35 (1997): 1, 11–13; Gretchen Gerzina, "The Black Presence in British Cultural History," *Perspectives* 35 (1997): 15–17.

42. Kwame Anthony Appiah, "Europe Turned Upside Down: Fallacies of the New Afrocentrism," *London Times Literary Supplement* (1993): 24–25.

43. Georges-Louis Leclerc, the Comte de Buffon, "The Geographical and Cultural Distribution of Mankind," in *Race and the Enlightenment: A Reader*, ed. Emmanuel Eze (Cambridge, Mass.: 1997), 22.

44. Cheikh Anta Diop, *The African Origin of Civilization: Myth or Reality* (New York: 1974); Cheikh Anta Diop, *Precolonial Black Africa: A Comparative Study of the Political and Social Systems of Europe and Black Africa, from Antiquity to the Formation of Modern States* (Westport, Conn.: 1987).

45. In this, we might ask if the historiography and epistemology must be coherent in the conventional sense. Again, contention among these scholars in relation to their notions of the history of the world can be regarded as healthy and therefore welcome.

46. Molefe Asante, "Multiculturalism and the Academy," *Academe* 82 (1996): 22–23; Molefe Asante, *Afrocentricity and Knowledge* (Trenton, N.J.: 1990), vi; Tsheloane Keto, *The Africa Centered Perspective of History: An Introduction* (Blackwood, N.J.: 1991), i, 1–2, 5–7, 18–19, 25; Keita, *Race*, 314–65.

47. Bernal, *Black Athena*, 433–37. Also see Keita, *Race*.

48. DuCille, *Skin Trade*; Valentine Y. Mudimbe, ed., *Surreptitious Speech* (Chicago: 1992).

12

"Modernity" and "Asia" in the Study of Chinese History

Wang Hui

In the study of Chinese history, some questions need to be answered first: What is China's "modernity"? How and when did it develop? What were its characteristics and driving forces? Since the 1970s, these questions have occupied researchers in the study of modern Chinese history. A new approach has emerged, which we can name "the inner development theory" (*neibu fazhan lun*). It has gradually replaced the former mainstream model, the challenge/response model, advanced by John K. Fairbank and others. As China scholars of the old generation looked for changes in China's response to outside challenges, historians in the 1970s and the 1980s became more interested in exploring elements of change inside Chinese society. In this methodological transition, the theory of inner development became associated with the idea of "local knowledge," and this convergence further led to the effort to explain the driving forces of modernity from the perspective of "local history."

But where did the theory of inner development originate? Within this approach, the use of the term modernity seems to suggest a break with Fairbank's use of "modernization"; whereas the latter was restricted to the political system, the former shifted its attention to social and political structures. But the effort to locate the emergence of Chinese modernity within China itself is not without precedent. Since the 1930s and the 1940s, this question has had two other perspectives. The first was a social historical approach, which examined the changes in the mode of production and its impact on social development. Marxist historiography is the most important school that represented this approach. The second model emphasized an "Asianist" approach, which regarded East Asia as an interconnected world-system; by examining exchanges and connections among the countries in the region, it analyzed the inner development and the occurrence of modernity in China, Japan, Korea, and Vietnam. These two approaches are not mutually exclusive, but their emphases are different. The first looks at social change and the occurrence of modernity as a result of the internal contradiction of the production mode. The second emphasizes that social disintegration and transformation (in the aspects of technology, division of labor, and culture) in a society take place as a result of long distance trade and intercultural confrontation. In many ways, there are some overlaps between the Asianist approach and the world-system model from Braudel and Wallerstein to the recent work by Andre Gunder Frank. In this article, I will analyze some books by Japanese scholars from half a century ago and put them in the new context of the world-system. But before I do this, I will first discuss the internal driving forces of modernity and then analyze the meaning of "Asia" in explaining the rise of modernity.

HOW TO UNDERSTAND THE SOCIAL CHANGE BEGINNING IN THE MID-QING

Inner Development Theory and Local History Orientation in the Study of Chinese History

In explaining the development of modernity, the inner development theory touches on many aspects of everyday life. But its focus remains on state, society, market system, legal system, new directions in Confucianism, and so on. The modernity concept suggests the possibility of the development of autonomy; many aspects of social life gradually break away from the control of the state and the monarchy and achieve some levels of self-discipline and autonomy. The state/society dualism in social theories provides a theoretical explanation for this "social autonomy." "Society" and "market" are often regarded as free, evolutionary, and becoming more self-disciplinary, obtaining an opposite position of the "state." The "civil society" theory in modern historical and social studies amplifies this thesis.

Historians trace modernity in many areas: Qing evidential scholarship, the writing of vernacular language after the Tang and Song dynasties, the professionalization of academic learning, the development of commerce in cities, the interchange between merchants and gentry, and so on. If earlier studies mainly paid attention to political changes in the state, the local history emphasis seen in more recent works has been more interested in the social change at the local level outside the state (the centralized state). But we are still unsure about their relation with the external factors after the Opium War—new technology, new ideas, and new models of social structure. There have always been changes in Chinese society, some of which could be considered structural changes, but the history after the late Qing, obviously, cannot be explained only by noticing the internal driving force. We cannot deny that new historical factors brought by the Opium War constituted the determinant force for changing the direction of history, nor can we ignore the influence of European capitalism and colonialism in modern Chinese history. We must continue to ask: Was modern Chinese history born in the 1898 Hundred-Day Reform or in the 1911 Revolution, or what was the modern element and its activity that resulted in the reform and revolution?

Let me begin with Philip A. Kuhn's outstanding book, *Rebellion and Its Enemies in Late Imperial China*. Kuhn turns the question of modernity into the question of "how to differentiate the decline of the Qing rule from the decline of traditional Chinese society as a whole"[1] and hence provides a basis for analyzing the causes of social change inside Chinese society. According to him:

> [The modern period began] when the "decline" we observe is no longer simply the waning of the Ch'ing (Qing) dynasty and its attendant social evils, but a more profound process that is leading Chinese history irrevocably out of its old paths and producing basic changes in social and intellectual organization. Such a process differs from the dynastic cycle in that never again can Chinese state or society be reestablished on the old pattern.[2]

Under this historical condition, "the motion of history is governed primarily by forces exogenous to Chinese society and Chinese tradition."[3] Then, exactly, what were the essential changes that caused this "modern" transformation? Kuhn points out that the structural change of the late Qing society was first seen in the process of putting down the Taiping Rebellion and the activities of the rebels, which resulted in local militarization and the power shift of the gentry class. Kuhn's consideration of the modernity question is based on the basic premise that Chinese history followed the cyclical process of dynastic succession. The significance of modernity therefore lies in that it marked the end of this cyclical movement of Chinese history.

In this process, many changes that had taken place in traditional society could turn to a new and very different direction because of new opportunities and circumstances. Kuhn argues that the Taiping Rebellion changed the state's relation with the gentry class. At the same time, there was a crisis in local militarization that resulted from the effort to put down the rebellion. These two changes not only became the determinant factors leading to the fall of the Qing Dynasty, but also indicated the total collapse of the traditional system of the Chinese Empire. The gentry elite used to play an indispensable role in mediating between the governmental bureaucracy and local villages, municipal administrative centers and the countryside in the inner land. But this traditional role was no longer played.[4] The effort to crack down on the Taiping and other rebels led quickly to local militarization and local autonomy. The key questions here are not whether these changes led to the fall of the Qing Dynasty (there is no dispute about it), but why these changes could become the cause for changing the traditional structure and why similar changes in the past didn't result in similar outcomes.

The Historical Evolution of the Gentry/ Monarchy Relation

Compared with the changing relationship between gentry and monarchy, or the local and central government in the mid-Qing, the new government reform that started in the late Qing was more responsible for undermining the legitimacy of the dynasty. In these political reforms, local gentry and merchant groups gained their legitimate political power, as shown in the political consultation bureau and the provincial assembly, which provided the new political basis for expanding the local political and military power. From 1909, when the Qing ruler decreed to establish provincial assemblies, to 1910, when constitutionalists in the provincial assemblies pleaded for establishing a national congress, the whole process formed the necessary political condition for the 1911 Revolution. The practice and theory of checks-and-balances in politics was not entirely new to Chinese history (especially if we look at the history during the third and the fifth centuries), but the theory and its practice had not led to modernity earlier. In fact, after the 1898 Hundred-Day Reform, both constitutionalists and revolutionaries believed in the republican system, despite their differences in explaining the term. This can be evidenced by their debate published in the *People's Journal* and the *New People's Miscellany*. We cannot overlook new political and cultural factors that appeared in a later period. In sum, if we would like to prove that certain changes would lead to a modern transformation, we must do much more than show the ineffectiveness of the old social structure.

We can also examine Kuhn's argument by placing it in a longer historical context to see its limit. First, the position of landlords and gentry and their relations with others were never very stable. From the Han and Tang dynasties onward, the gentry either united, disunited, or confronted the central government, feudal lords, official landlords, commoner landlords, and peasants in regard to the distribution of land and other social rights. Whenever the local feudal and/or official power became increasingly influential, the monarchy would unite commoner landlords and peasants to oppose feudal lords in order to get back both the tax-paying population and the tax-generating land. On the other side, when the monarchy over-expanded and controlled too much land, local forces and the landlord class would seek to limit the monarchical power and change the old land system, tax system, and social structure. Dynastic rulers, in order to protect and expand their own interest, allied either with feudal lords or with commoner landlords. From the early Tang Dynasty onward, the Equal Field System was undermined considerably. In order to curb the expansion of the plantations of feudal lords and Buddhist monasteries, dynastic rulers developed royal and official plantations. In the Song and Ming dynasties, official and royal plantations became a legally institutionalized system. Existing scholarship on the tax system of many dynasties, especially the Double Tax System in the Tang and the One-Whip-Tax System in the Ming, has shown that the monarchy at the center always acted in its own financial interest to repair the registration system of population and land, damaged by land exploitation and population loss, in order to secure a basis for generating stable revenue. The change in social classes did not obliterate the confrontation between the monarchical and local power for land and labor; it only indicated the change in the social content of such confrontation. From the Song and Ming dynasties onward, the local autonomous power and the monarchical power both expanded, which can be understood as a result of the disintegration of the Equal Field System.[5]

One can ask a further question: Was the new social hierarchy established on kinship or on bureaucratic ties?[6] For example, during the Northern Wei and the Tang dynasties, due to the existence of great noble families, dynastic rulers had to work on redistributing land in order to achieve a certain balance between the monarchical and local power.[7] During that period, social change was often characterized by changes in the land distribution system. From the Northern Wei to the Tang, the central government made great improvements in taxation based on the Equal Field System, which was perfected by the new tax policy of the Tang Dynasty that combined rent, corvée labor and military service. What really happened in that process was that the central government seized labor forces from local great families and disallowed them to conceal the headcount, thereby reestablishing the social system.[8] In the mid-Tang, the Equal Field System, which was by its nature a state landownership, began to fall apart due to land annexation, which resulted in the disintegration of the combined rent, corvée labor and military service tax system. Land annexation caused the emigration of the population, which made it hard for the government to continue its capitation system. As land, population, and taxes fell under the control of the local power, the Tang Dynasty had to start the tax reform and introduced the Double Tax System. The Double Tax System invented by Yang Yan aimed not only at levying tax on noble families but also at regaining control of the households hidden by them. It changed the traditional capitation system and replaced it with a property tax. It also consolidated corvée labor and military services and therefore eliminated the personal tax, and made labor force no longer attached to landownership. As the new tax system legally acknowledged private landownership and permitted peasants to migrate, it alleviated the problems and confrontations between central government and local power under the Equal Field and feudal systems; they both became economically independent.[9]

Along with the change of the class and political structure of society, the historical meaning of the relationship between gentry and monarchy also changed. Substituting the civil service examination for the old recommendation system and establishing the nine-category tax system according to the wealth of a household, in addition to the rise and fall of commoner and noble families, all affected class, political and economic structures.[10] Due to the civil service examination system and the land reform, landlords from the Song Dynasty onward were not only landowners but also government officials. In late imperial China, there even appeared the "role shift" of gentry and merchants, as noticed by Yu Ying-shih. Accordingly, Miyazaki Ichisada points out: "This new ruling class, which were both officials and landlords, were all over the country. Almost all the land was controlled by this rising new class."[11] This multifunctional new noble class rose from the ruins of feudal families and helped the establishment of absolute monarchy. In competing with feudal families for land and labor, this new class allied with the monarchy. But as the class consolidated its position and gained more political power, it ran into conflict with the expanding monarchical power. Social thinkers from the Song to the Qing Dynasties, such as Ye Shi, Gu Yanwu, and Huang Zongxi, all noticed the land annexation by the rich landlord class and believed that landlords and peasants were mutually dependent. Their positions suggest that achieving a certain autonomous power at the local level and limiting the monarchical power were two sides of the same coin.

The special role of the gentry class in Qing society was a product of historical change and its mediating role between the state and the local resulted from a series of institutional changes. From the Han Dynasty onward, Chinese rulers used the village as the basic unit to organize society; every dynasty developed slightly different organizations centering on the village. The main function of village organizations was to collect taxes, maintain public safety, and gather labor forces for large-scale public works.[12] But during the Ming Dynasty, this village system faced a crisis, coinciding with the rise of the landlord class. The landlord-village union thus gradually became the main form of maintaining the basic social order. The landlord-gentry class also was gradually becoming an opposing force to the monarchy toward the end of the Ming. For example, representing the interest of the gentry-landlord class, the Donglin Party campaigned for "public opinion" (*gonglun*) and sought more attention for local villages, in opposing the central power.[13]

The gentry and officials, sometimes even the prime minister, fought against the emperor and his eunuchs over mine taxation and village land. Their intention of sharing power with the emperor indicated a definite antimonarchical position. Huang Zongxi in his *Mingyi daifang lu* (A plan for the prince) pitted the concept of "people's land" against that of "king's land" and regarded the dynastic ownership of the land as "the big private" (*dasi*). He concluded that it was possible for a country not to have a monarch. Huang's "people" were not ordinary people, but "those powerful landlord class, including landowning peasants, and its partner, the urban artisans and merchants; or namely, the rich people class."[14] In other words, the rise of feudalism and the new land system in the late Ming suggested the resistance of the rich people's class and local gentry to land annexation by the monarchy.

The antimonarchical attitude of the gentry class in the late Ming was directly related to a new awareness of the right to redistribute official land. To defend the local gentry power and to challenge the traditional monarchical system suggested a conflict between monarchy and gentry over land and labor force and, to some extent, a conflict between the emperor and the prime minister. In other words, the egalitarianism of the sixteenth and the seventeenth centuries showed the rising social status of the gentry class and its resentment against the overexpansion of the monarchical power. If the Equal Field System during the Northern Wei and the Sui and Tang dynasties was aimed at attacking feudal lords and eliminating the graded landownership, the land reform ideas in the late Ming Dynasty were an effort to address the problem of land annexation by the autocratic state and to advance the interest of local villages by replacing the declining village organization with the gentry system. These ideas used the feudalism thesis as a political theory to make demands for decreasing central monarchical power and increasing the social position and wealth of the local gentry.

The gentry played a special role in the Qing because of the disintegration of Ming village organizations. But differing from the gentry in the late Ming that undermined the monarchy, the Qing gentry became an important ally of the monarchy in extending its rule into the bottom of society (especially villages). From the mid-Qing, particularly after the

Taiping Rebellion, land annexation became much more serious and local power expanded to an unprecedented level. As a result, although the discussion on feudalism and local autonomy in the late Qing addressed the same concerns as seen in the late Ming and the early Qing, its content apparently differed from the ideas found in Gu Yanwu and Huang Zongxi.[15] The discussion in the Qing reflected not only the struggle between the autocratic state and landlords for landownership and labor force, but also the desire of the lower class to compete with the landlord/gentry class for political rights, as well as the intention of the open-minded gentry and officials with some knowledge of the West to rebuild the state and social structure on a new political model.

This process contained two new factors not seen before. First, there was a great difference in terms of the sociopolitical structures of the Ming and Qing Dynasties. Having borrowed Arnold Toynbee's "external proletariat" idea, Yu Ying-shih has described the Qing Dynasty as "the rule of one single minority group." He has paid particular attention to the Qing's Eight Flag System and the political importance of the strict segregation between the Manchus and the Hans under the Qing's rule.[16] Second, the reform discussion of the late Qing occurred against the background of Western cultural influence. Both the "substance vs. function" thesis (Chinese learning as the substance and Western learning as the function) and the ideals for political reform, which emerged within the Qing government itself, and other more radical reform ideas advanced by the younger people, contained a knowledge system and political ideas that differed from those of the late Ming and the early Qing. Viewed in a long historical perspective, the depth and the breadth of these ideas were much deeper and broader than the "antimonarchical" idea of the late Ming. They were closely related to issues of nation-state and constitutionalism and republicanism.

Still, we should discuss the characteristics of the Qing social structure from a longer historical perspective. Under the Manchu minority rule, the gentry played an increasingly more important role as the village organization disintegrated. The demands made by Gu Yanwu and Huang Zongxi for village autonomy became institutionalized in the Qing. The rule of the gentry/landlord no longer had the antimonarchical characteristic. Rather, it now obtained political legitimacy. How could the Qing gentry/landlord class play such a role? Let us take a look at the explanations provided by scholars of Ming and Qing economic history. In his *The Open-up of Feudal Landownership in the Ming and Qing Dynasties*, Li Wenzhi analyzes in detail the opening up of landownership and the development of clan forces, and also describes the changes of landownership in the early Qing in three phases. First came the change in land distribution, namely the decrease of the land owned by feudal lords and the increase of the land owned by peasants. Second was the change in the relationship between the peasant and landlord class. The power of official landlords was relatively weakened and a number of contract laborers and tenant farmers were either liberated or improved their social status. Third, and most importantly, was that the decline of noble and feudal landlords led to an increase of landownership by commoners.[17] By introducing the policy that allowed pioneers to own the land cultivated by themselves, the Qing Dynasty reestablished the household registration system damaged by the peasant war and organized peasants into certain districts under village organizations in order to guarantee tax collection.[18] The opening of landownership and the disintegration of the Ming village organization produced a special social environment in which the gentry assumed the role of maintaining social order at the local level.

As the Qing emperors used the Eight Flag System to strengthen their position as minority rulers of Han China, they also made use of the structural changes of the late Ming society to consolidate their new dynasty.[19] The local militarization in the late Qing was, of course, related to the effort to put down the Taiping Rebellion, but it also was a product of the Qing political and economic structure. As minority rulers, Manchu nobles had to rely on Han landlords and gentry to maintain social order on the local level: To rule the whole country, Qing rulers had to keep a balance between its use of Han officials and gentry and its royal family and nobles. In this sense, as the demand for local autonomy and power sharing that was seen in the late Ming became legalized in the Qing, it was gradually incorporated into the basis of the Qing political and economic structure. It also became less antimonarchical. This is caused by an uncertain balance between monarchical power, ethnic power, and gentry power, as well as between state landownership, landlord ownership, and peasant landownership.[20]

Modern historians are not the first to have attributed the disintegration of the Qing Dynasty to the expansion of the local gentry power and local militarization; it was a conclusion already reached by late Qing revolutionaries.[21] What I want to add is that the changes of the state/local relation neither began nor ended at that time. Consequently, the late Qing revolutionaries and Philip Kuhn only partially explain the fall of the Qing by describing the social change in the mid-Qing. Although the reform in the late Qing somewhat challenged the monarchy, as a from the top-down, statewide reform movement, it was more interested in rebuilding the state system under the new historical circumstances. Accordingly, although the local autonomy reflected the increase of power at the local level, its ultimate goal, according to the principles of the late Qing political reform, was to put the now diverging local forces back on track for the state-building project in the late Qing. Local autonomy therefore also suggests the expansion of the state power to the local level. The idea of sharing power was not the invention of the revolutionaries but a product of the self-reform of the Qing state; its basis was the gentry-based village order that replaced the Ming village organizations and the village land-ownership as designed by the early Qing land system. And if the institu-tionalization of the landlord/gentry power detracted from the state-building project, it would be turned down.

Due to many social reasons, this state-building project did not achieve its goal but did accelerate the decline and fall of the dynasty. But when viewed in a longer historical context, we can find a similar process in modern times. In the 1898 Hundred-Day Reform, Kang Youwei and Liang Qichao enthusiastically advocated local autonomy. But when they saw that local autonomy would possibly weaken the state's capability of self-reform, they turned against it. Sun Yat-sen and Mao Zedong both had been advocates of local autonomy. But when they seized power, they immediately began land reform in order to weaken local autonomy and strengthen the centralized government. Thus viewed, it is inadequate to understand the historical meaning of these changes (or the occurrence of modernity) by looking at the state/local relation and/or the monarchi-cal/gentry power relation. What determined the historical meaning of these changes was not the changes per se, but the peculiar political and economic form in which these changes took place and their social and historical circumstances.

The Qing land system and its state/gentry relation also provide a pos-sible explanation for understanding the causes of the modern revolution. The gentry/landlord class had a double position in the dynastic rule and the social structure: It was at once the basis of the dynastic rule and the cause of its fall. In the Qing social structure and the late Qing local auton-omous movement, the expansion of the landlord/gentry power could not be simply seen as the opposing force to the monarchy because it also met the need of Qing state-building. Local autonomy undermined the central dynasty; there was certain connection between the Qing's fall and the fed-eralism shown in the autonomy of provincial alliances. Prasenjit Duara has noticed the changing meaning of the concept feudalism in the history of the late Qing and modern China. He points out that from the late Qing onward, the feudalism idea was closely related to the concepts of local, native land and so forth. It provided the basis for the federalist political demand of the autonomy of provincial alliances. But after 1927, the feu-dalism idea gradually deteriorated into "the Other of modernity." In his analysis, there were two distinctive notions of state in modern China: one centralist and the other federalist. Local political identity was both depen-dent on and contradictory to the dynastic rule because the provincial and local administration was closely connected with the gentry network.[22]

Due to this special political structure of the Qing Dynasty, rejecting the monarchy would eventually also involve its local basis. Lu Xun's well-known novel *The True Story of Ah Q* provides an appropriate example in this regard. It describes the failure of the 1911 Revolution in changing the local social order and therefore implies that a true revolution must thoroughly reorganize the political and economic relation at the local level. The novel became very influential because it showed a consensus among many revolutionaries and intellectuals that the ultimate goal of a revolution was not to seize the central power; rather the success of a revolution ought to be measured by its impact on changing the basic social structure, including the land system and the political structure. This book and other writings also reflected the increasingly strong sentiment against Confucian ritualism from the mid-Qing onward. For the radicals in the May Fourth/New Culture Movement, the failure of the revolution had a lot to do, historically, with the influence of the gentry/landlord class and Confucian ritualism. The fact suggests that after the 1911 Revolution, especially during the May Fourth era, the direction and the goal of the modern Chinese revolution underwent a transition, from that of abolishing the monarchy to that of reconstructing the local social organization and cultural foundations. Regardless of our moral attitude toward "revolution," we must understand the internal driving forces that caused the transition of the Chinese revolution from a political one to a social one. It can be seen at the outset of the revolution and was embedded in the reorganization of the sociopolitical structure during the late Ming and early Qing dynasties.

Can we explain convincingly the historical course after the late Qing by looking at the characteristics and changes of Ming and Qing political structure? My answer is no. The driving forces of social change were related not only to internal factors but also to the forces outside the Chinese tradition. We should not overstate the importance of the Chinese empire's continual border changes and foreign relations, but we should never overlook them either, for they helped generate new dynamics of change in China's knowledge and political system. These factors should not simply be regarded as external, because they themselves became the internal dynamics of change in Chinese society. Great social events such as the Opium War did not immediately change the internal structure of Confucianism, nor was the basic model of the dynastic reform completely "renovated." The ideological basis of the Westernization Movement was still rooted in the Confucian framework of "practical statecraft" in the Ming and Qing times. Even the 1898 Hundred-Day Reform utilized the Gong Yang scholarship.[23] A fundamental change of the Weltanschauung and the corresponding political changes and systematic reforms did not occur until the 1890s, particularly after the Sino-Japanese War (1895) and the Hundred-Day Reform. If we want to discuss the rise of modernity, we cannot separate it from the question of the nation-state, from the introduction of a modern knowledge and educational system, and from the capitalist "world history."

Historical Evolution and System Arrangement

The above is just a brief outline of the history from the middle imperial period onward. The complexity of historical change shows that the rise and fall of dynasties often hid the important and frequent structural changes inside traditional society. In fact, there have been scholars who have discussed the sprouts of Chinese modernity by studying the systematic changes (for example, the implementation of the civil service examination system) and economic activities (the development of commerce and consumer economy in urban areas) during the Tang and Song dynasties, and argued that a form of modernity had taken its shape in the Song. From the 1920s to the 1940s, some Japanese scholars regarded Song as the beginning of modern Chinese history (*jinshi*). The discussion of Chinese modernity thus concerns several critical moments in Chinese history, Tang-Song transition, Ming-Qing transition, and the mid-Qing moment.

It is one thing to recognize that some structural change indicated an irreversible reorientation in Chinese politics and society, but it is quite another to predict the direction and the form of change in Chinese society. As we broaden our vision from the political system to the entire social life, social relations, racial conflict, and assimilation, as well as the change in Weltanschauung and belief (including the change inside Confucianism), we must reexamine the image of the "ageless Orient." This image was created to be the opposite of European history and therefore is a product of modern historical interpretation. If we adopt a broader historical vision, we will see more clearly the meaning of the social thought in the late Ming and the early Qing as well as during the late Qing and the early Republican period.

In general, modern Chinese society was a product of a series of system arrangements rather than the outcome of some natural evolution. We should not regard the aim in designing a system as identical as the actual and unpredictable outcome of the system arrangement, nor should we regard the outcome of historical evolution as identical to the social form resulting from the system arrangement. On the contrary, system arrangement is often completed under certain historical circumstances; it is this process of arrangement that displays a certain autonomy of history/culture. For example, the rise of nation-states in Europe unfolded after the Middle Ages. The political form and national identity that resulted from it became an important sign of modernity in Europe. However, the political identity of China as a unified country and its evolution of political and educational systems can be traced back to a much earlier time.[24] This cultural and political identity was deeply rooted in history, which, along with political, economic, and educational institutions, provided the basic precondition for the institutional changes and reforms in modern China. When China entered the world-system as a modern state, it presented itself as a country that had its own long history and special political, cultural, and economic structures.

In discussing system arrangements, therefore, I not only explain the formation of modern institutions and their relations with various external forces, but I also examine the basic driving forces, limitations, and historical premises of such arrangement. On the one hand, system arrangement is not done without preconditions; it is rather a transformation limited by and based on the existing system. On the other hand, under the circumstances of the expanded communication networks, system arrangement also involves the effort to weave the old system and lifestyle into the much more broadly connected world-system. The form of sovereignty, legal system, educational system, and cultural identity of a nation-state may be regarded as a unique, but they still form an organic part of the new world-system. If we regard modern society merely as a result of natural evolution, we cannot understand the real driving force of the transformation of modern society as well as the way in which modernity was formed.

It is due to these reasons that when we talk about the new meanings of terms such as "state," "society," and "people," we must trace the social and intellectual origins of the new meanings. The works of Yu Ying-shih, Benjamin Elman, Philip Kuhn, and many Chinese scholars (most of them economic historians) have shown us that in order to understand China's modern transformation, we must understand the changes in Chinese societal structure after the Song and Ming dynasties. However, if we overemphasize the thesis of inner development, we will also underestimate the increasingly stronger influence of European capitalism on global history from the fifteenth and the sixteenth centuries onward. Modern sovereign states, market economies, educational systems, knowledge systems, and so on were not only the product of change in a single society and/or of the interactions in a continent, but also were the outcome of a global history in the age of colonialism. If we ignore the shock wave of European capitalism reaching many regional and traditional systems and cultures, we will be unable to understand the fundamental issue of the modernity question and discover the traditional elements that had real, long-lasting effects. As a result, we describe tradition as a host of aesthetic objects that have little to do with modern history. To some extent, the inner development theory is another modernization narrative. Can we then explain the development of modernity in China by looking at the communications among world regions rather than simply following the China–West dichotomy?

THE EXCHANGES AMONG WORLD REGIONS
AND THE ASIAN MODERNITY

Asia in the Multihistorical World and East Asian Civilization

It is not necessary to go back to challenge/response model after locating the restrictions of the inner development model. In the last half century, some Asian scholars have tried to link modernity to communications in Asia and to Asian relations to Europe. They ask: Were there elements and conditions that generated a modern transformation in Asia? We can put aside the ambiguous nature of the concept of "Asia"[25] and first examine whether there existed inside Asia elements that prepared its modern transformation. Against the background of colonialism and imperialist wars, Asian intellectuals followed the East–West dichotomy to understand history. The scholars who rejected Eurocentrism described the world prior to modern times as a macrocosm of a few independent civilizations. Some went as far as to argue that there were traces of the spheres of civilizations even in modern times. Before and after World War II, Japanese historians willingly accepted the idea of a self-developed East Asia and included both China and Japan into this East Asian world. For example, Nishijima Sadao believed that this "East Asian world" was a self-insulated cultural sphere. More precisely, this East Asian world circled China and included Korea, Japan, Vietnam, and the regions between the Mongolian and the Himalaya plateau. But the borders of this historical world were fluid and unfixed. Some areas, such as the Himalaya plateau, certain regions in central Asia, and regions in Southeast Asia, belonged to a different historical world because they lacked the characteristics of the East Asian world. These characteristics included Chinese character-based culture, Confucianism, legal and decree system, and Buddhism.[26]

East Asian ideology was closely related to the imperialistic foreign policy of modern Japan. That is the reason why Chinese academic circles and other Asian scholars are indifferent to the concept of "East Asia." But this does not mean that it is not important to take this Asian perspective into consideration. To some extent, Hamashita Takeshi's study of Asia's tributary system is an attempt to introduce this approach to the study of economic history. While recognizing regional interactions and their internal structure, Hamashita has attempted, on a theoretical level, to challenge F. Braudel and I. Wallerstein's Eurocentrism in their works. If we compare Hamashita's view and some of the questions raised by the Kyoto School about half a century before, we find that, while both emphasized the internal driving forces in East Asian nations, Hamashita does not share his predecessors' view that nationalism, similar to what we saw in Europe, also existed in the ancient East Asian world.[27] By describing an Asian trade system and its differences to that of Europe:

> [Hamashita] reveals an important fact that during its modern transition, East Asia did not have the same nation-states as in Europe. The histories of its different regions were connected through the tributary system that transcended the country border. . . . Asia was for the first time characterized as an organic unity with its intrinsic mechanism. In the tributary network centering around Chinese civilization, East Asia, Southeast Asia, South Asia and West Asia were linked together through trade and tributes into an orderly world, which had its own logic differing entirely from modern Europe. In the place of "state" there was the "center/periphery" geographical mechanism and its corresponding tribute/vassal relation.[28]

Japanese scholars' interest in Asian regions is related to their study of nationalism and its role in modern Japan. Consequently, the focus of their interest is on the economic, political, and cultural relations between Japan and China, the former as the periphery and the latter as the center. Karatani Kojin, for instance, argues that the sprouts of Japan's nationalism were first seen in the cultural movement that used the Japanese alphabet (*kana*) to replace Chinese characters (*kanji*).[29] In this sense, the origin of Japan's cultural nationalism had little to do with the "West." On the surface, Karatani's position is very different from Hamashita's idea of an organic Asia; he opposed overstating Japan's peculiarity. But regarding the rise of Japanese nationalism as an internal event within the region, Hamashita also tried to discuss modern Japan's historical logic by drawing attention to the China-centered trade network. From different angles, these studies prove that the idea of a sovereign state, a market system, a modern legal system, and cultural and educational system in Asia cannot be regarded simply as results of the stimulation of European civilization.

As a category of analysis, it seems that the Asian concept is more likely to be accepted by the scholars who study interregional economic and trade activities, less by those that examine intellectual and cultural history. Mizoguchi Yuzou drew a chart to illustrate the spread of neo-Confucianism in East Asia and used the case to examine social changes in China, Japan, and Korea. He based his analysis on cultural transmission and its related political geographic ideas (for example, East Asian–Confucianist cultural sphere). As did Braudel, Mizoguchi adopted the *longue durée* historical approach and explained the birth of "modern Asia" by looking at the exchanges (economic, political, and cultural) among its regions. But, different from the "world-system" model of Braudel, and especially of Wallerstein, Mizoguchi did not regard the birth of modern Asia as a consequence of the expansion of the Europe-centered world system. On the contrary, he believed that it resulted from the development of the China-centered Asian communicative system. It is not hard for us to trace, in Mizoguchi's study, the influence of the idea of the sphere of East Asian civilization in modern Japanese historiography.

Mizoguchi described the characteristics of East Asian civilization by outlining the spread of neo-Confucianism. According to Mizoguchi, some changes in certain East Asian regions were related internally to cultural exchange in East Asia, which made Asia's modernization different from the "cultural principles" of European modernization. To some extent, he echoed Nishijima Sadao's argument. For instance, he regarded the Song Dynasty, the Yi Dynasty, and the Edo period as thresholds of "modern" periods in tenth-century China, fourteenth-century Korea, and seventeenth-century Japan, respectively. In China:

> Neo-Confucianism rose in the historical transition of the fall of nobility and the rise of power of the civil servant officials. It had a rationalist cosmic view and world view on the one hand and advocated rule of morals rather than rule of law on the other, relying on the gentry class at village level.[30]

In a later period, Korea and Japan also witnessed the decline of nobility and the rise of commoners, either through civil service examinations or through the formation of a new peasant class and a samurai class. All this constituted a social order based on moral education and closely related to the spread of neo-Confucianism. In this sense, neo-Confucianism became "a modern Confucianism suitable to modern society."[31]

To analyze the historical evolution in East Asia from the perspective of the spread of neo-Confucianism helps to correct Eurocentrism and its methodological economic determinism in interregional studies. The revision of the world-system theories included two aspects. First, the internal change in China and other Asian countries did not result only from encountering European powers. Rather, cultural exchanges (the spread of neo-Confucianism) and trade-tribute relations, as well as the alienation between the central empire and its border regions within Asian regions, all provided internal driving forces for the rise of Asian nationalism. Second, the "long-distance trade" theory contains a strong bias toward economic determinism and the world-system theory defines nation-states as the political structures of the world system. Both pay little attention to cultural exchange and its role in social change. Mizoguchi's study shows a broadened vision that extends from the internal change of a single society to the interactions among many regions in Asia.

However, Mizoguchi's description of modern East Asia remains brief and sketchy. In fact, Mizoguchi's audacious argument is not buttressed by empirical study. Its importance lies in providing an explanation for China's and Asia's modernity based on the cultural exchange relations in East Asia. In his opinion, structural social change does not occur in a short time period; it already took place as early as the sixteenth and the seventeenth centuries.[32] This argument is not original per se. Chinese Marxist historians have always believed that the social change in the Ming and Qing dynasties constituted an important transition in Chinese history. For them, social change in the Ming and the Qing was rooted in the change of production relations of Chinese society. In this sense, Mizoguchi's and Chinese scholars' works both resonate, to some extent, with the theory of inner development. What differentiates Mizoguchi's study from that of Chinese Marxists is that he, echoing Hamashita's study on trade and tribute, considers long-distance trade and cultural exchange the key to understanding Asia's modernity.

Mizoguchi's thesis is based on the modern concept in Japan and the Asian perspective. Connecting closely the idea of modernity with the concept of Asia, he implies that neo-Confucianism and its social thought were a bridge for the modern transformation.[33] Mizoguchi paid special attention to the meanings of the "Heaven's principle" and "public/private" dichotomy that appeared in Chinese thought after the Song Dynasty and argued that these two phrases ran through both the intellectual and social history from the Song to the Qing. According to Mizoguchi, there were certain intrinsic connections between some aspects in the modern Chinese revolution, such as Sun Yat-sen's advocacy of people's livelihood and the land system in the Communist Revolution, and the discussions on land systems, the monarchy, and value systems in the sixteenth and the seventeenth centuries.

It is always very difficult, either from the perspective of economic relations or from the perspective of ideological order, to discover a certain principle in Asia's modernization. If we only try to observe the occurrence of modernity from a historical perspective, we tend to oversimplify the historical process. In the history of China after the mid-Qing, local militarization, the change of the gentry's status, and the social mechanism of professionalization were only organic parts of the total social transformation. These changes themselves were not single, isolated occurrences, nor could they point to the ultimate direction of transformation. In order to understand the rise of modernity, one must leave behind the often-arbitrary criteria and rules of being modern and deal with the change from a much broader perspective.

Asia in the Interactions of Historical Worlds

If the concept of "Asia" can be seen as a sort of category containing certain cultural principles, then there is some incomparability between social
developments in Europe and Asia. How can one explain modern development and capitalism in Asia? If the bases are incomparable but the civilizations are similar, how can one explain the relationship between the
incomparability and the similar historical factors? In addition, if one over-
emphasizes Asia's peculiarity in explaining the development of modernity, one will consequently regard a modern Asia as a result of the
expansion of Europe and overlook the multicultural meaning of the concept of "Asia." In the face of these many difficulties, we should look at
Asian scholars' answers to these questions from the 1940s onward.

In his *Manuscript of the Origins of Sui and Tang Institutions*, Chen Yinke
used the "medieval" (*zhonggu*) concept and considered the Sui and the
Tang "peaks of the medieval period." Obviously, he also examined institutional change in China within the ancient, medieval, and modern historical periods. However, his "medieval" concept is not located in the
linear development of history. Instead, he believed that Sui and Tang
"cultural and material systems spread very broadly, reaching the great
dessert in the north, islands in the south, Japan in the east and central
Asia in the west."[34] Because of this, Chen traced three origins of the Sui
and Tang systems in Northern Dynasties of the third and fourth centuries.
In the beginning chapter of his *Manuscript of the Tang Political History*,
Chen quoted a passage from Conversations with Master Zhu—classified
topically (Zhu Zi yulei): "Tang originated in northern barbarians; it is not
surprising to see (sexually) inappropriate behavior in young women"[35]—
to illustrate the connection between the Tang customs and those of northern national minorities. Noticeably, neo-Confucianism rose in the long-
lasting conflict between the Han Chinese and the northern national
minorities and was therefore strongly colored by antibarbarism. Chen
Yinke's historical study touched on many aspects of the history from the
third to the nineteenth centuries. However, except for his "Forward to
Deng Guangming's Evidential Investigation of the Official Treatise of the
Song History" (1943) and a few others, he did not produce systematic
work on Song history. But when he quoted Zhu Xi, his main attention was
paid to issues of "nation and culture" in Tang history, rather than on its
conservatism and ethic content, suggesting that his understanding of the
"medieval" concept focused on the relationship between the central and
border regions. In his article on "Minority Generals and Family Soldiers
in the Tang," he took the same approach in examining the change of the
system of minority generals and family soldiers, and concluded that
"although Tang's garrison generals were Han people, they acted like

minority generals, so were their armies, regardless of their racial composition."[36] At the methodological level, Chen Yinke's "medieval history" study can be understood as a "Chinese history with Asian perspective."

We can compare his Asian perspective with the discussion of the "modern Eastern civilization" among historians in postwar Japan. What differentiates them is that Chen Yinke did not use capitalism and other similar terms to describe Chinese history, whereas other scholars interested in regional interactions extensively borrowed terms of European history to study modern East Asia. For example, by analyzing the changes in trade and exchange during the Sui, Tang, and Five Dynasties period, Miyazaki asserted that "there was apparent capitalist tendency in Song society, which made it very different from that of medieval China."[37] Miyazaki might have misunderstood the history during the Tang and Song period since he filtered out historical phenomena not in line with a "capitalist" perspective. But his observations have important historical proof and inspiration.

Refusing to borrow concepts from European history amounts to an effort to return to one's own history. But it can also result in another kind of historical fundamentalism and eventually falls in the traps of dualistic comparison. However, as long as one does not view history from a teleological perspective and does not believe that every regional history follows the same track of development, it is acceptable to borrow concepts in European history to explain revolutionary changes in Chinese history. When modern scholars analyze nationalism in Japan, Korea, and other countries, as well as the China-centered Asian world-system, they often, consciously and unconsciously, use modern countries as basic units and categories of description and fail to consider that trade, culture, and labor divisions were often developed beyond political borders. As a unified political entity, China, of course, was formed in relation with its neighbors. But the meaning of this "frontier" (*zhoubian*) is not confined by "country," not even including Japan and Korea. In his *Inner Asian Frontiers of China*, Owen Lattimore described an Asian continent, with the Great Wall as its "center," that transcended political and national borders, providing us with a different perspective on understanding the center/periphery relation in history. The idea of this so-called center is that on both sides of the Great Wall, two parallel social entities existed: agricultural and nomadic. These two social entities kept long-lasting contacts along the Great Wall, which resulted in mutual impacts deeply affecting each society. Lattimore's idea of the center corrected the previous emphasis on agricultural society in the south and drew one's attention to the history of the frontier and the formation of nomadic tribes. Northern nomadic and southern agricultural societies developed synchronously;

the distance between the two produced "the frontier style."[38] In fact, the
political institutions of both the Sui and Tang dynasties were deeply
influenced by the northern dynasties. Yuan and Qing dynasties were central regimes established by northern national minorities. Their systems
were the results of the interaction between center and periphery.

Through his study of the communication of different regions, Miyazaki
attempted to connect their histories. From that angle, he explained such
terms as "Song capitalism," "modern Eastern civilization," and "nationalism." In some aspects, Miyazaki's study is similar to that of Andre
Gunder Frank's, which I will mention below. They both believe that a
mutually connected world existed prior to modern times. The peculiarities of civilizations cannot be used as evidence for the autonomous development of that civilization. This argument rejects the idea that prior to
modern times there existed several independent worlds in history that
had very different courses. In his *The Early Modernity in East Asia*, Miyazaki analyzed the national relations in Chinese history from the third century B.C.E. to the nineteenth century C.E. and argued that there were not
only "nationalist high tides" and more direct national contacts during the
Song Dynasty period (for example, the wars between Song and Liao and
between Song and Jin), but also a few "independent nation-states" in
southeast Asia, which were still "China's tributary states in name."[39] In
this sense, the development of nationalism in Asia paralleled that in the
West. Although this development was interrupted by the Yuan Dynasty,
it later stimulated the Han Chinese-centered nationalism of the Ming
Dynasty. In fact, the rise of the Qing Dynasty could also be seen as a result
of Manchu nationalism, which first urged the Manchus to achieve an
equal status in dealing with the Ming and later made them a conquering
force in battling with the Han Chinese. Thus viewed, it was nationalism
that contributed to the great unification of the modern East.[40]

To deal with the modernity question in Asia, one has to consider the
relationship between Asia and European colonialism and modern capitalism. But if there was indeed only one world in premodern times, or if
there were close connections among these historical worlds, then the discussion on the reshaping of Asia by modern European capitalism has to
analyze how the rise of European capitalism was related to Asia. Miyazaki firmly believed that "given the development of modern history after
the Song, it is time for us to use the development of modern Eastern history to examine that of modern Western history."[41] He asked: How could
the spices from Southeast Asia appeal to the Europeans and thereby spur
their activities on the sea? How did northern nomadic nations unite and
threaten China due to their love of Chinese tea? When he studied the history of the digging of the Great Canal, he even suggested that its significance should not be evaluated only in China. Instead, one should

consider the fact that the Great Canal not only improved China's domestic traffic but also connected the eastern part of both water and land highways across Asia. China was no longer the end of the communication between East and West but was chained to the circle of world communication.[42] If these important events inside China—such as the building of the Great Canal, the extension of trade routes, and the relocation of capitals (from Changan, Luoyang, the inconvenient cities in communication, to Kaifeng, the traffic hub and commercial city from the Five Dynasties to the Song)—influenced world trade and communication at that time, how can we attribute the change of modern China only to its inner development?

According to the works of Miyazaki Ichisada, Mizoguchi Yuzou, and others, the political, economic and cultural factors that characterized modern Asia were visible as early as the tenth and the eleventh centuries, earlier than in Europe by about three hundred or four hundred years. Then the question is whether the histories of these worlds paralleled each other or were just connected to each other. Due to the expansion of the Mongol conquest, the civilizations between East and West were very closely related to each other, which prompted Miyazaki to imagine that the renaissance of the East exerted great influence on the Western Renaissance. He cited the example of painting, and described how Chinese paintings, due to the Mongol conquest, entered the Islamic world in west Asia. As miniature painting reached its peak, there appeared the first phase of Italian Renaissance painting. Miyazaki's daring discovery shows some profound insight. In discussing the Industrial Revolution in eighteenth-century Europe and political revolutions in France, he also argued that the East, especially China, not only provided markets and raw materials for the Industrial Revolution but also nutrition for the humanitarianism in the French Revolution.[43]

From this perspective, Asia and Europe have been closely connected ever since the thirteenth and fourteenth centuries. When we want to explain the rise of modernity, we must start with the assumption that there was an interconnected world-system. Andre Gunder Frank points out: The rise of European capitalism from the fourteenth century onward coincided with the decline of the East in about 1800. European countries gained entrance to the expanding Asian market with the silver obtained from their colonies in the Americas. The Asian market in the world economy developed through the commercial and institutional mechanisms that were special and beneficial to Europe. As Asia began its decline, Western countries established the new industrial economy through the export and import mechanisms of the world economy. In this sense, the rise of European capitalism resulted more from Europe's relation with

Asia than from the change of production relations inside European society.[44]

Accordingly, in order to distinguish the modernity in the Tang and Song period and the modernization process after the late Qing, we need to look for an interpretation from the perspective of world history. Even scholars, such as Hamashita, who emphasize Asia's internal totality also acknowledged that the formation and change of financial trade and political systems in modern China had a close relation with the economic history of Western capitalism. In his "The Formation of the Capitalist Colonial System and Asia: The Infiltration of English Bank Capitals in 1850s China," Hamashita studied China's financial relations in the nineteenth century and pointed out that the deep involvement of Western capitalism in Asian finance was a result of the expansion of international financial markets due to the discovery of gold in the United States and Australia. From a financial perspective, modern Chinese economic history can be viewed as the process by which the Chinese economy was gradually woven into the London-based, unified international financial structure.[45]

We cannot understand the problems in China's semicolonial system without noticing this transition. For example, due to the proliferation of commerce, Chinese rulers after the Song levied taxes not only on land but on commodities as well (the salt tax was always an important item). The proportion of commercial taxes in the state revenue became higher and higher. But after the late Qing, due to the development of overseas trade, the tariff increased greatly. According to the statistics of the late Qing government, the tariff reached as high as 72 percent and the salt tax declined to 13 percent of the annual state revenue.[46]

The European capitalism that resulted from Europe's historical relation with Asia would never be a copy of the Asian model. On the contrary, it reconstructed its own complex appearance under the given historical condition. Conversely, although the rise of modernity in Asia had its own historical condition, it can be interpreted only by considering the larger historical interactions. Since the 1980s many studies of the history of Western imperialism have claimed that colonialism was not a one-way traffic but had a two-way influence; changes were seen not only in colonies but in the central regions of the metropolitan state.[47] Thus viewed, the "globalization" phenomenon referred to today is never an external event outside a society but is reflected in the many relations inside the society.

From the perspective of modern political economy, the basic task China faced in the nineteenth century was to renew the political systems, economic models, and cultural values associated with the previous dynastic system in order to adjust them according to the international relations in the age of colonialism. Policies in Japan and Korea did, breaking away from China's tributary relation and cultural dominance and establishing a more independent nation-state. However, this was not the solution for China. The world-system was not shaped simply by the course of development of Europe-based capitalism. Rather, it was a process that showed the interactions, struggles, influences of several historical worlds. Asian nationalism was not a copy of the nation-state model in Europe but resulted from the interactions among various regions in Asia. It is therefore possible that both the "challenge/response model" and the "inner development theory" have oversimplified, if not distorted, the course of history.

From the above discussion we can draw two conclusions with respect to methodology. First, the modernity question must be understood by placing it in a larger historical context. Second, it is not a question regarding one single society, but an outcome of the interactions of different historical civilizations. We must therefore examine the development of modern thought by situating it in the dual relations of both time and space.

NOTES

1. Philip A. Kuhn, *Rebellion and Its Enemies in Late Imperial China: Militarization and Social Structure, 1796–1864* (Cambridge, Mass.: 1970), 2–3.

2. Kuhn, *Rebellion and Its Enemies*, 2–3.

3. Kuhn, *Rebellion and Its Enemies*, 2–3.

4. Kuhn, *Rebellion and Its Enemies*, 1–10.

5. Compare Fu Yiling, *Mingqing tudi suoyouzhi lungang* (On Landownership of the Ming and the Qing Dynasties) (Shanghai: 1992), 10–11; Wu Jianguo, *Juntian zhi yanjiu* (A Study of the Equal Field System) (Kunming: 1992), 2–3.

6. See Hou Wailu, *Zhongguo sixiang tongshi* (A General History of Chinese Thought) (Beijing: 1959), 4: 101.

7. Compare Lin Ganquan and Tong Chao et al., eds., *Zhongguo fengjian tudi zhidushi* (A History of Land System in Feudal China) (Beijing: 1990), vol. 1.

8. Hou Wailu, *Zhongguo sixiang tongshi*, vol. 4. Also, Miyazaki Ichisada, *Toyo no Kinsei Riben xuezhe yanjiu zhongguoshi lunzhu xuanyi* (Modern East: Selected Translations of Japanese Scholars' Works on Chinese History) (Beijing: 1992), 1: 188–89.

9. Compare Chen Jiyu, "Zhongguo fengjian shehui tudi jiqi fushui zhidu bianqian de tantao" (An Investigation of the Evolution of Land and Tax Systems in Feudal China), *Journal of Yangzhou University* 3 (1998): 70–71.

10. Compare Miyazaki, *Toyo no Kinsei*, vol. 1: 194–95.

11. Miyazaki, *Toyo no Kinsei*, vol. 1: 181–83.

12. Nakamura Satoshi, "Zhongguo qian jindai shi lilun de chonggou" (Recon-

structing the Theory on Early Modern China), *Proceedings of the International Conference on Theories About Early Modern China*, (Wuhan: 1997), 18–19.

13. Compare Mizoguchi Yuzou, *Zhongguo qian jindai sixiang de yanbian* (The Intellectual Evolution in Early Modern China) (Beijing: 1997), 337–488. See also Mizoguchi Yuzou, *Chukogu no shiso* (China's Thought), trans. Zhao Shilin (Beijing: 1995), 102–3.

14. Mizoguchi, *Zhongguo qian jindai sixiang de yanbian*, 244.

15. Mizoguchi, *Zhongguo qian jindai sixiang de yanbian*, 16.

16. Yu Ying-shih, "Wuxu zhengbian jindu" (Reinterpreting the 1898 Hundred-Day Reform), *Twenty First Century* 2 (1998): 8.

17. Li Wenzhi, *Ming Qing shidai fengjian tudi guanxi de songxie* (The Open-Up of the Feudal Landownership in the Ming and the Qing Dynasties) (Beijing: 1993), 513–40.

18. Li, *Ming Qing shidai fengjian*, 542.

19. Mizoguchi, *Chugoku no shiso*, 103–4.

20. Mizoguchi, *Zhongguo qian jindai sixiang de yanbian*, 248.

21. Compare Wang Jingwei, "Manzhou lixian yu guomin geming" (The Manchu Constitutional Monarchy and National Revolution), *People's Journal* (8 January 1906) and "National Citizen," *People's Journal* (2 January 1906).

22. Compare Qi Yongxiang, "Lun xixue dongjian yu qianjia xueshu zhi guanxi" (On the Relationship Between Evidential Scholarship and Western Cultural Influence), *Traditional Culture and Modernization* 2 (1998): 11–17, and Benjamin Elman, *Classicism, Politics, and Kinship: The Ch'ang-chou School of New Text Confucianism in Late Imperial China* (Berkeley, Calif.: 1990), xxii.

23. Prasenjit Duara, Rescuing History from the Nation: Questioning Narratives in Modern China (Chicago: 1995), 178–204.

24. Compare Yang Liansheng (Lien-ssheng), *Guoshi Tanwei* (A Minute Investigation in National History) (Taipei: 1983), 27–28.

25. Lenin's and Japanese scholars', including Miyazaki, definition of Asia were different; see their works cited previously.

26. Nishijima Sadao, *Toua Sekai no Keisei* (The Rise of the Eastern World), *Riben xuezhe yanjiu zhongguoshi lunzhu xuanyi* (Modern East: Selected Translations of Japanese Scholars' Works on Chinese History) (Beijing: 1992), 2: 89.

27. Hamashita Takeshi, *Chongu Keitou to Kindai Ajia* (The tributary system and modern Asia) (Iwannami: 1997).

28. Sun Ge, "Yazhou yiwei zhu shenme?" (What Does Asia Mean?), Yaji wenhua yanjiu guoji huiyi: miandui yazhou (Inter-Asia Cultural Studies Conference: Problematizing Asia) (Taipei: 2000), 1: 319–42.

29. Karatani Kojin, "Minzoku Shugi to Seibun Gengo" (Nationalism and Ecriture), *Gakujin* (The Scholars), 6 (1995), 104–5.

30. Mizoguchi, *Chukogu no shiso*, 75.

31. Mizoguchi, *Chukogu no shiso*, 75.

32. See Mizoguchi Yuzou, "Chugoku no Rekishizou to Gendaizou" (China's Historical and Modern Images), unpublished manuscript.

33. Compare Ishida Kazuyoshi, *Wenhua shixue: lilun yu fangfa* (Cultural History: Theory and Method) (Hangzhou: 1989), 284, and Mizoguchi, *Zhongguo qian jindai sixiang de yanbian*, 296–97.

34. Chen Yinke, "Suitang Zhidu yuanyuan lue lungao" (Manuscript of the Origins of Sui and Tang Institutions), *Chen Yinke shixue lunwen xuanji* (Chen Yinke's Selected Works in History) (Shanghai: 1992), 515.

35. Chen Yinke, "Tangdai zhengzhi shi shulungao" (Manuscript of Tang Political History), *Chen Yinke shixue lunwen xuanji* (Chen Yinke's Selected Works in History) (Shanghai: 1992), 551.

36. Chen Yinke, "Lun Tangdai zhi fanjiang yu fubing" (Minority Generals and Family Soldiers in the Tang), *Chen Yinke Shixue lunwen xuanji* (Chen Yinke's Selected Works in History) (Shanghai: 1992), 383.

37. Miyazaki, *Toyo no Kinsei*, vol. 1: 168, 170.

38. Miyazaki Ichisada, *Dongyang de Jinshi* (The Early Modernity in East Asia), *Riben Xuezhe yanjiu zhongguoshi lunzhu xuanyi* (Selected Translations of Japanese Scholars' Work on Chinese History) (Beijing: 1992), 1: 153–242.

39. Owen Lattimore, *Inner Asian Frontiers of China* (New York: 1940), 59.

40. Lattimore, *Inner Asian Frontiers of China*, 211–13.

41. Lattimore, *Inner Asian Frontiers of China*, 240.

42. Lattimore, *Inner Asian Frontiers of China*, 163, 166.

43. Lattimore, *Inner Asian Frontiers of China*, 236–38.

44. Andre Gunder Frank, *ReOrient: Global Economy in the Asian Age* (Berkeley, Calif.: 1998).

45. Hamashita Takeshi, "Shihon Shugi Shoku Minchi Taisei no Keisei to Ajia: Jukyu Seiki Gojunerndai Eikoku Ginkou Shihon Tai Ka Sannyu no Katei" (The Formation of Colonial Capitalist System and Asia: The Entering of English Bank Capitals into China in the 1850s), *Riben Zhongqingnian xuezhe lun zhongguo shi: Song Yuan Ming Qing juan* (Young and Middle Aged Japanese Scholars on Chinese History: The Song, Yuan, Ming and Qing volume) (Beijing: 1995), 612–50.

46. Miyazaki, *Toyo no Kinsei*, 1: 178.

47. Compare James Hevia, "Cong Chaogong tizhi dao zhimin yanjiu" (From the Tributary System to Colonial Studies), *Readings* 8 (1998): 60–68.

13

Comparing Cultures in Intercultural Communication

Jörn Rüsen

The quest for intercultural communication in history is rooted in practical challenges. It is not free academic thinking that has brought about the problems we have to deal with, but practical needs of a general and fundamental importance. So I will begin with a few words about these practical challenges, and then, in my second part, develop some theoretical considerations concerning how to meet and to answer these challenges through intercultural communication. In the third and last part of the chapter I will outline some ideas on how to bring about intercultural communication in the special field of historiography. The challenge on which my argument focuses is ethnocentrism, sharpened and radicalized by modernization and antimodernism.

ETHNOCENTRISM

After 1989 the world of politics faced a deep crisis of orientation and a quest for a new global orientation. How do we have to look at the human world in general, in the broad perspective of world politics, and find a new pattern of orientation? Samuel Huntington's idea of "The Clash of Civilizations" has provided a remarkable and intensively debated proposal for a new paradigm of world politics coming from the United States; in the meantime, it has been enlarged from a widely debated article to a thick book, recently translated into German.[1] Huntington says that since the end of the cold war, we have been living in a situation in which different civilizations (I would prefer the category "cultures") are in severe tension—a "clash." This clash, Huntington claims, will be the most important factor of world politics in the future. He warns us to be aware of this decisive cultural factor and to prepare ourselves to manage it. This simply means that we have to win the battle by concentrating our strength against those cultures that are different from ours, mainly the Islamic and the Confucian ones. (In a threatening and paranoiac vision—worthy of the next Hollywood blockbuster film and of psychoanalytic treatment— Huntington draws a horrific picture of a threatening alliance of the Islamic and the Confucian world against the West.)

This famous and widely discussed concept is much more indicative of a problem of general orientation today than of a solution to it. It points to a problem that can be described on a more theoretical level as one of ethnocentrism as a cultural strategy of political orientation and identity construction. Speaking of a "clash" as a basic structure of intercultural relationship reveals large-scale ethnocentrism. It is by no means only a phenomenon of the West in its relationship to non-Western cultures. Instead, it is universal and anthropologically rooted in the depth of the human mind, close to nature. To say it philosophically: Every human has to realize a relationship to him/herself in which it distinguishes him/herself from others, thus gaining its identity as a necessary cultural condition for life. Ethnocentrism[2] is a widespread cultural strategy to realize collective identity by distinguishing one's own people from others. It simply means a distinction between the realm of one's own life as a familiar one from the realm of the lives of the others, which is substantially different; it also realizes this distinction with values that put a positive esteem into one's own group and a negative one into the other group (under specific conditions of self-criticism the valuations can be reversed).[3]

Ethnocentrism defines one's own identity by a specific distinction from the others': The otherness is placed beyond the limits of one's own form of life in such a way that the value system that regulates our relationship with our own people is different from the value system we use to deal with the others. We tend to attribute mainly positive values to ourselves; the contrary is true concerning the otherness of the others. Otherness is a negative reflection of ourselves. We even need this otherness to legitimate our self-esteem.[4]

A very remarkable finding in history and anthropology demonstrates this unequal evaluation in identity construction by the strategy of ethnocentrism. Most of the names that denominate the social unit to which one belongs, and to whose form of life one feels committed, simply mean "man" or "mankind." The others are not humans. Let me enumerate some of these names: Khoi-khoi, Bantu, Egyptian, Apache, Comanche.

This naming indicates ethnocentrism. Human values are concentrated in one's own group, and otherness is defined by a lack of them, or even worse, by something contrary to them.

Identity construction along the lines of this strategy of ethnocentrism inevitably leads to a clash of different collective identities. This clash is grounded on the simple fact that the others do not accept our devaluation; on the contrary, they assign negative values to us. The point of this deeply rooted and widely realized strategy of togetherness and separation from others is the tensional impact in its relationship between the two fundamental realms of togetherness and difference, of selfness and otherness. The clash is logically built in to this cultural strategy itself. The last word in the cultural relationship between different communities guided by ethnocentrism will be struggle, even war in the sense of Thomas Hobbes's description of the natural stage of social life (*bellum omnium contra omnes*).

Here lies the challenge. If we were to follow this logic of identity construction, which has been historically valid for many parts of the past in different countries, the clash of civilizations would be the last word in intercultural relationship. What does "clash" mean? Huntington illustrates it by a scenario of conflict and war. And indeed, war is only a physical realization of the cultural principle of ethnocentrism in identity construction. We start on the mental level with words and ideas; in the end weapons, blood, and death speak the language of the same strategy. We all know the challenging cases we have to look at: Yugoslavia, Rwanda, Chechnya, Tibet, the killing of foreigners in Algeria, xenophobia in Europe. It is all around us, and this is what I mean when I say we have practical challenges of intercultural communication. We have, of course, paradigmatic historical examples. The most negative and the most impressive and horrible one is, of course, the Holocaust. Is there no alternative?

Before I try to answer this question, I would like to sharpen our awareness of ethnocentrism by shortly featuring it in respect to modernity and antimodernity.

Modernization has brought about a very specific and complex form of ethnocentrism: a globalization of the Western way of life, in which a universalistic approach of rationality to cultural orientation of human life has become dominant. It has changed the lives of the people in most of the non-Western countries in a dramatic way, and it has been a threat to them up to the present. Globalization poses a threat to their cultural peculiarity, in the form of a universalizing rationality of European origin. This domination is largely perceived as a threat of losing one's own traditionally pregiven identity.

This rationality puts the variety of human forms of life under the unify-

ing force of technological progress, market economy, methodical rationality in the sciences, and other mechanisms of rationalization. This
rationalization is often seen as nothing but a globalization of Western
forms of life that allows no place for different cultures. In this respect
modernization is a threat to difference and variety in culture, the threat
of the "fury of desolation" (*die Furie des Verschwindens*), to quote Hegel's
critique of the political rationality of the French Revolution. This threat
has even been felt in Western self-understanding itself: Max Weber spoke
of an "iron cage" in which cultural creativity would be throttled.[5] Modernization has been discussed as a "tragedy of culture," and the two
world wars were seen as a horrible proof of it.[6]

This threat of modernization should not lead to a plea for postmodernism, because *antimodernism*, which at least partly includes postmodernism, is a threat of cultural identity as well. One should not overlook that
in the countermovement against the constraints of modernization there
is an urge to establish an order that radically denies the universalizing
principles of modernity by stressing the uniqueness of a particular form
of life. It uses the potentials of modernity in order to establish an antimodern system and to make it effective. Modernization has brought
about an antiuniversalist approach to particular identity, guided by the
principle of ethnocentrism. This reaction to modernity is visible not only
in non-Western countries, but can and has also occurred as a turn of
modernity against itself. Both types of reaction again bring about a "clash
of civilizations." We have two main examples for this threat: Nazism and
fundamentalism. I do not think that the Holocaust and the Nazi policy
reflect the substance and essence of modernity. On the contrary, Nazism
is a substantially antimodernist movement using essential elements of
modernity simply as means and not as goals of development. It is exactly
this antimodernist modernity that made Nazism so horrible and danger-
ous, so explosive and destructive. The same dialectics govern the different
fundamentalist movements and their antimodernism today.

So we find ourselves confronted with an open problem: an unbridgeable gap between cultural difference and a universalistic discourse. We
are left with an open question—must we decide in favor of cultural particularity or in favor of transcultural universality? I think this binary choice
is disastrous. So here we have a theoretical challenge the humanities have
to meet and to which an answer must be found.

HISTORY AND IDENTITY

The search for an answer brings history to the fore, since history is the
most important cultural strategy of bringing about and expressing iden-

tity. History is a medium of self-understanding, of expressing, articulating, and even forming one's own identity, and of shaping the otherness of those outside of one's own group. It represents the past as a mirror in which we can see the features of our world and ourselves in their temporal dimension. This is true for the individual person, as well as for group identity—for national, for gender, and for cultural identity. Identity is always delivered by history; it is shaped and formed, even constituted by memory and historical consciousness. Identity is the answer to the question of who I am or who we are. If we have to answer such a question, we usually do it by telling a story, by a historical narrative.

Concerning cultural identity, I would like to emphasize certain narratives that formulate and even bring about this wide range of collective identity. They are called *master narratives*. Master narratives are told in order to answer the question of cultural identity. In the Western world we now have a strong postmodernist criticism of master narratives, the most famous of which is presented by François Lyotard.[7] His declaration of the end of master narratives indicates a crisis of identity in the Western world. I doubt that there will be no further master narratives of the West, since master narratives belong to cultural identity. But in one respect Lyotard is right: We need structurally new narratives that tell us who we are now, since we do not simply remain what we have been in the past.

Historical narratives do not only present one's own cultural identity, but, of course, at the same time they describe the difference and otherness of the others. And here is a problem concerning the master narratives (not only of the West, because other cultures have their master narratives as well). Master narratives normally are universal histories.

In their universalistic attitude, master narratives allow no place for otherness (or at least only a very uncomfortable one). They integrate it into the patterns of the home culture (as a variant or an early stage or an example for general rules we feel committed to)—or they exclude it marginally, to wilderness and threat, or academically, to objects of ethnology. So what else does history bring about besides ethnocentrism?

If we want to move beyond the ethnocentric logic of identity construction, we cannot leave history, but we have to look for transgressing chances within it. The first chance is found in narratives that present historically identity-claimed truth because they are an important element in practical human life. They really deal with the substance of the people, with their social interrelationship. They must be plausible across all the differences of the people who share a common identity. They must be accepted when they present or interpret a pregiven social order. Without such a social consent on the ground of plausibility of the master narratives, a given social entity could not survive culturally. So history as a cultural practice of identity construction is essentially more than only an invention or fiction. Therefore the strategies of self-understanding and interpreting one's own world by telling historical narratives always include methodical elements to make their presentation of the past plausible. (These elements are traditionally called rhetoric.)

We have to look very carefully at these built-in truth claims of historical narratives, because here is a chance and a starting point for the intercultural communication we are asking for. I think this claim to truth is universal, and truth itself is universalistic in its nature. It belongs to the formal logical structure of historical narrative. I would therefore like to argue that historical narratives can bridge the gap between universalism and particularity by their truth claims.

Truth in history is not a single principle but a very complex relationship of different principles. It is related to different dimensions and realms of historical narratives. It is related to experience, to values, and to patterns of historical sense and meaning.[8]

I will not give any further details, but I can indicate only in general that truth is a matter of methodological regulation of thinking and I will pick up only one issue of this methodological regulation: the method of intercultural comparison.

Truth is a basic regulative idea of argument. It constitutes a dynamic discourse that is directed to understanding and consent (including consent on differences). Pursuing this kind of argumentation would be a cultural practice that contributes to solving the problem of mediating universality and cultural particularity.

But before I try to develop the principles of this mediation, I have to criticize a widespread concept of universality in historical thinking. I think of universality as a simple generalization of one's own particularity into a concept of universal history that, of course, marginalizes or even dissolves the otherness of the other. This has been the cognitive strategy of traditional world history, threatening those who are not willing to subsume themselves under a generalized self of the others. We can study it in most of the concepts of universal history (and not only in the West).

But I don't think that every concept of universality is nothing more than a generalized peculiarity excluding or suppressing otherness. There are some principles of conceptualizing historical narratives that take the other perspectives seriously. One is *criticism* in the relationship between different perspectives. We can use the different perspectives to move knowledge forward through criticism. Criticizing one perspective by means of another will bring both perspectives into movement, into change, in which they modify or even enrich each other. So criticism can lead to *integration*, which is the second strategy of conceptualization I would like to emphasize. We can sustain the difference, and by argument bring the perspectives into movement toward a comprehensive perspective that allows space for the differences and the dignity of the otherness.

This mutual enrichment is possible only under a certain condition that is expressed by the universalistic category of equality. The discussants have to concede each other the same reason of arguing, an equality in using reasons for the plausibility of their narratives. But this equality is not sufficient. It is abstract because it neglects the differences that shape the perspectives. Identity is not a question of what we have in common, but what makes us differ from each other and how it does so. This insistence on difference does not dissolve equality; it only leads us beyond it. We have to add a second principle to the category of equality, the principle of mutual recognition and acknowledgment of differences.

This principle of mutual recognition and acknowledgment of differences under the precondition of equality is very abstract, very philosophical. It is synchronic and in its simple form even timeless. So it has to be applied to change and development in the field of historical culture.

INTERCULTURAL COMPARISON

In the third and last part of this chapter I would like to carry out such an application in a special field of historical studies, namely intercultural comparative historiography.[9]

Traditionally, intercultural comparison in historiography is done in the following way: We start with a comprehensive idea of Western historiography and its development from Herodotus up to our time. Then we look at another culture and study its similarities and differences.

The logic of this comparison is clear: Here are we and there are the others, and the whole comparison is grounded on division and separation, guided implicitly by the logic of ethnocentrism. How can we avoid this?

First of all we should avoid a presupposition of comparison that appears at first to be a self-evident matter of treating cultures as the largest units of identity. An intercultural comparison presupposes cultures as the subject matter of its work. It is an open question, how these units of comparison should be looked at. Are there pregiven entities, well distinguished in time and space? If an intercultural comparison uses a theoretical framework, it has to be very careful not to start from problematic presuppositions. This can be easily shown with respect to sense criteria that constitute historical thinking in general. These sense criteria are an essential part of a cultural code that defines the units of comparison. Consequently cultures can and should be compared along the line of the fundamental concepts that define the forms and realms of reality and human self-understanding. These concepts, which we call the cultural code, are deeply rooted in the minds of people. The danger of the attempt to focus cultural differences on this code is its tendency to substantiate or even to reify the single cultures being compared. Their internal historicity, their manifold interferences and mutual conditionings are lost from sight. Comparison then is only a statement of dichotomy or clear alternatives: Historical thinking either follows this code or another one. The related forms of cultural identities look like spatial realms with clear borderlines. Nothing seems to exist beyond or across the single codes. Such a way of looking at cultures shares with ethnocentrism the essential factor of exclusion: cultures are clearly separated and exclude each other. A typology of cultural differences is methodically necessary as a hypothetical construct, but it has to avoid the constraints and misleading views of a concept of cultures as pregiven units and entities.

Now I would like to propose a method of theoretical conceptualization that avoids ethnocentrism as well as the presupposition of comparison that excludes cultures from one another. Ethnocentrism is theoretically dissolved if the specifics of a culture are understood as a combination of elements that are shared by all other cultures. Thus the specificity of cultures is brought about by different constellations of the same elements. The theoretical approach to cultural differences that is guided by this idea of cultural specifics does not fall into the trap of ethnocentrism. On the contrary:

1. It presents the otherness of different cultures as a mirror that enables us for a better self-understanding.
2. It does not exclude otherness in order to constitute the peculiarity of our own cultural features, but includes it.
3. It brings about an interrelationship of cultures that enables the people who have to deal with their differences to use the cultural power of recognition and acknowledgment.

Historiography as the subject matter of comparison is a manifestation of historical consciousness that cannot be understood without going back to a complex set of prepositions, circumstances, challenges, and functions that together shape its peculiarity. How is it possible to compare peculiarities? It is necessary to decompose them into their ingredients and reconstruct them as a specific relationship and synthesis of various elements. If it can be shown that these elements, or at least some of them, are the same in different manifestations of historiography, a comparative analysis can be done in a systematic way. So the first step to creating a theoretical parameter for comparing historiography is a theory of the main components of these specific cultural manifestations called historiography.

In order to do this, one has to identify anthropological universals in the works and results of historical consciousness. This universality consists of a specific experience of time and a specific mode of dealing with this experience. It is an experience of time that can be called "contingency." Contingency means that human life is embedded in a course of time that always irritates human life. It is the irritation of rupture, of unexpected occurrence in one's own world, like death and birth, catastrophes, accidents, disappointed expectations—in short it is the experience that can be described by Hamlet's words: "The world is out of joint;—O cursed spite that ever I was born to set it right."[10] "To set it right" means to develop a concept of the course of time, of temporal change and development, which makes sense of contingent occurrences with respect to the orientation of human activities vis-à-vis the continual changes to the world and to the people in question.

The experience of temporal change that structurally threatens human life and disturbs the concept of an unproblematic ongoing familiar process in one's own life and world, must be interpreted in order to adjust human activities and thought to it.[11] In order to do so people must insert disturbance into an idea of temporal order that gives an answer to the challenge of contingency. The work of historical consciousness can be described as a procedure by which the idea of a temporal order to human life is brought about. It deals with the experience of temporal change of life and world, which is stored in the halls of memory. It provides a sense of change by interpretation that can be applied to the understanding of today's world. Thus it enables people to expect the future and to guide their own activities by this future perspective according to the experiences of the past.

This work of historical consciousness is accomplished in specific activities of cultural life. I would like to call these the practices of historical narration. Through these practices "historiography" becomes a part of human life, a part of culture as a necessary element of the human form of life. Any intercultural comparison must systematically account for these practices and has to interpret their specific forms of the universal cultural activity of making sense of the past.

This activity of narration has a mental counterpart: "history" as a mental construct, in which the past is present as a determination or orientation of present-day life including its future perspective. What are the substantial elements of this mental construct called "history"? In order to distinguish it from the other elements of human memory, one should first of all explicate its specificity as a memory of a past, which goes beyond the limits of one's own personal recollection or (more objectively) beyond one's own lifespan. This temporal extension of memory is a necessary condition for giving the past the quality of being "historical." A perspective on futurity, opened by historical consciousness, transcends the limit of one's own lifespan as well. Historical consciousness enlarges the mental concept of the temporal dimension of human life into a temporal whole that goes far beyond the lifetime of the people who do the historical work of recollection.

The simple enlargement of the temporal horizon of memory is a necessary though not sufficient condition for the specific "historical" quality of going back to the past. The human mind has to fill this dimension with a specific "sense," which makes the past as experience significant for the present and future. This "historical sense" is an image, a vision, a concept, or an idea of time that mediates the expectations, desires, hopes, threats, and anxieties moving the minds of the people in their present-day activities with the experiences of the past. Recalled real time becomes synthesized with the projected time of the future; past and future merge into an entire image, vision, or concept of temporal change and development that functions as an integral part of the cultural orientation in the human life of the present. Examples for this idea of time as a meaningful order of human activities are the idea of regular and incessant change of order and disorder, the category of progress, the belief that God governs the world, or that there is an entire moral world order (such as *Tao*).

All these concepts are based on the idea of the order of time. So time concepts are the basis or the foundation of the sense of history; time related to the human world and its precarious balance between the experience of the past and the expectation of the future preforms any sense and meaning of the past as history. For comparative purposes a basic dichotomy has often been used: the difference between cyclic and linear time. This distinction as a simple alternative is not very useful to characterize fundamental modes of historical thinking, since there is no concept of history that does not make use of both of them. So the emphasis of disclosing characteristic time concepts should be directed to the modes of synthesis of cyclicity and linearity of time.

The comparative outlook on historiography has to identify these criteria of historical sense and meaning. Normally they do not occur in an elaborated form. Very often they are implicit principles or highly effective presuppositions—all the more reason to identify and explicate them. So a system of basic concepts can be explicated, governing the entire historiography, structuring its way of transforming the experience of the past into a meaningful history for the present. By such a system the semantics of history will be disclosed and prepared for comparison.

Today, these sense criteria are mainly considered to be fictional, inventions that have nothing to do with the reality. In this view the cultural creativity of historical consciousness is recognized, unfortunately, in a one-sided way, since one cannot deny the element of experience that molds the mental construct called "history" as well as the images, symbols, and concepts used to interpret it. Very often these interpreting elements are a part of the experience itself, so it is misleading to identify, explicate, and interpret them as being substantially fictional.

A typology of historical sense criteria is only a starting point of a theoretically conceptualized intercultural comparison of historical thinking. It has to be elaborated into a complex theory of historical conscience, which I am unable to present here. I only can enumerate the main points of this theoretical framework of comparison. It has to explicate the different possibilities of cultural practices of historical narration (in the wide range from dancing a myth to writing academic historiography). It has to deal with the linguistic and nonlinguistic forms of presentation and with the functions of representing the past in practical life.

These categories of comparison are synchronic. One has to complement them by diachronic perspectives, which refer to change in historiography. Here the main issue is a comprehensive direction of change.

Max Weber's concept of universal rationalization and disenchantment should be reformulated as a question for a comparative analysis of historiography. There is no historiography without rationality, that is, a set of rules, which bind the sense-making processes of historical consciousness into strategies of conceptualization, of bringing empirical evidence into the representation of the past, and of coherent argumentation. This rationality should be reconstructed and investigated with regard to its development toward the growing universality of its validity. The same should be done in respect to the norms and values that constitute historical identity. Do they show a directed development, which can be described as a process of universalization, and does the spatial extension of historical identity develop accordingly? I think we can observe such a process of universalization in many cultures:[12] It starts from a small social group in archaic times and leads to mankind in modern history. Alongside this universalization very often a corresponding regionalization takes place. Additionally one should look for a process of particularization and individualization; it may be a reaction to universalization or a consequence of it.

To give you an example of a theoretically conceptualized framework of diachronic comparison, I sketch a universal periodization of historical thinking that mainly relates to the media of historical narration and the elements of contingency and sense criteria of temporal change, and that makes use of my typology of historical narration (see figure 13.1).[13]

This kind of thinking follows the rules required to transcend the limits of ethnocentrism. I would like to characterize these rules as commitments to *reflect*, to *historize*, and to *universalize* the basic principles and determinants of historical thinking. With this strategy we should undertake a new approach to intercultural communication that could contribute to a historical culture of recognition and acknowledgment.

Figure 13.1 Universal periodization of historical thinking

Prehistoric	Sharp distinction between paradigmatic time of world order ("archaic" time of myth) and the time of everyday human life; the latter is meaningless for the order of world and self. Contingency is radically sorted out. Dominance of the *traditional* type of historical narration. *Medium of oral tradition.*		
Historic	Mediation of both "times." Contingent facts (events) are laden with meaning concerning the temporal world order.	Traditional	The entire order of time has a divine character. Religion is the main source for sense of temporal change. Dominance of the *exemplary type* of historical narration.
	Contingency is recognized as relevant for this order and bound into a concept of time that orientates practical activity and forms human identity. *Medium of scripture.*	Modern	Minimization of transcendent dimension of time-order. The entire sense of history tends to become inner-worldly. Human relationality is able to recognize it with the means of methodical research of the empirical evidence of the past. Dominance of the *genetic type* of historical narration
Posthistoric	No comprehensive order of time including past, present, and future. The past is separated into a time for itself. Facts of the past become elements of arbitrary constellations that have no substantial relationship to present and future. The human past becomes detemporized. Contingency loses its conceptualization by ideas of temporal order valid for present-day life and its future. *Medium of electronics.*		

Note: The typology of historical sense generation used here is explained in Jörn Rüsen, *Zeit und Sinn: Strategien historischen Denkens* (Frankfurt am Main: 1990), 153–230; Jörn Rüsen, *Studies in Metahistory* (Pretoria: 1993), 3–14. I have put three of the four types of historical sense-making into a clear periodical order. This is misleading, since they play a much more complex role in all periods. But nevertheless they can be used to characterize an epoch-related type of historical thinking.

NOTES

1. Samuel Huntington, "The Clash of Civilizations," *Foreign Affairs* 72 (1993): 22–49; Samuel Huntington, *The Clash of Civilizations and the Remaking of World Order* (New York: 1996); translated into German under the title *Der Kampf der Kulturen: The Clash of Civilizations: Die Neugestaltung der Weltpolitik im 21. Jahrhundert* (Vienna: 1996).

2. I use the word in a more general sense, not in its strict anthropological meaning where it is related to an identity focused on the social unit of a tribe.

3. Sato Masayuki provides illustrating examples of cartography: "Imagined Peripheries: The World and Its Peoples in Japanese Cartographic Imagination," *Diogenes* 44, no. 1 (Spring 1996): 132ff.

4. Compare Erich Neumann, *Tiefenpsychologie und neue Ethik* (Frankfurt am Main: 1985), 38ff. An excellent description of this ethnocentric attitude, based on broad-scale ethnographic evidence, is given by Klaus E. Müller, "Identität und Geschichte: Widerspruch oder Komplementarität? Ein ethnologischer Beitrag," *Paideuma* 38 (1992): 17–29.

5. Max Weber, *Die protestantische Ethik: Eine Aufsatzsammlung*, ed. Johannes Winckelmann (Gütersloh: 1965), 188.

6. Compare Friedrich Jaeger, "Bürgerlichkeit: Deutsche und amerikanische Philosophien einer Lebensform zu Beginn des 20. Jahrhunderts," in *Wege zur Geschichte des Bürgertums*, ed. Klaus Tenfelde and Hans-Ulrich Wehler (Göttingen: 1994), 171–206.

7. François Lyotard, *Jean-François Lyotard: Das Postmoderne Wissen: Ein Bericht* (Graz: 1986).

8. Compare Jörn Rüsen, *Historische Vernunft: Grundzüge einer Historik*, vol. 1, *Die Grundlagen der Geschichtswissenschaft* (Göttingen: 1983); Joyce Appleby, Lynn Hunt, and Margaret Jacob, *Telling the Truth About History* (New York: 1994).

9. Compare Jörn Rüsen, "Some Theoretical Approaches to Intercultural Comparison of Historiography," *History and Theory*, theme issue 35 (1996): 5–22. In what follows, I repeat the main arguments of this article.

10. Shakespeare, *Hamlet*, Act I, Scene V, 189sq.

11. In Chinese it is expressed by the term *pien* (change with meaning of turmoil).

12. I have tried to conceptualize such a process in respect to the question for the universality of human rights and the general issues of humankind, selfness, and otherness. See Jörn Rüsen, "Die Individualisierung des Allgemeinen," in Jörn Rüsen, *Historische Orientierung* (Cologne: 1994), 168–74; Jörn Rüsen, "Human Rights from the Perspective of a Universal History," in *Human Rights and Cultural Diversity: Europe—Arabic-Islamic World—Africa—China*, ed. Wolfgang Schmale (Frankfurt am Main: 1993), 28–46; Jörn Rüsen, "Vom Umgang mit den Anderen— Zum Stand der Menschenrechte heute," *Internationale Schulbuchforschung* 15 (1993): 167–78.

13. Rüsen, "Some Theoretical Approaches," 20.

Index

354

Index